CRYSTAL REPORTS® XI
FOR DEVELOPERS

D1529081

CRYSTAL REPORTS® XI
FOR DEVELOPERS

DAVID McAMIS

CHARLES RIVER MEDIA, INC.
Hingham, Massachusetts

Acquisition Editor: James Walsh
Cover Design: Tyler Creative

CHARLES RIVER MEDIA
25 Thomson Place
Boston, Massachusetts 02210
617-757-7900
617-757-7969 (FAX)
crminfo@thomson.com
www.charlesriver.com

This book is printed on acid-free paper.

David McAmis. *Crystal Reports XI for Developers*.
ISBN: 1-58450-411-0

Library of Congress Cataloging-in-Publication Data
McAmis, David.
  Crystal reports XI for developers / David McAmis.
     p. cm.
  Includes index.
  ISBN 1-58450-411-0 (alk. paper)
  1. Seagate Crystal reports. 2. Business report writing--Computer programs. I. Title.
  HF5719.M3865 2005
  651.7'8028557585--dc22
                      2005024576

Printed in the United States of America
06 7 6 5 4 3 2

To my mother, Evelyn Rose, who slipped away from this world
before this project was complete.
You will always be "The Most Beautiful Girl in the World."

Contents

Acknowledgments

There are a number of people behind the scenes who have made this book possible and who deserve a big thank you. First and foremost is Jim Walsh, who deserves credit for not only being a fantastic editor but also a caring and compassionate human being. Thanks also go to Bryan Davidson and the editorial and production teams at Charles River for an outstanding job editing the manuscript and putting together the finished product.

A special thank you to Colin, Alice, Melissa, Lisa and Daniel for putting up with this project for the past few months, as well as Tracy, Dave, Richard, Chang, and everyone at Business Objects Asia Pacific who have kept me "in the trenches" and continually challenged and inspired.

And to my family and friends, there are not enough words to express how much I appreciate your love, support, and encouragement. *Nunc scio quit sit amor.*

1 An Introduction to Crystal Reports

In This Chapter

- What Is Crystal Reports XI?
- What's New in Crystal Reports XI?
- What's New in Crystal Reports XI for Developers?
- Crystal Reports XI Versions?

INTRODUCTION

Reporting has been an important part of application development since the mainframe, and Crystal Reports® has been there nearly from the start. Bundled with early versions of Microsoft® Visual Basic® and Visual Studio®, developers have over the years developed a love-hate relationship with Crystal Reports. They love the functionality the product provides but sometimes are frustrated when trying to integrate reporting into their application. Hopefully, that is where this book can come in handy, because it was written specifically for application developers who want to use Crystal Reports to add feature-rich reports to their applications with minimum effort.

The book itself is organized into two major sections. The first half of the book covers report design, starting with the basics and working through more advanced report design topics. For developers who are new to Crystal Reports, tutorials help teach report design concepts; for developers who have some experience with Crystal Reports, this book provides a solid reference for Crystal Reports features.

The second half of the book is targeted at report integration and covers integration into a number of different platforms and application-development tools. Code samples and fully working sample applications are included that you can integrate into your own applications or use as a starting point for your own development.

Now, you may have flipped through the second half of the book already and seen that it is broken out into multiple chapters for Windows®, Web applications, and Java™ applications, with platforms ranging from Visual Studio .NET to Java Server Pages. You have to be thinking to yourself, "Is this guy crazy?" but you will soon see there is a method to the madness.

Most developers have had some experience with multiple development tools and platforms and sometimes are forced to use one tool or platform over another. This book was written to illustrate how to integrate reports into all of these platforms because you may end up using them one day.

It goes without saying that developers are notoriously hard to please when it comes to technical books and references. We all want to find the answer we need (and fast!), and we sometimes look to a book to cover every possible feature and usage scenario. Unfortunately, this is not always possible—not only would a book with 2,000 pages be hard to sell, it would be a back-breaker to boot.

The good news is that throughout the book are extensive resource listings and links to additional resources on the Web, including a dedicated Web site (*www.crystalxibook.com*) where you will find the latest information, updates, and sample code. With a product as complex as Crystal Reports and its related server technology, no one book can cover all of the integration methods and scenarios you may encounter, but with the wealth of code and resources in this book, on the CD-ROM, and on the dedicated Web site, this is the most complete reference available for Crystal Reports developers.

ON THE CD

WHAT IS CRYSTAL REPORTS XI?

Crystal Reports XI is the latest version of the popular report writer best known as the reporting tool originally included with Visual Studio. Crystal Reports XI was released in early 2005 and features a standalone report designer, shown in Figure 1.1, that can be used to design reports from a wide variety of data sources.

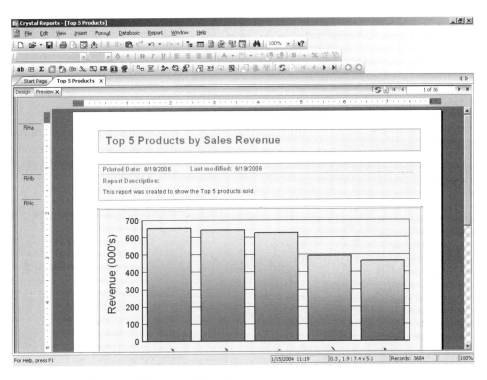

FIGURE 1.1   The Crystal Reports XI interface.

Crystal Reports XI features a number of different APIs for integrating reports into applications, including .NET, Java, and COM applications, to name a few. In addition to the standard developer APIs that come with Crystal Reports, a new product has been introduced with this version, Crystal Reports Server XI, which can be used to create robust, scalable applications that span multiple servers and processing tiers.

NOTE

The code base underneath Crystal Reports Server is the same code base used in BusinessObjects™ Enterprise XI, an enterprise framework for distributing reports, including security, scheduling, multitiered architecture, and more. For more information on BusinessObjects Enterprise XI, visit www.businessobjects.com/products/platform/enterprise.asp.

WHAT'S NEW IN CRYSTAL REPORTS XI?

Crystal Reports XI, the eleventh release of the product, is a significant upgrade over previous versions in terms of features and functionality. To help organize the new features in a logical manner in this chapter, they have been grouped by area, starting with what's new in the report designer itself.

Report Designer

The Crystal Reports XI Report Designer features an updated look and feel, borrowing some user interface elements from Microsoft Office. The first thing you will notice when you open Crystal Reports XI is the new start page, shown in Figure 1.2.

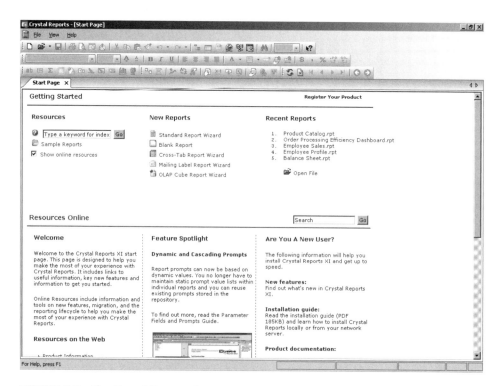

FIGURE 1.2   The Crystal Reports XI start page.

The top half of the start page features a quick help search box, links to sample resources, and the report wizards as well as a list of recent reports. The bottom half of the page is an HTML page that is downloaded from the BusinessObjects Web site and contains additional resources. You can stop these online resources from being displayed by checking the Show online resources box on the top of the page.

If we take another look at the report designer with a number of reports open, you will see that multiple reports can now be displayed using a tabbed interface, as shown in Figure 1.3.

FIGURE 1.3 Multiple reports are now shown as tabs within the report designer.

The Design and Preview tabs are still there but are now located below the other tabs. This makes it easier to switch between reports you may be working on, but it may be difficult to get used to if you are accustomed to using the Window menu to switch between reports and documents.

Another new concept in Crystal Reports XI is the Workbench, shown in Figure 1.4, which can be used to organize reports into projects.

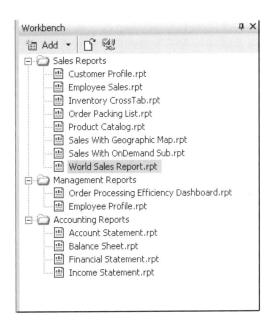

FIGURE 1.4 The Workbench.

Once you have created a project, you can then add multiple reports and publish the entire project to Crystal Reports Server or BusinessObjects Enterprise XI for viewing over the Web.

Speaking of the Web, one of the previous problems with designing reports for Web applications was that the report you designed in the report designer was not the same report you saw on the Web. In rendering the report to HTML, the spacing could be slightly off or some report elements weren't translated to HTML (such as rounded corners or vertical text). To solve that problem, Crystal Reports XI includes an integrated HTML Preview, shown in Figure 1.5, that you can use to preview your report as it will appear on the Web.

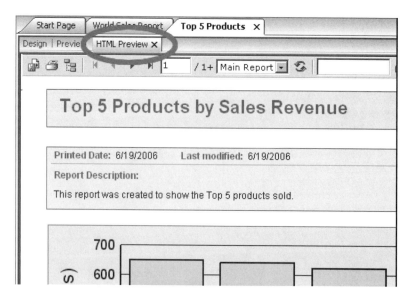

FIGURE 1.5 The HTML Report Preview pane.

This handy feature will save much time in switching between the report design and your application when you are trying to work out the formatting differences. You can now see what the report will look like in HTML and then switch back to your report's Design or Preview tab to make any required changes.

Another key feature for Web development that is new to this version is the ability to store image files outside of your report file. Previously, images had to be embedded into the report or stored in a database, but with Crystal Reports XI, these images can be stored on a network or Web server and included in your report.

Finally, if you are tired of trying to keep your copy of Crystal Reports up-to-date with the latest hot fixes and service packs, the product now includes an update service that alerts you when a patch is available.

Reporting Functionality

The real standout feature in terms of reporting functionality is the new dynamic and cascading parameter fields. Previously, when you created a parameter field in Crystal Reports, the pick list of values that you could add was static. In other words, the values that you added when you designed the report were saved with the report and couldn't be updated. So, if you created a parameter field on a Customer Name field and then a week later added a new customer, the new customer would not appear in the pick list. Most developers compensated for this by creating their own parameter interface and then just passed the selected values to Crystal Reports.

Now, with the new parameter fields in Crystal Reports XI, you can create dynamic parameters that are tied to your data source. When the report is run and parameters are required, the values in the list are generated dynamically from your database, as shown in Figure 1.6.

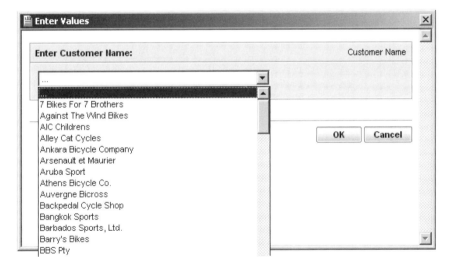

FIGURE 1.6 Dynamic parameters in action.

In addition, multiple parameters can be set to cascade so that parameter values are used to filter the other parameter values that appear. For example, if you were to select Canada from the Enter Country field, only the provinces that are in Canada would appear in the Enter Region field, as shown in Figure 1.7.

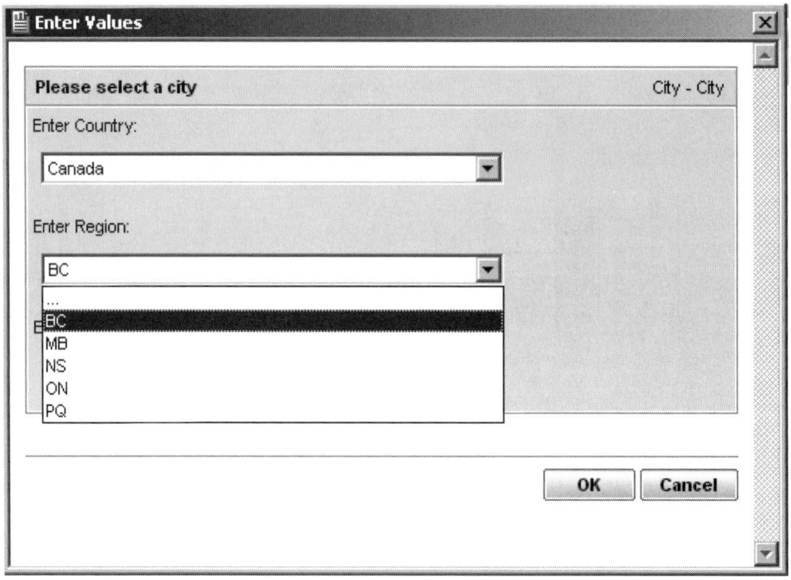

FIGURE 1.7 An example of a cascading parameter.

Another new feature that has been a long time coming is the click-once cross-tabs and charts. Previously, when you wanted to insert a cross-tab or chart, a dialog box would appear in which you would have to select your fields for a cross-tab, charting options, and so on. Then, when you were finished, you could click to place the cross-tab or chart in your report. However, if the section where you wanted to add the cross-tab or chart was suppressed or was so small that the object wouldn't fit, you often lost all of your hard work and had to start over.

The click-once concept means that when you insert a cross-tab or chart, it is attached to the tip of your mouse and you can click to place it on your report. In the case of a cross-tab, a blank cross-tab will be shown, which you can then edit. For charts, Crystal Reports will try to work out what type of chart you want to create from your report content. It can create a chart based on this information, applying the default formatting attributes, as shown in Figure 1.8.

If Crystal Reports is unable to work out what type of report you want to create, the Chart Expert will be shown, allowing you to select your chart fields and other elements. For easier formatting of charts, there is also a new Chart menu on the Crystal Reports menu bar, which will appear when you click a chart object in your report.

FIGURE 1.8 A chart created from data used in the report.

Another area that received some much-needed attention in this release is hier-archical grouping. Hierarchical grouping works on the concept that you have a data structure with a parent-child concept; for example, a table of employees where each has a Manager ID field that points back to the same table, or a general ledger table where the accounts are broken down into subaccounts.

Crystal Reports has had hierarchical grouping for a while, but it has not been very flexible. Most developers chose to use a combination of normal groups and formula fields to simulate the functionality of hierarchical grouping so they could have more control over the report layout itself, including indentation and group formatting.

Crystal Reports XI offers a new set of tools for working with hierarchical group-ing, including conditional formatting, which can be used to control the layout of your report and specify object position and indentation, to create complex reports in less time.

And finally, the last feature we'll look at is really the unsung hero of Crystal Reports XI—the new Dependency Checker. In earlier versions, debugging Crystal Reports was an arduous affair. As you wrote formulas, you had to check each formula field carefully to ensure that it worked; sometimes you found when you ran the report there was a formula field missing or a field name had changed. You would then get an error message and have to track down the missing or incorrect element of your formula field and correct it in order to run your report.

With the introduction of the Dependency Checker, shown in Figure 1.9, you can check the dependencies in your report to ensure that your report runs the first time.

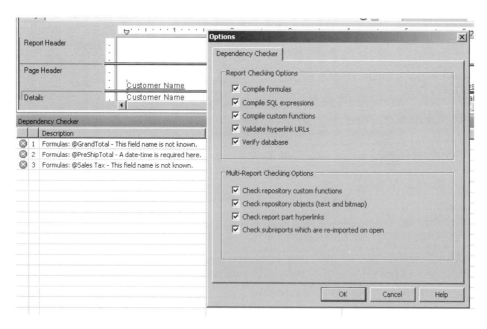

FIGURE 1.9   The Dependency Checker.

The checker can be used to perform the following checks on your report:

- Compile formulas
- Compile SQL expressions
- Compile custom functions
- Validate hyperlink URLs
- Verify databases

In addition, the Dependency Checker can also be used to check any subreports that have been reimported. Just this one new feature of Crystal Reports XI will save you time and effort when working with complex reports and can also ensure that any reports you have integrated into your application run correctly the first time.

Exporting

Reports delivered in Crystal Reports can be exported to multiple formats, including Microsoft Excel®, Microsoft Word, PDF, and HTML. This provides a flexible way to deliver information to users and gives them a way to further use the information contained in the report.

In previous versions, when you exported a Crystal Report, you had to select an export format and then set all of the options for that format, which could be time consuming. With Crystal Reports XI, the export formatting settings can now be saved so that you don't have to set them each time. For example, you can now set the default formatting options for exporting to Excel using the dialog box shown in Figure 1.10.

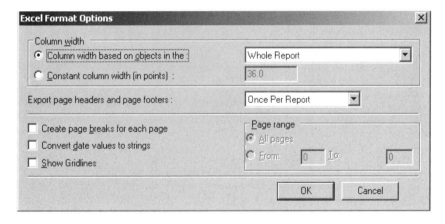

FIGURE 1.10   Setting Excel export options.

The next time you wanted to export to this format, the export options would be set automatically for you.

Another enhancement to exporting is a new editable RTF export format. When you exported a report from earlier versions of Crystal Reports to RTF, the information in the report was displayed in a number of text boxes in the RTF file. Although this made it possible to exactly mimic the report's design and layout, users found it difficult to edit this information or copy and paste it into other documents.

With the new editable RTF export format, you can now create RTF files that can be edited in Word, WordPad, and other editors. Also, the contents are easily copied and pasted into other applications, as shown in Figure 1.11.

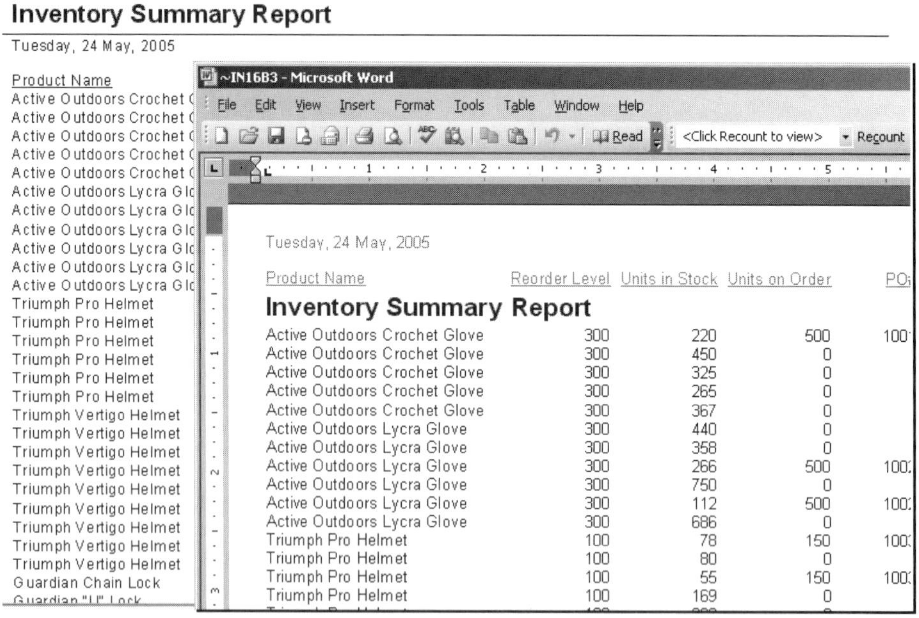

FIGURE 1.11   A report exported to the new RTF format.

Users can edit the report contents and add their own commentary and text to the exported report, which can then be used to create management reports.

WHAT'S NEW IN CRYSTAL REPORTS XI FOR DEVELOPERS?

In addition to a number of features in the report designer itself, Crystal Reports XI also includes a number of enhancements behind the scenes that make integrating reports into your own applications quick and simple.

In the following sections, we will look at some of these features broken down by development platform, starting with new features for Visual Studio .NET developers.

.NET Developers

Most .NET developers will be familiar with Crystal Reports from the version that is included with Visual Studio .NET 2002 and Visual Studio .NET 2003. The code base for this and other versions found in C# Builder® and Delphi® 2005 is almost two complete versions behind Crystal Reports XI, so there are definitely some features for which it is worth upgrading.

Starting at the top, both the Crystal Reports Winform and webform viewers have been updated to support all of the features found in Crystal Reports XI, including dynamic and cascading parameters and updated export formats. The look and feel of the viewer itself has been updated, and you can now turn off tool tips. The search facility on the Winform viewer has been replaced with a simple Find dialog box, and there is now an error event handler that gives you more flexibility in handling common errors and problems with the report. Another valuable enhancement is the more descriptive error messages that actually describe what the error is or what has happened, including passing-through-database error messages.

One of the most eagerly awaited enhancements to the developer side of things is the new XML database driver, which will allow you to report off of Web services and HTTP requests as a data source for your reports. This ability opens up a whole new set of options for accessing data, and it means Crystal Reports is a bit more flexible in the data sources it supports.

From the report integration API side, not much has changed. There is additional support in place for the new Crystal Reports XI features and some enhancements to database drivers.

Crystal Reports XI now features a single merge module for deployments, which is installed automatically when you install the product. Given the amount of trouble .NET developers have had over the years deploying their applications with the old merge modules, this feature is a major enhancement and well worth the price of the upgrade. There are also new deployment options that give the developer control over the database and exporting .dll files that are installed, which should also make a few developers happy—no more guessing what will be installed and where.

Java Developers

Crystal Reports has traditionally been known among Microsoft developers, but in the past few years, it has made real inroads in the Java community, including bundling an OEM version of Crystal Reports in a number of different Java IDEs, including JBuilder®, BEA® WebLogic Workshop™, and IBM® Rational® Application Developer.

For Java developers, Crystal Reports XI includes a Java Reporting Component (JRC) that has been updated to support Crystal Reports XI features, but unfortunately does not include dynamic or cascading parameters in this first release. Plenty of other enhancements for Java developers have been added, including the new XML data driver for reporting from Web services, which should help developers working in a services-oriented architecture.

The Java API has also been enhanced to bring it into rough parity with the other development APIs. It now allows developers to set the data source at runtime, set table location, and verify the database.

Another key enhancement is the introduction of Java User Function Libraries (UFL), which can be used to enhance the functions already found in Crystal Reports. These function libraries are similar to the function libraries Windows developers were able to create for Windows and Web applications through the use of .dll files. The difference is that Java UFLs leverage your existing Java skills and expertise, providing an easy way for you to create functions that you can reuse in multiple reports.

There is also a new JavaServer Faces viewer for Crystal Reports, which makes it a snap to integrate Crystal Reports into your existing applications using a custom set of JSF tags. These tags are a quick and easy shortcut for developers who may just be getting started with Crystal Reports and want to quickly integrate a report or two without having to learn the API.

Other Developer APIs

Crystal Reports XI also includes an updated version of the Report Design Component (RDC), which is a legacy API provided for COM and Visual Basic developers and is not recommended for new projects. This technology has been used for a number of years by Crystal Reports developers with Visual Basic 6, Delphi, and ASP applications, but it is definitely past its prime.

Many developers who have cut their teeth on the OEM version of Crystal Reports included in Visual Basic and in subsequent upgrades found the RDC to be their preferred integration method. But the *What's New* documentation that ships with Crystal Reports XI clearly states:

The new features in version 11 of the RDC are primarily focused on format compatibility with reports created in Crystal Reports XI. This focus includes maintaining compatibility with applications created in previous versions of the RDC.

That said, a number of Visual Basic 6 applications are still being developed and maintained, so we have featured a number of RDC sample applications on the Web site that accompanies the book (*www.crystalxibook.com*), but it may be time to start considering some of the other integration options available.

Another developer component that is missing from this release is the Report Application Server API, which is now part of Crystal Reports Server, a new server component introduced with Crystal Reports XI.

CRYSTAL REPORTS XI VERSIONS

Now that you have had a look at the new features in Crystal Reports, you are probably raring to run out to the store and buy a copy. But when you get there, a few different versions of the product are available to choose from—which one is the right one? As with previous versions of Crystal Reports, the product is split into different versions for different types of users. These versions include

- Crystal Reports XI Standard Edition
- Crystal Reports XI Professional Edition
- Crystal Reports XI Developer Edition
- Crystal Reports XI Server

The underlying report engine and report designer are the same for all of the different versions, but each version has its own list of features and functionality. A brief rundown of what is included in each edition follows, as well as a quick look at the licenses included in each edition. If you have worked with Crystal Reports before, you will be happy to know that the licensing for this version has been simplified and is much easier to understand.

As a general rule, the licensing information provided here is intended only as a guide. You should read the end user license agreement that comes with your product and the licensing white papers available from BusinessObjects for complete license terms, conditions, and interpretations.

Crystal Reports XI Standard Edition

The Crystal Reports XI Standard Edition includes a single report-design license and can be used to create reports from PC-type databases, including Microsoft Access, dBase™, and so on. Using this edition of Crystal Reports, you can create reports from these data sources, but there are no developer or server components included that you could use to integrate these reports into an application.

Crystal Reports XI Professional Edition

Crystal Reports XI Professional Edition includes a single report-design license and can be used to create reports from various data sources, through open database connectivity (ODBC), native database drivers, and more. Crystal Reports XI Professional Edition also includes a special introductory offer of a copy of Crystal Reports Server with five named-user licenses. This license will allow you to publish reports to Crystal Reports Server, and up to five users can connect to your Crystal Reports Server to view and interact with reports. No developer tools or APIs are available with this edition.

Crystal Reports XI Developer Edition

Crystal Reports XI Developer Edition includes a single report-design license and, like the professional edition, can be used to create reports from various data sources and runtime data sources, including ADO, RDO, CDO, and so on. Crystal Reports XI Developer Edition also provides all of the developer tools and components you will need to integrate Crystal Reports into your application.

This edition provides a royalty-free runtime for "fat client" Windows applications, which can be distributed within or outside or your organization, in addition to a free runtime license for any applications you create for internal use, including applications that run across multiple servers or processors. If you are developing an application that integrates Crystal Reports to distribute to other organizations, all you need to do is buy a copy of Crystal Reports XI Developer Edition for each organization that buys your application.

The Developer Edition also includes a copy of Crystal Reports Server with five named-user licenses. This license will allow you to publish reports to Crystal Reports Server, and up to five users can connect to your Crystal Reports Server to view and interact with reports. Crystal Reports Server also provides a robust platform for creating multitiered reporting applications, with all of the security and scheduling already built in.

SUMMARY

There you have it in a nutshell—all of the new features in Crystal Reports XI and in the APIs you can use to integrate reports into your own applications. Now it's time to roll up your sleeves and get your hands dirty. The next chapter starts the fun part, first looking at accessing your data source and then working through creating your first report.

2 Getting Started

In This Chapter

- Accessing Data with Crystal Reports
- Creating Reports Using the Standard Report Wizard
- Saving Your Report
- Working with the Report Designer
- Report Design Environment
- Customizing the Design Environment

INTRODUCTION

Regardless of what type of report you want to create, it all starts with a connection to a data source. One of Crystal Report's strengths is its ability to report from just about any database, from desktop and file-based data structures to data warehouses, relational databases, OLAP data sources, and enterprise resources planning (ERP) systems such as SAP®, Oracle® JD Edwards®, and more. In the first part of this chapter, you will learn how Crystal Reports accesses data, how to use features relating to data access, and how to report from these data sources.

The second half of the chapter is all about report design and, in particular, the Report Designer itself. You'll learn how to create a report quickly using the wizards available in Crystal Reports. Then we'll take a look at the report design environment itself, including how to preview and save your report.

ACCESSING DATA WITH CRYSTAL REPORTS

Crystal Reports can access data sources in two ways, either through a translation layer (like ODBC) or through a native driver or connection. A native connection from Crystal Reports to your data is accomplished through a specialized interface that is specific to your data source or application. Over the years, Crystal Reports has teamed up with database, application, and other vendors to create a number of native drivers for PC or file-type databases, relational databases, and ERP systems, including native drivers for Microsoft SQL Server, Oracle, and others.

Through a native-driver interface, you can access nontraditional data sources as well, such as log files, Microsoft Outlook®, and even the file system itself.

NOTE

The second data-access method uses a translation layer, which is most often ODBC. ODBC is a common interface for querying relational databases. Regardless of where the data resides, ODBC provides a reliable, stable platform that vendors can use to develop drivers and data-access methods.

Whether you use a native or ODBC connection depends on the data or application you are reporting from and the availability of a native driver or an ODBC for that connection. In terms of performance, it is always preferable to use a native driver when possible to eliminate the extra layer of translation that ODBC requires.

In addition to commercially available ODBC drivers, Crystal Reports includes drivers free of charge for some of the most popular databases.

NOTE

All of the data sources mentioned are accessed through the Database Expert, shown in Figure 2.1. The Database Expert is invoked when you create a new report and select a data source or when you are adding a new database or table to an existing report. It is arranged according to type. The following section describes the most common data types, as well as some basic instructions on how to use them in your report.

ON THE CD

The reports created in this chapter are located on the CD-ROM in the PROJECTS folder. You can either follow along with the instructions in the chapter to re-create the reports or you can copy the reports from the CD-ROM to your hard drive for editing.

Creating a Blank Report

This section contains a rundown of all of the data sources that can be used in your reports, broken down by type and listing the specific database formats that can be accessed. For each data source, step-by-step instructions are included for how to connect to the data source and create a blank report.

FIGURE 2.1   The Crystal Reports Database Expert.

Database Files

Crystal Reports can use a direct, native connection to report from file-type databases, including the following:

- Microsoft Excel (.xls)
- XML (.xml)
- Xbase (.dbf, .ndx, .mdx, .bde)
- Paradox® (.db)
- Pervasive® PSQL V8 (.ddf)
- Microsoft Access (.mdb)

Through this direct connection, Crystal Reports can extract data without having to submit a query to a database server. To create a report from these types of data sources, you can either create the report from scratch or use one of the report wizards, which we will look at a little later in this chapter.

To create a report based on one of these data sources, use the following steps:

1. Open Crystal Reports, and click File > New > Blank Report. The Database Expert opens.
2. Double-click the folder marked Create New Connection to expand the list of available data sources.
3. Double-click the Database Files folder, and using the standard File > Open dialog box, locate your database file and click OK to select. In this example, select the GALAXY.MDB database file from the CD-ROM.
4. A list of tables will now appear below your data source. Highlight the table or tables you want to use in your report, and click the right-arrow button to move them to the Selected list on the left. For this report, select the INVOICE table.
5. When finished selecting your tables, click OK to return to the Report Design window.

ON THE CD

A new report will be created and displayed in the Report Designer, as shown in Figure 2.2.

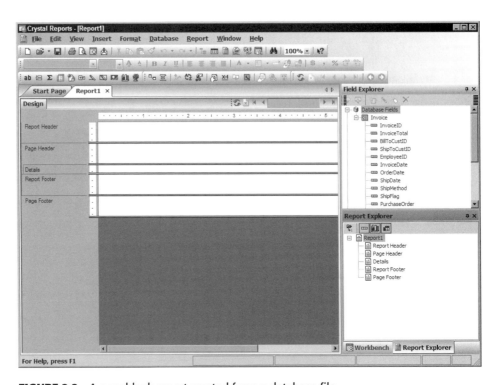

FIGURE 2.2   A new blank report created from a database file.

ON THE CD

A sample report named CONNECTNATIVE.RPT created using this method is located on the CD-ROM in the PROJECTS folder.

The Field Explorer is shown on the right side of the page, and the Database Fields node contains a list of all of the fields in the table you have selected. You can now drag and drop fields from this list onto your report.

Relational Databases

By far the most popular data-access method uses a native or ODBC connection to a relational database. Crystal Reports ships native and ODBC drivers for the most popular RDBMSs, including

- IBM DB2®, DB2/2®, DB2/400®, and DB2/600®
- IBM Informix®
- IBM Lotus Notes® and Domino® 4.5 and above, R5
- Microsoft SQL Server
- Oracle 7/8
- Sybase® Adaptive Server® release 10

Most of these native drivers require that the standard database client be installed and configured before they can be used. For example, if you want to access an Oracle database, you will need the Oracle client installed and configured locally on your computer. Chances are good that you probably already have the correct software installed on your machine. An easy way to tell is to check the Database Expert to see whether your data source appears under the heading More Data Sources.

In addition to using native driver access, you can also access these data sources through an ODBC driver. To access a database through ODBC, you will need to configure the appropriate ODBC driver through the ODBC Administrator (accessed through the Windows Control Panel) and then use the following steps:

1. Open Crystal Reports, and click File > New > Blank Report. The Database Expert opens.
2. Double-click to expand the folder marked Create New Connection, and then double-click the node marked ODBC (RDO). A list of available data sources appears, as shown in Figure 2.3.
3. To select a data source from the list, enter any required information, then click Finish. For the majority of examples in this book, we will be using the Xtreme Sample Database that is installed with Crystal Reports XI, so select the data source named Xtreme Sample Database 11, and click Finish. A list of the available tables, views, stored procedures, and so on within your data source is displayed in the Database Expert.

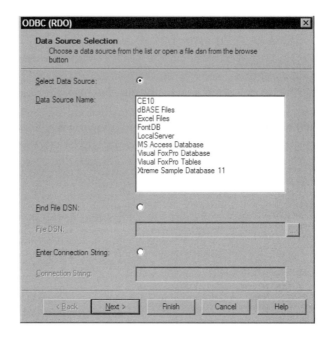

FIGURE 2.3   A list of available ODBC data sources.

4. Highlight the table or tables you want to use in your report, and click the right-arrow button to move them to the selected list on the left. For this report, select the EMPLOYEE table.
5. When finished selecting your table, click OK to return to the Report Design window.

You can now use the tables and fields you selected to build your report as you normally would.

A sample report named CONNECTODBC.RPT created using ODBC is located on the CD-ROM in the PROJECTS folder.

Crystal Reports logs on to your database to retrieve information and perform queries. Frequently, when you close a report and leave Crystal Reports open, the database connection will remain open as well. To log on or off of a database server, click Database > Log On or Off Server.

WORKING WITH THE VISUAL LINKING EXPERT

Relational databases are usually split into a number of different tables. These tables can be rejoined together to create complex queries. In Crystal Reports, these joins are created by using the Visual Linking Expert to visually draw a line between two key fields. If you select more than one table in the Database Expert, a separate Links tab will appear in the Database Expert. This dialog box, shown in Figure 2.4, is used to specify the relationship between the tables and views you have selected for your report.

You can make this dialog box larger by dragging the bottom-right corner.

The links that are shown in the Links dialog box correspond to the SQL joins that exist between the different tables in your data source.

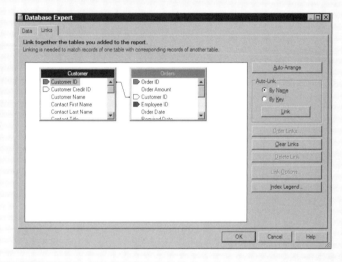

FIGURE 2.4 Use the Visual Linking Expert to indicate the relationship between your database tables or database files.

Crystal Reports will first go through the table, views, and so on that you have selected in your report and will attempt to auto-link these structures based on the keys and indexes it finds as well as the field name, type, and length.

If you are using a PC-type database such as Access or dBase, Crystal Reports will display the different indexes that are present in the table. You can click the Index Legend button to open a key to all of the indexes (for example, red = first index, blue = second index, and so on). →

Unless you are using a very well-structured database, smart-linking usually gets it wrong, so you can remove the links between tables or views by clicking the line between the two tables and pressing the Delete key on your keyboard. You can also use the Clear Links button to clear all of the links at once.

Once you have determine the correct links, you can add them to the dialog box by dragging one field on top of another to draw a line between the two tables. To change the type of join between tables, right-click the link you have drawn and click Link Options.

A dialog box opens that allows you to select the join type (inner join, outer join, and so on) as well as the type of link. Once you are finished specifying the join type, click OK to return to the Links tab. One final clean-up option you can use—if you are working with a large number of tables and links—is the auto-arrange button, which arranges them neatly on the Links page.

For more information on working with database linking and options, check out the resources on the companion Web site, www.crystalxibook.com

OLAP Data Sources

OLAP data (sometimes called multidimensional data) can be accessed through OLE DB for OLAP, a standard interface for accessing OLAP data, or through a number of native OLAP drivers that are included with Crystal Reports, including

- SQL Server Analysis Services
- Hyperion® Essbase®
- IBM DB/2
- Holos HDC

OLAP data provides a summary of information that is held in a relational database and can provide insight that millions of rows of data normally do not.

To report from an OLAP data source, use the following steps:

1. Open Crystal Reports, and click File > New > Blank Report. The Database Expert opens.
2. Double-click to expand the folder marked Create New Connection, and then double-click the node marked OLAP. The OLAP Connection Browser opens.

3. To add a new data source, click the Add button. The Connection Properties dialog box appears.

4. From the drop-down list at the top of the dialog box, select your OLAP data source. In this example, we will be using a sample Holos HDC cube that is included with the sample data provided with Crystal Reports. Select the option marked Holos HDC Cube (Local Client).

Holos was an OLAP software vendor that BusinessObjects (then Crystal Decisions) acquired and later integrated into various BusinessObjects products. Holos HDC Cubes are perfect a data source for demonstrating OLAP features in Crystal Reports, because they don't require a back-end OLAP server.

5. In the text box provided, enter a caption for your OLAP data source. In this example, enter Xtreme Sample OLAP Cube 11.

6. Use the Browse button to browse for your OLAP data source. The sample cube is available at *x*:\Program Files\Business Objects\Crystal Reports 11\Samples\En\Databases\Olap Data\Xtreme.hdc. (*x* is the drive where you installed Crystal Reports on your computer.)

7. Next, click the Test Connection button to test the connection to your cube. A message box stating Connection Successful opens.

8. To finish the setup, click OK to return to the OLAP Connection Browser, which should now look like the one shown in Figure 2.5.

FIGURE 2.5 The OLAP Connection Browser displaying your new connection.

9. Expand your new data source, and highlight the cube that you want to report from. In this example, expand your data source, select Xtreme, and click OK. You return to the Database Expert, and all of the available cubes in your data source appear in the OLAP folder below the data source name.

10. Highlight the cube(s) you want to use in your report, and click the right-arrow button to move them to the selected list on the left. For this report, select the CUSTOMER cube.

11. When finished selecting your tables, click OK to return to the Report Design window.

A list of fields will appear in the Field Explorer on the right side of the Report Designer. You can drag and drop these fields onto your report as you normally would. If the fields look a bit strange (for example, "Monthly, Level 0") don't worry too much about that now.

ON THE CD

A sample report named CONNECTOLAP.RPT created using an OLAP data source is located on the CD-ROM in the PROJECTS folder.

NOTE

Keep in mind that this setup procedure may be slightly different for the different OLAP data sources that Crystal Reports supports. For example, for the Essbase setup, you will need to enter a server name as well as a user name and password and may need to have the Essbase client software installed and configured on your computer.

Enterprise Data Sources

ERP systems generally run on top of a relational database, but they have their own business rules and data structures. Crystal Reports has a number of data drivers available for ERP systems, including

- SAP
- Baan™
- PeopleSoft®
- PeopleSoft Enterprise One (formerly JD Edwards)

NOTE

Some of these drivers may be sold separately from Crystal Reports XI.

To configure these drivers and access information, you will definitely need the help of your application administrator, because the setup is not for the faint of heart. A number of technical white papers are available at the BusinessObjects Web site (*http://support.businessobjects.com/library/docfiles/cps10/docs_en.asp*) that provide the technical background necessary to get started. Often there will be specific requirements for client software and configuration or specific OEM versions or add-ins to Crystal Reports required to use these drivers.

BusinessObjects Universes

Since the acquisition of Crystal Decisions by Business Objects and the integration of the two product lines, you can now report from BusinessObjects Universes as well. A Universe is a meta layer provided to mask the complexity of the underlying database, allowing a developer to create complex joins and manipulate data behind the scenes. From a user perspective, a Universe provides a well-organized view of the underlying data, including proper table and field names, view-time security, and more.

NOTE

To report from a BusinessObjects Universe, you will need to be using Crystal Reports in conjunction with BusinessObjects Enterprise, which is the enterprise distribution and scheduling framework for deploying reports. You can find more information about reporting from Universes in the documentation included on the BusinessObjects Enterprise XI CD-ROM.

Other Data Sources

Crystal Reports also includes a number of drivers for nontraditional data sources, including Act!®, Microsoft Exchange, and Microsoft Logs. Most of these data sources have their own setup and configuration requirements and do not fit into the standard data source categories that can be accessed through a native or ODBC driver. Some of the available formats follow:

- Act! 3.0
- Microsoft Exchange
- Microsoft Outlook
- Lotus Domino
- Web/IIS Log Files

All of these data formats are available in the Database Expert, either in the main or the More Data Sources section, as shown in Figure 2.6, and most require some additional parameters (file name, location, server name, and so on).

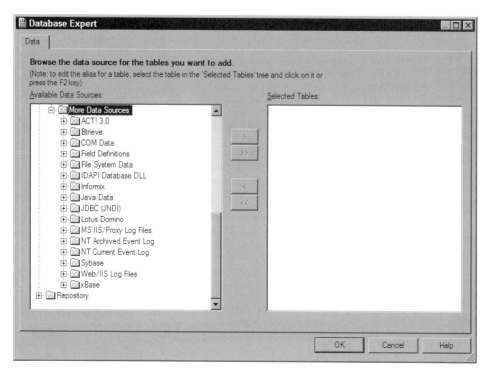

FIGURE 2.6   Additional data sources that are available in Crystal Reports.

For a complete list of the information required by these data sources, see the Crystal Reports Help file by clicking Help > Crystal Reports Help from within the Report Designer.

CREATING REPORTS USING THE STANDARD REPORT WIZARD

So far in this chapter we have looked at the first step in report design—connecting to your data source and creating a blank report. Once you have made a connection and selected the table, view, and stored procedure from which you want to report, you are presented with a list of fields in the Field Explorer that you can drag onto your report.

Although this is the most straightforward method of creating reports, there is an easier way to get started. Crystal Reports has a number of wizards that have been designed to walk you through the report design process and jump-start your report development. Most report developers will use the wizard to create a basic report and then customize it from that point.

Remember, anything you do using a Report Design Wizard can also be accomplished using the menus, commands, and icons in the Report Designer itself. If you prefer, you can use the techniques outlined at the beginning of the chapter to start from a blank page and add all of the elements of the report yourself. However, the wizards make the initial report design process easy.

When you first open Crystal Reports, you will see a start page that looks like the one shown in Figure 2.7.

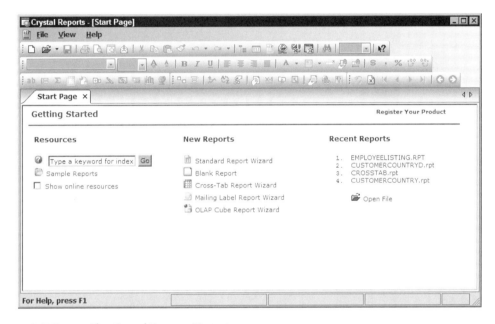

FIGURE 2.7 The Crystal Reports XI start page.

This page lists some resources you can use to get started and provides a list of the available report wizards, which you can access at any time by clicking File > New. A list of these wizards has been included in the next section, including a brief description of each and how they can be used.

Standard Report Wizard

The Standard Report Wizard is used the majority of the time. It allows you to create listing reports and to add grouping, sorting, summaries, formulas, and so forth.

You also can create reports for analysis using the Standard Report Wizard (such as, show me my top 10 customers), add graphs, and apply predefined styles to your report. An example of a report created with the Standard Report Wizard is shown in Figure 2.8.

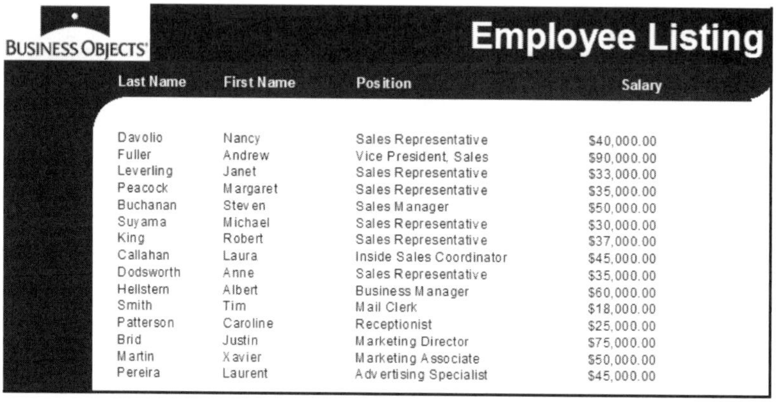
BUSINESS OBJECTS

Employee Listing

Last Name	First Name	Position	Salary
Davolio	Nancy	Sales Representative	$40,000.00
Fuller	Andrew	Vice President, Sales	$90,000.00
Leverling	Janet	Sales Representative	$33,000.00
Peacock	Margaret	Sales Representative	$35,000.00
Buchanan	Steven	Sales Manager	$50,000.00
Suyama	Michael	Sales Representative	$30,000.00
King	Robert	Sales Representative	$37,000.00
Callahan	Laura	Inside Sales Coordinator	$45,000.00
Dodsworth	Anne	Sales Representative	$35,000.00
Hellstern	Albert	Business Manager	$60,000.00
Smith	Tim	Mail Clerk	$18,000.00
Patterson	Caroline	Receptionist	$25,000.00
Brid	Justin	Marketing Director	$75,000.00
Martin	Xavier	Marketing Associate	$50,000.00
Pereira	Laurent	Advertising Specialist	$45,000.00

FIGURE 2.8 A report created with the Standard Report Wizard.

Blank Report Wizard

The Blank Report Wizard is what we have been using up to this point in the chapter. It is used simply to connect to a data source and create a blank report that you can then customize.

Cross-Tab Wizard

A cross-tab is a data presentation format that closely resembles a spreadsheet. The Cross-Tab Wizard is used to create a cross-tab that has rows and columns that can be stacked on top of each other to create a summarized, hierarchical view of your data. In addition to rows and columns, a cross-tab also has summarized fields that allow you to read the cross-tab quickly for the information you require, as shown in the report in Figure 2.9.

Mailing Label Wizard

Crystal Reports makes creating labels from your data source quick and easy with a number of the standard labels predefined. Using the Mailing Label Wizard, you can create labels quickly in various sizes and formats without having to work out the

Quarterly Sales by Country

		1/2000	10/2000	1/2001	4/2001	7/2001	10/2001
USA	AL	$1,067.50	$4,717.60	$14,060.26	$47,611.07	$38,824.45	$32,113.87
	AR	$0.00	$0.00	$0.00	$8,819.55	$0.00	$0.00
	AZ	$0.00	$0.00	$0.00	$91.40	$0.00	$0.00
	CA	$5,526.63	$2,860.65	$64,680.89	$47,630.29	$40,181.21	$55,095.34
	CO	$0.00	$0.00	$0.00	$161.70	$0.00	$0.00
	CT	$0.00	$0.00	$0.00	$43.50	$0.00	$0.00
	DC	$0.00	$0.00	$0.00	$13.50	$0.00	$0.00
	DE	$0.00	$0.00	$0.00	$52.50	$0.00	$0.00
	FL	$1,968.18	$1,316.50	$14,606.71	$20,369.23	$30,877.67	$10,357.65
	GA	$0.00	$0.00	$0.00	$17.50	$0.00	$0.00
	IA	$11,363.10	$5,893.09	$12,324.12	$25,836.51	$22,854.39	$25,926.82

FIGURE 2.9   A sample cross-tab report.

size, spacing, and so forth. If you are working with a label size or format that is not listed as a standard label, you can enter the dimensions and spacing to create a custom label, as shown in Figure 2.10.

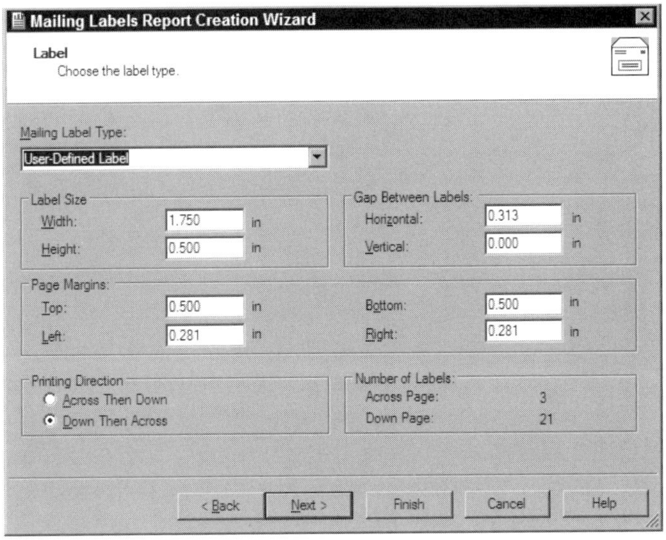

FIGURE 2.10   Setting up a custom label size.

Most of the standard labels are for letter-sized paper only and correspond to an Avery® label number. You can create a custom label if your particular label number is not listed.

Online Analytical Processing (OLAP) Wizard

The Online Analytical Processing (OLAP) Wizard can be used to create reports from OLAP data sources. Unlike relational databases, which store data in a number of tables in a two-dimensional view, OLAP data structures can be multidimensional. Instead of rows and columns (two dimensions), OLAP structures have multiple dimensions to help business users and managers analyze data extracted from their transactional systems, as shown in Figure 2.11.

Sales by Product/Country

Year Total

	All Products	Active Oudoors Crochet Glove	Active Oudoors Lycra Glove	Descent	Endorphin
USA	4,066,527	106,125	137,839	1,080,018	183,023
AL	259,943	12,276	855	78,257	27,407
Benny - The Spokes Person	35,525	1,570			2,780
Psycho-Cycle	121,566		855	50,903	3,147
The Great Bike Shop	102,852	10,706		27,353	21,479
AR	8,820			8,820	
Bikefest	8,820			8,820	
AZ	91		50		
CA	401,785	8,170	27,024	125,936	16,527

FIGURE 2.11   A report created from an OLAP data source.

Crystal Reports provides support for most of the major OLAP vendors, including Hyperion Cubes, IBM DB2 OLAP Server, Informix MetaCube®, Holos HDC Cubes, and many others using Object Linking and Embedding (OLE) Database (DB) for OLAP, including Microsoft SQL Server and Applix® TM/1®.

Each of these wizards will guide you through the steps for creating a new report with the specified features. Although there are a few to choose from, all of the wizards share some common steps, such as selection of the data source, fields, and so on. Once you are comfortable with the Standard Report Wizard, you can apply your knowledge of how it works to other wizards.

Selecting a Data Source

The first step in creating a report using the Standard Report Wizard is choosing the data source on which the report will be based.

The wizard will display a list of available data sources. This list is really just a number of different views of the data sources that you have available to use in your report.

Current Connections: This section of the Available Data Sources shows any databases or sources onto which you are currently logged.

Repository: If your system administrator has already configured a data source in the BusinessObjects Repository, it will appear here.

For more information on working with the Repository, see Appendix A.

Favorites: If you are familiar with Favorites in Internet Explorer, this option will be familiar; it works the same way, except that instead of saving frequently viewed Web pages, the Favorites option here allows you to save frequently used data connections.

History: The History section automatically saves connections you have recently used.

Create a New Connection: This command is used to create a new connection to your data source.

You have already seen some of these options in use earlier in the chapter when creating a simple blank report from a data source. (If you expand the node for Create New Connection, you will see a number of different data sources you can use in your report.)

For example, to create a report from an ODBC data source, you would expand the ODBC data source node. A second dialog box appears, prompting you to select the data source you wish to use. Once you have selected your data source, a separate node will appear under ODBC, showing the data source you have selected and all of the tables, views, stored procedures, and so on that are available for use.

To add a table to your report, expand the Tables node, and double-click to add to the list of selected tables on the right; alternatively, you could also highlight the table and use the arrows to move it across.

Linking Database Tables or Files

If you select one or more tables for your report, the Standard Report Wizard adds an additional step in the wizard titled Link, as shown in Figure 2.12. The best advice is to find a copy of the entity-relationship diagram that shows the relationships among the tables in your database and use this as your guide. You need to re-create these relationships in Crystal Reports by drawing visual links between the tables.

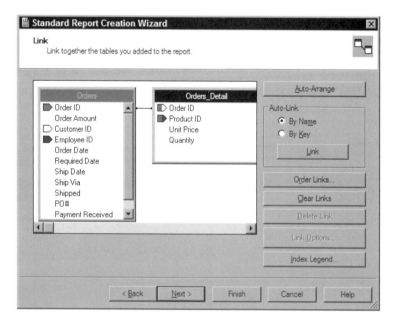

FIGURE 2.12   The Visual Linking tab helps you join two or more tables.

By default, Crystal Reports will perform the links or joins for you based on the name of the field or keys that are present in the table. Joining tables is covered in detail at the end of this chapter. For now, we need to select some fields to appear in our report.

Choosing Fields

The Fields page of the Standard Report Wizard, shown in Figure 2.13, is split into two sections. The left pane of the dialog box lists all of the fields that are available to be inserted into your report, grouped below their table name.

To add a field to your report, you need to move the field from the left pane to the right pane. You can accomplish this by double-clicking the field name or by highlighting the field and clicking the Add button. Additional buttons are also available to add or remove one or all fields.

To select multiple fields, press and hold the CTRL key while clicking.

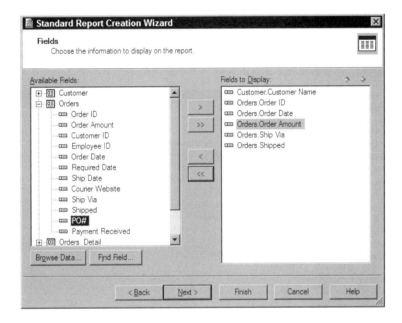

FIGURE 2.13   Using the Fields page to select the fields for your report.

If you are unsure of a field's definition or contents, you can click the Browse Data button to display a sample of the field's contents. Keep in mind that the sample returned is not based on the complete contents of the table; it is just a representative sample of up to (approximately) 200 records.

Another key feature of the Fields tab is the Find Field button, at the bottom left. This button allows you to search the selected tables for a field that matches your criteria.

And because we are just getting started with report design, we are not going to discuss the use of the Formula button to insert calculations and summaries at this time. If you can't wait to get started using formulas, you can go straight to Chapter 5, where formulas are covered in depth.

To change the order of the fields you are inserting in your report, you can use the up- and down-arrows that appear in the top-right corner of the dialog box to move fields up and down. At this point, you can also change the column heading associated with a field.

Grouping and Sorting

The next step in creating a report using the Standard Report Wizard is selecting the sorting and grouping to use in your report using the Grouping options shown in Figure 2.14. To select a field for grouping, you move it from the list on the left to the list on the right.

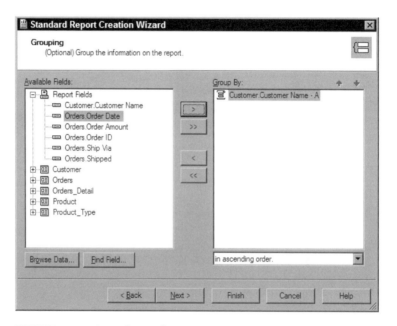

FIGURE 2.14   Grouping options.

By specifying a field on the Group tab, you can add control breaks or groups to your report. For example, if you were to group on the State field, your report would be printed with all the records for each state together, with a break between each state, as shown in Figure 2.15.

Customer by State

State	Customer Name	Address1	City
Alabama			
AL	The Great Bike Shop	1922 Beach Crescent	Huntsville
AL	Benny - The Spokes Person	1020 Oak Way	Huntsville
AL	Psycho-Cycle	8287 Scott Road	Huntsville
Arkansas			
AR	Bikefest	4301 President Way	Little Rock
Arizona			
AZ	Bicycle Races	3100 West Cactus Drive	Tempe
AZ	Biking and Hiking	76 Palm Drive	Phoenix
California			
CA	Changing Gears	1600 Hyde Crescent	Irvine
CA	Rowdy Rims Company	4861 Second Road	Newbury Park

FIGURE 2.15   An example of a report grouped by state.

Once you select a field, notice that you have a choice of sort orders in the drop-down list below the list of selected fields.

In Ascending Order: This option groups the records by the field you have specified and orders those groups from A through Z, zero through nine, and so forth.

In Descending Order: This option groups the records by the field you have specified and orders those groups from Z through A, nine through zero, and so forth.

In Specified Order: Using this option, you can name and define your own grouping criteria. You might want to use this option, for example, if you want to group states into sales territories. You could create a group called Bob's Territory and set the criteria to North Carolina and South Carolina. When the report is printed, all of the records from North Carolina and South Carolina will be grouped together under the group name, Bob's Territory.

In Original Order: If your database has already performed some sorting on the data, this option leaves the records in their original order.

The Grouping step of the wizard also features a Browse Data button that allows you to search for a field to use for your group.

Inserting Summaries

The Summaries options, shown in Figure 2.16, are used to insert Crystal Reports summary fields into your report; they appear only if you have inserted a group using the wizard. Crystal Reports provides these summary fields so that you do not have to create a formula every time you want to insert a sum, average, and so on.

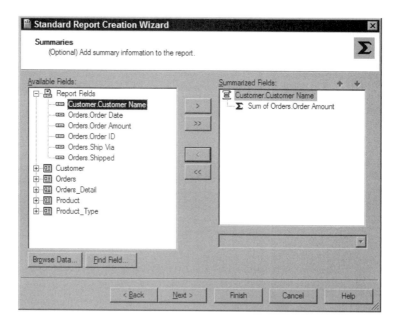

FIGURE 2.16   Inserting summary fields into your report.

You can insert a number of summary fields into your report; the types of summaries vary based on the type of field, as shown in Table 2.1.

For some of the statistical functions, you are asked to provide additional information, such as the value for N. For other functions, you specify that a summary is a certain percentage of a particular field.

When you add a summary to your report using the Standard Report Wizard, the summary appears immediately following each group, showing the summary for only that particular group. By default, if you have specified grouping for your report, Crystal Reports will add all of the numeric fields you have selected to be summarized.

TABLE 2.1   Crystal Reports Summary Operators

Summary Type	With Numeric Fields	With Other Field Types
Sum	X	
Average	X	
Maximum	X	X
Minimum	X	X
Count	X	X
Distinct Count	X	X
Sample Variance	X	
Sample Standard Deviation	X	
Population Variance	X	
Population Standard Deviation	X	
Correlation	X	
Covariance	X	
Weighted Average	X	
Median	X	
Pth Percentile	X	
Nth Largest	X	X
Nth Smallest	X	X
Mode	X	X
Nth Most Frequent	X	X

Using Group Sorting

Group Sorting (sometimes called Top N, Bottom N, and so forth), shown in Figure 2.17, is a powerful analytical feature that allows you to order data based on sub-totals or summaries and is an optional step when using most report wizards.

For example, if you have a report totaling each customer's sales for the past year, you can use group sorting to determine your top 10 or top 20 customers by ranking their sales totals. (Likewise, you can also find your bottom 10 customers.)

In addition to doing Top N and Bottom N analysis, this feature can be used to sort all of your customers, placing them in order from highest revenue to lowest (or vice versa).

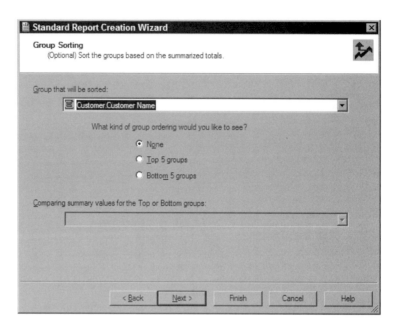

FIGURE 2.17   Group Sorting and Top N analysis can be used to analyze report data to identify trends.

When working with Group Sorting and the Report Wizards, you need to keep two things in mind. The first is that to use Top N analysis, you need to have a group inserted into your report and a summary field summarizing some information within that group. The second is that Group Sorting analysis can be applied to multiple groups. You may want to show your top 10 customers, for instance, and, for each customer, the top five products purchased.

Adding Charts

Crystal Reports uses a powerful third-party graphics engine to provide a wide range of graphs and charts, as shown in Figure 2.18. A number of standard chart types are available from within the wizard, including

- Bar
- Line
- Pie

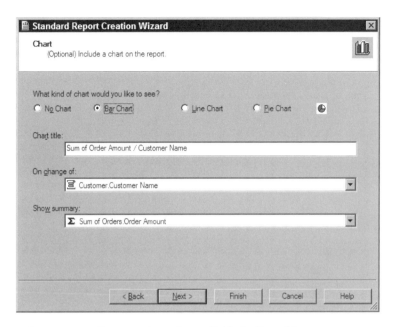

FIGURE 2.18   Charts and graphs available in Crystal Reports.

You also have the option of creating a custom chart type, based on your needs. In addition to the graph type, you can select the source of data for your graph. The wizard's charting function is based on a group you have inserted and some summary field. These graphs appear in the report header and represent some of the basic charting features available in Crystal Reports.

Crystal Reports can add complex charts and graphs after you are through with the Report Wizard. This functionality is available in the Report Designer and is detailed in Chapter 7.

Using Record Selection

One of the last steps in creating a report using the Standard Report Wizard is setting the record selection for your report using the Record Selection options, shown in Figure 2.19.

Record selection is important because you probably do not want to return every single record in the table for your report. You use record selection to narrow the data to get exactly the subset of information that you need. If you were creating a daily sales report, for example, you would probably want to return the sales records for only a single day.

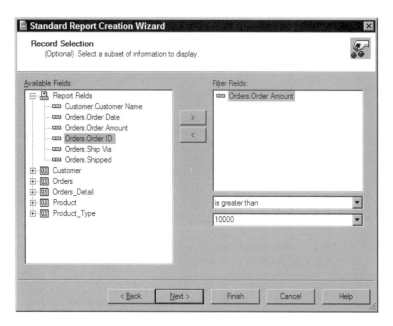

FIGURE 2.19 Choosing the record selection for your report.

Another key point about record selection is that you want to return only the records that you need for the report. It makes no sense running a report for 2 million customers when you are interested in only one particular customer. Using record selection, you can narrow your focus to that one customer and save on report-processing time.

Using this step of the wizard, you can specify a field to use and then set your record selection criteria based on that field. If you are creating your report from a relatively small database, you can skip record selection and move to select a template and preview your report.

Selecting a Template

The final step in the Standard Report Wizard, shown in Figure 2.20, is to apply a template to your report. A template is a set of formatting attributes that are applied to your report. If you select any of the predefined styles, you see a preview of what that particular style looks like on the right. You can also select a template that is not listed here by clicking the Browse button and selecting a template file.

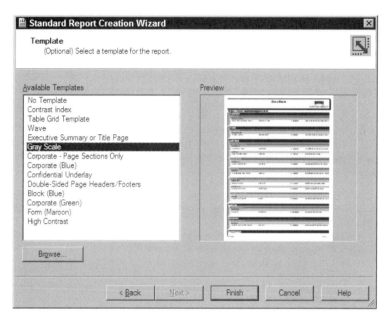

FIGURE 2.20   You can apply a preformatted report style to your report.

Once you have selected a template (or none), you are almost finished. With the Report Wizard settings complete, click the Finish button to preview your new report.

If you are a bit confused by the Design tab and Preview tab that appear, note that these subjects are covered in Chapter 3.

NOTE

Bringing It All Together

In the past few pages we have looked at all of the steps required to create a report using the Standard Report Wizard. Now it's time to put that knowledge to good use. In the following section we are going to walk through creating your first report using this expert. The report will display the Top 5 products sold and will include a chart at the top of the first page.

ON THE CD

This report, named TOP5PRODUCTS.RPT, is available on the CD-ROM in the PROJECTS folder .

To create this report using the Standard Report Wizard, use the following steps:

1. Open Crystal Reports, and click File > New > Standard Report.
2. Double-click the node marked ODBC (RDO) to open a list of available ODBC data sources.

3. Select the Xtreme Sample Database 11, and click the Finish button.
4. In the Database page of the wizard, expand the Xtreme Sample Database folder and then the Tables folder to display a list of available tables.
5. Double-click the Orders Detail and then the Product table to move it to the list of selected tables on the right side, and then click Next. The Links page will appear and by default, all of the links will be created for you.
6. Click Next to continue.
7. In the Fields page, double-click the Product table to expand it, and add the Product Name field to your selected fields. Repeat the procedure with the Quantity field, and then click Next.
8. In the Grouping page, double-click the Product Name field to add it to the selected fields, and then click Next.
9. In the Summaries page, verify that the Quantity field appears in the selected list on the right, and then click Next.
10. In the Group Sorting page, select the option for Top 5 Groups, and then click Next.
11. In the Chart page, select the option for Bar Chart, and then click Next.
12. Because we want to return all of the records in our table, in the Record Selection page just click Next.
13. And finally, in the Template page select the Corporate (Blue) template, and click OK to preview your report.
14. Next, click File > Summary info and enter a Title and Description for your report. Click OK. Your report should now look like the one shown in Figure 2.21:

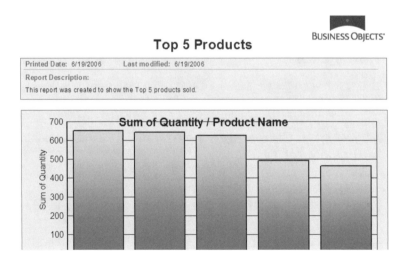

FIGURE 2.21   The finished report.

SAVING YOUR REPORT

After you have finished with the Report Wizard, you are returned to Preview tab of your report. At this point, you will probably want to save your report before we move on. You can save your report by clicking File > Save or by clicking the Save icon on the toolbar.

Save Options

On the File menu, the Save Data with Report option is selected by default. The only reason to leave this option selected would be if you were going to send the report to another Crystal Reports user who did not have access to your database. This user could open the report with saved data and view or print the results without having to go back to the original data source. Otherwise, this option will increase the report file size unnecessarily.

In addition, under File > Summary Info, shown in Figure 2.22, you can enter an author's name, keywords, and so forth. Although most people do not ever complete the summary information for any file that they save, you *should* complete this information. Crystal Reports treats these fields as special fields that can be inserted into your report. You can also select the checkbox at the bottom of the dialog box to generate a preview of the report. With this feature, when you are looking at a long list of reports, you can browse through a thumbnail picture of each report. This information is also used when you publish the report to the Web using BusinessObjects Enterprise, because the title, description, and thumbnail image can be viewed from the Enterprise front-end.

If your report is based on a data source that is being updated regularly, you can refresh your report at any time by clicking Report > Refresh Report Data or by pressing the F5 function key. If you are working off a database that has live data entry during the day, you may notice that your report results change as new data is entered or deleted.

File Format

In Crystal Reports 9, an .RPT file format was put in place to support Unicode. Unfortunately, this file format is not compatible with previous versions of Crystal Reports. The new file format is, however, supported by Crystal Reports 9, 10, and XI as well as Crystal Enterprise 9, 10, and BusinessObjects Enterprise XI. So, reports created in Crystal Reports XI can be opened using these previous versions and vice versa. But keep in mind that some features are not backward compatible, so if you open a version XI report in Crystal Reports 10, any report elements based on new features may be disabled or removed.

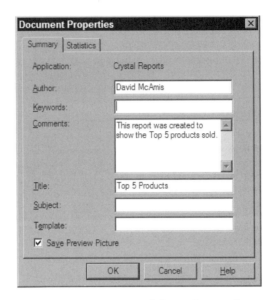

FIGURE 2.22 Summary information can be inserted into your report as a special field.

If you need to send reports to other users who have a previous version of Crystal Reports (or who don't use Crystal Reports at all), you may want to consider using one of the many export formats available.

Saving Data with Your Report

Another issue to consider when saving your report is whether to save the data with the report. When a Crystal Reports report is run, a saved record set is written to a temporary file on the hard drive. (You may notice this feature when you make a change to your report or record selection and you are prompted with Use Saved Data? or Refresh?) When you save your report with the Save Data with Report option enabled, this saved record set becomes a part of the report (.rpt) file and increases the size of the file dramatically. To turn off this option, click File > Save Data with Report to remove the checkmark.

WORKING WITH THE REPORT DESIGNER

With your first simple report created, it is time to take a look at the place you will spend the most time as a report designer: the Report Design environment. In this section, you learn the basic skills that you will need throughout the report design process. You will learn how to navigate through reports; to insert, move, and format different types of objects; and to use general report-formatting techniques.

REPORT DESIGN ENVIRONMENT

The report design environment is divided into several areas, each with its own purpose and unique properties. Some areas of the environment are standard with every report that you create, such as the Design and Preview tabs and the navigation toolbar and other toolbars.

Other areas, like report sections, depend on your report's design and may appear multiple times, depending on your needs. Understanding what is happening in the report design environment is the key to understanding report design, and this section gives you an overview of the various areas of the design environment and their use.

Design and Preview Tabs

You can view your report in two modes: Design and Preview. Design mode, shown in Figure 2.23, offers a behind-the-scenes look at your report, and each section of the report is displayed once. Any changes you make to a section or objects in a section while in Design mode are reflected throughout the report. For example, if you change the title that appears in the Page Header section, that change is reflected in every page header, regardless of whether your report is 1 page or 100 pages.

The Preview mode is a print preview that is prepared according to your default printer driver. It provides an accurate, multiple-page WYSIWYG (what you see is what you get) representation of your report. What you see in Preview mode is exactly what you see when you print your report.

For most operations, you can use either the Design or Preview mode, but it is sometimes easier to work exclusively in the Design mode because you can see precisely where you are placing objects. Also, when you are in the Design view of your report, you can view any objects that are suppressed or hidden in your report. (And believe me, this comes in very handy sometimes!)

Navigation Methods

The navigation toolbar, shown on the Preview tab in Figure 2.24, is used to navigate between pages in Preview mode. The arrows move you a page at a time through the report, and the arrows with the vertical lines move you to the first or last page of your report. In addition, you can close preview windows and stop report processing using the same set of buttons.

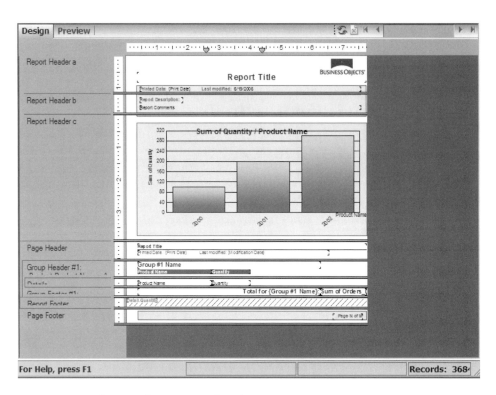

FIGURE 2.23   The Crystal Reports Design view.

FIGURE 2.24   The navigation toolbar can be used to move backward and forward through your report.

To navigate to a specific place in your report, you can also use the group tree that appears on the left side of the Preview window, shown in Figure 2.25. This tree will appear only if you have inserted one or more groups in your report. For quick access to information in your report, you can also search for a value using Crystal Report's Find function (CTRL+F).

FIGURE 2.25   The group navigation tree.

You can also jump to a specific page directly from the Report menu (CTRL+ G).

Sometimes you may see the page numbers shown as "1 of 1+." This means that Crystal Reports knows that there is enough data to fill additional pages, but it doesn't know exactly how many. If you click the right arrow, Crystal Reports will advance to the next page. If you click the right arrow with the line (indicating to jump to the last page), Crystal Reports will show you the total page count.

Toolbars

A number of toolbars contain buttons or shortcuts to commonly used menu items. These graphics are also shown on the menus, to help you quickly locate the corresponding button on the toolbar.

You can display four different toolbars and the status bar by right-clicking in the toolbar area and selecting a toolbar from the list. Figure 2.26 shows these toolbars, and a list of their associated functions follows.

FIGURE 2.26   Crystal Reports toolbars.

Standard: Provides the standard Windows buttons for opening, saving, printing, and refreshing reports as well as buttons for cut, copy, paste, undo, redo, and basic Crystal Reports operations. This toolbar appears by default when you start Crystal Reports.

Formatting: Supplies shortcuts to common formatting options, including font, size, and alignment. This toolbar appears by default when you start Crystal Reports.

Insert: Includes tools inserting fields and other objects, including database fields, groups, and summary fields.

Experts: Provides shortcuts to commonly used experts, including the Running Total Expert and the Highlighting Expert.

Navigation: Provides navigation controls for navigating through the report, including next and previous page.

Status Bar: Appears at the bottom of the report design page and shows object names, measurements, number of records, processing status, and so on. The status bar is shown by default when you start Crystal Reports.

Report Explorer

Another important concept to understand in the creation of reports is that the report is broken into separate sections. The different sections that make up a report are shown on the left side of the screen, as well as in the Report Explorer, shown in Figure 2.27, which can be opened by clicking View > Report Explorer.

The Report Explorer provides a look at all of the elements of your report at a glance and can be helpful when working with complex reports. Regardless of how complex your reports may be, the following sections may appear in your report and are commonly used as described here:

Report Header/Footer: These appear at the top of the first page of the report and at the bottom of the last page. The report title appears most often in the report header, and a record count or end-of-report marker may appear in the report footer (that is, "10,000 records processed—end of report"), in addition to any grand totals for your report.

Page Header/Footer: These appear at the top and bottom of every page. The page headers and footers are used to display information that is critical to understanding the data represented and may include field headings, page numbers, and the print date of the report.

Group Header/Footer: These appear immediately before and immediately after any groups you have inserted. The group header or footer usually contains the group name field, which provides a label for the group, and may also contain formulas, subtotals, and summaries based on the data in the group.

Details: This appears once for each record in your report and (unless you are creating a summary report) contains most of the report's data.

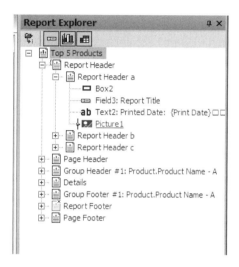

FIGURE 2.27 A number of sections make up a report.

On the Design tab, each of these sections is represented once, but when the report is previewed or printed, these sections are repeated as many times as needed, as shown in Figure 2.28.

It is easy to become confused when switching between the Design and Preview modes, especially when you are looking at a preview of a report and wondering where that field came from. One trick to help you understand where different objects are placed is to click the object to select it. When you switch back to the Design mode, the object will still be selected and you can see in which section it appears.

Note, too, that you can split report sections into multiples, so you may see Report Header A and Report Header B to indicate that the report header section has been split into two (or more) segments. You can use this technique to create complex reports that may be impossible to create with just a single section.

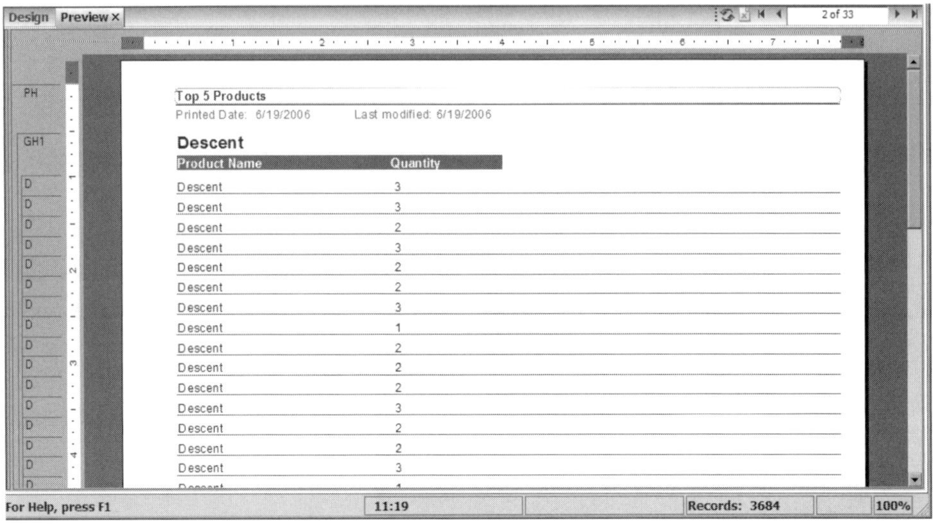

FIGURE 2.28 An example of a report preview.

For example, if you were creating a report for distribution in two different languages, you could have one report header set up with the English title, comments, and so on and a separate report header with the same information in Spanish. By looking at a database field (like a Country field), you could determine which header to display.

In the report we just created, the template we used split the Report Header section into three parts in order to display the title, description, and chart at the top of the report, as shown in Figure 2.29.

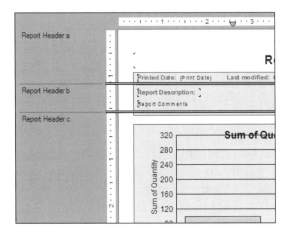

FIGURE 2.29 An example of a report with multiple sections.

CUSTOMIZING THE DESIGN ENVIRONMENT

The report design environment can be customized to suit the way that you work and the reports that you need to design. Environment settings are established using two main option sets: global options and report options.

Global Options

Clicking File > Options provides global options that affect all reports you create using Crystal Reports. Using the options shown in Figure 2.30, you can customize the layout of the report design and preview windows, define where reports are stored, and set other options that apply to the report design environment.

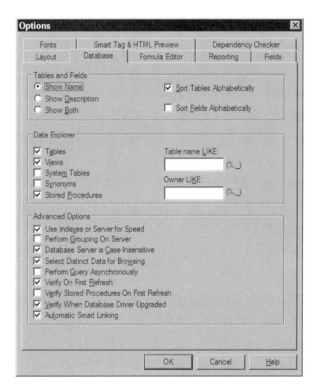

FIGURE 2.30   Options accessed using File > Options can be set globally and take effect with the next report you create.

Report Options

Clicking File > Report Options, shown in Figure 2.31, provides settings that apply to a specific report, and these settings take effect immediately. Report options specify how null fields are handled and whether data and/or summaries are saved with the report. Options also allow you to define preview page options and other properties.

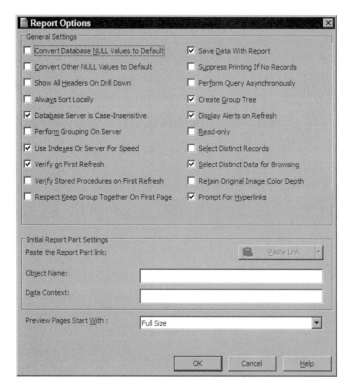

FIGURE 2.31 Options accessed using File > Report Options apply to a specific report only.

Layout Options

Everybody has his own work style and preferences when working with a software package, and Crystal Reports caters to your individuality. You can configure the design environment according to your preferences by clicking File > Options > Layout. You can control rulers that appear, guidelines (which we will talk about later), the display of section names, and more. Common layout options, shown in Figure 2.32, include options for both the Design or Preview view.

Which of these options you set is up to you. Some report designers prefer to view just the basics, without the rulers, guidelines, and so on to clutter up the design window, whereas others find that the rulers and guidelines help them get a feel for the report's dimensions and layout.

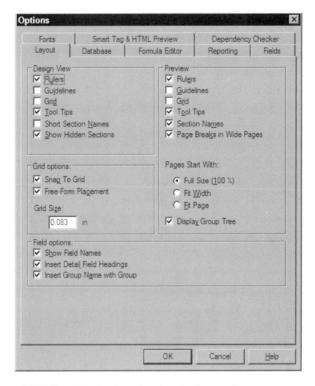

FIGURE 2.32   Options for the design environment.

There are also options that apply to the objects shown on your report. Some of the options available include the following:

Show Field Names: This option displays the full field name instead of a placeholder such as XXXXXXX.

Insert Detail Field Headings: When a field is inserted into the Details section, a text object is inserted automatically into the page header with the field heading.

Insert Group Name with Group: A group tree can be inserted to aid in report navigation and organization.

You can also choose options for the preview page, starting with the initial image set to Full Size (100 percent), Fit Width, or Fit Page. You can use the Display Group Tree checkbox to control whether a group tree is generated from the contents of your report.

Selecting Insert Group Name with Group will cause a group tree to be generated and appear on the left side of the report preview window. Choosing not to generate the group tree aids in report performance, because there is one item fewer for Crystal Reports to display.

And finally, to help you keep your report design evenly spaced, Crystal Reports has an underlying grid that can be used to align objects. Options for this grid include the following:

Snap to Grid: Aligns all inserted or moved objects to the underlying grid.

Free-Form Placement: Disregards the grid's placement of an object and places the object where you indicate.

Grid Size: Provides the size of the underlying grid in inches or centimeters, depending on your regional settings.

Alternatively, you could use a shortcut to access some of these options, following these steps: Switch your report to the Design mode by clicking the Design tab in the top-left corner of the report design environment. In any white space (where no objects are placed), right-click. A menu headed by Snap to Grid should appear, showing most of the options. Use the checkboxes that appear on this menu to configure the underlying grid.

SUMMARY

Crystal Reports can report from a wide range of data sources, using either a native connection, ODBC, or through special drivers specially designed to work with Crystal Reports. Connecting to a data source is a fairly straightforward process, but most report developers prefer to use one of the wizards to get started and take it from there. In the next chapter, we will look at where you will spend the most time when working with reports—report formatting and organization.

3 Report Formatting and Organization

INTRODUCTION

Formatting is an important part of the report-design process, and report developers spend a lot of their time formatting their reports, adjusting the look and feel to meet their own needs. In this chapter we will look at the formatting techniques you can use to customize your reports, including working with fields and sections.

In addition to formatting, we will also look at how to add value to the data from which you are reporting. One of the key goals of report design is the extraction and organization of data. Instead of just listing the data held within a particular database or table, you can use Crystal Reports to turn the data into information that people can use to make better decisions. Grouping and sorting both play key roles in organizing your report and in adding value to the information presented.

In the second half of this chapter, you will learn how to use grouping and sorting to organize your report, including hierarchical and specified grouping. You will also learn how to apply these techniques to create well-organized reports from your own data, including drill-down and summary reports.

UNDERSTANDING FIELD OBJECTS

Before we get too deep into formatting your report, we need to look at the basic building block for any report: field objects. Reports can include a number of different field objects, from database fields, to parameter fields, to fields that hold text that you enter directly into your report. Chances are that you will need to use all of these types of objects to achieve the results that you desire. The following sections describe the common field objects, how to identify them, and their use within your reports.

Database Fields

Database fields are drawn from the tables, views, or stored procedures used in your report. Database fields are represented with the designation {TableName. FieldName}. This information can be seen by clicking the field and looking in the bottom-left corner at the status bar. For example, if you were looking at a Phone Number field from a Customer table, the designation would be {Customer.Phone}. Database fields are used to display information from your database and are most commonly used in the Details section of your report, but they can also appear elsewhere.

Field Headings

When you insert a database field into the Details section of your report, a special type of text field is inserted to label the field. This field heading, which will appear in your page header, is derived from the field name stored in the database. When you move the database field, the field heading will move with the field itself.

Formula Fields

A formula field is a calculated field that can be inserted onto your report and is displayed the same as any other field is displayed. Backed by a powerful formula language that looks like a cross between Pascal, Excel's formula language, and Visual Basic, formulas can incorporate database fields, parameter fields, and so on to perform complex calculations and string, date, and time manipulations.

Formula fields are always prefixed with an @ symbol and are enclosed in curly braces, for example, {@commission}. Formula fields, which can be inserted anywhere in your report, have a wide range of uses, including mathematical calculations, string manipulation, and the execution of complex logical statements and outcomes. A formula field can be used just about anywhere you need a calculated or derived field.

Parameter Fields

Parameter fields are used to prompt report users for information. Parameter fields are prefixed by a question mark and are enclosed in curly braces, for example, {?EnterState}. Parameter fields can be used with record selection, formulas, and so on and can be inserted anywhere in your report.

Special Fields

Special fields generated by Crystal Reports include page numbers and summary information fields. Special fields are designated only by their field name, and all of the field names are reserved words. Special fields contain system-generated information and can be inserted anywhere they are needed in your report.

Running Total Fields

A running total field is a specialized summary field that can be used to create running totals, averages, and so on and display this information on your report. A running total field is prefixed by a hash symbol and enclosed in curly braces, for example, {#TotalSales}. Running totals frequently appear in the page footer or in the Details section with the detail data, but they can be placed in any section of your report.

SQL Expression Fields

A structured query language (SQL) expression field is similar to a Crystal Reports formula field, in that a SQL expression field can be used for calculations. However, with a SQL expression field, these calculations occur on the database server itself and take advantage of the server's advanced processing power. A SQL expression field is prefixed by a percent sign and enclosed in curly brackets, for example, {%CalcSummary}. A SQL expression field can be inserted anywhere in your report.

Summary Fields

A summary field can be used for calculations as simple as a subtotal or average or as complex as a standard or population deviation. At first glance, summary fields and formulas may appear to do the same thing, but the major difference is that a summary field does not require any coding. A summary field can be identified by the use of the summary type (Sum, Average, and so on), the word of, and the field that is being summarized, for example, Sum of Sales. A Summary field is generally placed in the group, page, or report header or footer, but it can be placed anywhere in your report.

Group Name Fields

A group name field is generated by Crystal Reports to label any group that you have inserted into your report. All group name fields can be identified by the same label—Group #n Name—where n is the number of the group with which you are working, such as Group #3 Name. Group names are generally inserted in their corresponding group header or footer. When a group name field is displayed on the Preview tab of your report, it will appear as the actual name of a group you have inserted. For example, if you inserted a grouping by state, the group name field might read Alaska, Alabama, and so on.

INSERTING FIELD OBJECTS

One of the most common formatting tasks when creating a report is the addition of fields to the report—in fact, sometimes it seems like a contest to see how many fields you can squeeze onto one page. To insert fields into your report, you use the Field Explorer, which can be opened by clicking View > Field Explorer. The Field Explorer is shown in Figure 3.1.

You can resize the Field Explorer by dragging the bottom-right corner of the Field Explorer window.

The Field Explorer displays all of the different types of fields that you can insert into your report, broken down by the field type. You can see the fields that are available in each category by clicking the plus sign beside the category name to expand the group.

If you click the plus sign beside the field type Database Fields, a list of all of the database tables you have selected is displayed; to find the field you need, you may need to expand the contents of each table. For the rest of the field categories, you can simply expand the category to see all of the fields contained within it.

FIGURE 3.1 The Crystal Reports Field Explorer.

If you have a large number of tables and fields, you may want to consider sorting alphabetically by the table name, the field name, or both. You can find this option by clicking File > Options > Database.

Because most of your time will be spent adding and arranging fields in your report, Crystal Reports tries to make this process as intuitive as possible. Fields can be dragged directly from the Field Explorer onto your report, or you can highlight a field and press the ENTER key to attach the field to the tip of your mouse. Then you can position it where you want using your mouse—click once to release it: it's that simple.

When you insert fields into the Details section of your report, you will notice that a special Field Heading object appears in the page header to label the field you have inserted. This action works only with fields that are inserted into the Details section. This feature can be turned off from the dialog box that appears when you click File > Options.

WORKING WITH FIELD OBJECTS

Once a field has been inserted into your report, you can to control the way the field looks: its properties, size, font, and so on. One way you can control the way a field looks and behaves is by editing its properties.

Formatting Field Objects

Every field object in Crystal Reports has properties associated with it. From the font that is used to display the field contents to the format of numbers contained within the field—you name it—there is a property to control it. To view the properties of a particular field, right-click the field and select Format Field from the shortcut menu that appears, shown in Figure 3.2.

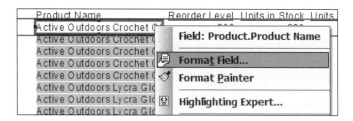

FIGURE 3.2 You can format a field by right-clicking the field and selecting Format Field.

The property pages for this object opens. In this example, we have selected a string field, so there are tabs for Common, Border, Font, and Hyperlink property pages. The property pages that appear depend on the type of field you select. For example, all field objects in Crystal Reports will display the property pages for Common, Border, Font, and Hyperlink, because all of these objects have these properties in common.

But when you compare a numeric field to a date field, you will notice some differences. A numeric field will have an additional tab with properties that relate only to numeric fields; likewise, a date field will have an extra tab with properties that can be set for date fields.

The following sections describe some of the most common object formatting properties.

Common Formatting Options

All of the different types of field objects in Crystal Reports have a common set of properties, as shown in Figure 3.3. There properties include the following:

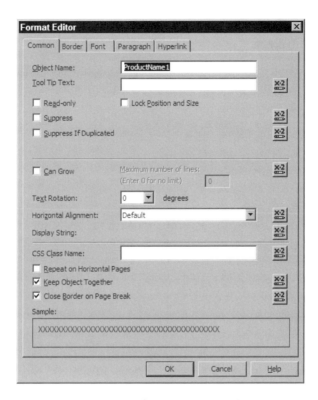

FIGURE 3.3 Common formatting properties.

Object Name: The name of the object. Crystal Reports will fill this field in for you, but you may want to rename the objects in your report to something more meaningful.

Tool Tip Text: Enable tool tip text to appear when the user moves the mouse over a particular object. You can enter the text directly into the text box provided or enter the text or a formula using the X+2 button located on the right side of the dialog box. You need to enter the tool tip text in quotation marks (for example, "This is tool text") in the formula, then click Save and Close when finished with the Formula Editor. The X+2 icon turns from blue to red to indicate that tool tip text has been entered.

Read Only: This setting determines if the object's properties are able to be changed.

Lock Position and Size: This setting locks an object into place on your report.

Suppress: Click this setting to enable suppression so that the object does not appear on your report. (The object will remain in your report design but will not appear when the report is previewed or printed.)

Suppress If Duplicated: Use this option to suppress a field if the contents are duplicated exactly. The object still appears in your report design, but the data itself does not appear when previewing or printing.

Can Grow: For multiline objects, select this option to ensure that the object can grow as needed, whether 2 lines or 20 are used. To control the maximum size of any object, you can also set the maximum number of lines. By default, this is set to zero to indicate no limit.

Text Rotation: Use this setting to rotate the text in an object either 90 or 270 degrees.

Horizontal Alignment: Select from the drop-down list provided to left-align, center, right-align, or justify the contents of the object. The default setting varies by type of field.

Display String: This setting is for displaying different types of fields using custom formatting.

CSS Class Name: If you are going to be using this report on the Web, a Cascading Style Sheet (CSS) file can be associated with the report. CSS is used to apply consistent formatting across multiple Web pages (or in this case, reports).

Repeat on Horizontal Pages: Enable this option to repeat this object on any horizontal pages that are created (most often used with page numbers and cross-tabs that run horizontally).

Keep Object Together: Enable this option to attempt to keep large objects on the same page.

Close Border on Page Break: Set this option for objects that have a border to ensure that the border extends to the edge of the page and that the border closes before the next page begins.

Formatting Numbers and Currency

For formatting numbers and currency, Crystal Reports also offers a number of specific properties. To make things easier, you can set these properties and formatting options by example, as shown in Figure 3.4. Instead of actually setting all of the properties, you can just pick a format that looks similar to what you want.

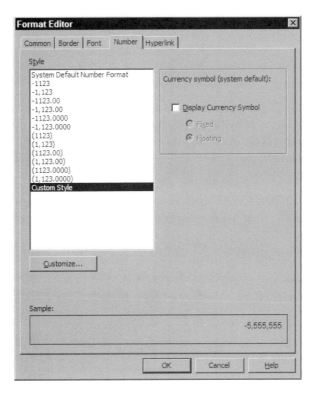

FIGURE 3.4   Selecting a numeric format by example.

To add a currency symbol, use the options at the top-right corner of the dialog box. You can also specify whether the symbol should be fixed in one position or floating beside the numbers.

To specify a custom numeric format, click the Customize button at the bottom of the dialog box. The following options are available for customization on the Currency Symbol and the Number tabs:

Enable Currency Symbol: Specifies whether the symbol will be shown.

Fixed/Floating: Specifies whether the currency symbol is fixed in place in the left margin of the field or floats next to the first digit.

One Symbol per Page: Places one symbol at the top of each page.

Position: Determines where the currency symbol will be displayed.

Currency Symbol: Specifies the currency symbol that will be used with numeric fields.

Use Accounting Format: Fixes the currency symbol at the left and displays negative amounts as dashes.

Suppress If Zero: Suppresses the display of a field if that field's value is zero.

Decimals: Specifies the number of decimal places, by example, to 10 decimal places of accuracy.

Rounding: Specifies the number of places to round to, from 10 to 1,000,000 decimal places.

Negatives: Displays a negative symbol before or after the number or uses parentheses to indicate negative numbers.

Reverse Sign for Display: Reverses the negative sign that would normally appear beside a negative value (that is, it displays a negative sign for positive numbers).

Allow Field Clipping: Specifies whether field clipping is performed. Field clipping occurs when a field frame is not large enough to hold the entire contents of the field. In situations where this occurs, Crystal Reports clips the field by default and shows only part of the field. If you uncheck this option, Crystal Reports displays number signs (#####) to indicate that a field is longer than the space allotted to it. To get rid of the number signs, you need to drag the field frame so that it is large enough to accommodate the entire contents.

Decimal Separator: Changes the decimal separator. By default, Crystal Reports uses a period to mark the place between a whole number and the numbers after the decimal point.

Thousands Separator: Changes the thousands separator and symbol. By default, Crystal Reports uses a comma to indicate the thousands place in a number.

Leading Zero: Adds a leading zero to any numbers displayed as a decimal.

Show Zero Values As: Displays zero values in the default format, which is zeros or a dash (-).

Any custom formats that you create cannot be saved and must be re-created each time you want to use them.

Formatting Date Fields

Date fields can also be formatted by example. Crystal Reports gives you a number of predefined formats to serve as a starting point. If you locate the date or time field that you want to format, right-click the field, and select Format Field, you'll notice that the properties include a Date/Time tab, which allows you to choose a date format by example (just like you did for numbers).

To select a custom style, click Customize at the bottom of the dialog box and specify a custom numeric format. Options available for customization follow:

- Date/time order
- Separator
- Date type
- Calendar type
- Format (month, day, year)
- Era/period type
- Order
- Day of week type
- Separator
- Enclosure
- Position
- Separators
- 12/24 hour
- AM/PM breakdown
- Symbol position
- Format (hour, minute, second)
- Separators

Bringing It All Together

With all of these formatting options, there are a number of ways we can improve the way a report looks. In the following walk-through, we are going to format the field objects of an existing Inventory Summary report (shown in Figure 3.5) to remove the thousands separator in the Purchase Order field and to format the Print Date field and Order Date field at the top of the report.

To apply these formatting changes, use the following steps:

ON THE CD

1. Open Crystal Reports, and open the INVENTORYSUMMARY.RPT report file from the CD-ROM.
2. Click the Design tab to switch to the Design view of your report.
3. Locate the PO# field in the Details section of your report, right-click the field, and select Format Field.
4. Click the Customize button, deselect the option for Thousands Separator, and then click OK twice.
5. Next, right-click the Order date field in the Details section, right-click, and select Format Field.

Inventory Summary Report

5/24/2005

Product Name	Reorder Level	Units in Stock	Units on Order	PO#	Order Date
Active Outdoors Crochet Glove	300	220	500	1,001	4/1/2004 12:00:00AM
Active Outdoors Crochet Glove	300	450	0		
Active Outdoors Crochet Glove	300	325	0		
Active Outdoors Crochet Glove	300	265	0		
Active Outdoors Crochet Glove	300	367	0		
Active Outdoors Lycra Glove	300	440	0		
Active Outdoors Lycra Glove	300	358	0		
Active Outdoors Lycra Glove	300	266	500	1,002	4/3/2004 12:00:00AM
Active Outdoors Lycra Glove	300	750	0		
Active Outdoors Lycra Glove	300	112	500	1,002	4/3/2004 12:00:00AM
Active Outdoors Lycra Glove	300	686	0		
Triumph Pro Helmet	100	78	150	1,003	4/5/2004 12:00:00AM
Triumph Pro Helmet	100	80	0		
Triumph Pro Helmet	100	55	150	1,003	4/5/2004 12:00:00AM
Triumph Pro Helmet	100	169	0		
Triumph Pro Helmet	100	200	0		
Triumph Pro Helmet	100	168	0		
Triumph Vertigo Helmet	100	89	0		
Triumph Vertigo Helmet	100	125	0		
Triumph Vertigo Helmet	100	220	0		
Triumph Vertigo Helmet	100	150	0		
Triumph Vertigo Helmet	100	92	150	1,004	4/8/2004 12:00:00AM
Triumph Vertigo Helmet	100	187	0		

FIGURE 3.5 An Inventory Summary report.

6. Select the option for 03/01/99, and then click OK.
7. Next, locate the Print Date field in the Page Header section, right-click, and select Format Field.
8. Select the option for Monday, March 1 1999 from the list, and then click OK.
9. Next, click the Preview tab to preview your report, which should now look like the report shown in Figure 3.6.

Inventory Summary Report

Tuesday, 24 May, 2005

Product Name	Reorder Level	Units in Stock	Units on Order	PO#	Order Date
Active Outdoors Crochet Glove	300	220	500	1001	04/01/2004
Active Outdoors Crochet Glove	300	450	0		
Active Outdoors Crochet Glove	300	325	0		
Active Outdoors Crochet Glove	300	265	0		
Active Outdoors Crochet Glove	300	367	0		
Active Outdoors Lycra Glove	300	440	0		
Active Outdoors Lycra Glove	300	358	0		
Active Outdoors Lycra Glove	300	266	500	1002	04/03/2004
Active Outdoors Lycra Glove	300	750	0		
Active Outdoors Lycra Glove	300	112	500	1002	04/03/2004
Active Outdoors Lycra Glove	300	686	0		
Triumph Pro Helmet	100	78	150	1003	04/05/2004
Triumph Pro Helmet	100	80	0		
Triumph Pro Helmet	100	55	150	1003	04/05/2004
Triumph Pro Helmet	100	169	0		
Triumph Pro Helmet	100	200	0		
Triumph Pro Helmet	100	168	0		
Triumph Vertigo Helmet	100	89	0		
Triumph Vertigo Helmet	100	125	0		
Triumph Vertigo Helmet	100	220	0		
Triumph Vertigo Helmet	100	150	0		
Triumph Vertigo Helmet	100	92	150	1004	04/08/2004
Triumph Vertigo Helmet	100	187	0		

FIGURE 3.6 The finished report with the formatting applied.

Resizing Fields

All of the fields you can insert onto your report can be resized. If you click a field object, you'll notice that four handles (or little blue boxes) appear on each side of the object. By moving these handles, you can resize the object.

Resizing objects in Crystal Reports works like resizing objects in Microsoft Office applications, such as Word and PowerPoint®.

As a time-saving feature, you can select multiple objects (even different types of objects), and when you resize one, all are resized in proportion. To resize multiple objects at the same time, use the following steps:

1. Locate the objects that you want to resize in your report, and multiple-select them. You perform a multiple-select operation by drawing a marquee box (sometimes called a stretch box) around the objects, or by clicking each while pressing SHIFT or CTRL.

You can also select all of the objects in a particular section by switching to the Design tab and right-clicking the section in the gray area on the left side of the screen. From the shortcut menu, select the Select all objects in section option.

2. Choose one of the objects, and resize its frame using the handles (or boxes) that appear on each side. Each object is resized proportionately to the object that you selected.
3. Click anywhere outside the selected fields to finish the operation.

If you need to resize a field with some precision, you can also specify the exact size and position of an object. Locate the object that you want to resize or position, and right-click it. From the shortcut menu that appears, select Size and Position. Using the dialog box shown in Figure 3.7, select the X and Y positions of your object and the object's height and width.

The height and width settings use the measurement unit defined in your Windows setup.

Moving Field Objects

When moving field objects, you have a couple of choices. The first, dragging and dropping, is more of a Windows skill than a Crystal Reports technique. By clicking an object, holding the mouse button, and moving the mouse, you can drag field objects around and drop them where you like by releasing the mouse button. If you

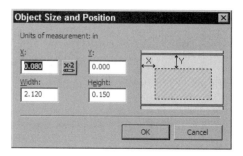

FIGURE 3.7   You can specify the exact size and location of objects in your report.

have used other Windows applications, chances are you have used this technique many times. Though it is the easiest way, it can also be the most time consuming, because you have to move each individual field, field heading, and so on. A much easier method is to use guidelines.

Another way to move field objects in the Design view of your report is to click the object to select it and then nudge the object around using the arrow keys.

Guidelines

Guidelines, shown in Figure 3.8, are invisible objects that can be used to align and move fields. The easiest way to think of a guideline is as a piece of string; you attach objects to that string, and when the string moves, everything attached to it moves as well.

Guidelines are invisible when you print your report. When working with the report design or preview, guidelines can appear as a dashed line in your report.

Guidelines can be added to your report by clicking anywhere in the ruler. A small icon (sometimes called a *caret*), shown in Figure 3.9, will appear, indicating that you have created a guideline.

Guidelines are also created with each new field that you add to the Details section of your report.

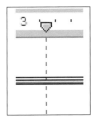

			2		3		4		5		6		7		
Inventory Summary Report															
Print Date															
Product Name		Reorder Level	Units in Stock	Units on Order		PO#	Order Date								
Product Name		Reorder Level	Units in Stock	Units on Order		PO#	Order Date								
													ge Number		

FIGURE 3.8   Guidelines can appear on both the Design and Preview tabs.

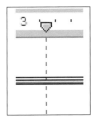

FIGURE 3.9   Guidelines
are marked by a caret.

Once you have created a guideline, you can then snap objects to it by moving them close to the guideline; Once you have ceated a guideline, you can then snap objects to it by moving them close to the guideline; you should see them jump a bit as you get closer. This appearance of jumping can be likened to the effect of a magnet; the object seems to want to stick to the guideline as you move the object closer.

When you move the guideline caret, the guideline and all of the objects attached to it move. To remove a guideline from your report, use the following steps:

1. Locate the guideline you want to remove, and drag the caret off of the ruler.
2. To remove all guidelines, right-click the ruler in the toolbar, and select one of the Remove All options from the shortcut menu.

Moving or Aligning Multiple Objects

An alternative to using guidelines is to move or align multiple objects at the same time. To use this technique, use the following steps:

1. First, locate the objects that you want to align in your report, and then multiple-select them. You perform a multiple-select operation by drawing a marquee box around the objects or by clicking each while pressing SHIFT or CTRL.

A standard Windows shortcut is to use the SHIFT key to select contiguous items in a list and the CTRL key to select distinct items.

2. After you have selected all of the objects that you want to align, right-click one of the objects, and from the shortcut menu that appears, select Align, as shown in Figure 3.10.

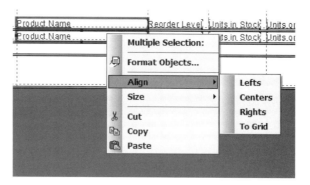

FIGURE 3.10 Alignment options can be found on the shortcut menu.

3. Select one of the options to align your fields, and then click anywhere outside the selected fields to finish.

Rulers, Guidelines, and Grids

Most of the user interface options for controlling the layout of your report are available by right-clicking a blank space in your report. A shortcut menu will open, allowing you to control the appearance of rulers, guidelines, and grids that may appear in the Design or Preview tabs.

Rulers are designed to show you the precise measurement of your report; guidelines and grids are used to control the position of elements on your report page.

If you are creating a report that mimics an existing report design or prototype, rules are the easiest way to ensure correct, precise alignment. You can measure the existing report or prototype to find the exact measurements and placement of fields.

Once you have established where all of the elements should be placed on the report, place guidelines using these measurements, so all of the fields on your report can be aligned.

Finally, if you have established a set gap between fields (that is, each field should be .05 inches apart), you can also change the underlying grid settings by clicking File > Options. These little tricks may not seem like much, but they can mean the difference between a few minutes and a few hours spent formatting your report.

Controlling Object Layering

Crystal Reports uses transparent object layering; that is, objects can be placed directly on top of one another. To control where objects sit within a layer, use the following steps:

1. Locate the object on your report that you want to use, and right-click it.
2. From the shortcut menu that appears (shown in Figure 3.11), select the layering option to control where the object is positioned.

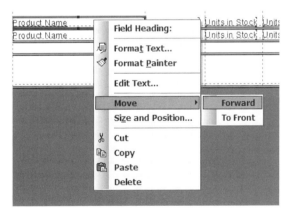

FIGURE 3.11   You can control object layering using this menu.

Text Objects

Text objects enable you to type text directly into your report. Text objects, simply labeled Text on the status bar, can be combined with database fields or formatted as paragraph text. Preformatted text, such as rich text format (RTF) and hypertext markup language (HTML), can be inserted directly into text objects. Text objects are used for report titles, field headings, and any text that needs to be inserted into your report.

Working with Text Objects

Text objects can be inserted anywhere in your report through the Insert menu. When you click Insert > Text Object, a crosshair icon will appear; use it to draw a text box in your report. Crystal Reports will immediately place the text object in Edit mode and place the tip of your mouse pointer inside the text object so you can start typing text. When you are finished editing the text, click anywhere outside the text object to leave Edit mode.

Once inserted on your report, text objects behave just like the field objects we saw earlier; they can be moved, resized, formatted, and so on. If you need to change the text you have entered in a text object, you can double-click the object to put it back into Edit mode, or you can right-click the object and select Edit Text from the shortcut menu.

For more control over a text object, you can also set paragraph formatting, including indentation, line spacing, character spacing, and tab stops.

Although text objects are most often used for report titles, column headings, and the like, they also can be combined with database and other fields where these formatting features come in handy.

Combining Text Objects and Other Fields

When working with Crystal Reports, you will reach the point where you are moving a field around in your report, and suddenly (and unexplainably) the field merges with a text object. Believe it or not, this is a feature. You can combine text objects with other fields to create form letters, statements, and so on. Imagine that you are writing a letter; you could merge the text *Dear:* with the database field containing the first name of your customer to create a personalized letter generated by Crystal Reports.

The mechanics of combining a text object with another field are simple—as mentioned earlier, you may have already done it by accident. In the walk-through that follows, we are going to use text objects to create a form letter like the one shown in Figure 3.12, integrating fields from a database with text you can enter or import. To get started, use the following steps:

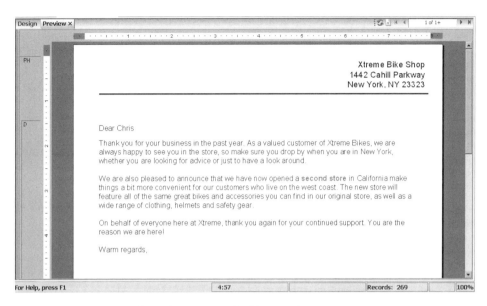

FIGURE 3.12 A typical form letter created with Crystal Reports.

ON THE CD

1. Open Crystal Reports, and open the BLANKLETTER.RPT report file from the CD-ROM.
2. Click the Design tab to switch to the Design view of your report.
3. To insert the text object for our salutation (*Dear XXX:*), click Insert > Text Object.
4. Use your mouse to draw a text object at the top of the Details section, and then enter the text *Dear*.
5. Next, click View > Field Explorer to open a list of available database fields.
6. Expand the Database Fields folder and the Customer table.
7. Drag the Contact First Name field from the Field Explorer to the text object you created. Your cursor will show your insertion point. Drop the field in the text object after the text.
8. Click the Preview tab to preview your report. As you go through the pages of the report, you will see that each page has its own salutation, as shown in Figure 3.13.

It may take some time to get the hang of the technique, but once you do, it is a handy trick to have up your sleeve.

FIGURE 3.13 Text objects can be used to combine text you enter with database fields.

Inserting Preformatted Text

When working with text objects and form letters or statements, you probably don't want to have to enter all of the text directly into Crystal Reports. Crystal Reports does not have a spell check or grammar facility, and it is difficult to type and format large amounts of text directly into a text object. To help you, Crystal Reports allows you to use a word processing application to create form letters and text and then bring that preformatted text directly into Crystal Reports.

To add the body text for the form letter we have been creating, use the following steps:

1. Open Crystal Reports and the report we have been working on in this section.
2. Click the Design tab to switch to the Design view of your report.
3. To insert the text object for the body of our letter, click Insert > Text Object.
4. Use your mouse to draw a text object at the top of the details section below your salutation.
5. Right-click in the text object you just created, and select Insert from File (shown in Figure 3.14), which allows you to insert a text, RTF, or HTML file into your text object. The CD-ROM contains an RTF file named LETTERTEXT.RTF—browse and insert this file into your text object.

ON THE CD

NOTE *If you do need more room on your form letter report or if you want to change the page size, you can click File > Page Setup to access the settings for page size, orientation, margins, and other printer options.*

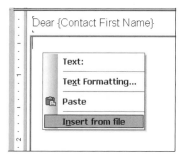

FIGURE 3.14 You can insert preformatted text into your text object.

WORKING WITH SECTIONS

A Crystal Report design can be broken down into a number of sections. In Chapter 2 we looked briefly at the basic sections that make up a Crystal Report. By default, each report you create with have a report header and footer, a page header and footer, and a Details section. (You may also have a group header and footer if you have any groups inserted into your report.)

For basic reporting, chances are you won't need more than one occurrence of the sections listed here, but Crystal Reports allows you to create multiple sections and set a number of section-specific properties to assist with tricky formatting problems you may encounter with complex reports.

An example of where the "multiple section" concept could come into play is if you were creating form letters for your company and wanted to show two different return addresses on the letter (one for your head office and one for a regional office, where appropriate). Using multiple sections, you could create two page headers and use conditional formatting to show the correct header for each page, based on the customer's address.

To accomplish this type of report, we need to insert two page headers (Page Header "A" and Page Header "B") and apply a little bit of conditional formatting to make this happen. Conditional formatting is something new, but if you have worked with Crystal Reports formulas before, this experience will come in handy. Conditional formatting allows you to create a formula, and if that formula is true, then something will happen.

If you have never worked with Crystal Reports formulas before, they are covered in-depth in Chapter 5, so you may want to flip ahead to get some background before working with conditional formatting.

Using the example of the two page headers, we could create two formulas and where the state was equal to "CA," we could show the header with the California return address; where the state was any other value, we could show the New York return address.

This is just one example of how multiple sections can be used to solve common formatting problems. Before we can get into the specifics of how sections can be used, we need to understand how to perform some basic operations, like inserting and removing sections and merging sections.

When working in the Design tab of Crystal Reports, each section has its own full-sized area on the left side of the design environment. If you were to right-click on this area to the left, a menu would appear, similar to the one shown in Figure 3.15.

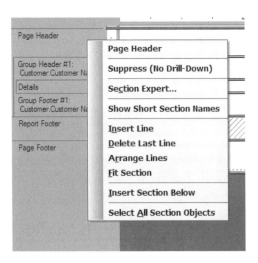

FIGURE 3.15   Each section can be edited through the Design tab.

This menu provides a quick and easy way to work with the different sections in your report, and it is where you will find the basic section functions (insert, merge, and so on).

The Preview tab also shows the different section names, but by default these are shown in abbreviated form (PH, GH1, and so forth).

Inserting a New Section

In the earlier example, we looked at a situation where you might want different page headers for your report in order to display two different return addresses for a form letter report you creates. To insert a new page header section into your report, use the following steps:

1. Open Crystal Reports and the Form Letter report we have been working on in this section.
2. Switch to the Design tab of your report.
3. Locate the page header section, right-click it, and select Insert Section Below.
4. Crystal Reports inserts a section immediately below the page header, as shown in Figure 3.16.

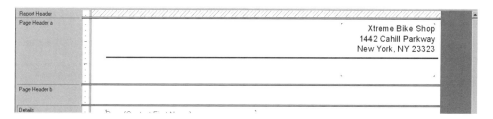

FIGURE 3.16 Sections you have inserted appear below the original section.

You'll notice that Crystal Reports has named this section Page Header B and your original page header Page Header A. Crystal Reports follows this naming convention throughout the different sections, so if you were to create a section below Page Header B, it would be labeled Page Header C.

Deleting a Section

When working with sections, you can also delete any unused sections you may have inserted by right-clicking the section and selecting Delete Section from the shortcut menu. Any objects that you have placed in that section will also be deleted, so if you want to keep any of them, make sure you have moved them out of the section before you delete it.

You will be unable to remove the following sections from your report using this method: report header/footer, page header/footer, group header/footer, and the Details section. You can delete a group header/footer by deleting the group to which they relate.

Resizing a Section

Another handy trick when working with sections is resizing. Sections can be resized to accommodate whatever information you need to insert, but they may not be larger than the page itself. To resize a section, use the following steps:

1. In the Form Letter report, locate the Page Header B section in the Design view of your report.
2. At the bottom of each section is a divider line. Move your mouse pointer over the divider line until the pointer changes to a double-headed arrow.
3. Using your mouse, you can drag the bottom border of the section up or down to resize. (It helps if you, select an area that is free of objects; otherwise, you may end up moving the object instead of the section border.)

Remember, you can always use Ctrl+Z to undo if you accidentally move an object instead of a border line.

Splitting a Section

Often, when resizing a section you will "split" that section by mistake. Splitting a section will just separate one section out into two (that is, the Details section becomes Details A and Details B). Using this method is very tricky and takes a little practice, but it comes in handy when you don't want to move a lot of objects around to get two separate sections.

To split a section of your report, use the following steps:

1. Using your own report, locate the section you wish to split, and move your mouse toward the left, along the bottom of the section, until you reach the intersection of the ruler line and the section's divider line.
2. Your mouse pointer should turn into the Split icon with a single line and one up-and-down arrow.
3. Use the Split icon at the intersection of the ruler line and bottom of the section, dragging your mouse down to split the section into two.

This technique take a little practice. Remember, a double line with an up-and-down arrow indicates that you can resize the section.

After spending a half-hour trying to get the technique down, a lot of people find it is just easier to insert another section and drag all of the objects down from the original section. Either way, it is up to you.

Merging Report Sections Together

When working with multiple sections, you may need to occasionally merge sections together to clean up or simplify the report's design. To merge two sections together, right-click the section above the one you wish to merge, and select Merge Section Below from the shortcut menu. When you merge two sections, all of the objects in those sections are retained.

One thing to note is that you can merge two sections only of the same type. For example, if you have Page Header A and Page Header B, you can merge them together, but if you try to merge Report Header A with Page Header A, it won't work.

Changing the Order of Sections

Finally, along with all of the other skills you have picked up for working with sections, you can also change the order of sections that appear in your report (without having to delete and recreate the same). To change the order of sections, simply drag-and-drop the section to its new location. When you first hold down the mouse button to drag, your cursor should change to the hand icon. Once you have positioned your section where you want it, release the mouse button to drop the section into place.

FORMATTING SECTIONS

The Section Expert, which can be opened by clicking Report > Section Expert, is key to understanding how the different sections of a report work together. All of the sections of your report are listed, as shown in Figure 3.17, and all of their formatting options are available from this dialog box.

A number of options deal specifically with creating, rearranging, and deleting sections of your report. Although some of these options are also available from the shortcut menu we used earlier, it may be easier to use the Section Expert to get the

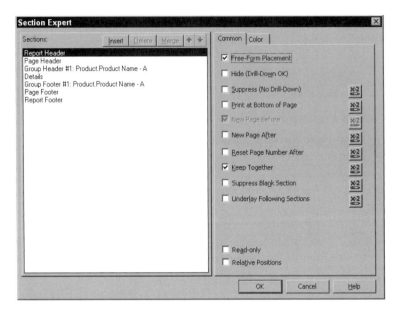

FIGURE 3.17 The Section Expert contains all of the formatting options for sections contained in your report.

big picture. These options can be found at the top of the Section Expert dialog box and are described in the following list:

> **Insert:** Inserts a new section into your report.
>
> **Delete:** Deletes a section that you have inserted into your report.
>
> **Merge:** Takes all of the objects out of two sections and merges them into one section.
>
> **Move Up/Move Down:** Changes the order of multiple sections you have inserted into your report.

Each section in your report also has a number of specific options associated with it that control the section's behavior and appearance. A list of available options follows:

> **Free-Form Placement:** Allows you to place objects anywhere in a section, disregarding the underlying grid and/or guidelines.
>
> **Hide (Drill-Down OK):** Hides a section of your report but still allows for drill-down, to show this section when required.

Suppress (No Drill-Down):   Completely suppresses a section of your re-port—you will not be able to drill down to show this section.

Print at Bottom of Page: Prints an entire section of your report at the bottom of the page.

New Page Before: Creates a page break immediately preceding a section.

New Page After: Creates a page break immediately following a section.

Reset Page Number After: Resets the page number immediately following a section.

Keep Together: Attempts to keep a particular section on one page to elimi-nate orphaning, or sections split between multiple pages.

Suppress Blank Section: Suppresses any sections that do not display any data, text fields, and so on.

Underlay Following Sections: Makes a section transparent and places it un-derneath the section immediately following.

Format with Multiple Columns: (Details section only) Creates multicolumn reports for mailing labels and the like.

Reserve a Minimum Page Footer: (Page Footer) Maintains the minimum page footer required by your printer or report design.

Color: Enables and sets the background color for a particular section.

We will be going through the most commonly used options a little later in this chapter.

Another option at the bottom of this list of properties makes the section read only, which would prevent users from making any changes to the section formatting.

Hiding or Suppressing a Section of Your Report

Earlier in this book, you learned how to create drill-down reports by hiding differ-ent sections of your report and summary reports by suppressing the details of your report. The Section Expert provides the same functionality and provides a quicker method for hiding or suppressing multiple sections. From the Section Expert, you will need to click to highlight a particular section name and then select the Hide or Suppress property from the options shown on the right side of the page. This method has the same effect as right-clicking the section name in Design view and selecting Hide or Suppress from the shortcut menu.

Showing Hidden Sections in Design

When you return to your report's design, it is sometimes difficult to determine what sections are present, hidden, and so forth, but you do you have some options to help you out. To show all of the hidden sections in the Design tab, use the following steps:

1. Click File > Options, and click the Layout tab.
2. From there, locate the Design View section, and click the option for Show Hidden Sections.
3. Click OK to accept your changes.

When you return to your report's Design view, the hidden sections in your report will now appear in the Design tab, but they will be grayed out.

Printing a Section at the Bottom of the Page

Another handy feature is the ability to print a section at the bottom of the page. This technique can be used with invoices to print a remittance slip or with form letters to include a "return comments" form. To use this technique, use the following steps:

1. Open Crystal Reports and your own report.
2. Switch to the Design view of your report to make things a bit easier, and identify the section you wish to print at the bottom of each page.

This section will be shown above the bottom page margin when the report is previewed or printed, but it will appear in the Design tab in its correct place.

3. Right-click the section, and select Section Expert from the shortcut menu.
4. In the Section Expert, select the option of Print at bottom of page.

This section will be printed at the bottom of the page. Where it appears in your report is subject to which section you select. If you select the report header, for example, the section will be printed on the bottom of the very first page and nowhere else. (Likewise, setting this option on the report footer would print the section on the bottom of the very last page.)

Creating a Page Break Before or After a Section

Often you want to create a page break before or after a section. This technique can be used with invoices (throwing a page break between invoice numbers), form letters (a separate page for each letter), or anywhere else you need to add a break. To create a page break before or after a section, you can set the properties within the Section Expert of New Page Before or New Page After. When your report is previewed or printed, a page break will occur in the location you have specified.

If you are using New Page Before, your report may show a blank page for the very first page. This is due to the report header appearing and then a page break is thrown. To eliminate this problem, suppress the report header section.

Resetting Page Numbering After a Section

When working with statements, invoices, form letters, or reports created for distribution to a number of different parties, you can reset the page number after a specific section to print pages that can be distributed, with each showing the correct page number. In this example, we are going to combine the New Page After option and Reset Page Numbering to throw a page break and reset the page numbering after a customer statement. To use these techniques, use the following steps:

1. Open Crystal Reports, and open the STATEMENT.RPT report file from the CD-ROM.

To reset page number after a section, always first make sure you have a Page Number field inserted in your report. If you don't, there won't be any way to tell if this option has actually worked.

2. Using the Design view of your report, click View > Field Explorer. Expand the section of the Field Explorer marked Special Fields, from the list select either the Page Number or Page N of M field, and drag it into your report in the Group Footer #1 section.
3. Right-click the Group Footer #1 section, and select Section Expert from the shortcut menu.
4. Using the properties on the right side of the Section Expert, select New Page After and Reset Page Number After.
5. Click OK to return to your report's Design or Preview.

When you preview your report, you should see that either the Page Number or Page N of M field you have inserted will reset after the section you have specified. In addition, your report will now run over multiple pages, with one (or more) pages for each statement, with the page numbering correct for each customer.

Suppressing a Blank Section

You can suppress a blank section to tighten up your report's design and get rid of any unwanted white space. This technique is frequently used when working with names and address. You can create two different sections for the address lines (here, Address1 and Address2, as shown in Figure 3.18) and enable the option for Suppress a Blank Section where there is no Address2 field. That way, when you report is printed, it won't appear as if a line is missing.

Details a	.	Customer Name
Details b	.	Address1
Details c	.	Address2
Details d	.	{City}, {Region} {Postal Code} {Coun
Details e	.	

FIGURE 3.18   Using the Section Expert you can suppress blank sections in your report.

To suppress a blank section, use the Section Expert and from the properties on the right side of the page, select Suppress if blank.

Creating a Multicolumn Report

Until now, all of the report designs we have seen have been single-column layouts; in other words, all of the fields and elements of your report were simply listed down the page. Through some special section formatting, reports can be created with multiple columns, allowing you to create flexible reports for phone lists, contact lists, and any other format that requires a large amount of information within a set area.

To create a multiple column layout, create a report as you normally would using the Standard Report Expert, inserting any fields you want to appear in your report as well as any groups or summary fields. Once you have a preview of your report, it is time for some multicolumn magic. In this example, we are going to create a multicolumn report to display an inventory stock list, which will have a list of products running across three columns with text boxes to enter the current inventory count, as shown in Figure 3.19.

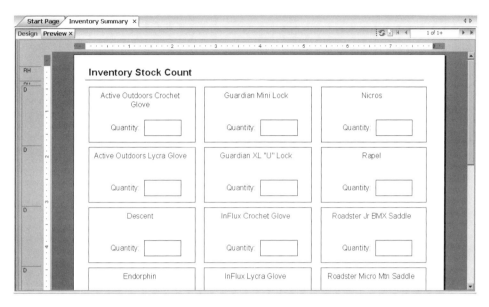

FIGURE 3.19 You can format your report with multiple columns to create complex report designs.

To create this multicolumn report, use the following steps:

ON THE CD

1. Open Crystal Reports, and open the STOCKLIST.RPT report file from the CD-ROM.
2. Switch to the Design view of your report.
3. Right-click the Details section of the report, and select Section Expert from the shortcut menu.
4. From the list of options on the right side, select Format with Multiple Columns.
5. Once you have selected this option, the Layout tab will appear at the top of the list of options. Click this tab to open the dialog box shown in Figure 3.20.
6. The first thing you will need to do is choose the width for your columns, as well as the horizontal and vertical gaps between each. For this report, enter a width of 2 or so inches.
7. In this dialog box, you will also need to select a print direction using the radio buttons shown, either Across then down or Down then across (the default). For this report, the default is fine.

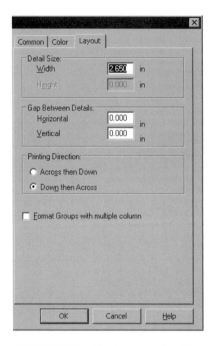

FIGURE 3.20 The Layout tab will not appear in the Section Expert unless you have specified you want the Details section formatted with multiple columns.

If you want to also format any groups you have inserted with multiple columns, click the checkbox at the bottom of the dialog box.

8. To finish, click OK to accept your changes and return to your report's Design or Preview.
9. Click Insert > Box to draw the boxes shown and adjust your fields and boxes as required.

The design view of your report will show gray section lines (see Figure 3.21) indicating the size of the column you have specified. Use this line as a guide to rearrange your report fields to fit in the columns you have created.

If you need to resize your column or change the horizontal or vertical spacing, you must return to the Section Expert by clicking Report > Section Expert and selecting the Details section.

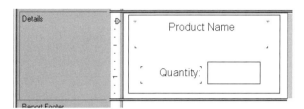

FIGURE 3.21   The gray section lines indicate the size of your column.

In addition to boxes, you can also draw lines on your report by clicking Insert > Line.

INSERTING GROUPS INTO YOUR REPORT

To this point, we have been working with some very simple reports, with columns and rows of data, and occasionally (as in the form letter example we used earlier) you may have noticed that we used groups. There is nothing really complicated about groups—a group, simply put, is a collection of related records.

When used in a report, groups allow you to put records together, in order, to analyze the information that they contain. If you were creating a sales report, for example, you may want to group your customer records by the countries where the customers reside, as shown in Figure 3.22. Alternatively, for an analysis of orders you have received, you may want to group the orders by the customers who placed them.

For each group that you create in Crystal Reports, a group header and footer is created, as shown in Figure 3.23. The group header or footer is usually where you put the name of the group as well as any summaries that are created from the group's data.

If you previously have worked with different types of reports, you may notice that groups in Crystal Reports closely resemble control breaks in other reporting tools and platforms. Both groups and control breaks share the same concept of putting like items together and placing space between the like items to indicate where one group ends and the next begins.

The reports created in the chapter are located on the CD-ROM in the PROJECTS folder. You can either follow along with the instructions in the chapter to re-create the reports, or you can copy the reports from the CD-ROM to your hard drive for editing.

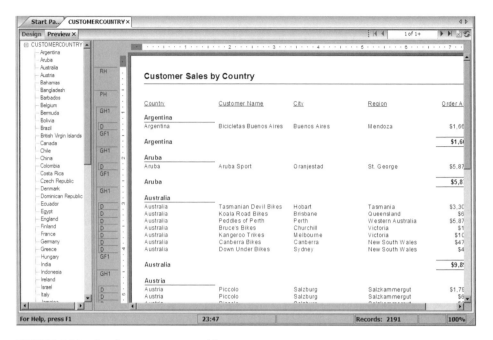

FIGURE 3.22   A sales report grouped by country.

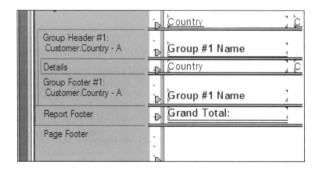

FIGURE 3.23   A group header and footer.

Groups can be based on any of the database fields, parameter fields, formula fields, or SQL expressions that appear in your report. To insert a group into your report, use the following steps:

ON THE CD

1. Open Crystal Reports, and open the CUSTOMERLISTING.RPT report from the CD-ROM.
2. Select Insert > Group. Using the dialog box shown in Figure 3.24, select a field to be used to sort and group the records in your report as well as the sort order for that particular group.

FIGURE 3.24   Basic group settings.

3. Select the Country field from the drop-down list, and select In ascending order for the sort order.

With grouping in Crystal Reports, the groups are not only separated by the field criteria that you specify but also are arranged in the order that you specify. You can choose to sort groups in ascending or descending order (A through Z, or Z through A), use the original sort order from the database, or specify your own order and groupings, which we will look at a little later in this chapter.

4. When finished setting your group options, click OK to insert the group into your report.
5. Save this report as CUSTOMERCOUNTRY.RPT (we will be using it a little later in the chapter).

The groups should now appear in the group tree on the left side of the page, and a group header and footer and a group name have been added to your report design.

To delete a group, switch to the Design tab, right-click either the group header or footer, and select Delete Group from the shortcut menu.

GROUP FORMATTING OPTIONS

With any group you insert into your report, you want to control how that group looks and the formatting options applied. Using the tips and tricks in the next section, you should be able to make a group do just about anything you need it to do.

Inserting Group Names

Group names, generated by Crystal Reports, are used to label the groups you create. You have already seen them in action—Crystal Reports automatically inserts them whenever you insert a group, and they usually appear in both the group header and footer.

There will be instances where you want to insert group names manually, and Crystal Reports lets you do this as well. To insert a group name, use the following steps:

1. To make it easier to see where you are going to place the field, switch to the Design view of your report by clicking the Design tab in the top-left corner of the screen.
2. Then click View > Field Explorer. This step opens the Field Explorer, shown in Figure 3.25.

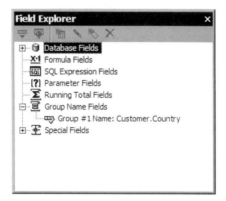

FIGURE 3.25   The Field Explorer can be used to insert group name fields onto your report.

3. Click the plus sign to open to the section for Group Name fields. A list of all of the group names in your report appears.

4. Select the field that you want to insert into your report, and press the ENTER key. This step attaches the field to the tip of your mouse, and as you move your mouse around the page, you should see the outline of the field follow.

5. Position your mouse in the area where you want to place the Group Name field, and click once to insert the field in your report. When your report is previewed, this field will be replaced with the name of the group it represents.

Customizing the Group Name Field

Group Name fields can be customized in a number of different ways. You can access the group options to customize a group name when you first insert a new group or when you are changing a group's properties.

To change an existing group, you can use the Group Expert by clicking Report > Group Expert.

As shown in Figure 3.26, you can choose a group name for an existing field by selecting Choose from Existing Field and then selecting a field name. A common example of when you would use this is when you have grouped on a company ID and want to display the company name.

FIGURE 3.26 You can customize the Group Name field based on an existing field, formula, and so forth.

You can also choose a group name based on a formula by clicking Use a Formula as Group Name and entering a formula using the X+2 button. This step opens the Crystal Reports Formula Editor and allows you to enter a formula that returns a group name. An example of when you would use a formula-based group name is when you have grouped by a sales rep code and want to display the sales rep's name. The formula in this situation follows:

```
If (Customer.RepNo} = 112 then "Nathan's Customers" else
If (Customer.RepNo} = 234 then "Kelly's Customers" else
If (Customer.RepNo} = 258 then "Jane's Customers" else
 "Other Customers"
```

After you have entered a custom formula for your group name and exited the editor, you'll notice that the X+2 button changes from blue to red and the pencil icon is moved from horizontal to slanted to indicate that you have entered formula text (see Figure 3.27).

FIGURE 3.27 The X+2 button changes from blue to red and the pencil icon changes its position to indicate that a formula has been entered.

Changing Group Criteria

After a group has been inserted, you may need to change the group criteria—there is a handy little trick to help you out. In Design mode, locate the group header or footer for the group that you want to change. After you have located the group that you want to change, right-click the group header or footer that appears in the gray area, and, from the menu shown in Figure 3.28, select Change Group.

You can then make any changes to the group using the Change Group Options dialog box. Click OK to accept your changes. The changes should be reflected immediately in the Report Design or Preview window.

Keeping a Group Together Across Multiple Pages

The option for keeping a group together attempts to prevent one section of the group from being orphaned on a separate page. Where possible, Crystal Reports tries to display the complete group on the same page. You can access the options to

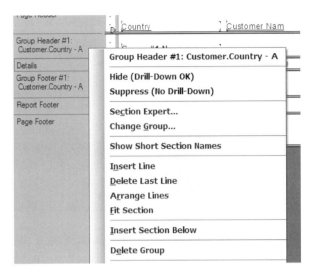

FIGURE 3.28   The Change Group Options dialog box.

keep a group together when you first insert a new group or when you are changing a group's properties.

From either the Insert Group dialog box or the Change Group Options dialog box, select Keep Group Together. Click OK to accept your changes. When your report is previewed or printed, Crystal Reports attempts to move all of the group records to a single page.

In any case where Crystal Reports is unable to fit all of the records on the same page, it places the records on separate pages, even with this setting turned on.

NOTE

Repeating a Group Header on Each Page

For long reports, a group header may be required on each page to identify each group because the group header and footer may be 10 or even 20 pages apart. To repeat a group header on each page, choose the group option Repeat a Group Header when you first insert a new group or when you are changing a group's properties. When your report is previewed or printed, the group header section is printed at the top of each page immediately under the Page Header section, as shown in Figure 3.29.

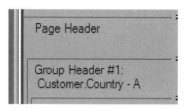

FIGURE 3.29 The group header can be printed at the top of each page

Creating a Page Break Between Groups

For readability, you may want to consider inserting a page break between the groups that appear in your report. To insert a page break, use the following steps:

1. Click Format > Section to open the Section Expert.
2. Locate the group footer of the group that you want to use as a page break. Highlight the group by clicking it.
3. From the options that appear on the right side of the page, select New Page After.
4. Click OK to return to your report.

NOTE

Alternatively, you can select the group header and select New Page Before.

Your report should now have a page break at the end of each group, making it a bit easier to read.

CHANGING GROUPS

Once you have a group inserted onto your report, you can change the options for the group without having to remove and add the group back again. You may want to change the group field or sort order or just have a look at the options you have set. In any case, you will want to get to know the Change Group Expert.

Using the Change Group Expert

The Change Group Expert can be used for changing groups and group options. To invoke the expert, click Report > Change Group Expert. As shown in Figure 3.30, select the group that you want to change, and then select Options.

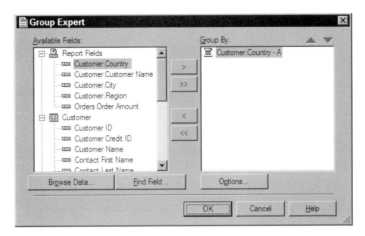

FIGURE 3.30 You can use the Change Group Expert to change
group criteria.

The standard Change Group Options dialog box appears, allowing you to make
changes to the group field, sort order, and so forth. Click OK to accept your
changes. The changes should be reflected in the report design immediately.

Reordering Groups

When working with groups, it is easy to get the hierarchy out of order (for example, by inserting a group for the country inside a group for the state). To reorder the
groups that appear in your report, you can simply drag and drop the sections using
the following instructions:

1. In Design mode, locate the group headers and footers in the gray area on
   the left side of the page.
2. Locate the groups that you want to reorder, and move these up or down by
   dragging the appropriate section of the report.
3. When you have a group selected, your mouse pointer appears as a hand
   cursor, as shown in Figure 3.31, which indicates that you have attached to
   a group.
4. While you are moving the group up and down, a thick bold line indicates
   where in the group hierarchy your group will appear.
5. After you are satisfied with the new location, drop the group into position
   by releasing the mouse button.

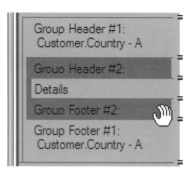

FIGURE 3.31   The cursor changes to a hand icon to indicate that you are dragging an entire group or section of the report.

Changing the Group Selection Formula

When a group is created, Crystal Reports automatically creates a group selection formula. Editing this formula gives you more control of the data that appears in each group. You can edit the group selection formula by clicking Report > Selection Formulas > Group. The Crystal Reports Formula Editor opens. You can then use the Formula Editor to enter your group selection formula.

If you are interested in writing your own formulas, you may want to skip ahead to Chapter 5.

Hierarchical Grouping

When working with groups and sorting, you sometimes make assumptions about the design of your database. For a report on international sales, for instance, you might assume that separate fields for the customer's country, region, and city are in the database. To create a hierarchical group based on these fields, you would then simply insert three groups: one for the country, one for the region, and one for the city.

What about the instance where the data that makes up the hierarchy is all stored in one table in one single field? That is when you need to use hierarchical grouping. A common example of where you need to use this feature is when working with employee data. Imagine that you have an employee table that contains all of the details for the employees that work at your company. In this table, a field indicates the manager of each employee, using the manager's employee ID.

How would you show this relationship on a report? If you attempted to use a simple group, you could produce a report that has a separate group for each manager, listing his or her employees. Unfortunately, that method would not show the hierarchical relationship among all of the employees (that is, Justin works for Morgan who works for Amy, and so forth).

If you use hierarchical grouping in this situation, you can specify a parent field for your group, and the report produced will display the complete hierarchical view of your employee data. Although it sounds complex, setting up a hierarchical group requires only one extra step.

To create hierarchical group, use the following steps:

ON THE CD

1. Open Crystal Reports, and open the HIERARCHY.RPT report from the CD-ROM.
2. Insert a group as you normally would, by clicking Insert > Group and choosing the field that represents the link to the next step in the hierarchy. In this example, we are working with an employee table that has a Supervisor ID field. You want to show the hierarchy of which employees work for whom, so select the Supervisor ID field for your group, and click OK.
3. Click Report > Hierarchical Grouping Options to open the dialog box, shown in Figure 3.32.

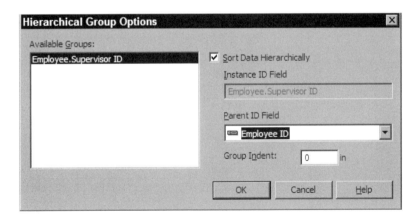

FIGURE 3.32 The Hierarchical Options dialog box.

4. Select the Sort Data Hierarchically option. From the Available Groups list, you would select the group that you want to group hierarchically.
5. Select the parent ID field on which this hierarchy is based. In the example here, the field is the Employee ID field.

6. Finally, set the indentation size for when your group is displayed. Click OK to accept your changes. The group that you have inserted should now reflect the hierarchy that you created.

SPECIFIED GROUPING

Specified grouping is a powerful feature that allows you to regroup data based on criteria that you establish. For example, suppose you have sales territories comprising of a number of states. You can use a specified group to create a separate group for each sales territory and to establish your own criteria (for example, North Carolina plus South Carolina is Bob's territory). To create a specified group, use the following steps:

ON THE CD

1. Open Crystal Reports, and open the SALESTEAM.RPT report from the CD-ROM.
2. Click Insert > Group, and select the Employee Last Name field.
3. In the same Insert Group dialog box, change the sort order to In Specified Order. A second tab, labeled Specified Order, should appear in the Insert Group dialog box, as shown in Figure 3.33.

FIGURE 3.33 The Specified Order option page.

For each specified group we want to create, we need to define a group name and specify the group criteria.

4. Type all of the group names you want to create, pressing the ENTER key after each, to build a list of group names.
5. Once you have all of the group names defined, highlight each one, and click the Edit button to specify the criteria.
6. To establish the criteria for records to be added to your group, use the drop-down menu to select an operator and value or values.

These are the same operators used with record selection.

7. You can add other criteria by clicking the New tab and using the operators to specify additional selection criteria, which are evaluated with an or statement between the criteria that you specify.
8. After you have entered a single group, another tab appears with options for records that fall outside of the criteria that you specify. By default, all of the leftover records are placed in their own group, labeled Others. You can change the name of this group by simply editing the name on the Others tab, which is shown in Figure 3.34. You also can choose to discard all of the other records or to leave them in their own groups.

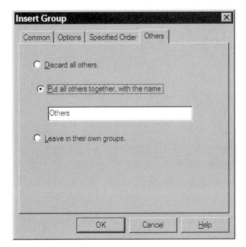

FIGURE 3.34 Options for dealing with other records.

9. After you have defined your specified groups and criteria and have reviewed the settings for other records, click OK to accept the changes to the group.

Your specified grouping is now reflected in your report.

GROUPING ON A DATE OR DATE-TIME FIELD

Grouping on a Date field requires you to specify how the dates are grouped. To create a group based on a Date field, you would simply insert a group by clicking Insert > Group, and then selecting a date or date-time field (Database, Formula, or Parameter) to be used to sort and group the records in your report.

You will need to select a sort order for your group (ascending, descending, specified, or original). Notice that Crystal Reports has added an additional option box for selecting the interval at which the group should be printed. The interval options are slightly different for dates and time fields. The options follow.

For dates:

- For Each Day
- For Each Week
- For Each Two Weeks
- For Each Half-Month
- For Each Month
- For Each Quarter
- For Each Half-Year
- For Each Year

For times:

- For Each Second
- For Each Minute
- For Each Hour
- For Each AM/PM

You can set any group options for customizing the group name, keeping the group together, and so forth. Once you have clicked OK and your group has been created, check the Design tab. You should see the group that you inserted represented by a group header and footer that appear in the gray area on the left side of the page.

When you preview your report, the group name is generated from the interval that you picked when creating your group. You can format this group name just like any other time- or date-time-type field.

Crystal Reports usually uses the last date in the interval to create a group name. If you selected a grouping by week, it would display the last day of each week as the group name.

RECORD-LEVEL SORTING

In addition to sorting records into groups, you can also use record-level sorting to sort records without separating them. For example, you may have a simple report that lists all of the invoices for a particular day. Because this is a simple list, you probably don't want to use grouping, but you do want to put the invoice in order on the report. This is where record-level sorting comes into play, because you can specify the sort order at the most basic level.

This method also works with groups inserted into a report, because you can sort the contents of a group using record-level sorting.

To add a record-level sorting to your report, click Report > Record Sort Expert to open the dialog box shown in Figure 3.35.

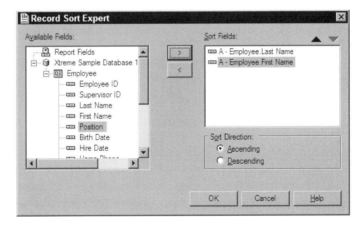

FIGURE 3.35   Options for record-level sorting.

In this dialog box, you move the fields you want to use in sorting from the left list to the right using the arrows in the middle of the dialog box. Highlight a field on the left, then click the right arrow to move the field to the list on the right. You can use the radio buttons below the list to select the sort order. The arrows on the top-right corner of the dialog box are used to specify the sort-order precedence.

You will see any groups you have inserted into your report shown here. Group sorting always takes precedence over record-level sorting. You cannot remove groups using this dialog box.

DRILL-DOWN AND SUMMARY REPORTS

Creating meaningful information from large volumes of data can be difficult. If a report is too long, report consumers generally tune out before they get to the section of data that is relevant to them. One trick for the concise presentation of information is to use a drill-down or summary report.

Drill-down and summary reports are similar because they contain a summary of information from your data. For a sales report, you may want to summarize a particular salesperson's sales for a given month, showing the total sales figure but not the details that it comprises.

Although drill-down and summary reports of this information look similar, one difference does exist. A drill-down report allows you to double-click the salesperson's name or any of the summary fields to display all of the details that make up that summary. In a drill-down report, the details are simply hidden from view, but they are still available when a user needs them. With a summary report, the details are suppressed from view and are not available to be seen by the user.

Each type has specific uses. If the report that you have created is likely to raise questions, such as "Why are John's sales up this month?" or "Why is that number negative?" a drill-down report can provide report consumers with the information they need to answer these questions without having to have another report created.

Drill-down reports can be used to drill down into the data as many times as required, and with each additional query, users open a separate Preview tab. This information can be printed independently of the main report; it can be exported as well. For report consumers, this flexibility provides a significant ad hoc capability. Instead of having to ask for a new report to be created for each request, they may be able to navigate through an existing comprehensive report and extract the information that they need. For this situation, a drill-down report is ideal.

On the other hand, if you are distributing a report that is a summary of expenses, including payroll figures that are confidential, you may not want to give users the ability to drill down into that information.

Regardless of which type of report you choose, both drill-down and summary reports can be used to add real value to the information that you present in your report.

Expanding on a report we looked at earlier, where a group had been inserted on the Country field, we could easily create a drill-down report that would show only the countries. The user could then double-click to drill down into the details of the report.

To create a summary report, use the following steps:

ON THE CD

1. Open Crystal Reports, and open the CUSTOMERCOUNTRY.RPT report we were working on earlier; you can also open a copy from the CD-ROM.
2. Switch to the Design view of your report, and locate the group header and footer for the group you are working with—in this case, the Country field.
3. Right-click the header in the gray area on the left side of the page, and select Hide from the shortcut menu.

Your report will now show only the summary information. To drill down into your report, move your mouse across a group header or footer field and double-click where your mouse pointer turns into the hourglass icon. An additional tab (beside Design and Preview) opens to display your drill-down data.

NOTE

If you wanted to show the headings when you drilled down, you would need to click File > Report Options and select Show All Headers on Drill-Down. Click OK to accept your changes.

You could then hide any other headers or footers by repeating the same process. Likewise, if you wanted to suppress the details (*not* show the details), you can right-click on the section and select the option to Suppress.

NOTE

A separate tab appears showing you the drill-down report you have selected. You can use the red X that appears on the navigation bar to close any drill-down tabs that you have opened.

Drill-down reports are the best means of quickly displaying an overview of the information contained within your report. Drill-down tabs can be printed individually, allowing a user to use one report for many sets of information. When combined with summary fields, drill-down reports offer a powerful analysis function, allowing users to see the details that make up a particular sum or total.

ON THE CD
You can also find additional examples of different drill-down reports and techniques on the CD-ROM in the PROJECTS directory.

SUMMARY

A large part of report design is formatting your reports and taking large amounts of data and condensing it into very concise pieces of information. In this chapter, we looked at some of the techniques to help you format and organize your reports to make the information more meaningful and easier to read. In the next chapter, we are going to look at another way of adding value to reports by analyzing the data they contain.

4 Analyzing Report Data

In This Chapter

- Summarizing Report Data
- Adding Summary Fields to Your Report
- Analyzing Report Data
- Using Record Selection to Filter Your Report
- Using Parameter Fields in Your Report
- Parameter Fields and Record Selection

INTRODUCTION

Reports can contain large amounts of data, and report users often find it difficult to sort and shift through hundreds of thousands of rows to find the information they need. Luckily, Crystal Reports provides the ability to summarize and filter report data to find only the relevant information the user needs. This chapter is dedicated to these techniques.

The first part of this chapter looks at the ways you can summarize report data, including some of the differences between Crystal Report's built-in summary operators and formula languages. This section will also look at how to analyze report data by sorting groups and summaries to order the data and highlight information that the user may have otherwise missed.

The second half of the chapter looks at parameter fields, which can be used to filter your report to show only the relevant information. In addition to entering parameters when the report is run, a feature that is new to Crystal Reports XI will allow you to tie parameter fields to your database fields, enabling users to select from a dynamic list of choices.

If you need to summarize large amounts of data and present it in a concise, meaningful way, this chapter is for you—let's get started.

SUMMARIZING REPORT DATA

One of the most common ways to analyze the data in your own reports is to display summaries of the underlying data. For example, you could have a report with groups that display the different salespeople in your organization and then show a summary at the bottom of each column to indicate their average sale, total sales, and so on, similar to what we see in Figure 4.1.

Employee Sales Summary

Employee Name	Average Order Amount	Total Order Amount	Number of Orders
Anne Dodsworth	$1,855.57	$682,849.21	368
Janet Leverling	$1,838.82	$649,101.99	353
Margaret Peacock	$1,858.23	$631,799.77	340
Michael Suyama	$1,909.68	$710,401.48	372
Nancy Davolio	$1,835.44	$660,756.95	360
Robert King	$1,876.58	$748,755.94	399

FIGURE 4.1 Example of a typical summary report.

You can display these summaries in a couple of ways. The following section will help you decide which is best for your report.

Summaries versus Formulas

When it comes to adding calculations to your report, you have two choices. You can either insert a summary field or create your own calculation, either using formulas or SQL Expressions. Summary fields are designed to eliminate the need to write formulas or SQL Expressions for common calculations, including sums, averages, counts, and others.

However, despite their ease of use, summary fields do have limitations. Summary fields are not as flexible as formulas that you write, and they are limited to the 19 summary operators currently available. Summaries are also tied to a particular group or the grand total for your report.

If you need full control of how a calculated field is derived or where it is placed, you probably need to create a formula field. Likewise, if you are familiar with writing SQL statements and want the calculation to be performed on the database server, you can create a SQL Expression.

If you are looking for a quick and easy standard calculation based on some grouping you have inserted into your report, summary fields may be for you. A list of the most popular summary fields and a description of how they are used follow:

Sum: Provides a sum of the contents of a numeric or currency field.

Average: Provides a simple average of a numeric or currency field (that is, the values in the field are all added together and divided by the total number).

Minimum: Determines the smallest value present in a database field. This field is for use with number, currency, string, and date fields.

Maximum: Determines the largest value present in a database field. This field is for use with number, currency, string, and date fields.

Count: Counts the values present in a database field. This field is for use with all types of fields.

Distinct Count: Counts the values present in a database field, but counts any duplicate values only once.

A number of statistical summary functions are also available for use, including

- Correlation
- Covariance
- Weighted average
- Median
- Pth percentile
- Nth largest
- Nth smallest
- Mode
- Nth most frequent
- Sample variance
- Sample standard deviation
- Population variance
- Population standard deviation

If this all looks like Greek to you, you may want to check out the Internet Glossary of Statistical Terms, available at www.animatedsoftware.com/statglos/statglos. htm. If you are not familiar with statistics, you can use this glossary as a guide to determine if any of these summary operators may be of use in your organization.

ADDING SUMMARY FIELDS TO YOUR REPORT

Simple summary fields include sum, average, minimum, maximum, and other calculations that do not require any additional criteria. In the following example, we are going to add a summary field to an existing sales report to make it easier to read and interpret the information that is contained within the report.

The reports created in the chapter are located on the CD-ROM in the PRO-JECTS folder. You can either follow along with the instructions in the chapter to re-create the reports, or you can copy the reports from the CD-ROM to your hard drive for editing.

To create a simple summary field, use the following steps:

1. Open Crystal Reports, and open the SALESLISTING.RPT report from the CD-ROM.
2. Locate and click the field that you want to summarize. In this case, it is the Order Amount field.

Make sure that you click the Order Amount field that appears in your report's Details section. You may want to switch to the Design view of your report before clicking to make things a bit easier.

3. Click Insert > Summary. In the dialog box, shown in Figure 4.2, select the summary operation you want to use from the Calculate this summary box, and select a location from the drop-down box at the bottom of the dialog box. For this example, select Sum; for the location, select Group #1: Employee.Last Name–A.
4. Click OK to accept your changes. Your summary field is inserted in the location you have selected, as shown in Figure 4.3.

As you scroll through the report, you will notice that underneath the Order Amount field column is now a Sum field that appears with each group. This field represents the total sales for a particular salesperson. Summaries are most often used with groups and appear on the group footer if a group has been selected. If you selected the option to create a Grand Total, these sums will always appear in the report footer on the very last page of your report, showing a total for the entire report.

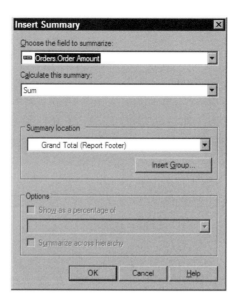

FIGURE 4.2   Options for inserting simple summary fields into your report.

Sales Listing

Order Date	Ship Date	Order ID	Order Amount
Davolio			
04/09/2005	04/14/2005	2903	$16.50
04/07/2005	04/13/2005	2895	$49.50
04/08/2005	04/10/2005	2897	$49.50
04/13/2005	04/23/2005	2909	$125.70
04/14/2005	04/14/2005	2910	$3,936.60
04/14/2005	04/19/2005	2915	$5,291.74
04/14/2005	04/23/2005	2916	$83.80
04/01/2005	04/02/2005	2881	$43.50
04/21/2005	04/25/2005	2957	$9.00
04/25/2005	04/26/2005	2964	$39.80
04/26/2005	05/01/2005	2969	$3,185.42
04/28/2005	05/01/2005	2974	$161.70
04/29/2005	04/29/2005	2977	$4,685.10
04/29/2005	05/02/2005	2982	$63.90
04/15/2005	04/17/2005	2922	$67.80
04/17/2005	04/21/2005	2933	$1,505.96
04/15/2005	04/15/2005	2920	$4,121.29
04/18/2005	04/22/2005	2936	$107.80
04/18/2005	04/21/2005	2937	$107.80
05/01/2005	05/02/2005	2989	$238.63
05/02/2005	05/03/2005	2998	$1,082.50
			$24,973.54
Dodsworth			
04/10/2005	04/10/2005	2949	$2,402.25

FIGURE 4.3   The report with the summary field in place.

Changing Summary Field Operations

After a summary field has been inserted into your report, you can change the summary operation by locating the summary field that you want to change on your report, clicking to select the field, and clicking Edit > Edit Summary. In the Edit Summary dialog box, use the drop-down list to change the summary operation, then click OK to accept your changes, as shown in Figure 4.4. The operator change should be reflected immediately in your report.

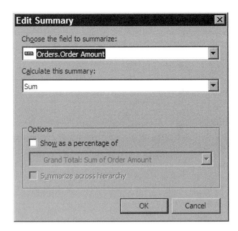

FIGURE 4.4   Summary field options.

 An important point to remember is that selecting a different summary operator may mean specifying additional parameters, depending on the summary operator you choose.

Inserting Summary Fields Shown as Percentages

The information in a summary field can be shown as a percentage of a grand total. For example, you may want to see what percentage a certain customer contributes to your total business. Or, using our earlier example, what percentage of sales a certain salesperson has contributed. If you insert a summary field shown as a percentage of the grand total of your report, that information is readily available.

To insert a summary field to be shown as a percentage in the Sales Summary report we have been working with, use the following steps:

1. Open Crystal Reports, and open the report we have been working with (SALESSUMMARY.RPT), or open a copy from the CD-ROM.
2. Click Insert > Summary.
3. In the dialog box, select the summary type you want to insert from the Calculate this Summary box. In this example, select the Sum operator.
4. Choose the field you want to summarize, and select a summary location. For this report, select the Orders.Order Amount field, and for the location, select `Group #1: Employee.Last Name – A.`
5. At the bottom of the dialog box, check Show as a Percentage Of. Using the drop-down list under Show as a Percentage Of, select the grand total field that you want to use to calculate the percentage (Grand Total: Sum of Order Amount), as shown in Figure 4.5.
6. Click OK to accept your changes and to add the summary field to your report.

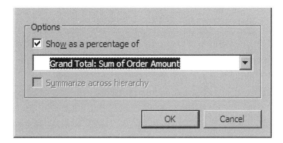

FIGURE 4.5   Options for showing a summary field as a percentage.

The report will now show how much each salesperson has contributed to the overall sales of the company. You can now format this field as a percentage using some of the techniques you learned in Chapter 2.

The show-as-percentage feature is especially handy when used alongside sums and averages. For instance, if you were creating a report on international sales, you could show the dollar amount (sum) for each country and the average sales as well as a percentage representing that country in the total sales.

NOTE

WORKING WITH STATISTICAL SUMMARIES

For the statistical functions available for use within summary fields, you may want to pull on a pair of boots, because we will be wading into deeper water. If you work with statistics, this information will make more sense, but if you are just starting out, check out the Web site mentioned earlier in the chapter for a detailed explanation of all of the statistical terms.

Correlation, covariance, and weighted averages are all related because they require a field to serve as the basis of the summary as well as a second field that is related.

To insert a correlation, covariance, or weighted average summary field, locate and select the field that will serve as the basis for your correlation, covariance, or weighted average. Right-click the field and click Insert > Summary. In the dialog box that opens, select the summary function you want to use.

When you select correlation, covariance, or weighted average, a With drop-down list appears. Select a field to be used when calculating your summary field from this list.

For a correlation or covariance, this will be the field against which you want to compare. For a weighted average, choose the field that contains the values that will weight the average denominator. (In a normal average, this defaults to 1 for each value, but for a weighted average it can be any number you specify.)

Select the summary location and click OK to accept your changes and return to your report. Your summary field is inserted into the group footer you specified.

Another handy statistical summary is the Pth percentile. The Pth percentile summary function can be used to determine the value of P in a numeric or currency field. For example, suppose you want to see where an employee's age falls within your company's distribution. If you enter 50 for the P value in your summary, Crystal Reports will return a value from the 50th percentile (for example, 42, meaning that 50 percent of your employees are younger than 42).

In addition, you may want to look at statistical functions that center around size and frequency. When creating a report, you may want to know what is the largest, smallest, or most frequent data item. Although you can use Group Sorting (which we will talk about later) to obtain similar information from your report, it is much easier to use a summary field. To insert one of these types of summary fields onto your report, use the same method to insert a regular summary field and then select the Nth Largest, Nth Smallest, or Nth Most Frequent Summary function. When you select any of these summary operators, an N Is text box appears. Enter a value for N in the box. It's that simple.

Inserting Grand Total Fields

Grand total fields appear in the report footer at the end of your report and are used to summarize the contents of your report. To insert a grand total field, use the following steps:

ON THE CD

1. Open Crystal Reports, and open the report we have been working with (SALESSUMMARY.RPT), or open a copy from the CD-ROM.
2. Locate and click the field you want to summarize with a grand total, in this case, the Order Amount field.
3. Click Insert > Summary. Using the same Insert Summary dialog box we have been working with, select a summary type and a summary location of Grand Total. Click OK to accept your changes. A summary field representing the grand total is inserted into your report footer.

NOTE

The term grand total is a little misleading. A grand total in Crystal Reports can be a value calculated with any of the summary operators, including Sum, Average, and so on.

ANALYZING REPORT DATA

In addition to calculated fields like summaries and formulas, Crystal Reports also includes a number of other options for analyzing information that appears in your report. Analysis methods range from simply reordering the data to presenting running totals alongside the data to highlighting areas of your report based on pre-set criteria. Regardless of which analysis options you choose to use in your report, you can quickly see the value they add.

Using TopN/BottomN Analysis on Groups

Group Sorting is a function of Crystal Reports used to sort groups according to a summary field that has been created based on that group. Most often, this function is used to determine the top 20 customers (that is, Top N where *N* is 20) or the top (or bottom) five products. Before you can use Group Sorting analysis in your report, you need to make sure that you have two things inserted onto your report: a group and a summary field. Without both of these present, you cannot use Group Sorting analysis.

To add Group Sorting analysis to your report, use the following steps:

ON THE CD

1. Open Crystal Reports, and open the ANALYSISREPORT.RPT report from the CD-ROM.
2. With any report, the next step should be to verify that your report has at least one group and summary inserted (otherwise, we wouldn't have any way to perform our analysis).

3. Click Report > Group Sort Expert. From the dialog box shown in Figure 4.6, you can select either Top N, Bottom N, Top N Percentage, or Bottom N Percentage. In this example, select Top N.

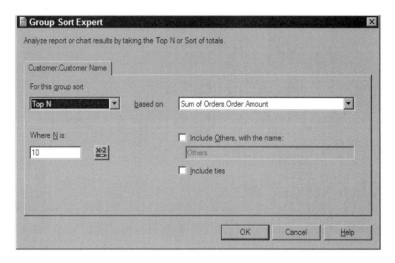

FIGURE 4.6 Options for Group Sorting analysis.

4. Using the drop-down list of available summary fields, select the field on which your analysis will be based. (You'll notice that this list is limited to the summary fields you have inserted in your report.) For this report, select Sum of Orders.Order Amount.

5. Next, enter a value for N. Because we want to create a Top 10 customer report, enter 10 for *n*.

6. There may be more than 10 groups in the report, so you can use the checkbox provided to include the other groups in your report; enter your own name for this group. If a group is not included in the Top (or Bottom) N you specify, it will get lumped into this group. If you would like to display the others, check the box provided and enter a name for the group.

7. Click OK to accept your changes and to apply Group Sorting analysis to your report.

Your report will now only display the Top 10 customers as well as any other records (if you selected that option). You could use this same method to create a Bottom N report or top or bottom percentage, that is, a Customers in the Top 50 Percent report.

Sorting Groups by Subtotal or Summary Fields

When working with groups, you may sometimes want to sort the groups according to some summary field that you have inserted in your report. This functionality is similar to Group Sorting analysis, except that it isn't limited to just a certain number of groups. Using the Crystal Reports Sort All functionality, you can order all of the groups by a summary value.

To sort the groups in your report by the value of a summary field, verify that your report has at least one group and summary inserted. Click Report > Group Sorting Expert. Then, in the dialog box shown in Figure 4.7, select All from the For This Group Sort drop-down list.

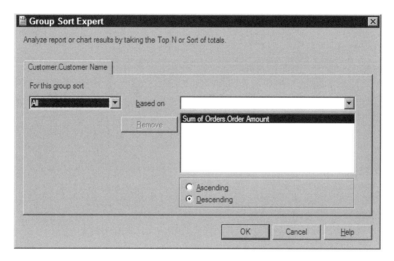

FIGURE 4.7   You can sort groups by a summary field that you have inserted into your report.

Using the drop-down list of available summary fields, select the field on which your analysis will be based. Select a sort order (Ascending or Descending), and click OK to accept your changes and to apply Group Sorting analysis and Sorting to your report. Your groups will now be ordered by the summary field you selected.

Running Totals

Running totals provide an at-a-glance look at cumulative values in your report and display a running summary beside each record. With each release of Crystal Reports, running totals have grown in functionality and can now be used for a wide range of summary and analysis tasks. Running totals also feature a flexible evaluation and reset function that makes complex analysis easier.

By using running totals in your report, you can quickly give users the information they need without have to wade through the report to get to a summary field or the end of a section. For example, suppose you want to create a running total that runs alongside a list of your customers and their last year's sales. With each record, you want this last year's sales figure added to the running total, as shown in Figure 4.8.

Running Totals

Customer Name	Last Year's Sales	Running Total
City Cyclists	$20,045.27	$20,045.27
Pathfinders	$26,369.63	$46,414.90
Bike-A-Holics Anonymous	$4,500.00	$50,914.90
Psycho-Cycle	$52,809.11	$103,724.01
Sporting Wheels Inc.	$85,642.56	$189,366.57
Rockshocks for Jocks	$40,778.52	$230,145.09
Poser Cycles	$10,923.00	$241,068.09
Spokes 'N Wheels Ltd.	$25,521.31	$266,589.40
Trail Blazer's Place	$123,658.46	$390,247.86
Rowdy Rims Company	$30,131.46	$420,379.31
Clean Air Transportation Cc	$23,789.25	$444,168.56
Hooked on Helmets	$52,963.82	$497,132.38
C-Gate Cycle Shoppe	$29,618.11	$526,750.49
Alley Cat Cycles	$298,356.22	$825,106.71
The Bike Cellar	$30,938.67	$856,045.37
Hercules Mountain Bikes	$18,000.00	$874,045.37
Whistler Rentals	$68,000.00	$942,045.37
Bikes and Trikes	$12,000.00	$954,045.37
Changing Gears	$26,705.65	$980,751.02
Wheels and Stuff	$25,556.11	$1,006,307.13

FIGURE 4.8   An example of a report with a running total.

You also can insert running totals from the Field Object menu (Insert > Field Object). Locate the section for running totals in the Field Explorer, right-click, and select New.

The first step in creating a running total is to locate and select the field that will serve as the base field. Right-click the field, and click Insert > Running Total. The dialog box shown in Figure 4.9 opens.

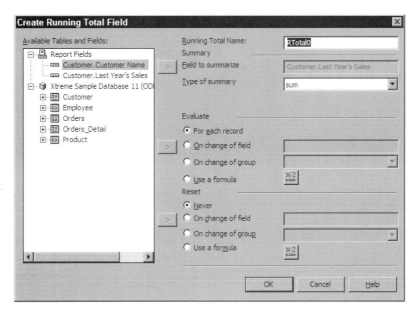

FIGURE 4.9   Running total options.

First you must type a name for your running total in the Running Total Name box. It can be any name you like, as long as it makes sense to you.

Crystal Reports will put the hash symbol (#) in front of your running total name so you can easily identify this field as a running total when it is inserted into your report.

The next step in creating a running total is selecting a field to summarize and then choosing a summary option, as shown in Figure 4.10. To select a field, locate it in the list on the left and then click the top-right arrow to move the field to the text box on the right.

From the drop-down list immediately below the summary field, select a summary operator. All of your old favorites are here: Sum, Average, and so on.

In this example you are inserting a running total that will run down the page, so you don't need to worry about the Evaluate and Reset options for the running total. Click OK to accept your changes and return to your report's Design or Preview. You'll notice that your running total field has been inserted into your report in the Details section.

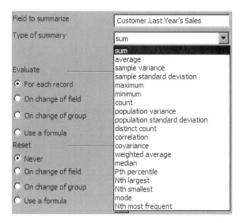

FIGURE 4.10   You need to select a field to summarize and a summary operator for your running total.

As you created your first running total field, you may have noticed two sections in the Create Running Total Field dialog box, marked Evaluate and Reset. These sections are for setting the options related to when your running total will be evaluated and when the total will be reset. For evaluation times, you can select a calculation time for your running total from the following options:

- For Each Record
- On Change of Field
- On Change of Group
- Use a Formula

For example, you would want to use these options if you were creating a running total to sum all of the international sales in a report. You could select the Use a Formula option and enter the following criterion:

```
{Customer.Country} <> "USA"
```

The resulting running total field would be evaluated only for those customers who are not in the United States.

Likewise, you can reset your running total field using the following options:

- Never
- On Change of Field
- On Change of Group
- Use a Formula

For example, you could reset the running total for each change of the Country field in your list. By using the Evaluation and Reset options, you can create running total fields for just about any use you can imagine.

To use these options, in most cases you will need to select the option and the corresponding field or group. For the Use a Formula option, you will need to select the option and then click the X+2 button to open the Crystal Reports Formula Editor and enter your criteria.

Just as with record selection, the formula you create here needs to return a Boolean value: either true or false. If the value is true, the record will be evaluated or the running total reset (depending on the option you are working with); likewise, if the condition evaluates to false, the action will not take place.

Highlighting Your Report

Just like a highlighter can be used to mark up a report physically, indicating values to be scrutinized, the Crystal Reports Highlighting Expert can do the same thing by changing the font, background colors, and borders when criteria are met. Created through a simple interface, multiple highlighting criteria can be established to mark problem areas that need to be addressed or data to be reviewed further. You may want to highlight customers whose sales have been under expectations or customers who have had exceptionally large sales in the past year. The criteria you specify is completely up to you.

To use the Highlighting Expert in your report, locate and select the numeric field that you want to highlight. Right-click the field, and from the menu that appears, select Highlighting Expert. The Highlighting Expert opens, shown in Figure 4.11.

The Highlighting Expert is easy to use. You simply enter a condition on the right side of the dialog box and then specify the formatting options that you want used when that condition is true. If you would like to enter multiple criteria, in the item list click New Item. To change the order of precedence for highlighting criteria (items), use the up and down arrows. After you have finished entering all of your criteria, click OK to accept your changes. The field that you selected originally should now reflect the options set in the Highlighting Expert.

Inserting Running Totals for a Group

In addition to setting running totals for a list of fields, you can set running totals for a group, allowing you to quickly summarize the contents of multiple groups in your report. To insert a running total for a group, select the field you want to summarize, right-click the field, and click Insert > Running Total.

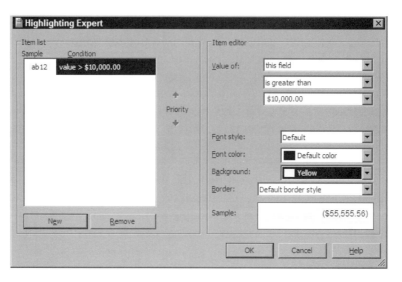

FIGURE 4.11 The Highlighting Expert.

Because you are inserting a running total for a group, select the For Each Record Evaluate option, and under Reset, select On Change of Group and select the group you want to use, as shown in Figure 4.12.

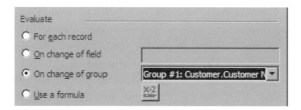

FIGURE 4.12 An example of creating a running total on a group.

Click OK to accept your changes. Your new running total should appear in your report in the group footer of the group you specified earlier.

USING RECORD SELECTION TO FILTER YOUR REPORT

When creating a report, chances are good that you don't want to use all of the records that are stored in your database. You may want to use a subset of records for a particular state, region, date range, and so on. The process used to cut down the number of records returned is called record selection. Record selection uses the Crystal Reports formula language to create a logical statement against which records are evaluated. A record selection formula might look something like the following code:

```
{customer.country} = "USA"
```

As records are read from the database, this formula is evaluated, and where it is true, those records are returned to Crystal Reports from the database. When the report is printed, you will see only records of customers in the United States.

If formulas make you squeamish, you are in luck—you don't have to write complex formulas to use record selection (although you can if you want to). Crystal Reports features a Select Expert that will do most of the work for you. The Select Expert, shown in Figure 4.13, is actually a set of specialized dialog boxes designed to help you quickly create record selection criteria without writing your own formula.

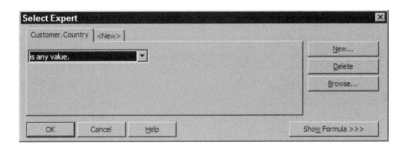

FIGURE 4.13   The Crystal Reports Select Expert.

The Select Expert can be used to apply record selection to a single field or multiple fields with a number of different record-selection operators. Regardless of how many fields or how complex the criteria, the Select Expert can take the choices you make and actually write the selection formula for you. The sections that follow describe some of the most common uses of record selection.

Applying Record Selection to a Single Field

Basing your record selection on a single field is the easiest way to see how the Select Expert works. Our earlier example showed a record-selection formula created on a single field that returned only customers within the United States ({customer. country} = "USA"). We could enter this formula directly, but we are going to let the Select Expert do the work for us.

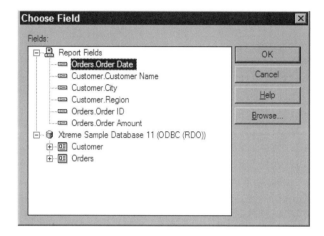

FIGURE 4.14 You need to choose the field that your record selection will be based on.

To get started, click Report > Select Expert. A list of fields that are available for you to use for record selection opens, as shown in Figure 4.14.

If you don't see this list of fields, you may have had a field selected before you clicked Report > Select Expert. In this case, Crystal Reports will assume you want to perform record selection using this field.

Select the field that will be used for your record selection criteria, and click OK. Using the dialog box shown in Figure 4.15, select a record selection operator and enter the required criteria.

From our earlier example, we could select the operator Equal To and then type in USA as our criteria. Click OK to accept your changes. Your report will now be filtered for only those customers that located in the United States.

You can also use the drop-down list to select values directly from the database, but this feature only returns around 200 records from the underlying table, so the value you are looking for may not be there.

In addition to Equal To are a number of other record-selection operators that can be used to narrow your report records to display only the records you need. Table 4.1 describes these operators.

FIGURE 4.15 The Select Expert.

TABLE 4.1 Record Selection Operators

Operator	Description
Is any value	Default option for record selection, allowing all records to be returned, regardless of value
Is equal to	Looks for an exact match to the criteria entered
Is not equal to	Looks for all records except those matching the criteria specified
Is one of	Is used to build a list of criteria, allowing you to select multiple values from one field (for example, is one of "USA", "Canada", and "Mexico")
Is not one of	Is used to build a list of criteria you don't want (for example, is not one of "Australia", "New Zealand", and "Japan")
Is less than	Brings back any records less than the criteria entered
Is less than or equal to	Brings back any records less than or equal to the criteria entered
Is greater than	Brings back any records greater than the criteria entered
Is greater than or equal to	Brings back any records greater than or equal to the criteria entered
Is between	Used to specify inclusive values as criteria; any records between the two inclusive criteria are returned
Is not between	The opposite of Is between; any records outside the two inclusive criteria are returned
Formula:	Used to enter a record selection formula directly without using the Select Expert

Applying Record Selection to Multiple Fields

The Select Expert can also be used to apply selection criteria to multiple fields. To establish criteria for multiple fields, you perform the same process as for a single field: click Report > Select Expert. Then click the New button, shown in Figure 4.16.

FIGURE 4.16 You can click the New button to add criteria for multiple fields.

After you have clicked the New button, a field list will appear, from which you can choose the second field you want to use in your record selection; then a second tab will appear, and you can specify the operator, values, and so on.

Whenever you use multiple fields for record selection, Crystal Reports makes the relationship between these two criteria an AND relationship (that is, Condition1 and Condition2 must be true for Crystal Reports to return a record).

NOTE

To delete criteria, click the tab for the field you want to delete and use the Delete button to remove that tab.

Using an OR Statement in Your Record Selection Formula

When using the Select Expert and using record selection on multiple fields, Crystal Reports assumes that the relationship between these two fields is AND, as shown in Figure 4.17.

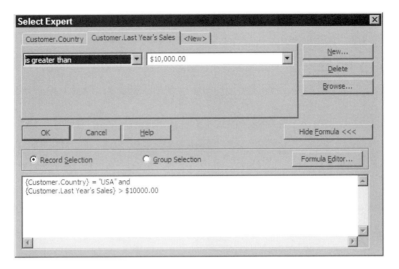

FIGURE 4.17   Crystal Reports places an AND between multiple fields
by default.

In this example, the records would be returned to your report only where the
Country was equal to the USA *and* the company's last year's sales was over 10,000.

If you do need to use the OR operator, you can click the Show Formula button
in the bottom-right corner and manually edit the record-selection formula in the
box shown.

*Once you manually edit the record-selection formula, you may not be able to use
the Select Expert to edit the formula. A message may appear stating "Composite
Expression: Please use formula editor to do editing." This message indicates that
the Select Expert doesn't know how to represent your record-selection formula in
the tabbed interface provided.*

Applying Record Selection Based on Date Fields

For date fields, an additional record selection operator is available, called In the
Period. This operator addresses some of the common types of record selection
based on dates.

To make your life easier, Crystal Reports has a number of predefined periods that can be used for record selection. These periods each generate their own internal list of dates based on each period's definition and the current date. For example, if you select the period MonthToDate, Crystal Reports builds a list of all of the dates that have passed since the first of the month and subsequently uses that list to select records from the database.

One of the most frequently asked questions about periods is: "Can we add periods to this list or change the definitions?" The answer is no. The periods reflected in the list are hard-coded in Crystal Reports. You can, however, create your own user-defined functions and include similar functionality.

The following periods are available for use when performing record selection on dates:

- WeekToDateFromSun
- MonthToDate
- YearToDate
- Last7Days
- Last4WeeksToSun
- LastFullWeek
- LastFullMonth
- AllDatesToToday
- AllDatesToYesterday
- AllDatesFromToday
- AllDatesFromTomorrow
- Aged0to30days
- Aged31to60days
- Aged61to90days
- Over90Days
- Next30days
- Next31to60days
- Next61to90days
- Next91to365days
- Calender1stQtr
- Calendar2ndQtr
- Calendar3rdQtr
- Calendar4thQtr
- Calendar1stHalf
- Calendar2ndHalf
- LastYearMtd
- LastYearYtd

To use these periods with a date field in your report, click Report > Select Expert. From the Choose Field dialog box, select the date field that you want to use in your record selection, and click OK. The Select Expert opens. Using the first drop-down list, shown in Figure 4.18, select either Is in the Period or Is Not in the Period. A second drop-down list appears with the periods listed.

FIGURE 4.18   When you use Is in the Period for record selection, a second drop-down list appears showing all of the available periods.

Select the period you want to use for record selection. Click OK to accept your changes to the record selection criteria and to return to your report, which should now reflect the data only from the period you specified.

Writing Record-Selection Formulas

In addition to the Select Expert, Crystal Reports provides a second method of record selection by allowing you to edit the record-selection formula directly. When looking at the Select Expert, you may have noticed a button in the bottom-right corner marked Show Formula, shown in Figure 4.19.

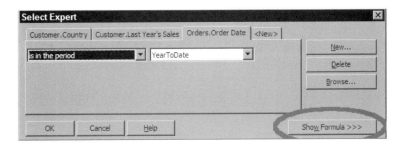

FIGURE 4.19   You can view the formula the Select Expert has created by clicking the Show Formula button.

By looking at the formula that Crystal Reports has created, you can pick up clues about how record-selection formulas work. To write your own selection formula, click Report > Selection Formulas > Record. The Record Selection Formula Editor opens.

You may be warned that you will not be able to keep any drill-down tabs that are open. Click OK to acknowledge this message and to continue writing your record-selection formula.

Using the Formula Editor, shown in Figure 4.20, you can create a record-selection formula that results in a Boolean value (meaning it can be evaluated as either true or false). Use the X+2 button on the toolbar to check the syntax of your record-selection formula. When you are finished working with the selection formula, click the Save button and the close button in the top-left corner to save your formula and close the Formula Editor. Your report should now reflect the record selection criteria you created.

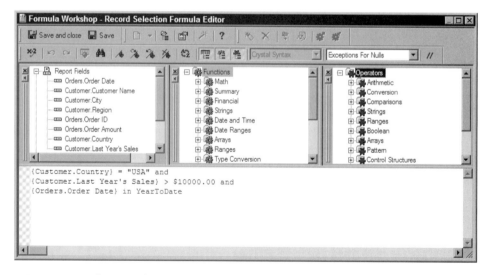

FIGURE 4.20   The Crystal Reports Formula Editor.

In the following sections, we will walk through creating some of the most common types of record-selection formulas.

If all this is just a bit too much, check out Chapter 5 for more information on work-ing with the Crystal Reports formula language and then revisit this section with those newfound formula skills.

Selecting Records Based on Discrete Values

For creating record-selection formulas based on a single, discrete value, you have a number of operators that are available for your use, and they are pretty easy to use because they match the mathematical operators you are probably already used to working with.

From our earlier example, if you wanted to create a report that returned records only from the United States, you could create a record-selection formula that looks like this:

```
{customer.country} = "USA"
```

And in addition to the equals operator, you could also use other operators to retrieve records. For example, if you wanted to retrieve all of the records where the customer's last year's sales were greater than $10,000, the formula would look like this:

```
{customer.last year's sales} > 10000
```

As you have probably already noticed, for comparison against string fields, we place the value in quotes; for numeric fields, no quotes or demarcation is required.

When working with date or date-time fields, we also can use these same oper-ators. For example, to return all database records for purchases made before August 1, the formula would look like this:

```
{Purchases.PurchaseDate} < Date (2003, 08, 01)
```

And if the Purchase Date field were a date-time field, it would look like this:

```
{Orders.Order Date} < DateTime (2003, 08, 01, 00, 00, 00)
```

As you have probably already noticed, using a date field in a record selection formula requires that we convert the values to a true date format, using either the Date or DateTime function provided by Crystal's formula language.

Selecting Records Based on Multiple Values

If you have multiple values that you want to use to select records, you can use a couple of different methods, depending on how the values are arranged.

If the values you want to use are naturally arranged in a range of values (that is, from 1 to 30, A to K, and so on), you can use the In operator and compare the database field against a range of values, separated by the keyword to.

```
{Customer.Last Year's Sales} in 10000 to 30000
```

And a similar formula using strings:

```
{Customer.Initial} in "A" to "K"
```

For values that don't fall into a range, you can also use the In keyword to compare a database field against an array of objects, separated by commands and enclosed in square brackets. For example, if you wanted to show records only for customers in the United States, Canada, and Mexico, the formula would look like this:

```
{Customer.Country} in ["Canada", "Mexico", "USA"]
```

Or for numeric values:

```
{Customer.Last Year's Sales} in [10000, 20000, 30000]
```

And to make things really confusing, you can also combine the two methods, using both a range and array in the same statement:

```
{Customer.Last Year's Sales} in [10000 to 20000, 30000, 40000]
```

As mentioned earlier in the chapter, Crystal Reports includes a number of built-in periods (MonthToDate, YeartoDate, etc.) and treats these as arrays, so you can use these in your record-selection formula the same way (that is, {Order.Order Date} in MonthToDate).

USING PARAMETER FIELDS IN YOUR REPORT

One of the goals of a good report design is that a single report should be able to deliver information to a number of people, eliminating the need for multiple reports that basically show the same information. One method we have for creating reports that fit many different types of situations is through the use of Parameter Fields. In the following sections, you will learn about Parameter Fields, how they are created, and how they can be used to enhance your report's design and usefulness.

Parameter fields are used in reports to prompt a user for information using a standard dialog box, like the one shown in Figure 4.21.

FIGURE 4.21   A typical parameter dialog box.

Parameter fields are just like any other fields in use in your report and can be displayed in your report, used in record selection, and more. If you have used Crystal Reports before, you have probably used parameter fields, although many report developers have been frustrated by some of the limitations that existed with previous versions of Crystal Reports.

Parameters have been dramatically improved in Crystal Reports XI and now include the ability to drive parameter pick lists from your data source as well as the ability to cascade parameter selections. For example, if you had two parameters for users to enter the Country and State fields for their report, they could select a Country and the State list would be filtered for just the states in that particular country.

With these new features, Crystal Reports XI now supports two different types of parameters:

Static Parameters: Like parameters found in previous versions, static parameters can display a list of values that are either entered or retrieved from your data source. These values are static and are stored with the report.

Dynamic Parameters: These parameters can be associated with your data source, so when you add a new value in the database, it will be added to the parameter pick list. Dynamic parameters can also be cascading, where one value determines what appears in the next list of parameter values.

In the following sections, we will cover both type of parameters as well as how they can be used with record selection to filter your report's results.

Working with Static Parameter Fields

To create a static parameter field to be used in your report, click View > Field Explorer. The Crystal Reports Field Explorer opens, as shown in Figure 4.22.

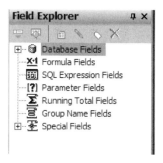

FIGURE 4.22 The Crystal Reports Field Explorer.

Right-click the section of the Field Explorer labeled Parameter Fields, and select New from the shortcut menu. Using the dialog box shown in Figure 4.23, type a name for your parameter field. In our example, we have named the parameter field Employee.

Next, using the combo-box labeled Value Type, select a data type for your parameter field from the following types:

- Boolean
- Currency
- Date
- Date-Time
- Number
- String
- Time

To create a static parameter field, the two required items are the name and type, so you can click OK to accept your changes and return to your report. Your parameter field should now appear in the Field Explorer, ready to be used on your report.

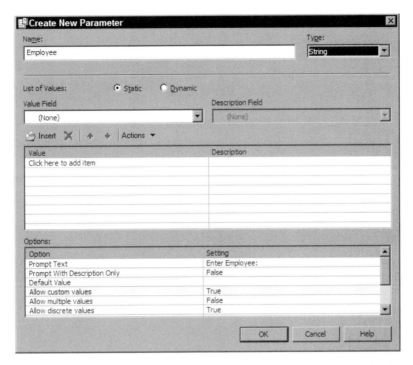

FIGURE 4.23   You can create a parameter field using this simple dialog box.

Inserting a Parameter Field on Your Report

To insert a parameter field that you have created, you can simply drag it from the Field Explorer onto your report's Design or Preview.

It is usually easier to place fields on your report if you use the Design view of the report.

Once you have dragged a parameter field into your report, you will be prompted to enter a value for the parameter the next time the report is previewed, as shown in Figure 4.24.

After you have entered a value for your parameter field, that value will be displayed in the report preview until you refresh your report and specify that you want to prompt for a new parameter value.

FIGURE 4.24 A typical Parameter prompt dialog box.

Setting Default Parameter Values

An easy way to help users complete parameter field prompts for static parameters is to give them some default values from which to choose. A list of default parameter values can be read from your database or entered manually, giving the users a list of values. An important concept when working with default parameter values is that this is a manual process with static parameters and can occur only when designing the report.

If you want to enter a list of values, you can click the Insert button in the Parameter dialog box and then enter a value and/or description in the grid area below. If you would prefer to read these values from your data source, use the following steps:

ON THE CD

1. Open Crystal Reports, and open the COMMISSION.RPT report from the CD-ROM.
2. Click View > Field Explorer to open a list of fields in your report.
3. Right-click the Parameter Fields heading, and select New from the shortcut menu. The Create New Parameter dialog box opens, shown in Figure 4.25.
4. In the Name field, enter Employee, and select a type of Number from the drop-down list on the right side.
5. Next, use the Value drop-down list to select the Employee ID field.
6. Use the Description drop-down list to select the Last Name field.
7. Click the Actions button, and select Append All Database values.
8. Click OK to return to your report.
9. Drag the Employee field into the Page Header of your report, and then preview the report.

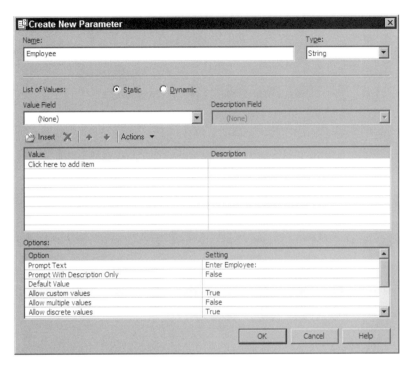

FIGURE 4.25 The Create Parameter dialog box.

The parameter you just created should now prompt you to use the list you just created, as shown in Figure 4.26.

Sorting Parameter Field Default Values

To make looking through these default values a little easier, we can sort the contents of the drop-down lists of values that the user sees. When working with the default values, click the header of either the Value or Description columns in the grid to sort the items to be in either ascending or descending order. This sort order will be reflected in the drop-down list when the user selects a value. With a sort order in place, users will have an easier time selecting the values they want.

Importing/Exporting a Parameter Field Pick List

When working with static parameter fields and default values, you may have multiple reports that use the same default values and descriptions. If you entered these values manually, retyping these values and descriptions in each time you want to use them is time consuming, so Crystal Reports has an easy way to work around

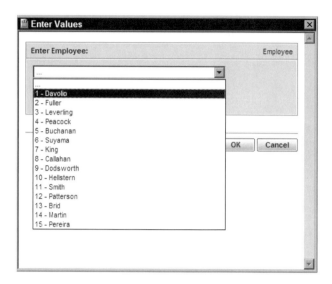

FIGURE 4.26 The parameter dialog should now show the default values you added.

this problem. If you frequently use the same parameter fields, you can export and import field pick lists, eliminating the need to establish default values and descriptions each time. The pick list files themselves are simply text files and can be used with any report you create.

To import/export a parameter field pick list, use the following steps:

1. Open the report we have been working on in this section.
2. Click View > Field Explorer.
3. Right-click the Employee parameter field, and select Edit to open the Edit Parameter dialog box. Under the Actions button, a drop-down list contains the following three options for working with pick lists:

   Clear: Removes all default values from the list.
   Import: Allows you to import a text file with default values.
   Export: Allows you to export a text file with all the values currently listed in this dialog box.

4. Select Export to export the default values for use another time.
5. Click OK to return to your report design.

You can then use Notepad to open the file to verify that the process ran correctly and check the format of the file, shown here in Figure 4.27.

FIGURE 4.27 You can export pick list values for use in other reports.

 Alternatively, you could also use the Import Pick List button to import an existing pick list as long as the text file you were importing was in the same format.

Customizing Parameter Prompts

Although users are prompted for parameters using a standard dialog box, you do have some control over how the parameter dialog box appears. On the bottom of the New Parameter or Edit Parameter dialog box shown in Figure 4.28, you will find the options you can use to customize the prompt that users see.

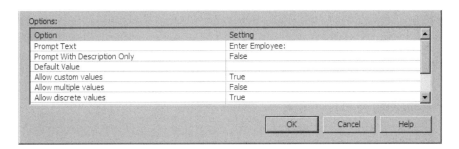

FIGURE 4.28 Options for customizing parameter prompts.

These options include:

Prompt Text: For entering text that will appear to instruct the user on what values to enter.

Prompt With Description Only: For prompting the user with the description only (rather than show the description and value, for example, CA—California).

Default Value: For setting the default value for a field.

Allow Custom Value: For allowing the user to enter his own custom value in the parameter.

There are also a number of other options that you can use with static parameters, but these are a bit more involved, so in the following sections we will look at these options in depth.

Creating a Multiple-Value Parameter Field

In addition to single and range values, parameter fields can be created that enable users to enter multiple values. What this means for you is that you can create one parameter field that can accept from one value to as many as you would like. You could create a parameter field for Country, for example, and then let users pick for which countries they want to run the report. From one country to three to thirty— it is their choice.

The only downside of using a multiple-value parameter field is that the values you enter can't be displayed on your report, which makes sense because there isn't enough room in the field to display the extra values.

To create a multiple-value parameter field, create a parameter field as you normally would, but this time, change the option Allow multiple values to True. Click OK to accept your changes and return to the Design or Preview of your report. When users are prompted for a parameter field, a dialog box similar to the one shown in Figure 4.29 will appear and allow them to build a list of values.

Limiting Parameter Input to a Range of Values

When using parameter fields, we can give users the option of entering a start value and end value, allowing them to use this field in record selection. Again, insert a parameter field, as you normally would, but this time use the drop-down list under the Options section of the dialog box to change Allow range values to True. When your parameter is inserted into your report or used with record selection and this setting is in effect, the dialog box shown in Figure 4.30 will be prompt you for a range of values.

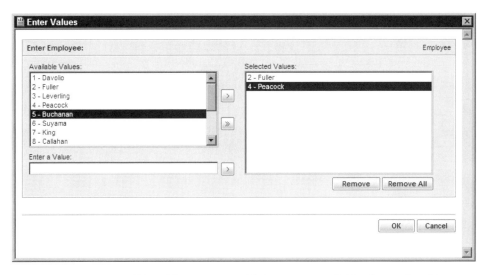

FIGURE 4.29   Users will be able to enter multiple parameter-field values using this dialog box.

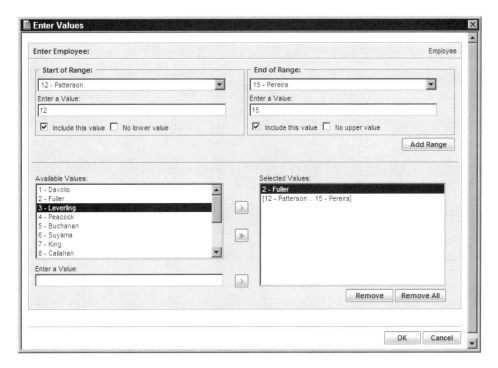

FIGURE 4.30   You can define a parameter to accept a range of values, a discrete value, or both.

A little later in the chapter, we will talk about how to use this type of field with record selection.

Using Static Parameters to Control Report Features

Boolean parameter fields can be used to prompt users for a true or false response and can be used to control report formatting, summary levels, and more. For example, you may want to create a report that prompts users to answer the question "Show Negative Numbers?" and then use the value they entered in a record-selection formula to filter out any negative numbers that may normally appear in the report.

Creating a Boolean parameter field is just like creating any other parameter field. To start, click View > Field Explorer. The Crystal Reports Field Explorer opens. Right-click the section of the Field Explorer labeled Parameter Fields, and select New from the shortcut menu. Using the Create New Parameter dialog box, type a name for your parameter field and change the type to Boolean. Next, using the Prompt Text option, enter any prompting text you wish to appear when users are prompted for information (for example, "Would you like to print all states?"). See Figure 4.31.

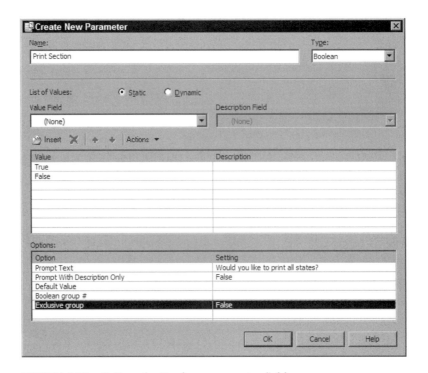

FIGURE 4.31 Options for Boolean parameter fields.

When users are prompted for a Boolean parameter field, a dialog box similar to the one shown in Figure 4.32 will appear, and they can enter a selection of True or False.

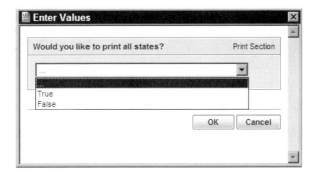

FIGURE 4.32   A typical Boolean parameter field.

If you are not really fond of just True and False, you can select how the Boolean value is entered (True/False, Yes/No, On/Off) by using the options at the bottom of the page. As a final step, you could use this formula field with conditional formatting to determine if a section or area of the report was printed.

ON THE CD
The CD-ROM contains a sample report that demonstrates this technique. Open the BOOLEAN.RPT report from the PROJECTS folder.

Working with Dynamic Parameters

Dynamic parameters, new to Crystal Reports XI, represent a significant enhancement over previous versions. Using dynamic parameters, you can tie a parameter field to a database table, view, or stored procedure and use the data to drive the pick list that is presented to users. For example, if you were to set up a parameter to prompt a user for a customer number, using a dynamic parameter would ensure that every new customer that is added to the database would appear in the parameter pick list.

The downside to dynamic parameters is that this can add to the processing overhead of the report. In this section we will look at how to use dynamic parameters in your reports as well as how to use SQL commands to minimize the amount of processing required to generate parameter pick lists.

But before we can get into that, we must look at how to create a dynamic parameter field. To get started, use the following steps:

1. Open Crystal Reports, and open the DYNAMIC.RPT report from the CD-ROM.
2. Click View > Field Explorer to open a list of fields in your report.
3. Right-click the Parameter Fields heading, and select New from the shortcut menu.
4. Enter a name for your parameter (in this case, Country), and select a type of String.
5. Use the radio button to select Dynamic, which will change the dialog box to be like the one shown in Figure 4.33.

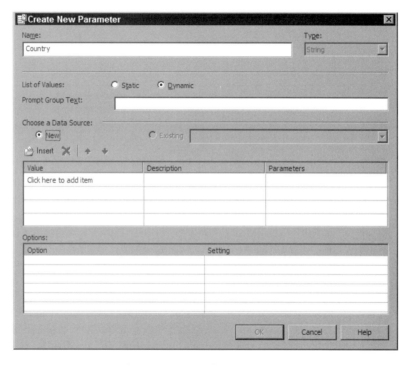

FIGURE 4.33 Dynamic parameter options.

6. Click the link marked Click here to add item, and select the Country field.
7. Next, enter any text that you want to appear when the prompt appears. In this example, enter the text, "Please select a country from the list."
8. Click OK to return to your report.
9. Drag the parameter field you just created into your report. A dialog box should appear and prompt you to select a value from a drop-down list.

The list of values that appear in this list is dynamic and will be refreshed from the database each time a user runs the report and is prompted for a parameter.

Using Dynamic Parameters with Cascading Values

Another option that is new to Crystal Reports XI is the concept of cascading parameters. Water cascades over a waterfall, down one rock to another, and so do cascading parameter fields. The selection you make in the first field is used to filter the second field, then the third, and so forth. An example of a cascading parameter field is shown in Figure 4.34.

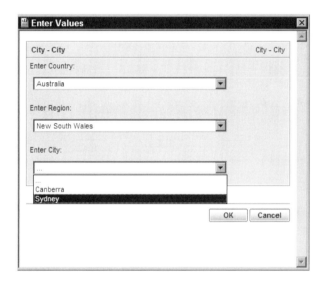

FIGURE 4.34   An example of a cascading parameter.

In this example, the user will select a Country field, which in turn filters the Region field to show only the regions related to that country. Then the user selects a Region field, which then filters the city list to only those cities that exist within that region.

You can easily apply this same technique to your own reports. In the following example we are going to re-create this scenario using a report based on one of our customer reports. To create a cascading parameter, use the following steps:

1. Open Crystal Reports, and open the CASCADING.RPT report from the CD-ROM.
2. Click View > Field Explorer to open a list of fields in your report.
3. Right-click the Parameter Fields heading, and select New from the shortcut menu.
4. Enter a name for your parameter (in this case, City), and select a type of String.
5. Use the radio button to select Dynamic.
6. Click the link marked Click here to add item, and use the drop-down list to select the Country field.
7. On the next line, click the same line and use the drop-down list to add the Region field.
8. And finally, on the line below, click the same link and use the drop-down list to select the City field. Your parameter field dialog box should now look like the one shown in Figure 4.35.

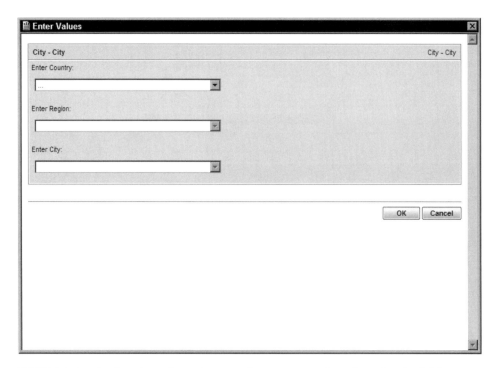

FIGURE 4.35 Settings for a dynamic, cascading parameter based on the city field.

9. Click OK to return to your report.
10. Drag the parameter field you just created into your report design.

The dialog box in Figure 4.34 should now appear and prompt you for the Country, Region, and City fields. As you make a selection in one drop-down list, the selections in the other lists will be filtered based on what you selected.

Splitting Cascading Parameters into Separate Fields

There will be times when you want to separate a cascading parameter into multiple fields. In our previous example, you may want to separate the parameter fields so you can use the values the user selected for the Country, Region, and City parameters.

To split the parameter fields into separate fields, use the following steps:

1. Open Crystal Reports, and open the cascading parameter report you were just working on.
2. Click View > Field Explorer to open a list of fields in your report.
3. Expand the Parameter Fields section, right-click the City parameter, and select Edit from the shortcut menu.
4. From the Edit Parameter dialog box, locate the grid that displays the value, description, and parameters field, and click to create a parameter on the `Customer.Country` field.
5. Repeat the same operation on the `Customer.Region` field.
6. Click OK to return to your report design.

Your report will now show the three parameters separately in the Field Explorer, as shown in Figure 4.36.

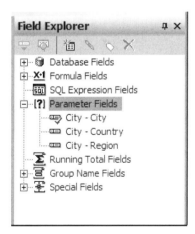

FIGURE 4.36 The parameters
split into separate fields.

You can use these parameter fields independently, but they are still part of a Parameter Group, so whenever you edit one of these fields, the entire prompt group will be shown in the Edit Parameter dialog box.

Using Command Objects for Dynamic Parameters

One way to cut down on the processing overhead required for dynamic parameters is to use an SQL command. We haven't covered SQL commands yet, but they can be used to write an SQL statement that is used as the basis of your report. We will look at this type of data source in-depth in the next chapter.

SQL commands for dynamic parameters are used to ensure that only the required amount of data is returned. For example, if we were to base a dynamic parameter for the user to enter a Country, and we used the customer table in our sample database, it would not be the most efficient way of populating the pick list. The customer table contains thousands of customer records, and some of these records repeat the same country. A much better technique would be to use a specialized lookup table (that is, a table that listed each country only once) or use an SQL command to bring back only a distinct list of countries from the customer table. And in the next example, that is just what we are going to do. Use the following steps:

ON THE CD

1. Open Crystal Reports, and open the PARAMETERCOMMAND.RPT report from the CD-ROM.
2. Click Database > Database Expert.
3. Click Create New Connection > ODBC RDO to open a list of available ODBC data sources.
4. Select the Xtreme Sample Database 11 option, and click Finish.
5. Next, below this data source double-click the Add Command option. The dialog box shown in Figure 4.37 opens.
6. Enter the following SQL statement in the text box provided:
   SELECT DISTINCT COUNTRY FROM CUSTOMER.
7. Click OK to return to the Database Expert, and then click OK twice to return to your report.
8. Next, click View > Field Explorer to open a list of fields in your report.
9. Right-click the Parameter Fields heading, and select New from the shortcut menu.
10. Enter a name for your parameter (in this case, "Country"), and select a type of String.
11. Use the radio button to select Dynamic.
12. Click the link marked Click here to add item, and use the drop-down list to select the Country field from the Command you entered earlier.

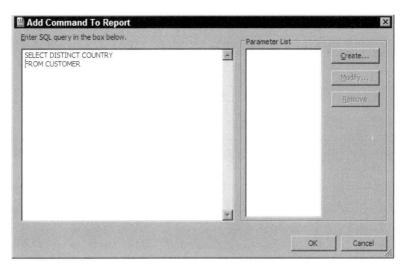

FIGURE 4.37   The Add Command dialog box.

13. Click OK to return to your report design.
14. Drag the parameter field from the list into your report.

Now when the parameter dialog box appears, the SQL command will be used to populate the pick list instead of querying the table underlying the report.

If you are publishing your report to BusinessObjects Enterprise, you can also sched-ule the generation of this pick list and share lists between reports. For more infor-mation, see the Administrators Guide available in PDF form in DOCS directory on your BusinessObjects Enterprise CD-ROM.

PARAMETER FIELDS AND RECORD SELECTION

Using parameter fields for record selection is a popular way to give users more control over the report at runtime. Setting up this functionality is quick and easy— there are only two steps involved.

The first is to actually create the parameter field used to prompt the user for information using the techniques learned earlier in the chapter. You will want to make sure that this parameter field is created with the same type as the field you want to use for record selection. (It will do you no good to create a string-type parameter field when you want the user to enter an invoice number.)

The second step is to set your record-selection formula using this parameter field. In its most simple form, your record-selection formula might look something like this:

```
{Customer.Country} = {?EnterCountry}
```

where `{?EnterCountry}` is the name of the parameter field you have created.

If formulas are not your thing, you can use the Select Expert to do most of the work for you.

NOTE

In this example, whenever the report is run, a dialog box will open and ask for a country to be entered, which we will assume is entered as "USA." Once this data entry has occurred, the record-selection formula will replace the parameter name with the actual value and make a request to the database to retrieve the correct records for companies in the United States.

To make things a little more complicated, parameter fields can also be created with the ability to enter multiple values. In this case, the formula looks exactly the same:

```
{Customer.Country} = {?EnterCountry}
```

When the dialog box opens and prompts for information to be entered for this Parameter Field, as shown in Figure 4.38, you can pick a list of values to be used—in this case we will assume "USA," "Canada," and "Mexico." These values are then used in the record-selection formula, and the appropriate records are returned.

This is often confusing to new report developers, because the proper record-selection operator for multiple values is One of. Crystal Reports stores these multiple values in memory and is smart enough to make the translation when processing occurs. Unfortunately, as was mentioned earlier, we are unable to display the contents of this array on our report. It can be used only for record selection.

The same concept also applies when we specify that a parameter field can accept a range of values. You will be prompted for a start value and end value, but Crystal Reports stores these values in its own internal memory and allows you to use the same record-selection formula of

```
{Customer.Country} = {?EnterCountry}
```

That said, it does not mean that Is equal to is the only record-selection operator you can use with parameter fields. Because parameter fields are treated just like any other field, you can use any record-selection operator or logic to achieve the desired results.

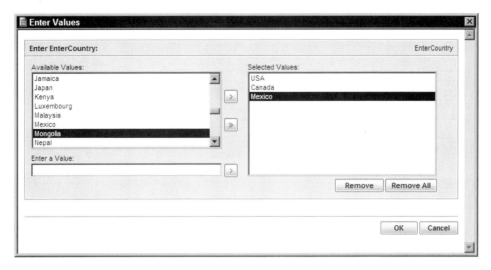

FIGURE 4.38 You can enter multiple values for parameters using this dialog box.

For example, if you wanted to create two parameters in a sales report where you created one parameter field for a StartDate and another one for an EndDate, you could use these in your record-selection formula just like you would any other values, as follows:

```
{Orders.Order Date} in {?StartDate} to {?EndDate}
```

Using a Parameter Field in Simple Record Selection

Parameter fields can be used in a number of different ways, but the most common use of parameter fields is in conjunction with record selection, prompting users for a value that will be used to narrow the results of a particular report.

To use a parameter field with record selection, determine which field from your database you want to use for record selection, and note the type and length of the field. You will then need to create a parameter field with the same field type as your database field. To use this field with record selection, click Report > Select Expert. A list of fields will appear. Choose the field from your database that you want to use for record selection. The Select Expert opens and allow you to choose a record-selection operator (Equal to, Is Not equal to, Is one of, and so on).

Once you have selected an operator, a second dialog box opens, as shown in Figure 4.39, which will allow you to select or enter a value to be used in your record selection. Use the drop-down list to locate and select the parameter field you have created.

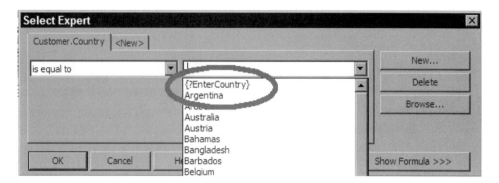

FIGURE 4.39 A second drop-down list should appear and allow you to select the parameter field you have created.

Click OK to accept your changes to your report's record selection and return to the report Design or Preview. When you next preview or refresh your report, a dialog box will open, prompting you for the parameter field you created. Once you enter this value, it will be used in the record-selection formula and subsequently passed to the database.

SUMMARY

Analyzing report data can be an effective way to bring real meaning and value to the information presented. In this chapter we looked at two different techniques to make that happen—analyzing report data using summaries, running totals, and so forth; and filtering reports using parameter fields. In the next chapter we will continue on with this theme, looking at how you can add calculations to your report.

5 | Expressions, Formulas, and Functions

In This Chapter

- Formula Overview
- Working with Formulas
- Creating Simple Arithmetic Formulas
- Using Crystal Reports Functions
- Adding Logic to Formulas
- Understanding Formula Evaluation Times
- Debugging Formulas
- Working with Custom Functions
- SQL Commands and Expressions

INTRODUCTION

Crystal Reports offers a flexible environment for adding calculations to your reports, leveraging both its own formula languages and SQL command and expressions that can take advantage of your database server's processing power.

In this chapter you'll first learn how to use the Crystal Reports formula languages to create and debug formulas to add calculations and logic to your reports, and you will gain an understanding of the behind-the-scenes processing that makes Crystal Reports tick. You'll also learn how to reuse your formula code to create custom functions that you can employ as required.

In the second half of the chapter, we'll look at how to create SQL commands and expressions and use them in your reports. SQL commands offer a way to reuse

SQL statements as the data source for your report and push more processing back to the database server. If you don't want to write full-blown SQL, you can still use SQL expressions to add calculations to your report. SQL expressions offer only a subset of the functions and operators found in Crystal's own formula language, but they have the added bonus of being evaluated by the database server (instead of locally). The material at the end of the chapter drills down into how to create and use SQL commands and expressions, including some common usage scenarios and examples.

FORMULA OVERVIEW

By now, you are already somewhat familiar with the Crystal Reports formula language—it is used throughout the product in record selection, conditional formatting, and more. But the Crystal Reports formula language goes beyond those uses, giving you the ability to add complex calculations to your reports and manipulate report fields and elements.

If you have ever worked with a programming language or development tool, the Crystal Reports formula language will seem familiar. Likewise, if you are new to software development but have had some experience creating formulas in Excel, you should be able to transfer your skills to Crystal Reports easily. (In fact, many of the functions work just like the ones you find in Excel.)

Formulas are written using the Crystal Reports Formula Editor, shown in Figure 5.1. A formula can consist of any number of database or other fields, operators, functions, text, numbers, and control structures such as If...Then statements. Before we can start our discussion of how formulas are put together, we need to look at the Formula Editor and see how it works.

Using the Formula Editor

The Formula Editor is the tool you will use to add or edit formulas that appear in your report. To open the Formula Editor, use the following steps:

1. Open Crystal Reports and any existing report on which you have been working.
2. Click View > Field Explorer.
3. Locate the Formula Fields section, right-click the section header, and choose New.
4. You will be prompted for a name for your formula. Enter a name and click OK. The Crystal Reports Formula Editor opens.

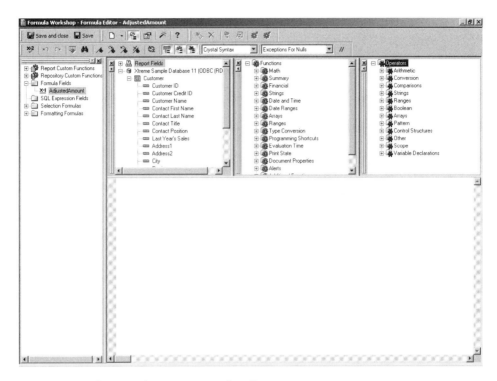

FIGURE 5.1 The Crystal Reports Formula Editor.

5. The Formula Editor consists of five main areas:

The Workshop Tree: Located on the left side of the page, this allows you to navigate through and access formulas and custom functions wherever they may appear in your report.

The Toolbar: Contains icons for creating a new formula, switching between formulas, finding and replacing, and more (see Figure 5.2).

The Report Fields section: Lists all fields present in your report, followed by your data source and all of the tables and fields it contains.

FIGURE 5.2 The Formula Editor toolbar.

The Operators list: Contains a hierarchical view of all of the operators available in Crystal Reports (all of the arithmetic operators, variable declarations, comparison operators, and so on).

Some of the operators, such as +, –, /, and *, may be easier to just type, but you can double-click any operator in this list to add it to your report.

The Functions section: Lists all of the available functions. They range from simple summaries (sum, average, and so on) to type conversion and field manipulation functions to functions for complex statistical and financial analysis.

The largest section in the Formula Editor is used for the formula text you enter. This area behaves similarly to other text editors (such as Notepad) or word-processing applications you may have used in the past.

When working with formula text, you may notice that Crystal Reports uses different colors for words or phrases in your formula text. This color-coding is designed to identify reserved words, functions, and comments. You can control this and many other aspects of the Formula Editor's appearance by clicking File > Option > Editors.

Over the past few versions of Crystal Reports, the Formula Editor itself has come a long way in terms of functionality and features for the developer. For example, the editor has an auto-complete function that you can use to complete code, similar to the Intellisense feature in Visual Studio. To use the auto-complete function, press CTRL+spacebar to open a drop-down list with the most likely text to complete the text you are entering.

Crystal vs. Basic Syntax

Just as English has its own syntax that dictates how words and sentences are put together, so does Crystal Reports—in fact, it has two types of syntax: Crystal syntax and Basic syntax. Crystal syntax has been around the longest, and up until version 8.0, it was the only choice for report developers. Crystal syntax has no direct relationship to any programming language (although it does resemble Pascal or dBase at times), and for report and application developers, it was difficult to learn.

With the release of Crystal Reports 8.0 came a new formula syntax, Basic, with structures and functions that closely resemble those used in Visual Basic. For application developers, the Crystal Reports Formula Editor then became familiar territory, because they could apply the concepts and functions they knew from Visual Basic. For new report developers, Basic syntax provides a better frame of reference and some additional functionality.

In Crystal Reports XI, both types of syntax can be used, side by side, in different formulas in your report, according to your needs. To select a syntax for your formulas, locate the drop-down list in the top-right corner of the Formula Editor and select the appropriate syntax. When it comes to actually choosing a particular syntax, there is no clear winner—you will find most of the functions you need in both.

If you are just starting out with Crystal Reports, it would probably be a good idea to learn Crystal syntax first, because the record-selection formulas in Crystal Reports are written using *only* this syntax. However, Basic is easy to pick up if you have some programming experience.

To illustrate the difference between the two syntaxes, an example works best. The same formula is shown in the next examples, first written in Crystal Syntax:

```
{Orders.Order Amount} * 1.06
```

and then again in Basic Syntax:

```
Formula = {Orders.Order Amount} * 1.06
```

You can see that the syntax is almost identical, except the Basic syntax requires a `Formula =` to indicate what the output of the formula should be. And to make things even easier, most of the functions in Crystal Reports are the same for both Crystal and Basic syntax, as shown first in the following sample formula with Crystal Syntax:

```
Sum({Orders.Order Amount})
```

And then again in Basic syntax:

```
Formula = Sum({Orders.Order Amount})
```

Some cracks start to show, however, as formulas become more complex. In the next two examples you can see the difference between how Crystal and Basic syntax handle returning information to the report. First, in Crystal syntax we see a simple `If…then` that returns a string if the condition is met:

```
If Sum({Orders.Order Amount})>10000 then "Good Sale"
```

In this example, the string to be returned is simply enclosed in quotes, and it is assumed that this will be the value returned to the formula field. And in the second example, you see the same formula in Basic syntax, only this time instead placing the Formula = at the start of the formula text, it is used to assign what will be returned to the report:

```
If Sum({Orders.Order Amount})>10000 then Formula = "Good Sale"
```

Finally, the last major difference we are going to point out between Crystal and Basic syntax is the way variables are declared. To declare, use, and display a variable in Crystal syntax, you may write something that looked like the following:

```
CurrencyVar OrderAmountWithTax;
OrderAmountWithTax = {Orders.Order Amount} *1.06;
OrderAmountWithTax
```

The first line dimensions a variable called OrderAmountWithTax and then performs a calculation and returns it to the report. Note that each line has a semicolon as the continuation character, and to display the results on the report, you just need to repeat the variable name. The Basic syntax version of the same formula would look something like the following:

```
Dim OrderAmountWithTax As Currency
OrderAmountWithTax = {Orders.Order Amount} *1.06
Formula = OrderAmountWithTax
```

You can see that the Basic syntax example follows conventions you may have used in Visual Basic, including the Dim statement to dimension a variable with a particular type.

So now that you have seen a little bit of the difference between the two, it is time for you to groan. For the examples and projects in this chapter, we will use Crystal syntax: the main reason is that key Crystal Reports features that are formula based (such as record selection) rely on this syntax. Therefore, if you want to use these features, you need to know Crystal syntax.

ON THE CD Because the audience for this book is primarily software developers, on the accompanying CD-ROM you will find all of the examples from this chapter shown in Basic syntax as well. A number of reports are also included that demonstrate formula concepts covered in the chapter as well as some we didn't have room for, including both Crystal and Basic syntax examples.

Another key point is that this chapter is not an exhaustive reference on every function and operator available within Crystal Reports; rather it covers the most popular functions and operators. If we were to cover every function and operator in depth, that could be a book in itself.

WORKING WITH FORMULAS

Before we can get into the nitty-gritty and look at the specific operators, functions, and text that make up formulas, we need to look at some of procedures for working with formulas.

Creating a New Formula

Like most fields in Crystal Reports, formula fields can be created and inserted using the Field Explorer. To create a new formula in a report, use the following steps:

ON THE CD

1. Open Crystal Reports, and open the FORMULAS.RPT report from the CD-ROM.
2. Click View > Field Explorer; you should see a section named Formula Fields.
3. To insert a new formula, right-click the section marked Formula Fields, and select New from the shortcut menu, shown in Figure 5.3.

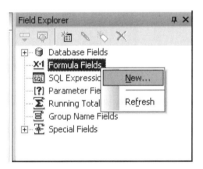

FIGURE 5.3   You create new formulas from the Field Explorer dialog box.

4. In the next dialog box that appears, enter a name for your formula, and click OK. The name you select can be anything that makes sense to you and can include spaces or special characters. In this example, name the formula OrderWithDiscount, because we are going to calculate the order amount with a $200 discount applied as a simple first example.

NOTE

If you are going to create multiple formulas, you may want to consider a naming convention (for instance, SalesTax1, SalesTax2, *and so on) for your formula names.*

5. The Formula Editor appears, and you can enter your formula text. Expand the Report Fields section, and under the Orders table, double-click the `Orders.Order Amount` field to insert it into your formula.
6. Next, type a space, then a negative symbol, and then 200. Your formula should now look like the following:

```
{Orders.Order Amount} -200
```

At any time, you can check the syntax of your formula by clicking the X+2 button on the toolbar, but remember that Crystal Reports also performs a syntax check whenever you exit the Formula Editor.

7. When you are finished editing your new formula, click the Save and Close icon located in the top-left corner of the Formula Editor. You will then be returned to your report's Design or Preview view, where you will be able to insert your newly created formula into your report.

Inserting a Formula into Your Report

Inserting your formula into your report may be easier from the Design tab of your report. From there you can see all of the sections clearly and understand where you are placing your formula field.

To insert the formula field you just created, use the following steps:

1. In the Field Explorer (which you open by clicking View > Field Explorer), your formula should be listed under the section named Formula Fields.
2. From the Field Explorer, drag and drop your formula field onto your report into the details section.
3. Alternatively, you can click to select the field and then press ENTER, which will attach the field to the tip of your mouse. When you have the field positioned on your report, click once to release the field and place it in your report.

Editing an Existing Formula

Crystal Reports identifies formula fields you insert into your report by placing the @ symbol in front of the name and {} (curly braces) around the name. For instance, the field name for the `OrderWithDiscount` formula would appear as `{@OrderWithDiscount}`.

You can edit any existing formula that has been inserted into your report by locating the formula field you want to edit and right-clicking that formula field. Then select Edit Formula from the shortcut menu, shown in Figure 5.4. This opens the Crystal Reports Formula Editor, where you can edit the formula field.

FIGURE 5.4 To edit an existing formula, right-click the formula shown in your report.

When you are finished editing your formula, click the Save, and then the Close icon in the top-left corner to close the Formula Editor and save your changes. You will be returned to your report's Design or Preview view, and your changes should be reflected in the formula results.

Renaming a Formula

Often you will want to revisit your report design and clean up the names of formulas, parameter fields, and running totals that appear in your report, to make it easier for other report designers or users to understand the logic behind your report design. To rename a formula, click View > Field Explorer to open the Field Explorer, locate the Formulas section, and find the formula you want to rename.

If you right-click the formula name, you should see the Rename option in the shortcut menu, shown in Figure 5.5. Select Rename to edit the formula name.

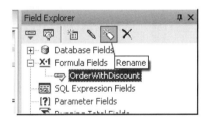

FIGURE 5.5 You can edit a formula name from the Field Explorer.

When you are finished editing the formula name, click anywhere outside of the formula name to accept your changes.

Even if the formula is used on your report multiple times or referenced in multiple other formulas, the name change will be propagated everywhere it used.

NOTE

CREATING SIMPLE ARITHMETIC FORMULAS

The most basic formulas use one of the simple arithmetic operators (+, –, *, /) and perform a calculation. To see how arithmetic formulas are written, we are going to write a Crystal Reports formula that will add on a flat shipping amount and then calculate the sales tax on the Order Amount field. We know that there is a field in our database that contains the Order Amount figure, that shipping is a flat $20, and that sales tax is 6 percent; the rest is up to Crystal Reports.

To create a simple arithmetic formula, use the following steps:

ON THE CD

1. Open Crystal Reports, and open the FORMULAS.RPT report that we have been working with, or open a copy of the report from the CD-ROM.
2. Click View > Field Explorer and, from the Field Explorer, right-click the section named Formula Fields and select New from the shortcut menu.
3. In the next dialog box, you enter a name for your formula field—in this case, Sales Tax—and click OK. The Formula Editor will appear and allow you to enter your formula text.
4. In this example, we need to locate the field Order Amount. Look in the Fields pane of the Formula Editor, shown in Figure 5.6; locate the Last Year's Sales field. All of the fields that appear in your report are located in the top section, named Report Fields.

FIGURE 5.6 The Fields pane of the Formula Editor contains all of the fields that appear in your report as well as all of the fields available from your report's data source.

If you want to use a field that does not appear in your report, you can do so. All of the tables and fields in your data source are available in the list.

5. To place a reference to a particular field in your formula text, double-click the field name. The reference should immediately appear in the formula text below. In this example, double-click the `Orders.Order Amount` field.

You'll notice that database fields are represented in the format of `TableName.FieldName`, with a set of curly braces around the entire lot. This format indicates that this is a database field.

All of the Formula Editor panes—Fields, Functions, and Operators—behave the same way; double-click any of the items listed, and it will be inserted into your formula text.

6. For this formula, not only do we need a reference to the Order Amount field, we also need to do some simple arithmetic to multiply this field by 0.06 (6 percent) and then add $20 on to this total (because there is no sales tax on shipping). To do this, move to the Operators pane.

The Operators pane, shown in Figure 5.7, contains all of the operators that are available in Crystal Syntax. These operators are separated into categories: Arithmetic operators, Conversion operators, and so on.

7. In this instance, we know that multiplication is an arithmetic operator, so we can expand the Arithmetic section, locate the operator for multiplication (*), and then double-click it to insert it into our formula text.

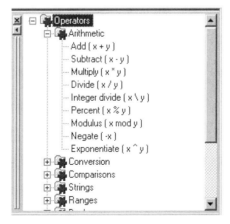

FIGURE 5.7 The Operators pane lists all of the operators available in Crystal Reports.

It is also sometimes just as easy to type the operator yourself, once you are familiar with them.

8. Now all we need to do is enter the 1.06 value, to show the order amount plus 6%. The formula should then look something like the following:

```
{Orders.Order Amount} * 1.06
```

9. Next, we need to add the $20 flat sales tax to our formula. Because Crystal Reports follows a logical order of operation for all calculations, it is always a good idea to use parentheses to indicate which part of the calculation should be performed first. So, surround your formula text with parentheses and then add + (the plus operator) and the 20 value. Your formula should now look like the following:

```
( {Orders.Order Amount} * 1.06 ) + 20
```

Congratulations—that's all you need to do. If you were to place this formula in the Details section of your report, it would calculate the sales tax on the Order Amount field and add the shipping cost for every customer in your report, like in the report shown in Figure 5.8.

Customer Name	Order ID	Order Date	Order Amount	With Sales Tax
Deals on Wheels	1002	12/02/2003	$5,060.28	$5,383.90
Warsaw Sports, Inc.	1003	12/02/2003	$186.87	$218.08
Bikes and Trikes	1004	12/02/2003	$823.05	$892.43
SAB Mountain	1005	12/03/2003	$29.00	$50.74
Poser Cycles	1006	12/03/2003	$64.90	$88.79
Spokes	1007	12/03/2003	$49.50	$72.47
Clean Air Transportation Cc	1008	12/03/2003	$2,214.94	$2,367.84
Extreme Cycling	1009	12/03/2003	$29.00	$50.74
Cyclopath	1010	12/03/2003	$14,872.30	$15,784.64
BBS Pty	1011	12/03/2003	$29.00	$50.74
Piccolo	1012	12/03/2003	$10,259.10	$10,894.65
Pedals Inc.	1013	12/03/2003	$1,142.13	$1,230.66
Spokes 'N Wheels Ltd.	1014	12/04/2003	$29.00	$50.74
Cycle City Rome	1015	12/04/2003	$43.50	$66.11
SAB Mountain	1016	12/04/2003	$563.70	$617.52
Tyred Out	1017	12/05/2003	$72.00	$96.32
Has Been Bikes (consignme	1018	12/05/2003	$115.50	$142.43
Spokes for Folks	1019	12/05/2003	$43.50	$66.11
Extreme Cycling	1020	12/05/2003	$67.80	$91.87
Canal City Cycle	1021	12/06/2003	$5,237.55	$5,571.80
Belgium Bike Co.	1022	12/07/2003	$2,792.86	$2,980.43
Tienda de Bicicletas El Parc	1023	12/07/2003	$890.61	$964.05
Tandem Cycle	1024	12/07/2003	$33.00	$54.98
SAB Mountain	1025	12/07/2003	$8,819.55	$9,368.72
Wheels Inc.	1026	12/07/2003	$33.00	$54.98
The Great Bike Shop	1027	12/07/2003	$2,972.85	$3,171.22

FIGURE 5.8 An example of a formula in action on a report.

ORDER OF OPERATIONS

Crystal Reports follows the standard order of operations, reading formulas from left to right and in the following order:

- Parentheses (any formula text enclosed in parentheses)
- Exponents (such as in x^2)
- Multiplication
- Division
- Addition
- Subtraction

When working with the order of operations, make sure that you use parentheses to force calculations that may not fall under the scope of normal algebraic equations.

For example, if you are attempting to calculate someone's age from a database field that holds the person's birthday, you could use a formula that looks like the following:

```
Today - {Staff.BirthDate}
```

The only problem with this formula is that when you insert it onto your report, it shows the number of days, instead of years. An easy solution would be to divide by 365.25 (the 0.25 accounts for leap years), making your formula read as follows:

```
Today - {Staff.BirthDate} / 365.25
```

When you attempt to save this formula or perform a syntax check, an error will occur, due to the order of operations. When Crystal Reports attempts to calculate the division part of the formula first, it doesn't understand how to divide a date field by 365.25, so an error results.

If you add parentheses to your formula, as shown in the following code, the formula will work correctly:

```
(Today - {Staff.BirthDate}) / 365.25
```

In these special cases, where a function or operator cannot be immediately used with the field you need, you will need to use parentheses to force a type conversion or other manipulation and then use the result in your formula.

As long as you keep the order of operations in mind and plan what calculations need to occur first, everything should work fine.

USING CRYSTAL REPORTS FUNCTIONS

Functions extend the Crystal Reports formula language and can be used to simplify complex calculations. If you expand the Functions pane of the Crystal Reports Formula Editor, you will see all of the available functions, arranged by function type. To insert a function into your formula text, double-click the function name.

Functions generally require one or more arguments, enclosed in parentheses and separated by commas. When you insert a function into your formula text, Crystal Reports automatically adds the parentheses and commas to indicate the arguments required, as shown in the following code for the Round function:

```
Round ( , )
```

In this example, you would need to specify a number to be rounded and the number of decimal places to be used, as follows:

```
Round ({Orders.OrderAmount}, 2)
```

Crystal Reports includes more than 200 functions, and keeping track of all of their names, parameters, and syntax can be tough. To find an explanation of a Crystal Reports function, go to Crystal Reports online Help. First press the F1 key from within Crystal Reports (or click Help > Crystal Reports Help) to display the main Crystal Reports Help screen, shown in Figure 5.9.

Select the Index tab, type Functions in the text entry box, and press ENTER. This action will take you to the function listing by category. Click a category to see all of the functions of that type; click the link to go to the specific property page for a function. The Help page lists the function's required and optional arguments, the information that is returned, and some examples of the function. Click the close button in the top-right corner to close the Crystal Reports online Help when you are finished.

In addition to Crystal Report's own built-in functions, you can also create your own custom functions, which we will look at a little later in this chapter. These functions can be reused in a report or shared in the repository to be used in multiple reports.

NOTE

Summary Functions

You can use summary functions to summarize fields that appear in your report. The most common summaries are performed on numeric or currency fields, but you can also apply summary fields to other field types, for example, to create a count of

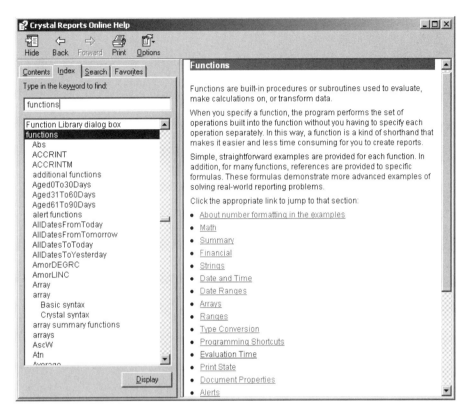

FIGURE 5.9 The Crystal Reports Help screen.

countries represented in a report. Numerous summary functions are available in Crystal Reports, but the ones listed in Table 5.1 are the most popular.

String Functions

The Crystal Reports formula language also includes a number of functions for manipulating string fields. *String* fields contain alphanumeric characters and are the most common field type; you can put just about anything in a string field.

One of the handiest tricks for working with strings is concatenation. Using special concatenation operators, you can combine two or more string fields for use in your report. For example, you may have separate First Name and Last Name fields in your data, but when this information is displayed on your report, you may want the information from the First Name field to appear followed by a space and then the information from the Last Name field. Crystal Report's special concatenation operators make this possible.

TABLE 5.1 Common Summary Functions

Summary	Syntax	Usage
Sum	Sum( )	Calculates the sum of a particular field; for example, Sum({Orders.Order Amount})
Average	Avg( )	Calculates the average for a particular field; for example, Avg({Orders.Order Amount})
Min	Min( )	Finds the minimum value; for example, Min({Orders.Order Amount}) would return the lowest Order Amount value
Max	Max( )	Finds the maximum value; for example, Max({Orders.Order Amount}) would return the greatest Order Amount value
Count	Count ( )	Returns a count of all values; for example, Count({Orders.OrderId}) would return a count of all orders
Distinct Count	DistinctCount( )	Returns a distinct count of all values, meaning that each item is counted once; for example, if you create a formula using DiscountCount({Orders.OrderId}), and if OrderId includes duplicates, each distinct record will nevertheless only be counted once

Two concatenation operators are available within Crystal Reports: + and &.

The plus sign (+) operator works just like the operator for adding together two numbers, but it applies to string fields. Using this operator, the formula for the example mentioned earlier would look as follows:

```
{Customer.First Name} + " " + {Customer.Last Name}
```

The formula text in the middle—the space surrounded by double quotation marks—adds a space between the first and last names. Likewise, if you want to include any other specific text in the concatenation, you would enclose it in quotation marks, for example, ("Mr" + {Customer.Last Name}).

NOTE

The ampersand (&) concatenation operator can be used just like the plus sign:

```
{Customer.First Name} & " " & {Customer.Last Name}
```

The difference between the two operators is that the ampersand is a bit more flexible and can be used to concatenate numeric and other types of fields as well (without having to convert them to strings). Extending the earlier example, for instance, we can show the customer's first name, last name, and customer ID using the ampersand.

```
{Customer.First Name} & " " & {Customer.Last Name} &
{Customer.CustomerID}
```

If you tried to create this same formula using the plus sign operator, Crystal Reports would return an error, because the `Customer.ID` field is numeric, and the + operator works only with strings.

Now that you know how to put strings together, what about ripping them apart? Crystal Reports includes a function called Subscript that numbers each position within a string.

Using the Subscript function, you can rip off a particular position of a string. For example, you can display the first initial of a customer's first name by using the following formula:

```
{Customer.First Name}[1]
```

Likewise, if you want to display both the first initial of a customer's first name followed by the customer's last name, you can combine the two types of string functions we have worked with so far, as follows:

```
{Customer.First Name}[1] + " " + {Customer.Last Name}
```

In addition to ripping strings apart and putting them back together, Crystal Reports also includes functions for converting strings to all uppercase or lowercase characters, determining the length of a string, and trimming blanks from the start and end of a string. Table 5.2 lists some of the most commonly used string functions, along with an example of how each is used.

TABLE 5.2 Common String Functions

Function	Purpose	Usage
Uppercase( )	Converts strings to all uppercase	Uppercase({Table.FieldName})
Lowercase( )	Converts strings to all lowercase	Lowercase({Table.FieldName})
Length( )	Calculates the length of a string	Length({Table.Fieldname})
Trim()	Deletes extra spaces at the start and end of a string	Trim({Table.Fieldname})
Left(String, Length)	Returns the number of characters from the left side of the string	Left({Table.Fieldname}, 4)
Right(String, Length)	Returns the number of characters from the right side of the string	Right({Table.Fieldname}, 6)

Type-Conversion Functions

In using Crystal Reports, you may run into problems related to the types of fields contained in a particular database. The field types may be set by the database or application developer, and you can't change them without changing the database or application itself. For example, you can find numeric information, such as an order amount, stored in a field that has been defined as a string field. With the information held as a string, you can't apply all of the handy summary functions within Crystal Reports.

If your organization has developed the database or application from which you are reporting, you may be able to submit a change request to get the information stored in a more appropriate field type. But even if you are using a commercial application, or if your own database or application can't be changed, don't give up. Instead of changing the type in the database, you can let Crystal Reports do the type conversion.

The Conversion section of the function list includes a number of functions that can convert field types. To find the appropriate function, first determine the target type (that is, the type you want the field to be when you are done). Then select a function from Table 5.3 and create a formula to perform the conversion.

TABLE 5.3 Type-Conversion Functions

Target Type	Function	Input
Text	ToText( )	Number, Currency, DateTime, Date, Time
Number	ToNumber( )	String, DateTime, Date, Time
Boolean	Cbool( )	Number, Currency
Currency	Ccur( )	Number, Currency, or String
Date Time	CdateTime( )	Number, String, DateTime, Date, Time
Integer	CDbl( )	Number, Currency, String, or Boolean
String	Cstr( )	Number, Currency, String, DateTime, Date, or Boolean
Date	Cdate( )	Number, String, DateTime, Time, Ctime() Number, or String

With all of these functions, the formula text will look something like the following:

```
ToText({Orders.Order Amount})
```

In this example, the values in the Order Amount field would be converted to text and displayed on your report.

Some of the functions listed in Table 5.3 may have additional, optional parameters that can be passed to control the output. For example, the `ToText()` function can be passed a number of decimal places to convert, as shown in the next example:

```
ToText({Orders.Order Amount},0)
```

In this example, no decimal places will be displayed.

Remember that you can find a complete list of functions and their parameters by clicking Help > Crystal Reports Help > Functions and searching on the function name.

Period Functions and Date Fields

Crystal Reports has a number of predefined periods for use with dates. Until now, we have applied date periods only to record selection. However, you can use these same periods in the Formula Editor.

When you work with periods, Crystal Reports does all of the hard work for you. When you use the MonthToDate period, for example, Crystal Reports goes behind the scenes to check today's date and then builds a list of all of the dates that should be in MonthToDate—you don't need to lift a finger.

Periods in the Formula Editor are used most often in conjunction with an operator called In that determines whether a specific date is within that period. An example of the In operator is shown here. This snippet of formula text looks at the Order Date field, and if a date is in the period Over90Days, then it displays the words "PAST DUE ACCOUNT!" on the report.

```
If {Order.OrderDate} in Over90Days then "PAST DUE ACCOUNT!!"
```

You can also use this technique with the other date periods, listed here and found in the Date Ranges section of the Function list:

- WeekToDateFromSunday
- MonthToDate
- YearToDate
- Last7Days
- Last4WeeksToSun
- LastFullWeek
- LastFullMonth
- AllDatesToToday
- AllDatesToYesterday
- AllDatesFromToday
- AllDatesFromTomorrow
- Aged0to30Days
- Aged31to60Days
- Aged61to90Days
- Over90Days
- Next30Days
- Next31to60Days
- Next61to90Days
- Next91to365Days
- Calendar1stQtr
- Calendar2ndQtr
- Calendar3rdQtr
- Calendar4thQtr
- Calendar1stHalf
- Calendar2ndHalf

In addition to using these period functions with dates, Crystal Reports allows you to perform some simple arithmetic on date fields. For instance, Crystal Reports allows you to calculate the difference between two dates as well as add a number of days to a particular date, where the result is also a date field. Date arithmetic is especially handy when calculating aging or an invoice due date.

For example, suppose you want to look at the difference between when an order was placed and when it was actually shipped. Using the subtraction operator (–), you can find out how many days have passed.

```
{Orders.ShipDate} - {Orders.OrderDate}
```

The value returned will be in days. If you want to determine how many years this represents (as when calculating age, for example), enclose the existing calculation in parentheses and divide by 365.25.

Likewise, if you want to calculate a due date, say, in 30 days, you can add 30 days to the ship date, as follows:

```
{Orders.ShipDate} + 30
```

You can add and subtract dates, but you cannot multiply or divide them.

Keep in mind that when performing calculations between dates, you may need to use parentheses to force the order of operation. Crystal Reports will display an error message when you try to combine calculations involving dates with calculations involving numbers.

ADDING LOGIC TO FORMULAS

At this point, we have talked about simple arithmetic formulas, strings, and date fields and periods, but we really haven't gotten into adding any logic to your formulas. Crystal Reports has a number of different ways you can add logic, and we're going to start our coverage with the most common, the `If...then...else` statement.

Writing `If...Then...Else` Formulas

In a few examples earlier in this chapter, you might have noticed the use of `If....then` statements. These statements work on the simple premise that if some condition is true, then something will happen (if A is true, then B will happen).

To see how If...then statements can be used, we are going to look at a common example. In the previous examples, we worked with an Order Amount field. If we want to flag all Order Amount values that are over $1,000, we can use an If...then formula that looks something like the following:

```
If {Orders.Order Amount} > 1000 then "Great Sale!"
```

If we place this formula beside the Order Amount field on the detail line, this formula will be evaluated for every record in the table. Where the condition is true (for orders greater than $1,000), then the message "Great Sale!" will appear on the report, as shown in Figure 5.10.

Customer Name	Order ID	Order Date	Order Amount	Sales Flag
Deals on Wheels	1002	12/02/2003	$5,060.28	Great Sale!
Warsaw Sports, Inc.	1003	12/02/2003	$186.87	
Bikes and Trikes	1004	12/02/2003	$823.05	
SAB Mountain	1005	12/03/2003	$29.00	
Poser Cycles	1006	12/03/2003	$64.90	
Spokes	1007	12/03/2003	$49.50	
Clean Air Transportation Co	1008	12/03/2003	$2,214.94	Great Sale!
Extreme Cycling	1009	12/03/2003	$29.00	
Cyclopath	1010	12/03/2003	$14,872.30	Great Sale!
BBS Pty	1011	12/03/2003	$29.00	
Piccolo	1012	12/03/2003	$10,259.10	Great Sale!
Pedals Inc.	1013	12/03/2003	$1,142.13	Great Sale!
Spokes 'N Wheels Ltd.	1014	12/04/2003	$29.00	
Cycle City Rome	1015	12/04/2003	$43.50	
SAB Mountain	1016	12/04/2003	$563.70	
Tyred Out	1017	12/05/2003	$72.00	
Has Been Bikes (consignme	1018	12/05/2003	$115.50	
Spokes for Folks	1019	12/05/2003	$43.50	
Extreme Cycling	1020	12/05/2003	$67.80	
Canal City Cycle	1021	12/06/2003	$5,237.55	Great Sale!
Belgium Bike Co.	1022	12/07/2003	$2,792.86	Great Sale!
Tienda de Bicicletas El Parc	1023	12/07/2003	$890.61	
Tandem Cycle	1024	12/07/2003	$33.00	
SAB Mountain	1025	12/07/2003	$8,819.55	Great Sale!
Wheels Inc.	1026	12/07/2003	$33.00	
The Great Bike Shop	1027	12/07/2003	$2,972.85	Great Sale!

FIGURE 5.10   An example of an If . . . then formula in action.

With If...then statements, we also have the option of adding an Else statement to the end. An If...then formula states some condition and what will happen if the condition is true; an Else statement goes into effect when the If condition is not true.

Using the previous example, we can add an Else statement that prints "Good Sale" for all of the Order Amount values less than $1,000. That formula would look like the following:

```
If {Orders.Order Amount} > 1000 then "Great Sale!" else "Good Sale"
```

In this case, if the condition is true (the Order Amount value is greater than $1,000), then the first condition will fire, printing "Great Sale!" on the report; otherwise, if the condition is false (the Order Amount value is less than $1,000), the "Good Sale" message will be printed.

Regardless of whether you use the Else statement on the end, If...then formulas can be combined with other functions and operators you have learned about in this chapter to create complex formulas to calculate the values you need.

 For examples of other types of control structures and loops, including Select statements and looping, see the reports located in the CONTROLSTRUCTURE.

ON THE CD ZIP file, located on the CD-ROM in the PROJECTS folder.

UNDERSTANDING FORMULA EVALUATION TIMES

Crystal Reports is a multipass reporting tool. Traditionally, it has been agreed that when a report is processed, Crystal Reports will perform two passes to accommodate advanced features like grouping, sorting, summaries, and grand totals.

If you have been working with Crystal Reports formulas long, you may have noticed that when you place a formula on your report, it does not give the results that you expected. One of the major reasons for this (other than the formula being incorrect) is actually the time at which the formula is processed by the report.

You can correct this problem and force your formulas to be processed using Evaluation Time functions. You can specify the following four evaluation times:

- BeforeReadingRecords
- WhileReadingRecords
- WhilePrintingRecords
- EvaluateAfter (formula name)

Each of these evaluation functions can be used in conjunction with your existing formula text and will determine when the formula will be processed during report execution. An example of one of these functions follows:

```
WhilePrintingRecords;
NumberVar SalesCount
SalesCount := SalesCount + 1;
SalesCount;
```

The formula itself is used to perform a manual running total on the number of sales orders placed. In order to understand how these functions work, we need to drill down a little further into how a report is processed.

BeforeReadingRecords

Formulas marked to evaluate `BeforeReadingRecords` will be evaluated before any database records are returned to Crystal Reports. This evaluation time can be used only to evaluate "flat" formulas that do not include any database records or calculated elements from the report. Because most formulas include some reference to database or other fields that require processing at a later time, this evaluation time is used infrequently.

WhileReadingRecords

Formulas marked `WhileReadingRecords` will be evaluated as the database records are read from the database. This evaluation time function is most often used when you want to perform a calculation or conversion on a database field (that is, changing a string to a number), as shown in the next example:

```
WhileReadingRecords;
ToText({Orders.Order Amount})
```

This evaluation time is often used for formulas behind the scenes that need to be calculated early in the report processing, but not necessarily shown on the report itself to be printed out.

WhilePrintingRecords

The most popular evaluation time function is `WhilePrintingRecords`. This evaluation time is used to force formulas to run when the report records are printed on the page. This function can be used with manual running totals, counters, and so on, and is often required to make formulas on your report return the required results. An example of this evaluation time formula in action follows:

```
WhilePrintingRecords;
NumberVar StatusCounter;
If (Customer.Status} = "Overdue" then StatusCounter :=
StatusCounter + 1;
StatusCounter;
```

For an example of a manual running total field created with `WhilePrinting-Records`, open the MANTOTAL.RPT report from the PROJECTS directory on the CD-ROM.

EvaluateAfter (formula name)

The `EvaluateAfter` function is used to force the processing of one formula after another. For example, if you had a formula that calculated an Order Total, you may want to set your formula for Sales Tax to evaluate after, so you could ensure that the Order Total was calculated before the sales tax was calculated and added on.

The CD-ROM includes sample reports that use all three of these evaluation time functions. They are located in the EVALTIME.ZIP file in the PROJECTS directory on the CD-ROM.

DEBUGGING FORMULAS

When you use formulas, you need to make sure that the syntax you have entered for your formulas is correct. As luck (or good design) would have it, Crystal Reports includes its own syntax checker, and it can be invoked in two ways.

When you save your formula by clicking the Save icon on the toolbar, shown in Figure 5.11, Crystal Reports automatically performs a syntax check, just to make sure there are no missing parentheses, misspelled words, and so on.

FIGURE 5.11 Make sure you save your formula before exiting the Formula Editor.

The second method of invoking the syntax checker is to click the X+2 icon, also shown in Figure 5.11. You can click this icon at any time while working in the Formula Editor. If you are building a complex formula, you may want to check the syntax each time you add a major piece, to make sure that what you have entered is correct syntactically.

Regardless of which method you use, the syntax check Crystal Reports performs is very simple: it makes sure you have spelled all of the function and field names correctly, that you have used the correct function values, and so on.

If the syntax checker does return an error, your cursor will be moved to the place in the formula that the error occurs to pinpoint which part of the formula you need to modify.

Another method, new to Crystal Reports XI, is the Dependency Checker, shown in Figure 5.12.

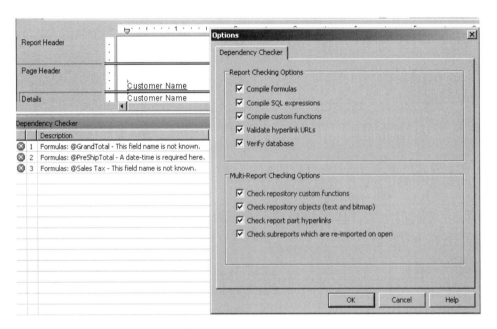

FIGURE 5.12 The Dependency Checker in action.

When invoked, the Dependency Checker will run through your report and find any errors or determine any dependencies that are not met. For example, if your report had a formula that references a group summary and you delete the group, the formula would appear in the Dependency Checker as an error, and you would need to fix the formula before it would run. Likewise, if there is a field missing or misnamed, the Dependency Checker will pick this up; it provides a quick way of finding all of the errors in a report.

You can set the options for the Dependency Checker by right-clicking the toolbar above the list of dependencies. Select Options from the shortcut menu.

With both of these methods, there is still no guarantee that your formula will return the correct values, but you can be assured that the syntax is correct and that all of the required dependencies have been met—the rest is up to you.

WORKING WITH CUSTOM FUNCTIONS

Crystal Reports has always provided the ability to add your own functions to the Formula Editor. This traditionally has been accomplished through writing a UFL, or User-Function Library, that was compiled to a .dll used with the Report Designer and distributed with your application. This was not always the best method, because UFLs were difficult to create and maintain. A much better alternative was introduced a few versions back with the addition of custom functions.

A custom function is simply a formula field that you have saved and can reuse in other formula fields in your report. In addition, if you are using BusinessObjects Enterprise, there is a piece of server technology called the Repository, which will allow you to save your custom functions and use them in other reports. The advantage of using the Repository to store your custom functions is that when you change the function in the repository, all of the other reports can utilize the updated function, eliminating the need to reopen each report where the function is used.

For more information on adding functions to and working with the Repository, see "Appendix A: Working with the Repository."

But before we get too deep into working with custom functions, we need to take a look at how to create them. There are two methods you can use to create custom functions—you can either extract a function from an existing formula field or you can use the Formula Editor to create the custom function from scratch. We'll start our coverage of custom functions looking at the first method, creating functions from existing formula fields.

Extracting Functions from Existing Formulas

If you have been working with Crystal Reports for a while, chances are that you have already created a number of formula fields. The easiest method of creating a function is to use these existing formula fields as the basis for custom function and extract all of the logic, variables, and so on that you need from them.

To extract a function from an existing formula, use the following steps:

1. Open CUSTOMFUNCTION.RPT from the CD-ROM.
2. Click View > Field Explorer to open the list of available fields.
3. Expand the Formula Fields section, right-click any of the formulas, and select Edit. The Formula Editor opens.
4. Using the drop-down menu beside the New icon, select Custom Function, as shown in Figure 5.13.

FIGURE 5.13 Creating a new custom function.

5. In the dialog box that opens, enter the name of your custom function—in this example, we'll call the function ShipMethod.
6. Once you have entered the name of your function, click the Use Extractor button. The Extract Custom Function from Formula dialog box opens, as shown in Figure 5.14.
7. From the left column, click the @Shipper formula field. This will display the formula field in the text box and change the properties dialog box to show any arguments that need to be passed to the function.
8. In the arguments section, the argument name is listed by default as v1. Click this box and change the argument name to OrderAmount. This is what needs to be passed to this function to make the logic work.
9. You may notice that there is a button on the top-right corner named Enter More Info. This step is optional; it opens a set of property pages where you can add a description of the function, the author name, and some Help text for the user.

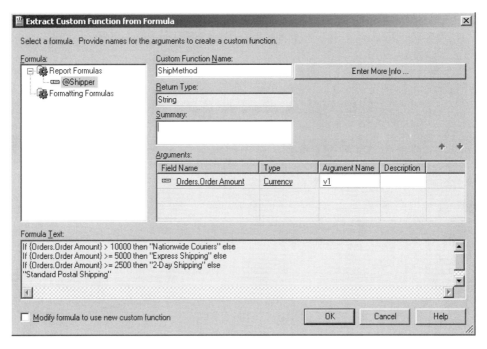

FIGURE 5.14   The Custom Function dialog box.

10. Next, click the checkbox in the bottom-left corner to Modify formula to use custom function, and click OK.

11. This will take you to the formula text to review your custom function text, which will look like the following:

```
Function  (currencyVar OrderAmount)
If OrderAmount > 10000 then "Nationwide Couriers" else
If OrderAmount >= 5000 then "Express Shipping" else
If OrderAmount >= 2500 then "2-Day Shipping" else
"Standard Postal Shipping"
```

12. Click the Save and Close button to return to your report's Design or Preview view.

The original formula, @shipper, has been modified to use the custom function you created. You can now use this same function in your report without having to redefine or copy and paste the text into other formula fields.

You'll also notice that in the Formula Editor your custom function appears in both the function list as well as in the workshop tree on the left side, as shown in Figure 5.15.

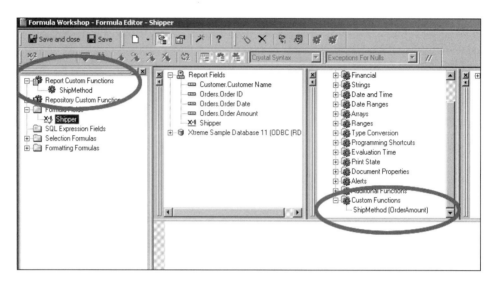

FIGURE 5.15 Custom functions as they appear in the Formula Editor.

To edit the formula, double-click it from the workshop tree to open the formula in the editor. To add the formula an existing formula, double-click from the function list in the middle of the page.

Creating Custom Functions from Scratch

If you don't have any existing formulas to use as the basis of your report, you can create custom functions from scratch, just by entering the formula text yourself.

To create a custom function using this method, use the following steps:

ON THE CD

1. Open FUNCTIONFORMULA.RPT from the CD-ROM.
2. Click View > Field Explorer to open the list of available fields.
3. Expand the Formula Fields section, and right-click any of the formulas and select Edit. The Formula Editor opens.
4. Using the drop-down menu beside the New icon, select Custom Function. A dialog box appears, prompting you for the name of the function. Enter CountryGrouping, and then click the Use Editor button. The Crystal Reports Formula Editor opens.

5. Enter the formula text as follows:

```
Function  (stringVar Country)
If Country= "USA" then "Domestic" else
If (Country = "Mexico" or Country = "Canada") then "North
America" else
"Rest of World"
```

6. When finished, click the Save and Close button in the top-left corner.
7. To create a formula to use this function, click View > Field Explorer.
8. Right-click the Formula Field heading, and select New from the shortcut menu.
9. Enter a name for your formula—in this example, name the formula `Country Flag`.
10. Next, enter the formula text as follows:

```
CountryGrouping({Customer.Country})
```

11. When finished, click the Save and Close button to return to your report's Design view.
12. From the Field Explorer, drag this formula field onto your report into the Detail section. Your report should look something like the one shown in Figure 5.16.

Customer Name	Order ID	Order Date	Order Amount	Sales Flag
Deals on Wheels	1002	12/02/2003	$5,060.28	Express Shipping
Warsaw Sports, Inc.	1003	12/02/2003	$186.87	Standard Postal Shipping
Bikes and Trikes	1004	12/02/2003	$823.05	Standard Postal Shipping
SAB Mountain	1005	12/03/2003	$29.00	Standard Postal Shipping
Poser Cycles	1006	12/03/2003	$64.90	Standard Postal Shipping
Spokes	1007	12/03/2003	$49.50	Standard Postal Shipping
Clean Air Transportation Co	1008	12/03/2003	$2,214.94	Standard Postal Shipping
Extreme Cycling	1009	12/03/2003	$29.00	Standard Postal Shipping
Cyclopath	1010	12/03/2003	$14,872.30	Nationwide Couriers
BBS Pty	1011	12/03/2003	$29.00	Standard Postal Shipping
Piccolo	1012	12/03/2003	$10,259.10	Nationwide Couriers
Pedals Inc.	1013	12/03/2003	$1,142.13	Standard Postal Shipping
Spokes 'N Wheels Ltd.	1014	12/04/2003	$29.00	Standard Postal Shipping
Cycle City Rome	1015	12/04/2003	$43.50	Standard Postal Shipping
SAB Mountain	1016	12/04/2003	$563.70	Standard Postal Shipping
Tyred Out	1017	12/05/2003	$72.00	Standard Postal Shipping
Has Been Bikes (consignme	1018	12/05/2003	$115.50	Standard Postal Shipping
Spokes for Folks	1019	12/05/2003	$43.50	Standard Postal Shipping
Extreme Cycling	1020	12/05/2003	$67.80	Standard Postal Shipping
Canal City Cycle	1021	12/06/2003	$5,237.55	Express Shipping
Belgium Bike Co.	1022	12/07/2003	$2,792.86	2-Day Shipping
Tienda de Bicicletas El Parc	1023	12/07/2003	$890.61	Standard Postal Shipping
Tandem Cycle	1024	12/07/2003	$33.00	Standard Postal Shipping
SAB Mountain	1025	12/07/2003	$8,819.55	Express Shipping
Wheels Inc.	1026	12/07/2003	$33.00	Standard Postal Shipping
The Great Bike Shop	1027	12/07/2003	$2,972.85	2-Day Shipping
Bikes and Trikes	1028	12/08/2003	$296.87	Standard Postal Shipping

FIGURE 5.16 The finished report with the function-based formula in place.

And like functions created using the extract, custom functions written by hand can also be reused in other formulas in your report.

Using Custom Functions in Formulas

Because custom functions look just like another other function field you would find in Crystal Reports, you can simply add them to your formula text using the same syntax as you just used (that is, `function(parameter1, parameter2, etc.)`). But if you don't want to go to the trouble of actually typing out a formula field just to use the function, there is another method of using functions.

To see this method in action, use the following steps:

ON THE CD

1. Open FUNCTIONIWIZARD.RPT from the CD-ROM.
2. Click View > Field Explorer to open the list of available fields.
3. Expand the Formula Fields section, right-click, and select New. The Formula Editor opens.
4. From the Toolbar, click on the Magic Wand icon to invoke the Custom Function Expert, as shown in Figure 5.17.

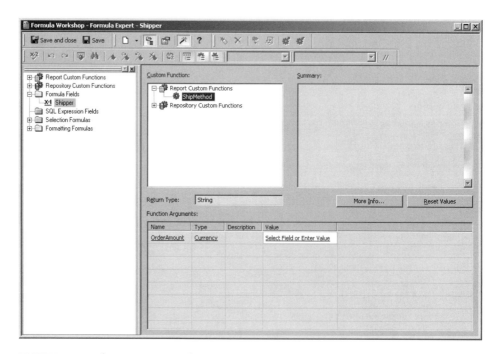

FIGURE 5.17 The Custom Function Expert.

5. Expand the list of Report Custom Functions, and click the `CountryGrouping` function. The bottom of the dialog box displays the values that are expected by this parameter.

6. Click the link Select Field or Enter Value, and enter a value or use the drop-down list to select Choose other field, which will open the Field Selector dialog box shown in Figure 5.18.

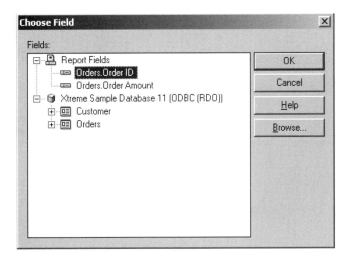

FIGURE 5.18 The Field Selector.

7. Select a field from the list, and click OK.

8. Next, click Save and Close to return to your report.

9. You can now drag your formula field onto your report and preview your report to see the results.

Whether you use the Custom Function Expert or just bang in the formula yourself, the results are the same. If you are planning to create a simple formula where you want to just use the function, the Expert is probably a good choice because it is quick and simple. If you want to write a more complex formula or want more control over the formula text, it is probably better if you write the formula yourself.

SQL COMMANDS AND EXPRESSIONS

One of the most powerful features of Crystal Reports is its ability to write the SQL for your report, as you select tables, links, fields, and so on. In early versions of Crystal Reports, this functionality was handy for new users who didn't know how to write SQL but was frustrating for database administrators and developers who knew exactly what they wanted.

As the product matured, the ability to modify parts of the SQL statement and add expression fields written with SQL was introduced, but this still didn't go far enough. It wasn't until the concept of SQL Commands was introduced that developers were able to fully leverage the power of the database server itself.

Working with SQL Commands

So what is an SQL Command? In Crystal Reports, it is a SQL statement that is passed to the database server, and the result set is treated as a virtual table that can be used as the basis for your report.

For example, you could write a the following simple SQL Command to retrieve all of the results from the customer table in your database:

```
SELECT * FROM CUSTOMER
```

When this SQL command is used in your report, all of the resulting fields will appear in the Field Explorer, and the records that are returned can be used as the data set for your report.

Remember as we go through the following sections that the purpose of this part of the chapter is not to teach you how to write SQL—there are entire volumes and references written on the subject, and each SQL syntax may be slightly different. Rather, this section teaches you how to use the SQL you write as the data set for your reports.

Creating SQL Commands

In our first example of creating an SQL Command, we are going to use a similar SQL statement of some fields and a number of records that we can use as the basis for our report. To keep the SQL simple we will select all of the items from a table with a where clause to filter the number of records returned.

To create a report based on an SQL Command, use the following steps:

1. From the Start menu, open Crystal Reports.
2. Click File > New > Blank Report. The Database Expert opens.

3. Double-click Create New Connection, and then expand the ODBC (RDO) folder to open a list of available data sources.
4. Select the data source named Xtreme Sample Database 11 and click Finish. A node is added underneath the data source name in the folder.
5. Click the Add Command option, as shown in Figure 5.19. The SQL Command window opens.

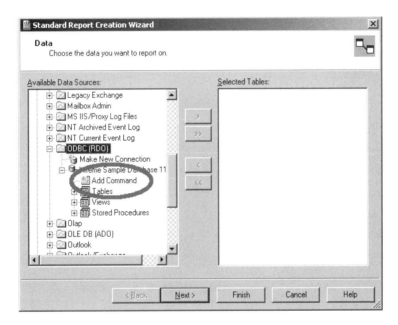

FIGURE 5.19 The Add Command option appears below your data source name.

6. Enter the following SQL code in the large text box on the left side:

```
SELECT * FROM CUSTOMER WHERE COUNTRY='USA'
```

The SQL command window should now look like the one shown in Figure 5.20.
7. Click OK to return to the Database Expert, and then OK to return to your report design.
8. Click View > Field Explorer to open a list of available fields. The available fields will be listed under the heading Command. You can drag and drop them on your report.
9. Save your report as SQLCOMMAND.RPT. We will be adding to the report as we go along in this section.

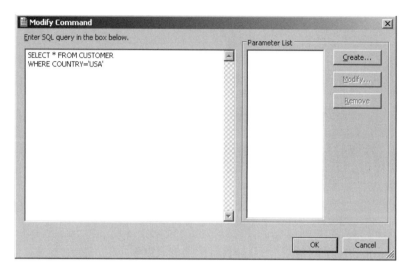

FIGURE 5.20   The SQL command dialog.

This is just a simple example of an SQL Command. The rules of creating an SQL Command are pretty simple. First off, the SQL Command itself must contain SQL code that can be processed by your database. For example, if you had some SQL syntax that was specific for DB2 and tried to use it to write an SQL Command, it would not work. The SQL syntax that you write for an SQL Command must run exactly as it is entered.

A good practice is to test your SQL statement in a query tool before you actually paste it into an SQL Command. If there is an error in your SQL Command, Crystal Reports will return the error message from the database, but sometimes it is easier to debug SQL in a "native" environment. For example, Query Analyzer for SQL Server has definite advantages when writing SQL, because you can browse databases and tables and confirm field names. Once you have the SQL query running there, paste it into an SQL Command.

Second, the SQL Command should be able to run and return a result set to Crystal Reports. You can make your use of SQL as complex as required, using unions, subselects, and so on, but the query must return a result set. Often developers new to Crystal Reports will get frustrated because they see SQL Commands as a way to run SQL on the database server and will try to update records and use complex SQL normally reserved for stored procedures in their SQL Commands.

Remember, SQL Commands form the data set for your report and need to return columns, records, and so on. If you need to do some complex processing where you need to insert, update, or otherwise manipulate records or advanced multipass SQL usually reserved for processing records, use a stored procedure. You can then use a SQL Command to return a data set from the table or view that you created.

Editing SQL Commands

Because SQL Commands can be revised a number of times during the course of writing a report, Crystal Reports makes it easy to edit the SQL Command through the Database Expert. To open the Database Expert, click Database > Database Expert, then right-click the Command object itself. In the shortcut menu you will see options to Edit or View the SQL Command that will open the SQL Command window.

Another handy trick for SQL Commands: to rename an SQL Command, click the command, then press F2 and type a new command name. When finished, press the ENTER key.

From the SQL Command window, you can edit your SQL statement as required and then click OK to return to your report.

Adding Parameters to SQL Commands

Parameters are a popular feature in Crystal Reports, because they allow you enter and select information when the report is run. With SQL Commands, you can create parameters that are included as part of the SQL statement itself, so the processing of these parameters will always occur on the database server itself.

To add parameters to a SQL statement, use the following steps:

1. Open the SQLCOMMAND.RPT report that we were working with earlier in this section.
2. Click Database > Database Expert.
3. Right-click the Command object on the right side of the dialog box, and select Edit Command from the shortcut menu to open the SQL Command window.
4. From the right side of the dialog box, click Create to create a new parameter and open the dialog box shown in Figure 5.21.
5. Enter a name for your parameter, as well as some prompting text, a value type, and any default value you want to assign to the parameter field. In this example, name the parameter Country and define the type as "String".
6. When finished, click OK to return to the SQL Command window.

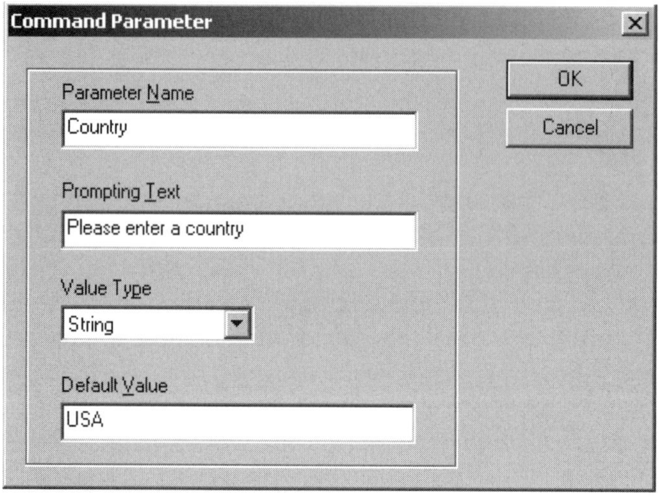

FIGURE 5.21   The SQL Command parameter dialog box.

7. Next, modify your SQL Command to include the following parameter in the `where` clause.

```
Select * from customer where Country = '{?Country}'
```

8. Click OK to return to the database expert and OK again to return to your report design.
9. Press F5 to refresh your report. You should be prompted for a Country value, which will be used to filter your report.

The key points to remember about parameters in SQL Commands is that they are referenced just like other Crystal Reports parameters (that is, with a question mark and curly braces around the field name (`{?Country}`), and the values entered are translated literally. For example, in the SQL Command we just saw, the parameter itself was enclosed in quotes in the `where` clause. The reason for this is that when the SQL Command is executed, it will replace the parameter field with the actual values you enter.

You will also notice that when you are setting up parameters in SQL Commands, the dialog box does not have as many options as when you created a normal parameter in the Report Designer. Parameters in SQL Commands are passed directly back to the database, so you won't find all of the capabilities you might find with normal parameter fields.

However, you can use a combination of SQL Command parameters and normal parameter fields in your reports if required, and in some instances, you can use normal parameter fields in record selection that can be evaluated on the database server for more efficient processing and flexibility.

Parameters can be used with SQL Commands for all sorts of things, including creating Top N reports that are processed on the database, executing stored procedures, and passing stored procedure parameters. For more examples of using advanced SQL Commands, see www.crystalxibook.com.

Working with SQL Expressions

SQL Expressions are SQL statements that are like formulas that get submitted to and evaluated by your database server. The difference between SQL Commands and SQL Expressions is that SQL Expressions can be used with reports created from tables, views, and so on and are an easy way to push more processing back on the database server. It's important to note that you can't have SQL Expressions in a report that is based on an SQL Command (because if you are using a SQL Command, you can just put the required SQL code in the command itself).

For reports based on database tables, however, SQL Expressions can definitely reduce report-processing time, because they are evaluated on your database server, as opposed to Crystal Reports formulas, which are evaluated locally.

To create a new SQL Expression in your report, use the following steps:

1. Open the SQLEXPRESSION.RPT report from the CD-ROM.
2. Open the Field Explorer by clicking View > Field Explorer, and then right-click the node marked SQL Express and select New. A dialog box appears and prompts you for the name of your SQL Expression.
3. Enter a name and click OK to open the SQL Expression Editor, as shown in Figure 5.22. If this interface seems familiar, it should—the SQL Expression Editor is based on the Formula Editor and features the same panes across the top of the dialog box, showing Fields, Functions, and Operators.

You'll notice that the functions list displays generic SQL functions that you can use in your SQL Expression instead of the usual Crystal Reports functions.

4. Using the text box at the bottom of the editor, enter your SQL expression, following correct SQL syntax and operator usage. If you are unfamiliar with which SQL Expressions are available for your particular database, your database administrator should be able to help you find out.

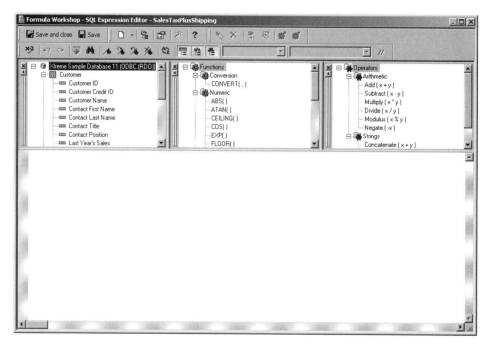

FIGURE 5.22   The SQL Expression Editor.

5. Once you have finished entering your SQL Expressions, click the Save and Close button to return to your report design. You can now drag your SQL Expression into your report as you would any other field.

SUMMARY

Adding calculations and logic to your reports is an easy way to add value and provide insight into the data presented. Using the formula languages available in Crystal Reports, you can create formula fields quickly using the hundreds of functions and operators that are available, or you can create your own custom functions that can be shared between formulas or even reports.

And finally, for complete control over the report data set and to push processing back to the database server, SQL Commands and Expressions return control of the data set squarely back in the developer's hands.

This all provides a good background for the next chapter, where we start looking at building more complex reports, building on the concepts learned so far.

6 Building Complex Reports

In This Chapter

- Working with Subreports
- Formatting Subreports
- Working with Cross-Tabs
- Formatting Cross-Tabs
- Analyzing Cross-Tab Data

INTRODUCTION

In the past few years, organizations have seen an explosion in the amount of data that they must analyze and present. Often this data is from multiple data sources, including order entry applications, accounting systems, manufacturing systems, databases, e-mails, and spreadsheets. Often, they are required to show information from these different sources side-by-side in a single report. Because these data sources can be stored many different ways, it has previously been difficult to display heterogeneous data in a single report. Fortunately, Crystal Reports has a feature called subreports that makes this possible.

Subreports are a flexible feature in Crystal Reports that allows you to insert multiple instances of reports into a single report file. Subreports have many different uses, including displaying related or unrelated data in a single report and providing at-a-glance reports with multiple pieces of information displayed on a page to create packages of reports that allow multiple reports to be run and printed at the same time.

In the first half of the chapter, you will learn how to create both linked and un-linked subreports and how to use them in a report. We'll also see how to format a subreport and learn about techniques for managing the use of subreports.

Another key requirement when creating reports is the consolidation and presentation of data. Crystal Reports includes a powerful cross-tab feature that allows you to show your report data in summarized rows and columns. You can use this feature to consolidate large amounts of data into an easy-to-read format. In the second half of the chapter, you will learn how to create and format and modify a cross-tab.

WORKING WITH SUBREPORTS

You may sometimes want to display information from two different data sources in the same report. If these two data sources have a common key and are compatible, you can create a report easily using both of these data sources. For example, if you have an employee database that contains employees' names, employee numbers, and so on, and a payroll database that also stores the employee numbers in the same format, you can join these two data sources together easily to create a report that lists information from both sources.

But what if the payroll database doesn't store the employee number in the same way? For example, suppose that the employee table stores the number in a true number field, and the payroll database stores it as a string. This is where a subreport comes in handy. You can create a report from the employee table and then insert a subreport to display the payroll information from the other data source, as shown in Figure 6.1.

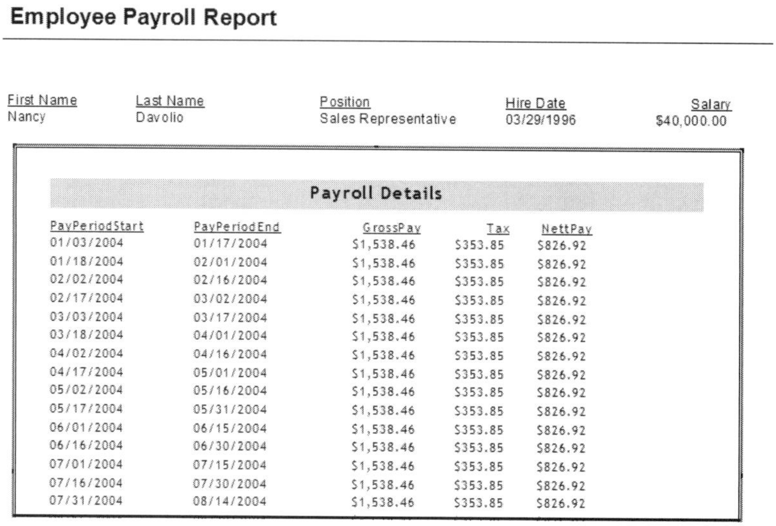

FIGURE 6.1 An example of a linked subreport.

Subreports come in two flavors: linked and unlinked. In the previous example, you would use a linked subreport, so that each employee is shown with the correct payroll details. When working with linked subreports, Crystal Reports passes a parameter between the main report and subreport, which the subreport uses for record selection.

Crystal Reports sometimes uses the term main report *or* container report *to indicate that a report contains subreports.*

For an unlinked subreport, Crystal Reports does not pass any parameters between the main report and subreports, so the subreport displays all of the records available.

The reports created in this chapter are located on the CD-ROM in the PROJECTS folder. You can either follow along with the instructions in the chapter to recreate the reports, or you can copy the reports from the CD-ROM to your hard drive for editing.

In our example report, you could add an unlinked subreport to your employee report to show national salary averages. Because the data in the main report and the subreport are not linked, you can show totally unrelated data side by side, as shown in Figure 6.2.

Employee Payroll Report

National Average Salary by Year

First Name	Last Name	Position	Hire Date	Salary
Nancy	Davolio	Sales Representative	03/29/1996	$40,000.00

Payroll Details

PayPeriodStart	PayPeriodEnd	GrossPay	Tax	NettPay
01/03/2004	01/17/2004	$1,538.46	$353.85	$826.92
01/18/2004	02/01/2004	$1,538.46	$353.85	$826.92
02/02/2004	02/16/2004	$1,538.46	$353.85	$826.92
02/17/2004	03/02/2004	$1,538.46	$353.85	$826.92
03/03/2004	03/17/2004	$1,538.46	$353.85	$826.92
03/18/2004	04/01/2004	$1,538.46	$353.85	$826.92
04/02/2004	04/16/2004	$1,538.46	$353.85	$826.92
04/17/2004	05/01/2004	$1,538.46	$353.85	$826.92

FIGURE 6.2 An unlinked subreport showing unrelated data.

When working with subreports, an important concept to remember is that subreports are both an element of the main report and an individual report in their own right. Each subreport you insert into your main report will be shown in the section where it is inserted, but it will also have its own Design tab, as shown in Figure 6.3.

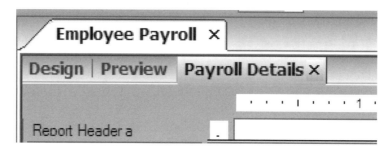

FIGURE 6.3 A subreport Design tab.

If you preview a subreport independently, you will see a separate Preview tab for each subreport as well.

You can edit the attributes of both the subreport object shown in the main report and the subreport itself—but before we get too far down that road, we need look at how subreports are inserted.

Inserting an Unlinked Subreport

An unlinked subreport doesn't require a parameter to be passed to the main report and can display any information you require. The information can be totally unrelated and can be from different databases with different formats, tables, and so on. When working with unlinked subreports, you can either select an existing report to insert or create one from scratch. To get started, click Insert > Subreport to open the dialog box shown in Figure 6.4.

You may want to switch to the Design tab before inserting a subreport, so you can see the sections and their boundaries easily.

Use the radio buttons to indicate whether you will choose a subreport or create one. If you select Choose an Existing Report, click the Browse button to locate a Crystal Report that you have created earlier. If you select Create a Subreport with the Report Wizard, you will need to enter a name for your subreport and then click the Report Wizard button to invoke an expert to create your report. When you are finished, click OK to return to the Insert Subreport dialog box.

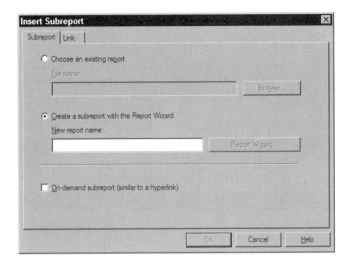

FIGURE 6.4   You can insert an existing report or create a new one.

When you are finished with the Insert Subreport dialog box, click OK. Your subreport will be attached to the tip of your mouse pointer. You can then position the subreport on your main report and click to place it.

You should choose the location of your subreport carefully. Where you position it determines how many times it is processed. If you place your subreport in the report header or footer, for example, the subreport will be processed only once for each report. If you place the subreport in the page header or footer, the subreport will be processed for every page, which can cause significant performance problems when your report is run or refreshed.

Inserting a Linked Subreport

Working with linked subreports is just as easy as working with their unlinked counterparts. The only difference is that you will need to specify a field in both the main report and subreport that will determine the relationship between the two. In the Insert Subreport dialog box shown in Figure 6.5, there is an additional tab for Link.

The first step in linking the two reports is to decide which field in your main report to use. From the list of available fields on the left side of the dialog box, select a field and use the right arrow to move the field from this list to the one on the right.

Once you have selected a field, additional options appear at the bottom of the dialog box, as shown in Figure 6.6, to allow you to select a field in your subreport. You'll notice that a parameter field is created automatically for you; all you need to do is select a field in use in your subreport.

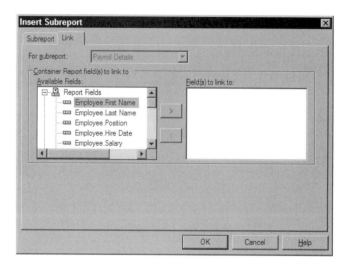

FIGURE 6.5   You can specify the links between your main report and subreport.

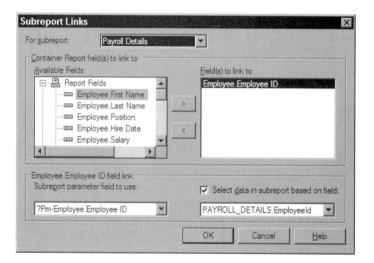

FIGURE 6.6   You will need to select a parameter field and a field from your subreport.

If you don't want the value in the parameter field to be used for record selection, you can remove the checkmark from the Select Data in Subreport Based on Field box. The subreport will be linked and the parameter field value will be passed, but the parameter will not be used in record selection.

You can select multiple fields in your main report for linking in the same manner. You will need to specify a field in the subreport for each. When you are finished, click OK to accept your changes and place the subreport in your main, or *container*, report.

Again, it is important where you place a linked subreport. A subreport will be processed once every time the section appears. If you have a report with 500 detail records and place the subreport in the Detail section, it will be processed 500 times, adding to the total report processing time.

Bringing It All Together

To demonstrate some of the techniques you just saw for linked and unlinked subreports, the project that follows recreates the Employee Payroll report we looked at earlier in the chapter. We will start off with a simple employee listing report and then add a subreport to display the payroll details from a separate data source. To re-create this report, use the following steps:

ON THE CD

1. Open Crystal Reports, and open the PAYROLL.RPT report from the CD-ROM.
2. Switch to the Design view of your report, and click Insert > Subreport to open the Insert Subreport dialog box.
3. Click the option to Create a subreport with the Report Wizard, and enter a name for your subreport. In this example, call the subreport Payroll Details.
4. Click the Report Wizard button to open the Standard Report Creation Wizard.
5. In the Data dialog box, expand the node for Create New Connection, then double-click Access/Excel DAO to open the dialog box shown in Figure 6.7.
6. Click the browse button (…), browse to the CD-ROM, and select the PAYROLL.MDB file. Then click the Finish button.
7. Expand the Tables node of your data source, and double-click the PAYROLL_DETAILS table to add it to your list of selected tables. Then click Next.
8. In the Fields dialog box, click the double-arrow to move all of the fields from the table to the selected area.
9. Click the Finish button to return to the Insert Subreport dialog box.
10. Click OK to finish the expert. The subreport will now be attached to your mouse pointer.
11. Click to place the subreport in the Details section of your report.
12. Preview your report to verify that the subreport is working correctly.
13. Next, we need to set the linking for your subreport, so right-click the subreport, and select Change Subreport Links to open the dialog box shown in Figure 6.8.

FIGURE 6.7 Access/Excel Data Connection options.

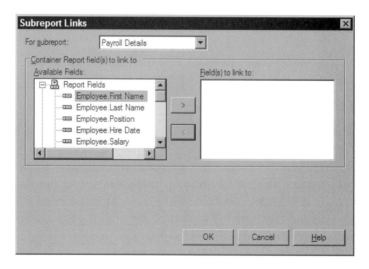

FIGURE 6.8 The Change Subreport Links dialog box.

14. Select the Employee ID field, and use the right arrow to move it to the list of selected fields on the right. A parameter field is created and appears at the bottom of the dialog box.

15. On the right side, select the option for Select data in Subreport based on Field, and use the drop-down list to select the Employee ID field. Then click OK to return to your report.
16. Your subreport results should now be filtered for each employee, so only the payroll details will be displayed, as shown in Figure 6.9.

Employee Payroll Report

First Name	Last Name	Position	Hire Date	Salary
Nancy	Davolio	Sales Representative	03/29/1996	$40,000.00

1/3/2007

PayPeriodStart	PayPeriodEnd	GrossPay	Tax	NettPay
1/3/2004 12:00:00AM	1/17/2004 12:00:00A	$1,538.46	$353.85	$826.92
1/18/2004 12:00:00A	2/1/2004 12:00:00AM	$1,538.46	$353.85	$826.92
2/2/2004 12:00:00AM	2/16/2004 12:00:00A	$1,538.46	$353.85	$826.92
2/17/2004 12:00:00A	3/2/2004 12:00:00AM	$1,538.46	$353.85	$826.92
3/3/2004 12:00:00AM	3/17/2004 12:00:00A	$1,538.46	$353.85	$826.92
3/18/2004 12:00:00A	4/1/2004 12:00:00AM	$1,538.46	$353.85	$826.92
4/2/2004 12:00:00AM	4/16/2004 12:00:00A	$1,538.46	$353.85	$826.92
4/17/2004 12:00:00A	5/1/2004 12:00:00AM	$1,538.46	$353.85	$826.92
5/2/2004 12:00:00AM	5/16/2004 12:00:00A	$1,538.46	$353.85	$826.92
5/17/2004 12:00:00A	5/31/2004 12:00:00A	$1,538.46	$353.85	$826.92
6/1/2004 12:00:00AM	6/15/2004 12:00:00A	$1,538.46	$353.85	$826.92
6/16/2004 12:00:00A	6/30/2004 12:00:00A	$1,538.46	$353.85	$826.92
7/1/2004 12:00:00AM	7/15/2004 12:00:00A	$1,538.46	$353.85	$826.92
7/16/2004 12:00:00A	7/30/2004 12:00:00A	$1,538.46	$353.85	$826.92
7/31/2004 12:00:00A	8/14/2004 12:00:00A	$1,538.46	$353.85	$826.92
8/15/2004 12:00:00A	8/29/2004 12:00:00A	$1,538.46	$353.85	$826.92
8/30/2004 12:00:00A	9/13/2004 12:00:00A	$1,538.46	$353.85	$826.92

FIGURE 6.9 The finished report with a linked subreport for the payroll details.

Creating an On-Demand Subreport

On-demand subreports are subreports that are run when the user requests them. Unlike the subreports we have looked at so far in this chapter, on-demand subreports do not add any additional processing overhead to our report, because they are not run until the user requests them.

To create an on-demand subreport, use the following steps:

1. Open Crystal Reports, and open the Payroll report we have been working on in this section.
2. Right-click the subreport, select Format Subreport, then click the Subreport tab to open the dialog box shown in Figure 6.10.
3. Select the option for On Demand Subreport. The subreport will then be shown as a link on your report.
4. To control the text that appears either on the on-demand link and Preview tab, click the X+2 option beside either of these options and enter the caption in quotes (for example, "Click here for Payroll Details").

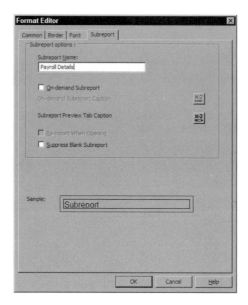

FIGURE 6.10 Subreport formatting options.

5. Click OK to return to your report, which should now look like the one shown in Figure 6.11.

Employee Payroll Report

First Name	Last Name	Position	Hire Date	Salary
Nancy	Davolio	Sales Representative	03/29/1996	$40,000.00
Click here for Payroll Details				
Andrew	Fuller	Vice President, Sales	07/12/1996	$90,000.00
Click here for Payroll Details				
Janet	Leverling	Sales Representative	02/27/1996	$33,000.00
Click here for Payroll Details				
Margaret	Peacock	Sales Representative	03/30/1997	$35,000.00
Click here for Payroll Details				
Steven	Buchanan	Sales Manager	09/13/1997	$50,000.00
Click here for Payroll Details				
Michael	Suyama	Sales Representative	09/13/1997	$30,000.00

FIGURE 6.11 A report with an on-demand subreport.

FORMATTING SUBREPORTS

Once you have inserted a subreport into your report, you can apply a number of formatting options and techniques to integrate the main report and subreport into one seamless presentation.

Changing the Subreport Name

When you insert an existing subreport into your main report, by default Crystal Reports names the subreport the same name as the report file you have inserted. For example, if you inserted MySales.rpt, the subreport would also be named MySales.rpt. To rename the subreport, right-click the subreport and select Format Subreport from the shortcut menu. Using the option shown on the Subreport property page and the Formula Editor, shown in Figure 6.12, you can rename your subreport. Whenever the subreport name is shown (for example, in the main report, tool text, on a design tab for the subreport, and so on), this new name will be used.

FIGURE 6.12 You can rename the subreport to something more meaningful using the Formula Editor.

Changing the Border

By default, Crystal Report places a border around any subreports you have inserted into a main report. This is usually the first default formatting option you will want to turn off. To change the border around a subreport, right-click the subreport, select Format Subreport, then click the Border tab to open the dialog box shown in Figure 6.13.

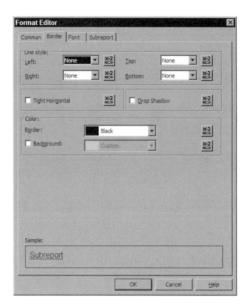

FIGURE 6.13 You can control subreport formatting from the shortcut menu.

From the Border tab in the Format Editor dialog box, you can change all four of the Line Style drop-down boxes from Single to None. Alternatively, if you want a border around your subreport, you can use the drop-down boxes and options to select a line style (Single, Double, Dashed, Dotted) and color, as well a background color and drop shadow. When you are finished editing the borders and colors for your subreport, click OK to return to your report Design or Preview view, shown in Figure 6.14.

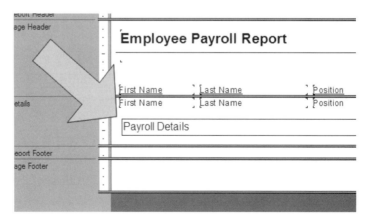

FIGURE 6.14 You can remove or format the border that appears around your subreport.

For precise control over the where the subreport appears and its size on the page, right click the subreport and select Size and Position from the shortcut menu. Here you can enter precise dimensions and positioning coordinates.

Changing Subreport Links

Subreport links are usually set up when you first insert a subreport, but you can change subreport linkage as your needs and report structure change. You will need to locate the subreport you want to change, right-click it, and select Change Subreport Links from the shortcut menu. The Subreport Links dialog box you saw earlier opens.

To select a field for linking, locate a field in the list of available fields, click to select it, and use the right arrow to move it to the list on the right. Once you have selected a field, a second set of drop-down lists and options will appears, allowing you to select fields in your subreport.

When you are finished changing the links for your subreport, click OK to accept your changes. The next time your report is refreshed, these changes should be reflected.

You can refresh your report at any time by clicking the Refresh icon or pressing F5.

WORKING WITH CROSS-TABS

Cross-tabs provide an easy way to add complex data summarization and analysis to your report. As the main feature of a report, or as a supporting object within an existing report, they provide an at-a-glance view of information in your database. In this chapter, you will learn how to create, format, and manipulate cross-tabs, adding instant analysis and summarization to your reports.

Cross-tabs, like the one shown in Figure 6.15, are composed of rows and columns of summarized data and either can be placed in the structure of existing reports or can be the main focus and content of their own reports.

Cross-tabs look similar to a spreadsheet, but it is important to remember that cross-tabs are database driven. In the Design view of your report, a cross-tab presents a simple row-and-column display. When viewed in the preview of your report, these rows and columns are filled with the data you have requested. The size of the cross-tab varies based on the number of records returned.

To facilitate the creation of reports specifically for use with cross-tabs, Crystal Reports includes a Cross-Tab Expert that walks you through the process of creating a cross-tab report. In addition, you can insert cross-tabs as an element of an existing report.

International and Domestic Sales

		International Sales	Domestic Sales	Total
Competition	Descent	$16,903,532	$9,095,823	$25,999,355
	Endorphin	$10,244,249	$3,618,778	$13,863,027
	Mozzie	$8,040,145	$4,952,752	$12,992,897
	Total	$35,187,926	$17,667,354	$52,855,280.12
Gloves	Active Outdoors Crochet G	$8,170,838	$5,013,556	$13,184,394
	Active Outdoors Lycra Glo	$10,507,918	$6,719,969	$17,227,887
	InFlux Crochet Glove	$4,252,417	$1,961,401	$6,213,818
	InFlux Lycra Glove	$2,449,197	$2,494,682	$4,943,879
	Total	$25,380,370	$16,189,607	$41,569,977.61
Helmets	Triumph Pro Helmet	$10,647,611	$5,655,971	$16,303,582
	Triumph Vertigo Helmet	$14,107,961	$7,560,351	$21,668,312
	Xtreme Adult Helmet	$10,249,214	$4,661,505	$14,910,720
	Xtreme Youth Helmet	$2,541,981	$1,341,177	$3,883,158
	Total	$37,546,768	$19,219,004	$56,765,771.82

FIGURE 6.15 A typical cross-tab summarizing domestic and international sales.

From the Insert menu, click Insert > Cross Tab. A blank cross-tab is attached to your mouse pointer. Click to place the cross-tab on your report, then right-click the cross tab and select Cross-Tab Expert to open the dialog box shown in Figure 6.16.

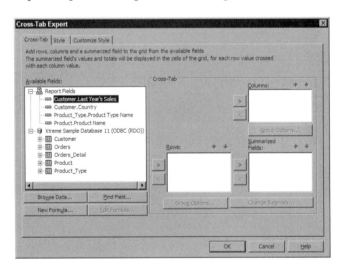

FIGURE 6.16 The Cross-Tab Expert.

To create a cross-tab, you need three elements: rows, columns, and summarized fields. For a basic cross-tab, you need only one of each. To create new rows, columns, or summarized fields, you can drag a field from the Available Fields box to the corresponding box for rows, columns, or summarized fields.

You can also highlight a field in the Available Fields box and click the arrow button next to text boxes for the Rows, Columns, and Summarized Fields.

To remove a field from a cross-tab, highlight the field and click the left arrow button beside the text box to remove it from the list of selected fields.

If you are curious about the contents of a particular field, you can view some of the values held in the field by highlighting the field name and clicking the Browse button at the bottom-right corner of the dialog box. This action will return about 200 records at a time for you to look through, but keep in mind that on large databases, this process may take some time.

With cross-tabs, you can add as many fields for the columns, rows, and summarized fields as required. When your cross-tab is printed, the fields you specified for the columns and rows will be used to create the cross-tab, and the summarized field you specified will be calculated at the intersection of the columns and rows. For example, in the cross-tab shown in Figure 6.17, the fields for Product Class and Product Name have been used for the rows, with an Order Date field used for the columns. A Quantity value appears in the summarized field.

Quarterly Sales Report

		QTR1	QTR4	QTR1	QTR2	QTR3	QTR4
Accessory	Active Outdoors Crochet Glove	11	25	27	89	57	75
	Active Outdoors Lycra Glove	4	37	59	94	75	73
	Guardian "U" Lock	0	2	5	15	11	13
	Guardian ATB Lock	0	2	7	15	10	4
	Guardian Chain Lock	0	6	10	14	19	14
	Guardian Mini Lock	3	12	10	16	5	7
	Guardian XL "U" Lock	0	1	10	24	7	15
	InFlux Crochet Glove	0	4	31	30	30	39
	InFlux Lycra Glove	9	15	18	36	32	41

FIGURE 6.17 A typical cross-tab summarizing orders over a number of quarters.

By default, the summary operator used for numeric fields is Sum. A little later, you'll learn how to highlight and change the summary operator for summarized fields, but for now it is important to remember that the summarized field is calculated by Crystal Reports at the intersection of rows and columns.

To help you understand how you can create your own cross-tabs, we are going to create a new cross-tab and insert it into an existing report. To do so, use the following steps:

1. Open Crystal Reports, and open the QUARTERLYSALES.RPT report from the CD-ROM.
2. Switch to the Design view of your report, and click Insert > Cross Tab. Then click to place a blank cross-tab in the Report Header in your report.
3. Right-click the cross-tab, and select Cross-Tab Expert from the shortcut menu.
4. Drag the Product Class and Product Name fields from the list of Available Fields to the Rows box.
5. Drag the Order Data field from the list of Available Fields to the Columns box.
6. Drag the Quantity field from the list of Available Fields to the Summarized Fields box. The Cross-Tab Expert should now look like the one shown in Figure 6.18.

7. Click OK to return to your report.

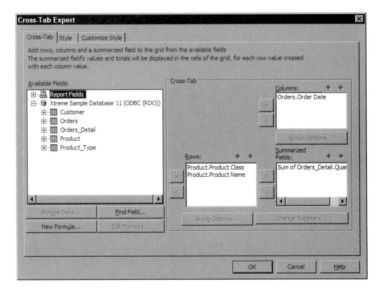

FIGURE 6.18 The Cross-Tab Expert with all of the required fields selected.

When your preview your report, the data will be filled into the cross-tab and shown using the rows, columns, and summarized fields we selected earlier.

It's important to note that when adding a cross-tab to your reports, Crystal Reports allows you to insert a cross-tab into only a report or group header or footer. If you insert your cross-tab into the report header or footer, the cross-tab will display the entire data set you have requested, showing all records. If you place a cross-tab in a group header or footer, your cross-tab will display only the records that relate to that one particular group, as shown in Figure 6.19.

Quarterly Sales Report by Product

Active Outdoors Crochet Glove

		QTR1	QTR4	QTR1	QTR2	QTR3	QTR4
Accessory	Active Outdoors Crochet Glove	11	25	27	89	57	75
	Total	11	25	27	89	57	75
Total		11	25	27	89	57	75

Order ID	Customer Name	Order Date	Product Name	Quantity
2600	Furia	14-Jan-2005	Active Outdoors Crochet Glove	1
2006	Spokes	21-Aug-2004	Active Outdoors Crochet Glove	3
2010	Rough Terrain	22-Aug-2004	Active Outdoors Crochet Glove	2
2013	To The Limit Biking Co.	22-Aug-2004	Active Outdoors Crochet Glove	3
2951	Psycho-Cycle	19-Apr-2005	Active Outdoors Crochet Glove	1
2017	Bikes, Bikes, and More Bike	24-Aug-2004	Active Outdoors Crochet Glove	2
2622	Wheels and Stuff	21-Jan-2005	Active Outdoors Crochet Glove	2
1374	To The Limit Biking Co.	27-Feb-2003	Active Outdoors Crochet Glove	1

FIGURE 6.19   A cross-tab placed in a group header will be filtered by the group.

One of the most common mistakes when placing a cross-tab is trying to place it in the wrong section. If you are inserting a report in the Preview tab, keep an eye on the cursor as you move across sections of your report. Where the "circle with a line through it" symbol appears, you can't add your cross-tab to that section. A good practice is to put it into the Report Header until you figure out where you want to place it on your report or use the Design view to place the cross-tab.

Customizing Grouping Options

As with reports, you can control the way information is displayed in a cross-tab through the use of grouping. You can apply the same grouping concepts to your cross-tab by using the shortcut menu shown in Figure 6.20 to edit your cross-tab, then highlight the row or column field you want to change and click the Group Options button.

The Cross-Tab Group Options dialog box, shown in Figure 6.21, opens. Here, you can select a sort order from the following options:

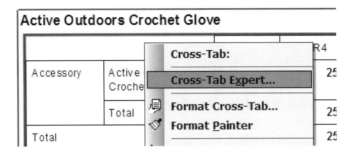

FIGURE 6.20 To edit a cross-tab, right-click in the top-left corner of the screen, and select Cross-Tab Expert.

FIGURE 6.21 A number of grouping options are available for use with cross-tabs.

- Ascending
- Descending
- Specified Order

When you use these options to select the sort order, remember that this sort order affects only the items in a single cross-tab. If you were using a cross-tab as the summary page for a long, detailed report, you would also need to change the report sort order so the cross-tab and report would reflect the same sorting.

Reordering Grouped Data

Ascending and descending order is easy to work with, but what about when you want to reorder the data itself, not just sort it? The functionality that allows you to create your own groups is called Specified Grouping. The Specified Order option with cross-tab groups works just as it does for other specified groupings you insert into your report. You need to name each group and then specify the criteria for each.

You might use specified grouping with a cross-tab if you have a particular product grouping not represented in the database. You could use a specified grouping to create separate groups and to establish your own criteria (for example, in our fictional bike company, all the gloves, helmets, and so on could be grouped as Personal Accessories, and saddles and other items could be grouped together as Spare Parts).

Once you have selected Specified Order, a second tab should appear in the Cross-Tab Group Options dialog box, as shown in Figure 6.22.

FIGURE 6.22 The Specified Order tab.

The next step is to define a group name, and then you need to specify the group criteria. Start by typing all of the group names you want to create first, pressing the ENTER key after each. This process will build a list of group names.

Once you have all of the group names defined, you can highlight each and click the Edit button to specify the criteria. To establish the criteria for records to be added to your group, use the drop-down menu to select an operator and values.

These are the same operators that were used with record selection.

You can add criteria by clicking the New tab and using the operators to specify additional selection criteria, which are evaluated with an Or operator between the criteria that you have specified.

Make sure that you delete any groups you may have added by accident. Even if the criterion is set to Any Value, it can still affect report performance.

After you have entered a single group, another tab appears with options for records that fall outside of the criteria that you specify. By default, all of the leftover records are placed in their own group, labeled Others, shown in Figure 6.23. You can change the name of this group by simply editing the name on the Others tab. You also can choose to discard all of the other records or to leave them in their own groups.

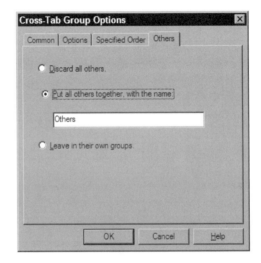

FIGURE 6.23   Options for handling other records.

After you have defined your specified groups and criteria and have reviewed the settings for other records, click OK to accept the changes to the group options. Your specified grouping is now reflected in your cross-tab, as shown in Figure 6.24.

An example report named XTABGROUP.RPT with a cross-tab with specified grouping is available on the CD-ROM.

Customizing the Group Name Field

Another handy option for formatting groups is the ability to select the Group Name field that appears in your cross-tab, using the dialog box shown in Figure 6.25.

Sales by Target Market

	QTR1	QTR4	QTR1	QTR2	QTR3	QTR4	QTR1	QTR2	Total
Boys Bikes	95	182	556	727	670	604	638	172	3,644.00
Girls Bikes	68	252	508	878	664	786	537	273	3,966.00
Total	163	434	1,064	1,605	1,334	1,390	1,175	445	7,610.00

FIGURE 6.24 A cross-tab with specified grouping.

FIGURE 6.25 You can also set some of the same grouping options that are available for groups inserted into your report.

For selecting the group name, you can customize the group name either by selecting a database field or by using a formula. If your database has a table that contains the name you wish to use, you could specify the name of the field that holds the proper name.

For example, if you were creating a cross-tab using the field Product ID, you could customize the group name and select the field Product Name so that the correct product name would appear instead of a numeric Product ID.

If the names of your group are not stored in one of your database tables, you can always create a formula to use as a group name. For example, in an Order Summary report, a cross-tab could be created using the Order Date field. The grouping options could then be set to For every quarter, which would produce some pretty ugly group names using the dates.

A much better solution is to use a formula as the group name. To create a formula for this purpose, click the X+2 button beside Use a Formula as Group Name. The Formula Workshop opens and allows you to enter a formula to be displayed as the group name.

From our example, we wanted to display a quarter number based on the month of the Order Date, so our formula looked like the following:

```
If Month({Purchases.Order Date}) in [1,2,3] then "QTR1" else
If Month({Purchases.Order Date}) in [4,5,6] then "QTR2" else
If Month({Purchases.Order Date}) in [7,8,9] then "QTR3" else
If Month({Purchases.Order Date}) in [10,11,13] then "QTR4"
```

You can create any formula you like, as long as it is designed to return a string as a group name.

Working with Summary Fields

Summary fields are used to summarize the information contained your cross-tab. All of the standard Crystal Reports summary fields are available for use. By default, Crystal Reports uses Sum for numeric fields you have inserted into your summarized fields and Count for any string or other type of field. You can change the summary type by highlighting a summarized field and clicking the Change Summary button.

There are a number of summary fields that are available for use within cross-tabs, including

- Sum
- Average
- Minimum
- Maximum
- Count
- Distinct Count
- Correlation
- Covariance
- Weighted Average
- Median
- Pth Percentile
- Nth Largest
- Nth Smallest
- Mode
- Nth Most Frequent
- Variance

- Standard Deviation
- Population Variance
- Population Standard Deviation
- NthSmallest

In addition to these standard summary field types, some summary types that are specific to cross-tabs follow:

- Percent Of Sum
- Percent Of Average
- Percent Of Maximum
- Percent Of Minimum
- Percent Of Count
- Percent Of Distinct Count

Some of these functions may require that you specify an additional field or value, such as the one shown in Figure 6.26, which shows the summarized field as a percentage of the total sum.

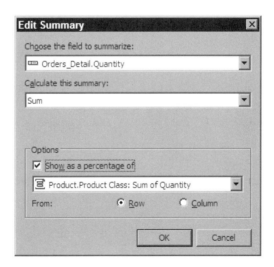

FIGURE 6.26   Some summary fields may require an additional field or value to be specified.

Inserting Formula Fields

In addition to database fields, you can also use formula fields in your cross-tabs. Using the Crystal Reports formula language, you can add complex calculations and analysis to your cross-tab. To insert a formula field into a cross-tab, click the New Formula button on the right side of the Format Cross-Tab dialog box.

To edit an existing cross-tab, right-click the cross-tab object and select Format Cross-Tab from the shortcut menu.

As always, the first thing you will need to do is enter a name for the formula you want to create. Click OK to open the Crystal Reports Formula Editor, and enter your formula text, as shown in Figure 6.27.

FIGURE 6.27 You can create a formula using the Cross-Tab Expert.

Using the Formula Editor, enter the text for your formula. When you are finished editing your formula, click Save and then the Close button at the top-left corner of the Formula Editor to close your formula and return to the Format Cross-Tab dialog box.

Your formula should now appear in the section marked Available Fields, shown under the Report Fields node. You can then drag the formula to the Row, Column, or Summarized Field box to add it to your cross-tab. When your report is previewed and the cross-tab created, this formula will be evaluated and displayed, as shown in Figure 6.28.

FIGURE 6.28   An example of a cross-tab with a formula field inserted.

FORMATTING CROSS-TABS

Now that you understand how to insert a cross-tab into your report and control its structure, it's time to take a look at formatting your cross-tab.

Changing Field, Column, and Row Size

If you have worked with Excel and resized columns, you may try to resize columns in your cross-tabs by resizing the actual column. In Crystal Reports, the column size is determined by the actual fields within the column itself. Just like Excel, column widths are set for the entire column at once (regardless whether the column has summarized fields, totals, or both).

You can resize a field by clicking the field to select it and then using the handles to change the width or height of the field. You can also right-click the field and select Size and Position from the shortcut menu to open the dialog box shown in Figure 6.29, which gives you precise control over the field's size.

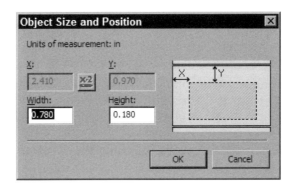

FIGURE 6.29   The Object Size and Position dialog box.

When you are finished resizing your fields, columns, or rows, click anywhere outside of the cross-tab to deselect the object with which you were working.

Applying a Preformatted Style

Because the majority of time spent working with cross-tabs is for formatting them, Crystal Reports includes a number of preformatted styles for which the formatting attributes have been set for you. This eliminates the need to individually change each of the formatting settings and also provides a way to apply uniform formatting to cross-tabs that may appear on different reports.

To apply a preformatted style to your cross-tab object, insert or edit an existing cross-tab and, in the Cross-Tab dialog box, click the Style tab to open the dialog box shown in Figure 6.30.

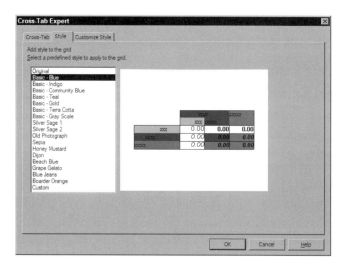

FIGURE 6.30 You can apply a preformatted style to your cross-tab or OLAP grid.

To see a preview of the style's formatting, click the style. The pane on the right side of the dialog box will display a preview of a sample cross-tab with the formatting attributes applied. When you have found the style you want to apply, click OK to return to your report and see the style applied to your cross-tab.

One of the most-often asked questions is, "Can I add my own style to this list?" At this time, Crystal Reports does not support adding custom styles. You can, however, use the styles as a starting point for your own formatting, which may make things a little easier.

Customizing a Style

If you don't particularly care for some of the formatting attributes of a particular style, you can customize the style using the Customize Style tab, also found in the Cross-Tab Expert and shown in Figure 6.31.

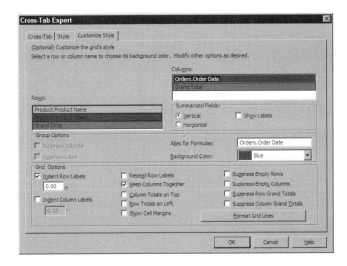

FIGURE 6.31   You can further customize a preformatted style using the Cross-Tab Expert.

To change the formatting of a particular row of column, highlight the row or column from the lists provided, and then use the drop-down box immediately below to change the background color and set other options, including the showing of labels, aliases for formula fields, and so on.

On the bottom half of the dialog box are the options for formatting the grid that appears around your cross-tab by default. Table 6.1 summarizes the gridline options available on the Customize Style tab.

TABLE 6.1   Cross-Tab Style Options

Option	Description
Show Cell Margins	Displays the internal cell margins in your cross-tab
Indent Row Labels	For each row, indents the labels that appear on the left side of the cross-tab
Repeat Row Labels	Repeats row labels on any new pages
Keep Columns Together	Attempts to keep all columns together on the same page →

Option	Description
Row Totals on Top	Moves the row totals from their default location at the bottom of the cross-tab to the top
Column Totals on Left	Moves the column totals from their default location on the right side of the cross-tab to the left
Suppress Empty Rows	Suppresses any empty rows in the cross-tab
Suppress Empty Columns	Suppresses any empty columns in the cross-tab
Suppress Row Grand Totals	Suppresses the grand totals that would appear by default at the bottom of the cross-tab
Suppress Column Grand Totals	Suppresses the grand totals that would appear by default on the right side of the cross-tab

You also can control the grid lines that appear in your cross-tab by clicking the Format Grid Lines button to open the dialog box shown in Figure 6.32.

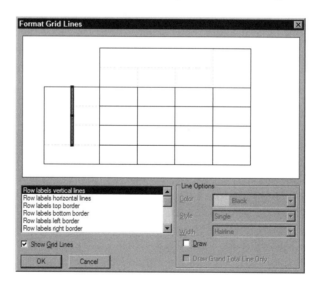

FIGURE 6.32 You can format individual grid lines as well.

Using this dialog box, select the part of your cross-tab or OLAP grid that you want to format and choose the line color, style, and width. The following grid lines are available:

- Row Labels Vertical Lines
- Row Labels Horizontal Lines
- Row Labels Top Border
- Row Labels Bottom Border
- Row Labels Left Border
- Row Labels Right Border
- Column Labels Vertical Lines
- Column Labels Horizontal Lines
- Column Labels Top Border
- Column Labels Bottom Border
- Column Labels Left Border
- Column Labels Right Border
- Cells Vertical Lines
- Cells Horizontal Lines
- Cells Bottom Border
- Cells Right Border

When you are finished setting the grid lines for your cross-tab or OLAP grid, click OK to return to your report design. The changes you have made should be reflected in your cross-tab.

ANALYZING CROSS-TAB DATA

In addition to summarizing data, the data in cross-tabs can also be manipulated to help analyze the data presented and find information quickly.

Using the Highlighting Expert

The Highlighting Expert can be used to quickly highlight exceptions or abnormal values in a cross-tab. To use the Highlighting Expert, use the following steps:

ON THE CD

1. Open Crystal Reports, and open the XTABHIGHLIGHT.RPT report from the CD-ROM.
2. Right-click the field in your cross-tab that you want to highlight. In this example, right-click the Quantity field. From the shortcut menu, select the Highlighting Expert to open the dialog box shown in Figure 6.33.
3. Click the New button on the left side of the dialog box.
4. Next, in the Item Editor section on the right side of the dialog box, select an operator from the pull-down Value Is list. In the box immediately below the operator, enter the criteria to specify when the highlighting should occur. For this report, select Is less than and then enter 10000.

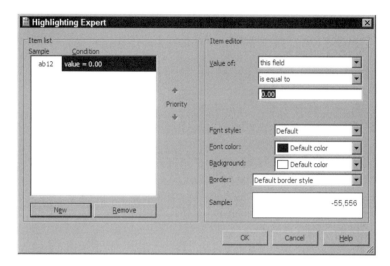

FIGURE 6.33 The cross-tab Highlighting Expert.

5. Now select the font color, background, and border that will be triggered when this criteria is met. For this report, select a background color of Yellow. If you want to enter multiple criteria, click New in the Item List on the left.

To change the order of precedence for highlighting criteria, use the up and down arrows.

6. After you have entered the criteria and formatting options, click OK to exit the Highlighting Expert.

When you preview your report, the field you originally selected in your cross-tab should reflect the options set in the Highlighting Expert.

Changing Cross-Tab Orientation

Sometimes when creating cross-tabs, we don't have a good indication of what the resulting summarized data is going to look like. To make cross-tabs a bit easier to read and to bring at least one of its features into line with Microsoft Excel, you can pivot cross-tabs by right-clicking the cross-tab and selecting Pivot Cross-Tab from the shortcut menu.

This action will cause the rows and columns in the cross-tab to be switched, so a report with different countries across the top in columns would then have the countries showing as rows.

This feature is available only at design time—when users view the report through any of the export formats or through one of Crystal Report's Web delivery methods, this feature is not available. You would have to pivot the cross-tab to the desired configuration before distributing or publishing your report.

Cross-Tab Uses and Limitations

Traditionally, Crystal Reports developers have either loved or hated cross-tabs. One of the main reasons that report designers are sometimes unhappy with cross-tabs is that they look at a cross-tab and see rows and columns, similar to a those in a Excel spreadsheet, and they expect the same functionality. However, a cross-tab and a spreadsheet are not the same.

For starters, a cross-tab's rows and columns all share the same height and width. For example, you can't show ten columns of data and have one column wider than the rest. Another key point is that any formatting you apply to a field in a cross-tab will be applied to every field in the cross-tab grid.

Over the different versions of Crystal Reports, improvements have been made to fix problems with page breaks, formatting, gridlines, row and column suppression, and so on that really do make cross-tabs a viable analysis and presentation option, but you must understand and work within the framework presented.

If you do need some of the specialized formatting features found in Excel and other spreadsheet programs, Crystal Reports does include a number of export formats that allow you to export to a spreadsheet file. What you do with the data at that point is up to you. The advantage of using a cross-tab is that even though it may not have all of the formatting functions of a spreadsheet, the information presented is data driven and does not require manual updating as a spreadsheet would.

SUMMARY

Subreports are a handy way you can use to show data from two or more disparate sources in the same report. Offering the flexibility of being either related or unrelated to the underlying report data, subreports can often make impossible reports seem possible. Another handy trick you learned in this chapter was the use of cross-tabs to display data in summarized rows and columns, presenting information clearly and concisely. And in the next chapter, we'll take that concept even further with details on how to use charts and graphs effectively within your reports.

7 Adding Visual Elements

In This Chapter

- Adding Charts to Your Reports
- Advanced Formatting

INTRODUCTION

In recent years, organizations have seen an explosion in the amount of data that they must collect. With the majority of business applications and systems tied to a backend database, an organization can have millions of rows of records that need to be condensed, analyzed, and displayed. Crystal Reports is the obvious solution for this problem, because even a single report can distill millions of rows of information into a clear, concise format.

You have already seen some of the ways that Crystal Reports can turn raw data into information, using summary and drill-down reports, running totals, summaries, and more. Until now, all of the summary methods we have looked at have been text-based and provided exact numbers and totals that reflect the underlying data in a report.

In this chapter, we are going to explore the different ways you can display data visually, providing report results at a glance using graphs and charts. Using these graphics you can distill millions of rows of data into a concise graph or chart that is easy to read and understand, like some of the examples shown in Figure 7.1.

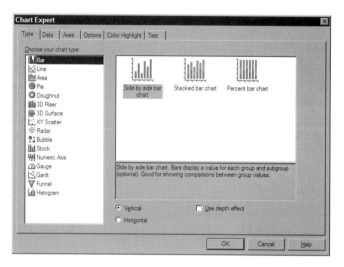

FIGURE 7.1 An example of some of the chart types Crystal Reports supports.

Driving these charts is a sophisticated graphing engine that provides support for a wide range of business and scientific charts, with more than 40 templates to select from. These charts can be customized to meet your specific needs, and numerous formatting attributes are available to achieve the desired result.

Using charting in your reports means that you can convey the meaning of a report and the data it represents at a glance, as shown in some of the examples in Figure 7.2.

In this chapter, we will look at charting in detail, starting with a look at the different chart layouts that are available.

ON THE CD
The reports created in the chapter are located on the CD-ROM in the PROJECTS folder. You can either follow along with the instructions in the chapter to recreate the reports, or you can copy the reports from the CD-ROM to your hard drive for editing.

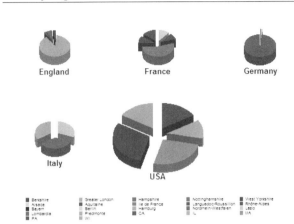

Sales by Region

FIGURE 7.2 An example of side-by-side charts embedded into a report.

ADDING CHARTS TO YOUR REPORTS

Crystal Reports supports a number of different chart formats, including bar charts, pie charts, and line charts. These formats may determine the look and feel, but Crystal Reports charts generally fall into four distinct types or layouts: advanced, group, cross-tab, and OLAP grid, as shown in Figure 7.3.

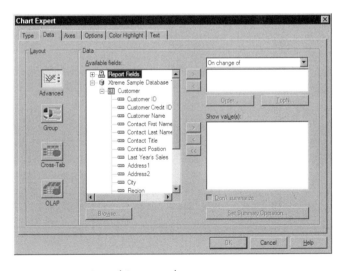

FIGURE 7.3 Crystal Reports chart types.

Advanced Charts

Advanced charts work like the charts you may remember from high school math: you plot a chart or graph based on *x* and *y* values. Crystal Reports' implementation of this type of charting is a little more sophisticated; you can specify summary fields to be generated, perform complex analysis, and control how the information is grouped when displayed on your graph.

Group Charts

Group charts are commonly used in reports and can be used wherever you have inserted a group into your report and created a summary field based on that group (Sum, Average, and so on). A group chart can appear once, representing the data in the entire report, or you can present one chart for each group.

Group charts can be used to create a drill-through effect, where you start with a graph of the highest level of data (the whole report) and then drill down through the different groups, with a graph displayed for each group, all the way down to the details.

ON THE CD An example of a drill-through report (DRILLTHROUGH.RPT) is included on the CD-ROM in the PROJECTS folder.

Keep in mind that the difference between advanced and group charts is that advanced charts don't require a group or summary field to be inserted into your report. Frequently, advanced charts are used with formula fields and can be used to create complex graphs that would not normally have been possible with just a group graph.

Cross-Tab Graphs

Cross-tabs are used to display summarized rows and columns of information in your report, similar in presentation to an Excel spreadsheet. You can create a chart directly from cross-tab data, providing a way to visualize the data that has been summarized in the cross-tab grid, as shown in Figure 7.4.

Annual Sales by Country

	2001	2002	Total
USA	$1,941,447	$771,234	$2,712,682
Canada	$188,984	$58,426	$247,410
Italy	$92,763	$16,360	$109,123
Germany	$58,866	$11,396	$70,261
England	$57,803	$8,137	$65,940
Total	$2,861,205	$957,190	$3,818,395

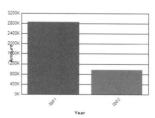

FIGURE 7.4 A cross-tab grid and chart.

OLAP Grid Charts

OLAP grids are similar to cross-tabs, except that OLAP grids display multidimensional OLAP data, as opposed to cross-tabs, which display relational data. Other than that distinction, they behave in the same manner and share most formatting attributes.

Inserting an Advanced Chart

Advanced charts are drawn based on *x* and *y* values, commonly referred to in Crystal Reports as On Change of field and Values to be Displayed. In the following steps, we create an advanced chart using the Order Listing report from the CD-ROM as a starting point.

ON THE CD

1. Open Crystal Reports, and open the ORDERLISTING.RPT report from the CD-ROM, as shown in Figure 7.5.

Order Listing Report

Order Date	Customer Name	City	Region	Order ID	Order Amount
12/02/2000	City Cyclists	Sterling Heights	MI	1	$41.90
12/02/2000	Deals on Wheels	DeKalb	IL	1002	$5,060.28
12/02/2000	Warsaw Sports, Inc.	Warsaw	Warsaw	1003	$186.87
12/02/2000	Bikes and Trikes	Sterling Heights	MI	1004	$823.05
12/03/2000	SAB Mountain	Bern	Cantons	1005	$29.00
12/03/2000	Poser Cycles	Eden Prairie	MN	1006	$64.90
12/03/2000	Spokes	DeKalb	IL	1007	$49.50
12/03/2000	Clean Air Transportation Co.	Conshohocken	PA	1008	$2,214.94
12/03/2000	Extreme Cycling	Clearwater	FL	1009	$29.00
12/03/2000	Cyclopath	Kingston	RI	1010	$14,872.30
12/03/2000	BBS Pty	London	Greater London	1011	$29.00
12/03/2000	Piccolo	Salzburg	Salzkammergut	1012	$10,259.10
12/03/2000	Pedals Inc.	Madison	WI	1013	$1,142.13
12/04/2000	Spokes 'N Wheels Ltd.	Des Moines	IA	1014	$29.00
12/04/2000	Cycle City Rome	Torino	Piedmonte	1015	$43.50
12/04/2000	SAB Mountain	Bern	Cantons	1016	$563.70
12/05/2000	Tyred Out	Santa Ana	CA	1017	$72.00
12/05/2000	Has Been Bikes (consignment)	Kingston	RI	1018	$115.50
12/05/2000	Spokes for Folks	Hightstown	NJ	1019	$43.50
12/05/2000	Extreme Cycling	Clearwater	FL	1020	$67.80
12/06/2000	Canal City Cycle	Amsterdam	Noord Holland	1021	$5,237.55
12/07/2000	Belgium Bike Co.	Brussels	Brussels	1022	$2,792.86
12/07/2000	Tienda de Bicicletas El Pardo	Madrid	Madrid	1023	$890.61
12/07/2000	Tandem Cycle	Nampa	ID	1024	$33.00
12/07/2000	SAB Mountain	Bern	Cantons	1025	$8,819.55
12/07/2000	Wheels Inc.	Des Moines	IA	1026	$33.00

FIGURE 7.5 The Order Listing report provides a good starting point for creating an advanced graph.

2. Switch to the Design view of your report, and then click Insert > Chart. Click to place the chart in your Report Header section and to open the Chart Expert dialog box shown in Figure 7.6.

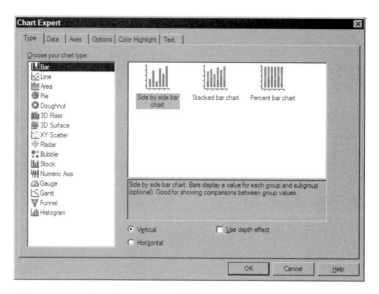

FIGURE 7.6 The Chart Expert dialog box.

3. Click the Type tab, select a Bar chart type, and then click the first icon on the right side to select a Side-by-side chart.
4. Click the Data tab at the top of the dialog box. The dialog box shown in Figure 7.7 opens.

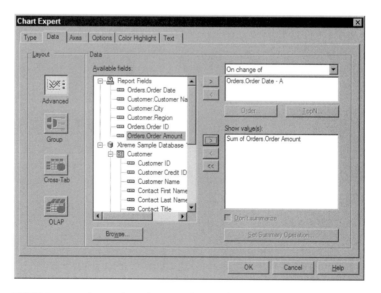

FIGURE 7.7 The options for an advanced chart.

In this example, we are going to create an advanced chart that displays the amounts of each order, sorted by the order date. This chart will be displayed in your report header and will appear on the first page of the report. By default, the placement will be set to One per report and Header, but you could as easily change this placement to put the chart in the report footer.

5. First, click to select the `Orders.OrderDate` field, and then click the right-arrow button near the top of the dialog box to move it to the On change of field, which is the equivalent of an *x*-axis value (if you remember your high school algebra).

When working with this *x*-axis value, you have three options for how this field will be used:

On Change Of: When the value contained in the field changes, a new bar, pie piece, and so on will be generated.

For Each Record: A new bar, pie piece, and so on will be created for each record in the database.

For All Records: One bar, pie piece, and so on will be created for all of the records in the database.

6. Because the chart in this example calls for one bar to be shown for each order date, leave the drop-down list to read On Change Of.
7. Next, click to select the `Orders.Order Amount` field, and then click the right-arrow button closer to the bottom of the dialog box to move it to the Show values field, which could also be considered the *y* values for your chart.

You'll notice that you can choose multiple x-axis values in an advanced graph. This allows you the flexibility you need to create complex graphs that require multiple x-axis values. But be warned that not all of the different graph types support multiple x axes.

8. Click the Text tab at the top to set the text labels for your chart. As with other graph types, Crystal Reports creates text labels for your chart by default, but you can change and format this text as you see fit.
9. To override the default values, uncheck the Auto-Text boxes, and enter the text you want to see on your chart.
10. To change the formatting attributes associated with this text, select an item (title, subtitle, and so on) from the list at the bottom-right corner of the dialog box. Click the Font button to change these attributes.

11. Click OK at the bottom of the Chart Expert to insert your advanced chart into your report, which will now look like Figure 7.8.

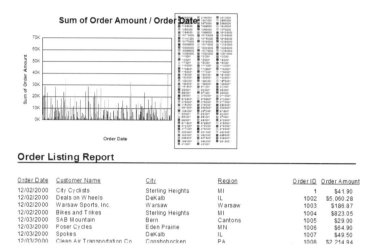

FIGURE 7.8 Your finished report with an advanced chart inserted.

Changing the Sort Order

Unfortunately, the chart we just created doesn't really tell us much about the underlying data, because there are too many bars or data points for us to make any sense of the chart. Some reorganization of the chart data would definitely come in handy, and we can change the sort order of this chart to make it a bit more readable.

On the Data tab of the Chart Expert, you may have noticed a button for Order, as shown in Figure 7.9. This button is grayed out until you actually select one of the On Change Of or *x*-axis fields.

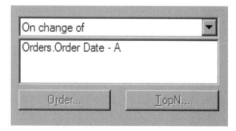

FIGURE 7.9 Data options for your chart.

You can use this button to order and summarize the data that appears on your chart by using the following steps:

1. From the Order Listing report we have been working on, right-click the advanced chart we just created, and select Chart Expert from the shortcut menu to open the Chart Expert.
2. Click the Data tab.
3. Locate the `Orders.Order Date` field in the text box below the drop-down box labeled On Change Of, and click to select it.
4. Click the Order button to open the Sort Order dialog box shown in Figure 7.10.

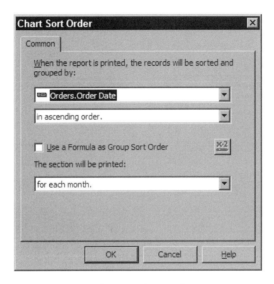

FIGURE 7.10   Chart-sorting options.

The following four sorting options are available:

Ascending: A to Z, 0 to 9, and so on.

Descending: Z to A, 9 to 0, and so on.

Specified: Similar to specified grouping option with groups inserted into your report. This option is for naming a group and specifying the criteria for the values that should be included in that group.

Original: The original order of the data.

5. By default, Ascending is selected. This is the sort order we want, so leave the dialog box as shown.

Because we have created an advanced chart on a date field (that is, Order Date), a third drop-down box appears with grouping options specifically for use with date fields (for each day, week, month, and so on).

6. To make this chart a bit more readable, change this drop-down list to read For each Month, and click OK.
7. Click OK again from the Chart Expert to return to the Report Designer. Your report should now look similar to the one shown in Figure 7.11.

FIGURE 7.11 The same report with a monthly grouping.

Applying Top N/Sort All Analysis

Top N and sorting are popular analysis methods in reports because they draw attention to trends in the data. For example, the *N* in Top N stands for a number, so you could create a Top 5 report to see your top five suppliers, according to how much you purchased from each. In addition, the Sort All functionality allows you to put groups in order by their totals or summary fields. You could take that same supplier report and use Sort All to put the suppliers in order from the supplier with whom you spend the most money to the supplier with whom you spend the least.

In addition to using this functionality in your report, you can also apply this functionality to your charts. To apply Top N/Sort All analysis to your chart, use the following steps:

1. Right-click your existing chart, and select Chart Expert.
2. In the Chart Expert, click the Data tab.
3. Locate the field that controls sort order in the text box below the pull-down box labeled On Change Of, and click to select it.
4. With the field highlighted, the Top N button is enabled. Click to open the Top N/Sort dialog box.

Three types of analysis are available using this feature, and each has its own parameters.

Top N: Enter a value for N to determine the Top N values based on the y field you have selected.

Bottom N: Enter a value for N to determine the Bottom N values based on the y field you have selected.

Sort All: Choose this option to sort all data items in either ascending or descending order based on the y value.

With Top N and Bottom N, you must also determine what to do with the values that are not included in your N sample. Just as with Top N/Bottom N analysis on a report, you can discard the other values, keep them in a group called Other, or simply leave them in their own groups—it's up to you.

5. When you are finished setting the Top N/Sorting options, click OK to accept your changes and return to your report's Design or Preview view. Your graph should now reflect the analysis options you have selected.

Changing the Summary Operation

Another report feature that can be used in charts is summary operators, which we looked at in Chapter 4. By default, an advanced chart type will use a Sum summary operator, but you can change this to any of the other summary types that Crystal Reports supports. To change the summary operator, use the following steps:

1. Right-click your chart, select Chart Expert, then click the Data tab.
2. Click the summarized field you want to work with in the Show Values dialog box at the bottom-right corner of the dialog box.

3. With the field highlighted, the Set Summary Operation button is enabled. Click it to open the dialog box shown in Figure 7.12.

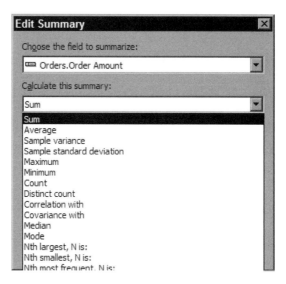

FIGURE 7.12 Summary operators available for use in your chart.

A number of summary operators appear in the drop-down list, depending on the field type; the most popular follow:

Sum: Provides a sum of the contents of a numeric or currency field.

Average: Provides a simple average of a numeric or currency field (that is, the values in the field are all added together and divided by the total number of values).

Minimum: Determines the smallest value present in a database field; for use with number, currency, string, and date fields.

Maximum: Determines the largest value present in a database field; for use with number, currency, string, and date fields.

Count: Provides a count of the values present in a database field; for use with all types of fields.

Distinct Count: Similar to Count, except any duplicate values are counted only once.

4. Click OK to accept your summary type change and return to the Chart Expert.
5. When you are finished editing your chart options, click OK to accept your changes and return to your report's Design or Preview view.

Inserting a Group Chart

Now let's move on to the most common type of graph: the group graph. To use a group graph, you will need two things in your report. The first is a group; this group can be created from a database field, formula field, and so on. The second requirement for a group graph is that you have some sort of summary field inserted onto your report.

Although this field is most frequently a summary on a numeric field, it can also be a summary on another type of field, such as a count of customers. (See Chapters 3 and 4 for information on inserting both groups and summary fields.) Again, to make things a bit easier, we are going to use a report from the CD-ROM as a starting point for our chart. The report CUSTOMERCOUNT.RPT is available in the PROJECTS directory on the CD-ROM.

ON THE CD

To insert a group chart into this report, use the following steps:

1. Open Crystal Reports, and open the CUSTOMERCOUNT.RPT report from the CD-ROM, as shown in Figure 7.13.

Customer Count by Country

USA	90
France	32
England	14
Canada	10
China	9
Germany	8
Australia	7
Brazil	6
Mexico	6
New Zealand	6

FIGURE 7.13 A typical customer report with a group and summary inserted.

2. Switch to the Design view of your report, click Insert > Chart, and click in the Report Header section to place your chart. Your chart will appear automatically with the default settings in place. To change these settings, right-click the chart and select the Chart Expert.

The first step in customizing a group graph is selecting the type of graph you want to create.

3. Referring to the descriptions of the different types of graphs, click the Type tab and select a chart type from the list on the left, then click an image of the specific type of graph you want to create.

4. The next step is selecting where the data will come from. Click the Data tab to open the dialog box shown in Figure 7.14. From the layouts on the left side of the page, select Group.

If you don't have a group inserted into your report, this option will be unavailable.

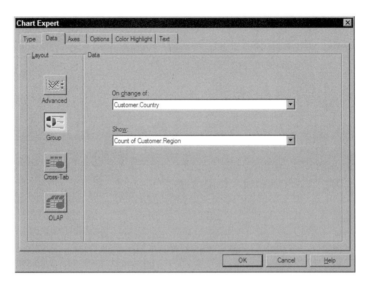

FIGURE 7.14 You need to select the source of your graph data.

5. You need to specify where you want your new group chart placed. If you have only one group and summary in your report, this task is easy; your only options will be to place the graph in either the Report Header or Report Footer section. If you have multiple groups and summaries, you can place the graph in the group headers.

6. In the middle of the page, you need to select On Change Of and Show Values. These two options correspond directly to the groups and summaries you have inserted onto your report. You should see all of the groups you have inserted in the On Change Of drop-down list, and all of the summaries should appear in the Show drop-down list.

7. The last step in creating a group graph is setting the text (that is, title, axis labels, and so on) that will appear on your graph. Click the Text tab to display the dialog box shown in Figure 7.15.

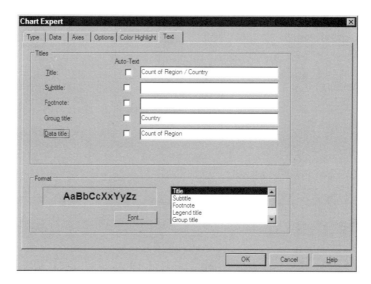

FIGURE 7.15   You can enter or edit the text for your chart.

By default, Crystal Reports creates text labels for your graph. To override these values, uncheck the Auto-Text checkbox found in the Text tab and enter the text you want to see on your graph. To change the formatting attributes associated with this text, select an item from the list at the bottom-right corner of the dialog box, and click the Font button to change the attributes.

    8. Now click OK. Your new chart options are applied to the chart you added to your report.

A little later in the chapter, we will look at some of the formatting options for charts, but now it's time to get a little practice with the other graph types.

Inserting a Cross-Tab Chart

Cross-tabs are special objects that can be inserted into your report to provide complex summary and analysis features (for more on cross-tabs, see Chapter 6). To take those capabilities even further, you can insert a graph based on the data in a cross-tab.

First, you need to make sure you've added a cross-tab to your report's design and that it is working correctly. You can open a good example of a cross-tab report from the CD-ROM for use in this section. The report is named CROSSTAB.RPT and can be found in the PROJECTS folder.

To add a chart to a cross-tab report, use the following steps:

1. Open Crystal Reports, and open the CROSSTAB.RPT report from the CD-ROM.
   a. Preview the cross-tab to make sure data appear in the rows, columns, and summarized fields.
   b. Switch back to the Design view of your report, click Insert > Chart, click to place your chart, and from the Chart Expert, select a chart type.

By default, Crystal Reports sets chart options automatically, reducing the number of formatting options required. If you want more control over your report, you can turn off this setting by unchecking Automatically Set Chart Options in the Chart Expert. Additional tabs will appear in the Chart Expert dialog box.

2. Click the Data tab to progress to the next step of the Chart Expert. In the dialog box that appears, click the Cross-Tab layout type, and select the placement for your chart. The options for Cross-Tab layout are set by the cross-tabs you have inserted into your report and their locations. If your report contains only one cross-tab, you can place the graph only in the report header or footer. If you have placed a cross-tab in the group header or footer, you can place a chart alongside it.
3. Using the combo boxes in the middle of the Data page (see Figure 7.16), specify how the chart will be printed, including how its components will be broken out (On Change Of), how they will be split within those breakouts (Subdivided By), and what values will be shown (Show).

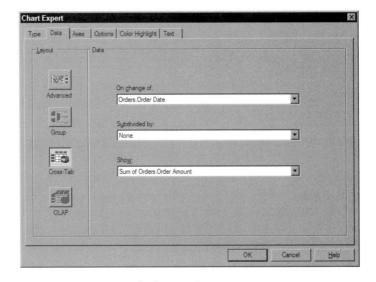

FIGURE 7.16 Cross-tab chart options.

4. Click the Text tab to advance to the final step of the Chart Expert, and choose the text that will appear on your chart and the format of each text object. By default, Crystal Reports will choose the text, but you can override this by unchecking the Auto-Text box and typing your own text in the box provided.
5. When you are finished editing your chart's text, click OK to finish.

Crystal Reports will show a placeholder graph on the Design tab, so your data may not appear immediately. To see your own data, preview your report.

Your report should now look like the one shown in Figure 7.17.

Annual Sales by Country

	2001	2002	Total
USA	$1,941,447	$771,234	$2,712,682
Canada	$188,984	$58,426	$247,410
Italy	$92,763	$16,360	$109,123
Germany	$58,866	$11,396	$70,261
England	$57,803	$8,137	$65,940
Total	$2,861,205	$957,190	$3,818,395

Sum of Order Amount / Order Date

FIGURE 7.17 The finished report with the cross-tab and chart side-by-side.

Formatting Charts

Regardless of what type of graph or chart you have created, some common formatting options can be applied to all. Most of the formatting options are available through shortcut menus that appear when you right-click your graph or chart.

Moving Charts

Charts can be placed almost anywhere on your report, depending on the type of chart you have created. To change a chart's position within a section, click the graph, and drag and drop the chart to its new position.

To move a chart between sections (for example, between the page header and a group header), use the Chart Expert. To move a chart, use the following steps:

1. Right-click the chart, select Chart Expert, and then click the Data tab.
2. Using the pull-down box at the top of the page, select a new section for your chart. Use the radio buttons to specify whether the chart should be included in the header or footer of that section.

The options available at this point depend on what type of graph, groups, and so on you have inserted. All of your available options will be shown.

3. Click OK to accept your changes. Your chart should now be in the section you have specified.

Changing a Graph from Color to Black and White

By default, Crystal Reports charts appear in full color. However, you can choose to use black-and-white shading and patterns instead, for better visibility when printing on a monotone printer.

To switch a chart to black-and-white mode, use the following steps:

1. Right-click the graph you want to work with, and click Format > Chart Expert.
2. Click the Options tab to open the dialog box shown in Figure 7.18.

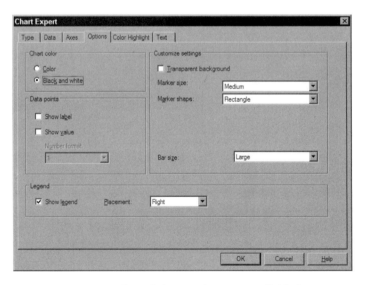

FIGURE 7.18 A number of chart options are available for you to customize from within the Expert.

3. Click the radio button marked Black and White, and then click OK to accept your changes. Your graph will now be recolored using only black and grayscale solids and patterns.

Showing a Graph Legend

Crystal Reports generates a legend for the charts and graphs you install automatically. To work with legend options found in the Chart Expert, use the following steps:

1. Right-click the chart you want to work with, and click Format > Chart Expert.
2. On the Type tab of the Chart Expert, turn off Automatically Set Chart Options, and click the Options tab that appears.
3. Locate the section marked Legend, and select the checkbox to enable the legend.
4. Use the pull-down list next to this setting to choose the placement of the legend (right, left, or bottom).
5. Click OK to accept your changes.

Controlling Chart Grid Lines and Scale for Bar and Area Graphs

Grid lines are an easy way to add value to your chart or graph and provide an instant reference to the grid's dimensions and values. To control the grid lines and scale within your graph, use the following steps:

1. Right-click a grid line in the chart, and select Format Grid Lines. A dialog box with multiple tabs, shown in Figure 7.19, opens.
2. Click either the Scales or Layout tabs.
3. On the Layout tab, choose one of the grid line options for this axis, which include the following:

    ■   Show Gridlines
    ■   Grid Style (regular, grids and ticks, inner ticks, outer ticks, spanning ticks)
    ■   Draw Custom Line As

4. Click the Scales tab to set the options for scaling, which include the following:

    ■   Use Logarithmic Scale
    ■   Always Include Zero
    ■   Use Manual Settings for Minimum Value
    ■   Use Manual Settings for Maximum Value

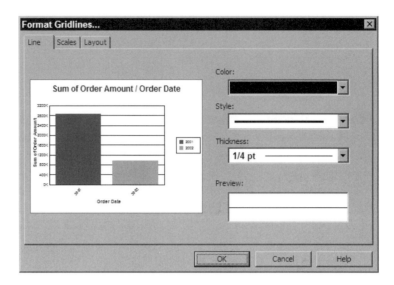

FIGURE 7.19 You can set grid formats using these options.

5. When you are finished setting grid and scale options, click OK to accept your changes.

Changing the Graph Type

You can apply a number of different chart types to your report data. In addition to the standard types of bar, pie, and so on, some chart types suit statistical data, radar and bubble graphs, three-dimensional graphs, and more. To change the graph type, use the following steps:

1. Right-click the chart you want to change, and select Load Template from the shortcut menu.
2. From the Gallery tab, select a new chart type by clicking an item on the list.

The preview image and options on the right side of the page will change according to the graph type you choose.

3. For custom chart types or any templates you may have saved, click the User Defined category. In this dialog box, click to select a category. A preview of all of the charts in that category appears on the right side of the page.

Any templates you have saved can be found in the category called User Defined.

4. Click a chart preview image to select it.
5. Click OK to accept your change and return to your report's design or preview.

Setting Chart Titles and Text

As mentioned earlier, chart titles and text are set by default by Crystal Reports. To create your own chart titles and text for your graph, use the following steps:

1. Right-click your graph or chart, select Chart Options from the shortcut menu, then click on the Titles tab.
2. Enter the text you want to appear for the title, subtitle, and so on.

Changing the text that appears in this dialog box is the equivalent of unchecking the Auto-Text option in the Chart Expert and entering text.

3. When you are finished entering your text, click OK to accept your changes and return to your report's Design or Preview view.

ADVANCED FORMATTING

Beyond the basic options, Crystal Reports offers more granular control over your charts and their data, which you can access by right-clicking a chart and choosing Chart Options. Here are some of the more advanced options you can apply.

Controlling Font Size and Color

One of the most common formatting tasks you'll perform is changing the font, type size, and color. To do so, use the following steps:

1. Locate the element of your graph that you want to change, right-click it, and select Format XXX to open the Formatting dialog box.
2. Using the dialog box shown in Figure 7.20, select the font, size, style, and color for the object you selected.
3. When you are finished, click OK to return to the report's Design or Preview view.

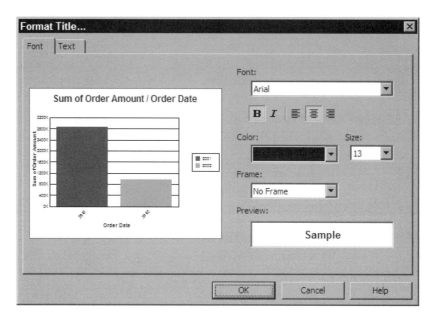

FIGURE 7.20 You can control the attributes of a specific element of your graph or chart.

Auto-Arranging Your Chart Contents

If you need a hand getting your graph or chart organized, you can use the Auto Arrange feature to have Crystal Reports do the arranging for you. To auto-arrange your chart contents, right-click anywhere on the graph, and select Auto Arrange Chart from the shortcut menu. Your graph contents will be rearranged, and the automatic changes should be reflected when you preview the report.

Resizing a Chart

Charts and graphs may be just one element of a Crystal Report, and trying to get all of the elements to fit in the allotted space can be tricky. You can resize your chart or graph body so it fits within your report. To resize a chart, click to select the chart you want to resize. A blue handle should appear on each side of your chart. Drag the blue handles to resize your chart.

Alternatively, right-click the graph and select Object Size and Position from the shortcut menu. This option will allow you to control the size and position of your graph or chart precisely within the Design or Preview tab.

SUMMARY

Regardless of whether you have 10 records or 10,000, charts and graphs are an easy way to consolidate and present information in a report. Crystal Reports supports a wide variety of report layouts and formats.

8 Report Integration Overview

In This Chapter

- Deciding on an Integration Method
- Selecting Your Data Source
- Selecting a Reporting Architecture

INTRODUCTION

Now that we have covered how to design reports, it's time to look at how to actually integrate reports into your application. You may have noticed that the remaining chapters cover integrating Crystal Reports with Windows, Web, and Java applications. Before we actually get into coding for each of these scenarios, we need to make some key architectural decisions about your reports and how they are integrated into your application.

An easy way to think of this chapter is as a blueprint for integrating reports into your own application—although the languages and platforms may be different, the basic concepts are the same.

Specifically, this chapter covers how to decide on an integration method, that is, whether you are going to create a simple view-only application for viewing reports or customize the reporting experience for users. Second, this chapter looks at selecting a data source for your report and covers options ranging from reporting from existing database tables to using stored procedures to reporting off of application data.

Finally, we will look at the best architectures for creating robust, scalable applications that can cater to from one to one thousand users. This coverage will also include some common application architectures that you may want to use for your own applications, based on a decade of experience integrating Crystal Reports into applications of all shapes and sizes.

We start our coverage looking at how to decide on an integration method for integrating reports in your application.

DECIDING ON AN INTEGRATION METHOD

If you were to survey application developers who are using Crystal Reports to integrate reports into their applications, one question you would want to ask is, "How do you plan to integrate reporting with your application?" Chances are, a large number of these developers would tell you that they plan to design reports based on their own database and then provide users with a menu of reports or other simple mechanism that would allow them to select a report and run it. This type of view-only integration, one of the methods shown in Figure 8.1, is the most common among application developers, because it satisfies the users' basic need for output with a minimum of coding required.

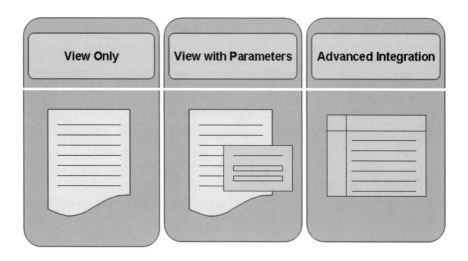

FIGURE 8.1   Common report integration options.

Viewing Reports

For example, to view a report from a Windows application created with Visual Studio .NET 2003, all you need to do is drag the report viewer onto your form and use the following line of code to set the report source:

```
CrystalReportViewer1.ReportSource = "c:\reports\sales.rpt"
```

And like all of the integration methods we will look at, users can run and view reports, drill-down, search, navigate through the report, export the report to multiple formats, and print the report or any part thereof using one of the standard report viewers, like the one shown in Figure 8.2.

FIGURE 8.2 Standard report viewer for Windows .NET applications.

All of the viewers for the different languages and SDKs offer a rich viewer object model that goes along with this integration method and allows you to control most aspects of the viewer and the report itself, including the look and feel of the viewer's toolbars and buttons as well as database logon information for the report, record selection formulas, and more.

Viewing Reports with Parameters

The next type of integration is driven by users who have more sophisticated requirements and want to select the data for their report at runtime using parameters. In this scenario the developer will create reports from the database with a number of parameters used to filter the report for just what the user wants to see.

This view-with-parameters method is just as easy as creating the view-only integration; in fact, the code is exactly the same—Crystal Reports actually handles the parameter dialog boxes and report filtering for you. An example of the same Windows application shown with the standard Crystal Reports parameter dialog boxes appears in Figure 8.3.

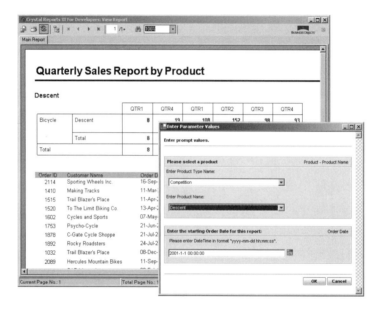

FIGURE 8.3   Viewing a report with parameters in a Windows .NET application.

In previous versions of Crystal Reports, only static pick lists were available for parameters. Most application developers built their own custom frontend to display values from a database and pass these values to the Crystal Reports parameters behind the scenes. With Crystal Reports XI, we now have dynamic and cascading parameters, and the parameter dialog boxes have been improved, reducing the need to create a custom user interface.

Another option to consider is the use of stored procedures, which can have their own parameter fields. We'll discuss using stored procedures a little later when working with databases, but you can use a stored procedure as the data source for your report. When the report is run, the user is prompted for any parameters that are required by the stored procedure. This is another way you can leverage the standard dialog boxes to create dynamic reports that are easy to develop and maintain.

Advanced Integration

Because two three options don't cover every integration scenario for developers who may be integrating Crystal Reports into their application, a third category, which we will label Advanced Integration, covers developers who need complete control over the report that is presented and use the API to excise control of the report at runtime.

These advanced methods could include creating a custom report viewer to embed into your application, using the report part viewers to view only a part or section of a report, or using any of the advanced features in the Crystal Reports APIs for working with reports.

The chart shown in Figure 8.4 shows a breakdown of how often each of these integration methods is used.

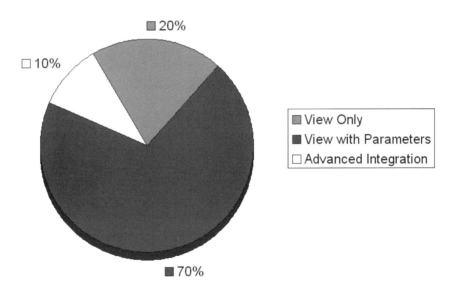

FIGURE 8.4   Report integration methods.

So why is viewing a report with parameters so popular? It turns out it is an easy way for application developers to aim for the middle of the road, between catering to user requirements and keeping development time to a minimum. A few applications are created solely for reporting, so this method enables developers to quickly integrate the reporting components and then get on with developing the application itself.

In addition, with the new parameter features in Crystal Reports XI, it is now possible to offer users dynamic lists of values from which to select without any additional coding required. And if you have worked with Crystal Reports before, you will appreciate the time that has gone into redesigning the parameter dialog boxes, which are now a viable user interface for entering parameters that doesn't require any form development or behind-the-scenes code to work.

The best place to start is with either the simple view-only integration or by allowing users to view reports with parameters. The cost of these two methods is very low because only a few lines of code are required to view the report, with the benefit of having Crystal Reports handle all of the parameter dialog boxes, dynamic pick lists, and passing of values and filtering of your report data.

If you are considering some of the advanced integration techniques to create a custom viewer and tightly integrate reporting into your application, it is recommended that you carefully consider the user requirements and review the technical specifications before getting started. One of the most common problems found when creating complex custom reporting applications is that the scope of the work is not clearly defined.

For example, the author has worked on applications where the report specifications include a parameter dialog at the top of the report, with the parameter fields running down two to three columns and the report itself shown in the bottom half of the page. After working for a week or so on a prototype for this user interface, it was discovered that the end-user who requested the report never actually requested the specific user interface shown in the specification—it was created as a "mock-up" only. After showing the end-user the standard parameter screens and report viewer, they were quite happy to use the standard dialogs and cut down on development costs. Often this will be the case, with the cost outweighing the real benefit that is delivered.

If after a thorough evaluation you are convinced that custom coding is required to deliver a specific report, take a step back and think about not only this report but also all of the other reports you plan to integrate into your application. If you are going to create a custom user interface, can this UI be shared with other reports?

If so, try to plan for a component-based architecture where the same dialog boxes and code can be reused with multiple reports. The last thing you want to do is find you have an application with 20 reports integrated, each with its custom form for entering parameters, viewing reports, and so on. A little bit of planning now can help you save time in the long run.

SELECTING YOUR DATA SOURCE

After you have some idea of how you want the integration to work, you need to get some reports. Before you can get down to actually designing the reports, you need to determine the data source for the reports. The diagram shown in Figure 8.5 outlines some of the approaches we will be looking at in the following sections.

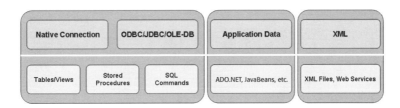

FIGURE 8.5   Data source options.

Native versus ODBC Database Access

The most common type of data source is a database, with reports developed from the tables, views, and so on that are contained within the database. Databases can be accessed either through a translation layer (like ODBC, JDBC, OLE-DB, and so on) or through native access.

Crystal Reports XI Professional and Developer Editions ship with a number of ODBC and native drivers for most popular relational database platforms. In addition, ODBC and JDBC are both standard interfaces for accessing data, so if a driver is not included with Crystal Reports for your database platform, an ODBC driver is probably available from the vendor or a third party.

The native database drivers in Crystal Reports have been provided for direct access to data sources and don't require the translation layer in the middle. Some of these data sources have been developed in conjunction with a database or application vendor to ensure quick, reliable access to the data you need.

Table 8.1 displays some of the most commonly used data sources and indicates which access methods are supported for each.

TABLE 8.1 Common Data Sources Used with Crystal Reports

Database	Native	ODBC	JDBC	OLE-DB
Oracle 8.17	X	X	X	X
Oracle 9.2	X	X	X	X
Oracle 10.1	X	X	X	X
IBM DB2 8.1	X	X	X	X
IBM DB2 8.2	X	X	X	X
Sybase ASE 12.5	X	X		
Teradata v2R5, R6		X		
Microsoft SQL Server 2000 SP3		X	X	X
Microsoft SQL Server 7.0 SP4		X		X
MySQL 4.0		X	X	
Microsoft Access 2000	X	X		X
Microsoft Access 2003	X	X		X
Microsoft Excel 2000	X	X		X
Microsoft Excel 2004	X	X		X
Microsoft Exchange	X			
ADO.NET	X			
JavaBeans™	X			
XML		X		
All Other ODBC Drivers		X		
All Other JDBC Drivers			X	

Just because your data source is not listed doesn't mean it won't work with Crystal Reports. A number of database and application providers have created ODBC, JDBC, and native drivers for use with Crystal Reports, and your database or application may be included. The best way to find out of a driver is available is to contact the vendor directly and ask.

Crystal Reports can also access a number of OLAP (Online Analytical Processing) data sources for reporting from multidimensional data. For a complete list, see the platforms.txt file included on the Crystal Reports installation CD-ROM.

Selecting a data source is one thing, but how you use it is another. When first starting out with Crystal Reports, most developers will use the tools in Crystal Reports to select database tables, specify links, pick fields, and so on and let Crystal Reports write the SQL for them. But for more control over the report results, you can also write your own SQL Command. The result set from that command can be used as the data source for your report.

The more experienced you become with Crystal Reports, the more you will mix these two methods—for simple reports, it is often quicker to let Crystal Reports write the SQL for you, but for complex requirements, it may be easier to get in there and write it yourself. Writing your own SQL Command also means that you can add parameter fields that are embedded in the SQL and run on the database server, making for more efficient coding.

And that's not to say that regular Crystal Reports parameter fields can't be passed to the database. There are instances where parameter values are passed through to the SQL statement, but parameters in SQL Commands are always passed to the database and are the most efficient method of filtering a report.

Another popular option is to create reports from database-stored procedures. With previous versions of Crystal Reports, before SQL Commands were introduced, this method was one of the only ones that developers could use to get complete control over the SQL and to increase report performance, because all of the processing could be pushed back to the database server itself. Stored procedures are still a popular and viable option for report data sources, because they bring so much more flexibility to the report developer. A stored procedure can pass parameters, perform advanced SQL processing that may not be possible in a SQL Command, and leverage cursors, looping, and so on for complex record processing.

Application Data

Another popular data source for reports is the data within the application itself. Often applications will use complex datasets behind the scenes to drive the application, and application developers may want to report from this data at runtime.

For example, if an application developer created an application with a data grid that contained a table of information, he may want to use Crystal Reports to print this information directly from the application data. This view-with-dynamic-data integration is a bit more complicated to code, but there is a definite benefit to using application data as the data source for your report—you don't have to go back to the database to get the data for the report.

With Crystal Reports XI, you can use data held in data sets stored in ADO.NET data sources, COM data providers, or JavaBeans, depending on your platform.

XML and XML Web Services

Another viable data source for your reports is XML files and XML Web services. Crystal Reports XI includes a flexible XML driver that can be used to report from both XML files stored locally and on a Web server and XML Web services. This data-access method provides a flexible alternative to reporting from a database or application data, because the Web service can be decoupled from the reporting application itself. With the push to more service-oriented architectures for applications, this method opens up a number of possibilities for working with data held both within and outside your organization.

If you have to choose between one of these database-access methods, your best bet would be to report from a database using ODBC or one of the other translation layers like JDBC or OLE-DB, because this is frequently the easiest method to use. In particular, ODBC drivers are easy to install and configure and can be tested by a number of different applications, so if a problem docs arise, it is easy to use a generic query tool, or even Excel, to test the ODBC driver and setup.

On the other hand, for maximizing the speed of database queries and the result sets that are returned, native access is the best method, and one of Crystal Reports's native drivers may be useful to you. Keep in mind that most of these native drivers require some supporting files or database client installed in order to work, which could add extra overhead and work for you.

With the last two data sources—application data and XML—the decision here is driven by the applications and services with which you are working. If your application performs a large amount of business logic or calculations that are used in the user interface, there is no reason to reinvent the wheel and create the same logic from scratch while developing your report. Likewise, if you have data that is stored in XML or that is available through an XML Web service, you should leverage this data to make report integration easier.

SELECTING A REPORTING ARCHITECTURE

One of the goals for any developer is to create applications that are scalable and can be accessed by multiple users. One of the key decisions that can make or break an application is the architecture behind the application. In the following sections we will look at some of the most common reporting architectures in use with Crystal Reports and Crystal Reports Server, including some of their advantages and trade-offs.

Thick-Client Application

A thick-client application is one in which the majority of application components are installed locally on a user's PC, as shown in Figure 8.6.

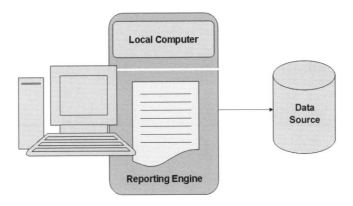

FIGURE 8.6 A thick-client application.

Most developers and users are familiar with this type of application because most Windows applications are thick-client ones. Although the majority of components may be on the local machine, thick-client applications can also be considered to be client-server applications because there is usually some backend database or application server that provides the data, business logic, and so on that the application requires.

In terms of Crystal Reports, a thick-client application is one that is installed locally and includes the report engine to process reports on the local PC. Crystal Reports has featured a free runtime license for a number of versions, so a number of commercial applications use this architecture to integrate reports into applications.

One of the advantages of distributing reports using this architecture is that everything that is required to view a report is installed locally. Another advantage is that users can view and interact with reports on their local machine, including reports created from local data sources. This enables developers to create standalone applications that don't require a backend server to process reports.

The disadvantage of this type of architecture is that the reports all run locally, so users may have to wait for a report to process. In addition, distributing a thick-client application requires distributing a number of Crystal Reports runtime components; in the past, this process has not always been a smooth one. If you move to a new version of Crystal Reports, you must update each application and its runtime files and redistribute it to users.

With that said, thick-client applications are here to stay (just look at Microsoft Office), and there will always be the need for reporting to be embedded into these applications. Choose this architecture type if your application is going to be installed locally on each user's machine and if local report processing is not an issue.

Single-Tier Application

A single-tier application adds an additional layer to the mix, with a backend server (usually a Web server) used to process reports and display the results, as shown in Figure 8.7.

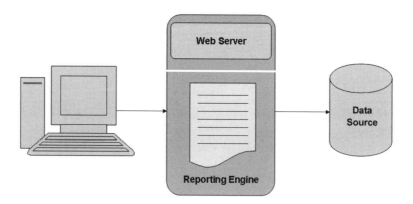

FIGURE 8.7   A single-tier application.

This type of reporting application grew out of a set of legacy tools available with Crystal Reports that were used to create Web applications. They caused an entire generation of application developers to question whether Crystal Reports could be used as a scalable solution for Web applications. Often this was a case not so much of Crystal Report's capabilities but of selecting the right toolset and architecture.

The problem with these traditional single-tier applications is that all of the report processing would occur on the same Web server where the application itself was running. As a result, this would often bring the primary application to a screeching halt because the report-processing time would often interfere with the application itself.

For scalability and a host of other reasons, this type of architecture is not recommended beyond small- to medium-sized applications. That is not to say that you need multiple servers to create a scalable reporting application. What you do need, however, is a component-based architecture that can expand as required to push processing to other servers and services, as shown in our next architecture, the multitiered application.

Multitiered Applications

For true scalability to hundreds or thou0sands of users, you should consider developing a multitiered application, like the one shown in Figure 8.8.

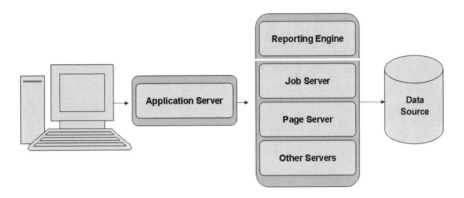

FIGURE 8.8   Multitiered architecture.

In a multitiered application, the components that actually process and render the report are compartmentalized, which allows you to add additional components or separate these components onto additional servers as the demand for reports grows.

This type of architecture is supported through the use of Crystal Reports Server and BusinessObjects Enterprise, which both have been built on the same underlying servers and framework. By utilizing backend servers to process reports, you can take the processing load off of your application server and provide better performance to reporting users. In addition, both of the server products mentioned include a host of other features and functionality that go beyond simply viewing reports. The two servers also provide batch scheduling, security, report distribution, and more.

Which of these architectures you decide to use depends on the type of application you plan to create. For Windows applications that will be installed locally on each user's computer, you will probably be using the thick-client approach and will distribute the runtime files required to view and work with reports.

For most small- to medium-sized Web applications, most developers will choose to use the single-tier model and will leave the reporting components on the same server as the application. This decision is often due to the cost involved with purchasing the additional servers and software required to implement a multitiered application. There is also a large reliance on the "wait and see" method, to see how reports affect server and application performance before moving to a multitiered solution. The key factor that most people will overlook in this exercise is that a little bit of planning goes a long way. If you believe that your application will require a more robust backend for processing reports, or if you can leverage the functionality provided through the associated server technology, plan from the start for a multitiered application.

You could even start the project with all of the components on a single server, which could also be the same server where your application is running. The advantage of planning for a multitiered solution from the start is that when the time comes to scale your application, you are simply adding servers instead of redeveloping the entire application and recutting code.

SUMMARY

No single chapter of a book can cover all of the different ways you can integrate Crystal Reports into your application. The purpose of this chapter was to get you thinking about the "how" as opposed to the "how-to," which is covered in the following chapters for the different languages and platforms that Crystal Reports supports. Most importantly, you should remember the two areas where most developers run into problems integrating Crystal Reports.

The first is that you need to start with the basics and then move on from there—don't try to create a complex application when a simple one would meet users' requirements. As your skills and experience increase, you can add on features and functionality, but get the basics right and everything that follows will be easy.

The second is that some forethought and planning go a long way. Time and time again, developers have just thrown together some reports, downloaded some sample code, and tried to make everything work—and they failed miserably. Sit down at the start of your project and plan your integration method, find where the data for your reports resides, decide how you are going to access that data, and pick an architecture that will support your application through its entire lifecycle. Don't be afraid to test your thoughts and ideas during this process by developing reports and stub applications as a proof of concept.

For example, if you are trying to decide between two different data drivers or access methods, create a simple report using each method and test it out for yourself. Likewise, if you want to create your own custom viewer, try creating a stub application and working with the API. The lessons learned during this proof of concept phase will help make the key decisions that will make your report integration go smoothly.

But enough about that already—at this point, you are probably dying to get into the code. And that is where we pick up in the next chapter—integrating reports into Windows applications created with Visual Studio .NET.

9 Integrating Reports into Windows Applications

In This Chapter

- Getting Started
- Working with the Report Viewer Object Model
- Working with the Report Document Object Model

INTRODUCTION

Over the past few years Windows applications have dominated the desktop software market, covering most personal and business applications, with everything from word processors, spreadsheets, databases, and presentation programs to special-purpose business applications for managing customers, finances, inventory, and more. Most of these business applications manage large amounts of data and make it easier to turn this data into useful information. A common requirement for these types of applications is the ability to present this information in a clear, concise format—and that is where Crystal Reports comes in.

One company that recognized the power and flexibility of using a tool like Crystal Reports was Microsoft. Crystal Reports has been part of the Microsoft development platform since Crystal Reports 2.0 was shipped with Visual Basic 3.0 in

1993. Over the years a version of Crystal Reports has been included with each new version of the Microsoft development platform, right up to Visual Studio .NET 2003 and later.

The main focus of this chapter is on integrating Crystal Reports into Windows applications created using Visual Studio .NET 2003 and the .NET framework. Although Crystal Reports can be used with a number of different development tools and platforms that can create Windows applications, Visual Studio .NET—and in particular, the .NET framework—provides a rich development environment for creating robust Windows applications.

ON THE CD

And if you are developing applications using another toolset that supports the .NET framework (like Delphi 2005), don't despair! This chapter includes code examples written in VB .NET and on the CD-ROM we have provided the sample applications also written in C#, so you use the same code in your own application even without Visual Studio .NET.

NOTE

Some developers are still using Visual Basic 6.0 to develop applications and aren't likely to move across to Visual Studio .NET anytime soon. (It's the old concept of "If it ain't broke, don't fix it.") So, if you are still developing applications using VB6 and want to integrate Crystal Reports using the legacy RDC component, a list of resources, tutorials, and links to sample applications are available on the Web site accompanying this book (www.crystalxibook.com).

The examples and walk-throughs in this chapter assume that you have Visual Studio .NET 2003 installed with the correct language option enabled. In addition, it is assumed that you have Crystal Reports XI Developer Edition installed on the same machine. Having this will update the OEM version of Crystal Reports that is included with Visual Studio .NET 2003, so you can edit any reports embedded in your project directly from within the IDE. Alternatively, if you would like to use the standalone report designer, right-click your report and select Open With to open the dialog box shown in Figure 9.1.

Select the option for crw32. You can edit your report using the standalone report designer that ships with Crystal Reports XI.

Another important note is that the majority of the sample reports used in this chapter are based on the Xtreme Sample Database 11, which is an Access database that is installed and configured by default when Crystal Reports is installed. In addition to this sample database, some of the examples show code that is specific for SQL Server, Oracle, and other databases. You will need to have the correct database platform and sample databases installed and configured for these examples to work.

ON THE CD

All of the sample applications and reports are located on the CD-ROM that accompanies this book. You can find also find additional samples and code at the companion Web site at *www.crystalxibook.com*.

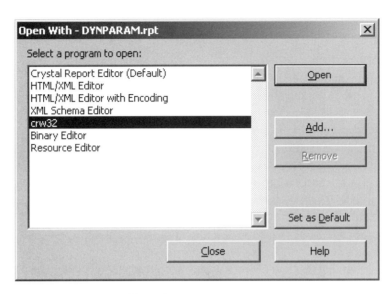

FIGURE 9.1 Open With options.

GETTING STARTED

With Crystal Reports XI, you can use two main object models to integrate reporting into your .NET application. The first is the `CrystalReportViewer` object model, which provides all of the properties, methods, and events you will need to view your report and some simple customization of the report at runtime. This object model is aimed primarily at viewing reports and passing a few simple options to control the report output. For complete control over the report, you will need to use the `ReportDocument` object model, which provides a rich set of properties, methods, and events that you can use to work with the report itself.

Which object model you decide to use depends on the type of application you want to create. In Chapter 8, we looked at the different types of integration methods that you could use in your applications, including view only, view with parameters, and so on. For these simple applications, the `CrystalReportViewer` object model is a good choice because it provides the basic options you will need to preview, print, and export reports from your application. You can also pass parameters to the viewer using this object model as well as log on to secure databases.

If you have more complex integration requirements, such as passing ADO or ADO.NET data sets to the report, printing to a specific printer or printer tray, exporting to a specific format, and controlling formula fields and report formatting, you will need to use the `ReportDocument` object model.

In this chapter we will look first at the `CrystalReportViewer` object model and run through its features and functionality. In the second half of the chapter, we will look at the `ReportDocument` object model and see what it has to offer. There will be some duplication of topics as we go through each of the object models—for example, when we look at working with parameter fields a section near the front of the chapter discusses how they work with the `CrystalReportViewer` object model. Toward the end of the chapter, you may see the same topic again, only this time covering how parameters work with the `ReportDocument` object model and any advanced features this object model provides.

It is important to stress at this point that you should never mix the two object models. If you do have a look through the `CrystalReportViewer` object model and decide that you need more control over the report, make sure that you write all of your code using the `ReportDocument` object model and use the `CrystalReportViewer` object model only to view the resulting report.

Mixing the two object models is not only a bad programming practice, it also can lead to unpredictable results when running reports, especially if you set some properties in one object model and some properties in the other.

WORKING WITH THE REPORT VIEWER OBJECT MODEL

Two components are involved in viewing a report using the `CrystalReportViewer` object model. The first is a .NET control that you can drag and drop onto your Windows forms; the second is the actual code behind it that controls the appearance and behavior of the viewer itself. You can use the properties, methods, and events associated with the object model to control both the report and the viewer itself.

Throughout the rest of this section, we will be looking at some of the most common customizations that developers make to the viewer and how it is used with their reports, including previewing, printing, and exporting reports as well as passing parameters and more. These customizations are grouped together logically based on their function, making it easier to find what you need.

For a complete list of all of the properties, methods, and events in the `Crystal ReportViewer` *object model, use Visual Studio .NET's Object Browser to browse through the class under the CrystalDecisions.Windows.Forms namespace.*

Previewing Your Report

You need only one line of code to view a report from your application. To view a report in your application, all you will need to do is drag the `CrystalReportsViewer` onto your form and set the `ReportSource` property.

You can set this property either through the property page associated with the viewer itself or through a single line of code. The latter is actually the preferred method, because you may want to use this same form to view a different report later.

This process is called binding, and it is simply the process of associating a report with the viewer itself. Crystal Reports supports a number of methods you can use to bind reports to the viewer. In the following example, we are going to use the file-name method, in which you will specify a filename and path to the report with which you want to work. All of the examples in the first half of the chapter will use this method. In the second half of the chapter, when we look at using the Report Document *object model, we will look at some different binding methods you can use to embed reports directly into your application.*

When you build and run your application, the form and report viewer will be displayed with a preview of your report. To see this one line of code in action, use the following steps:

1. From the Start menu, open Visual Studio .NET 2003.
2. Click File > New > Project.
3. From the New Project window, click the Visual Basic Projects folder, and then select Windows Application.

If you are developing in C#, don't worry— A C# version of each of the sample projects in this chapter is also provided on the accompanying CD-ROM.

4. Enter a name and location for your project, and click OK. For this example, we have called the project VB_ViewReport. A new project will open with a blank Windows form.
5. Click View > Toolbox and locate the CrystalReportViewer control. Drag the control onto your form, and set the Dock property of the viewer to Fill.
6. Next, double-click the form to access the code behind it, and add the following line in the Form Load subroutine. The sample report, ROSTER.RPT, is included in the PROJECTS folder on the CD-ROM. You may need to modify the file location depending on where you have saved this file.

VB .NET:

```
CrystalReportViewer1.ReportSource = "d:\projects\roster.rpt"
```

7. Finally, click Debug > Start or press the F5 key to start your application. The form opens, and the viewer that you added earlier should now display the Employee Roster report, as shown in Figure 9.2.

FIGURE 9.2 A simple report preview.

For some developers, this may be the only line of code you need, depending on the level of report integration you are trying to achieve. By default, the viewer is displayed with a toolbar at the top that includes the following buttons:

Export: Opens the Save dialog box, which you can use to export your report to Word, Excel, PDF, and so on

Print: Opens the print dialog box

Refresh: Refreshes the report against the database

Group Tree: Shows or hides the group tree on the left side of the report

Page Navigation Buttons: Provides navigation through report pages

Find: Opens the Find dialog box for entering text to find in the report

Zoom: Controls the magnification factor

Chances are, you may want to use the viewer just as it is, but you can customize the look and feel of the viewer using some options that we will look at in the next section.

Modifying Viewer Appearance

The viewer itself has a number of properties that you can use to set different options for controlling its appearance. The first set of properties has to do with the overall appearance of the viewer; the second set deals with specific icons that appear on the viewer's toolbar.

The first set of properties are shown in Table 9.1.

TABLE 9.1   Viewer Properties

Method	Description	Type
`DisplayToolbar`	Controls whether to display the toolbar at the top of the viewer	Boolean
`DisplayBackGroundEdge`	Controls the border that appears around the viewer	Boolean
`DisplayGroupTree`	Controls the display of the group tree on the left side of the viewer	Boolean

If you wanted to hide either the group tree or the viewer's toolbar, you could add the following code to the Form Load code we looked at earlier:

VB .NET:

```
CrystalReportViewer1.DisplayGroupTree = False
CrystalReportViewer1.DisplayToolbar = False
```

If you use this code to turn off the group tree and toolbar, the report viewer would now look like the one shown in Figure 9.3.

As mentioned earlier in the chapter, the viewer provides two sets of properties for controlling its appearance and functionality. This second property set is for controlling the individual icons that appear on the toolbar. By controlling the icons on the toolbar, you also control how users interact with the report. For example, if you don't display a print button, users won't be able to print their reports from the viewer.

FIGURE 9.3 The report viewer minus the group tree and toolbar.

These properties follow:

- ShowCloseButton
- ShowExportButton
- ShowGotoPageButton
- ShowGroupTreeButton
- ShowPageNavigationButtons
- ShowPrintButton
- ShowRefreshButton
- ShowTextSearchButton

All of these properties are Boolean, so to hide the Print button from our earlier example, the code would look like the following example:

VB. NET:

```
CrystalReportViewer1.ShowPrintButton = False
```

When you view your report, the viewer would now omit the Print button, as shown in Figure 9.4.

FIGURE 9.4   The report viewer minus the Print button.

Printing and Exporting Your Report

Now that you can control the appearance of the report viewer, it's time to look at the methods available to invoke different actions from the viewer. The first of these actions we are going to look at is printing your report using the aptly named `Print Report` method. Although the report viewer itself features a print button that users can click to print a report, you may want to invoke the print dialog box from another location, such as the main menu.

In this example, we create a form, add the report viewer, and then add a main menu and a Print Report option on the File menu. When a user clicks File > Print Report, the standard Windows print dialog box will open and allow the user to select a printer, the number of copies to printed, and so on.

To create this application, use the following steps:

1. From the Start menu, open Visual Studio .NET 2003.
2. Click File > New > Project.
3. From the New Project window, click the Visual Basic Projects folder, and then select Windows Application.
4. Enter a name and location for your project, and click OK. For this example, we have called the project VB_ViewReport.
5. A new project opens with a blank Windows form. Click View > Toolbox and locate the `MainMenu` control. Drag the control onto your form. In the Type Here box, type File. In the box that appears below it, type Print Report, as shown in Figure 9.5.
6. Next, locate the `CrystalReportViewer` control in the toolbox, and drag the control onto your form. Set the `Dock` property of the viewer to `Fill`.
7. Next, double-click the form to access the code behind it, and add the following line in the Form Load subroutine. The sample report, ROSTER.RPT, is included in the PROJECTS folder on the CD-ROM. You may need to modify the file location, depending on where you have saved this file.

ON THE CD

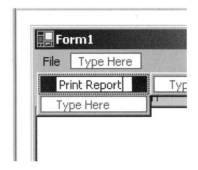

FIGURE 9.5. Your form with the main menu control added and configured.

VB .NET:

```
CrystalReportViewer1.ReportSource = "d:\projects\roster.rpt"
```

8. Back on your form, double-click the Print Report option on your main menu, and enter the following code:

VB .NET:

```
CrystalReportViewer1.PrintReport()
```

9. Click Debug > Start or press the F5 key to start your application. The form opens and displays your report. When you click File > Print Report, the standard Windows print dialog box appears, as shown in Figure 9.6.
10. Save your project as VB_PrintExportReport; we will continue this project in the next section.

In addition to printing your report, you also can export your report using the ExportReport method. This method will open a standard Windows Save As dialog box, which will allow you to select your export format as well as enter a file name and location for the exported file.

Remember, there are two different object models you can use to interact with your report. This is the method that is included with the CrystalReportViewer *object model. If you want more control over the export process, you could use the* ReportDocument *object model to export your report and control the export format and settings.*

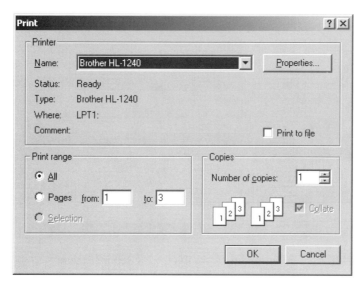

FIGURE 9.6 The `PrintReport` method in action.

To add export functionality to your application, use the following steps:

■ From the Start menu, open Visual Studio .NET 2003.

■ Click File > Open > Project.

■ Open the VB_PrintExportReport project you were working with earlier in this section.

■ On your form's design, locate the main menu control you added earlier. Below the Print Report option, in the Type Here box, enter the text Export Report.

■ Next, double-click the Export Report menu option to open the code view to show the code behind this menu option.

■ Enter the following code:

VB .NET:

```
CrystalReportViewer1.ExportReport()
```

■ Click Debug > Start or press the F5 key to start your application. The form opens and displays your report. When you click File > Export Report, the standard Windows Save As dialog appears.

■ Use the Save as type drop-down list at the bottom of the dialog box to select your export format, as shown in Figure 9.7.

■ Enter a file name for your exported file, and click the Save button to save the file.

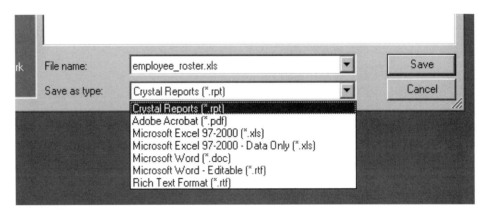

FIGURE 9.7 Export options from the Crystal Reports viewer.

The CrystalReportViewer object model supports the following export file types:

■ Crystal Reports (.rpt)
■ Adobe Acrobat (.pdf)
■ Microsoft Excel 97–2000 (.xls)
■ Microsoft Excel 92–2000 Data Only (.xls)
■ Microsoft Word (.doc)
■ Microsoft Word—Editable (.rtf)
■ Rich Text Format (.rtf)

The difference between the two Excel formats is that the default Excel format will attempt to retain the formatting that is present in your report, whereas the Data Only option will export only the data that is in your report and will not include the report formatting.

The other format that may not be familiar to you is the editable Microsoft Word format. This option is new for Crystal Reports XI. It produces an RTF document that you can edit in Word. In previous versions of Crystal Reports, the Word export option created a document that had the same formatting as the report but used text boxes and other tricks to get the formatting right, making it almost impossible to edit.

For complete control over the export processing or to create a custom interface, see the second half of this chapter, which illustrates how to export using the Report Document *object model.*

Modifying Report Record Selection

Record selection is the process Crystal Reports uses to filter report records. It accomplishes this through the use of a record-selection formula, such as the following example:

```
{Customer.Country} = "USA"
```

Record-selection formulas are written using Crystal syntax and can be created either when you design the report or at runtime when you are viewing the report. You can view any record selection currently in use in your reports by opening the report in Crystal Reports and clicking Report > Selection Formulas > Record. The Record Selection Formula Editor, shown in Figure 9.8, opens.

FIGURE 9.8 The Record Selection Formula Editor.

Any record selection you create in this tool is saved with your report. When integrating reports into your application, you can two different properties to set the record selection at runtime. The first property, `SelectionFormula`, can be used to get or set the record-selection formula. This property can be used to overwrite any existing record selection that is present in the report, in effect giving you complete control over the records that are returned.

The second property, `ViewTimeSelectionFormula`, is used to append a record-selection formula onto the existing record-selection formula used in the report.

For example, if your report already had an existing record selection of

```
{Customer.Country} = "USA"
```

and you were to use the `ViewTimeSelectionFormula` property to set the record-selection formula to bring back a specific state in Australia, as follows:

```
{Customer.State} = "NSW"
```

the resulting record-selection formula would become

```
{Customer.Country} = "USA" AND {Customer.State} = "NSW"
```

This combination would not actually bring back any records—the first part of the record selection would look for all customers who are in the United States, whereas the second part would look for customers who are in the state of New South Wales. Therefore, you need to be careful if you plan to use the `ViewTime SelectionFormula` property, because you could end up not showing any records at all if the formula doesn't work out correctly.

Let's look at an application that sets the record-selection formula at runtime. To create this application, use the following steps:

■ From the Start menu, open Visual Studio .NET 2003.

1. Click File > New > Project.
2. From the New Project window, click the Visual Basic Projects folder, and then select Windows Application.
3. Enter a name and location for your project, and click OK. For this example, we have called the project VB_RecordSelection.
4. A new project opens with a blank Windows form. Click View > Toolbox and locate the `CrystalReportViewer` control. Drag the control onto your form and set the `Dock` property to `Fill`. Set the Dock Padding > Top property to 100. This will give us some room at the top of the form to add drop-down boxes to use to set the record-selection formula.
5. Next, double-click the form to access the code behind it, and add the following line in the Form Load subroutine. The sample report, DYNSE-LECT.RPT, is included in the PROJECTS folder on the CD-ROM. You may need to modify the file location depending on where you have saved this file.

ON THE CD

VB .NET:

```
CrystalReportViewer1.ReportSource = "d:\projects\dynselect.rpt"
CrystalReportViewer1.DisplayGroupTree = False
```

6. Now with the report viewer control in place and the report source set, you can do a quick check to make sure that you can preview your report. Click Debug > Start or press the F5 key to start your application. The form opens and displays your report.

7. Next, you will need to drag a label, a combo box, and a button from the toolbox onto the top of your form, placing the objects as shown in Figure 9.9.

FIGURE 9.9   The toolbox items in place on your form.

8. Change the label text to read Select a Country. Change the Combo Box text to read All Countries. Finally, change the Button text to read View Report. Your form should now look something like the one shown in Figure 9.10.

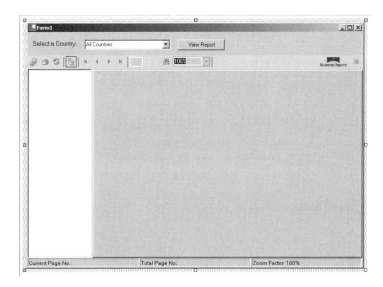

FIGURE 9.10   The finished form.

9. Now we want to give the users some countries to select from, so select the properties of the Combo Box, and edit the Items property to include the following collection items:

- USA
- Australia
- Canada
- Mexico

Additional countries are represented in the report, but we are looking at a quick example here. If this were a real application, you would probably want to dynamically connect to the underlying database table to populate this list.

10. With the list of countries complete, we need to go add some code behind the View Report button to create the record-selection formula and pass it to our report. Double-click the View Report button to switch to the code view, and add the following code behind the form:

VB .NET:

```
If ComboBox1.Text = "All Countries" Then
    CrystalReportViewer1.SelectionFormula = ""
Else
    CrystalReportViewer1.SelectionFormula = "{Customer.
    Country} = '" & ComboBox1.Text & "'"
End If
CrystalReportViewer1.RefreshReport()
```

11. Finally, click Debug > Start or press the F5 key to start your application. The form opens and displays your report. You can use the combo box to select a country. When you click the View Report button, your record selection will be applied and your report refreshed.

This is just a simple example of how record selection can be used. You could create a record-selection formula as complex as you require.

Working with Parameter Fields

If you read through the first section of this book and followed along with the projects, you have probably already seen the Crystal Reports parameter dialog boxes. These dialog boxes are a dramatic improvement over those offered in previous versions of Crystal Reports. They can use both dynamic and cascading parameters so that you can read values from a data source and then pass the selected values back to your report.

These enhanced parameter fields and dialog boxes make using the default user interface (shown in Figure 9.11) a viable option for developers who have simple integration requirements.

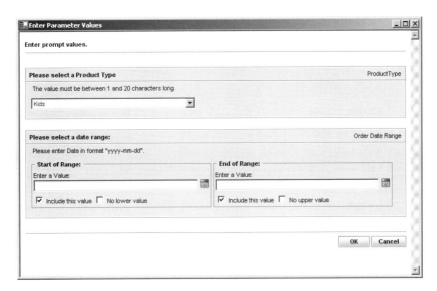

FIGURE 9.11   Default Crystal Reports parameter dialog boxes.

If you need more control over the parameter dialog box or if you want to create a custom dialog box, you will need to pass the parameter values to the report viewer using the `ParameterField` class. This class contains the properties you will need to retrieve and set parameter information at runtime. Also, there is another class called `ParameterFields` (note the plural), which holds all of the parameter fields in your report.

To start working with parameter fields, we are going to look at how to retrieve information from the report about the parameter fields in your report.

Retrieving Parameter Field Information

In addition to setting parameter field information, you can also retrieve information about the parameter fields in your report. Their basic properties include the following:

Name: Name of the parameter.

ReportParameterType: Type of parameter (string, date, and so on)

ParameterValueType: Type of value expected by the parameter (string, date, and so on).

PromptText: Text that is displayed to the user when the parameter prompts the user for a value (for example, "Please enter a state").

ReportName: Name of the report or subreport where the parameter appears. If it appears in the main report, this property will be blank.

HasCurrentValue: Indicates whether this parameter has a default value associated with it.

MinimumValue: Returns the parameter's minimum value that will be accepted.

MaximumValue: Returns the parameter's maximum value that will be accepted.

EditMask: A mask representing the excepted input, format, and any other place-holders, used to ensure the correct value is entered.

By reading these properties, we can retrieve information about the parameter and then use this information to build and populate a custom parameter dialog box, using the parameter definition from the report with which we are working.

To demonstrate how these properties work, in our next example we are going to retrieve some of the properties and display these properties in a message box from your application. This project will lay the groundwork for the rest of the projects in this section as we work through different parameter features. To get started, use the following steps:

From the Start menu, open Visual Studio .NET 2003.

1. Click File > New > Project.
2. From the New Project window, click the Visual Basic Projects folder, and then select Windows Application.
3. Enter a name and location for your project, and click OK. For this example, we have called the project VB_Parameters.
4. A new project will open with a blank Windows form. Click View > Toolbox and locate the CrystalReportViewer control. Drag the control onto your form, and set the Dock property to Fill. Set the Dock Padding > Top property to 100. This will give us some room at the top of the form to add some extra features later.
5. Next, double-click the form to access the code behind it, and add the following line in the Form Load subroutine. The sample report, PARAMINFO.RPT, is included in the PROJECTS folder on the CD-ROM.

ON THE CD

You may need to modify the file location depending on where you have saved this file.

VB .NET:

```
CrystalReportViewer1.ReportSource = "d:\projects\paraminfo.rpt"
CrystalReportViewer1.DisplayGroupTree = False
```

6. Now, with the report viewer control in place and the report source set, you can do a quick check to make sure that you can preview your report. Click Debug > Start or press the F5 key to start your application. The form opens and displays your report.

7. Our next order of business is declaring some variables so we can access the `ParameterFields` collection and each `ParameterField` so we can read some of the properties associated with each. Double-click your form to open the code view, and enter the following code in the Form Load section below your `ReportSource` declaration:

VB .NET:

```
    Dim ParameterFields As CrystalDecisions.Shared.ParameterFields
    Dim ParameterField As CrystalDecisions.Shared.ParameterField
    ParameterFields = CrystalReportViewer1.ParameterFieldInfo
    Dim DisplayText
 For Each ParameterField In ParameterFields
    DisplayText = "Parameter Name: " & ParameterField.Name & Chr(13)
    DisplayText = DisplayText & "Parameter Type: " &
    ParameterField.ReportParameterType.ToString & Chr(13)
    DisplayText = DisplayText & "Parameter Value Type: " &
    ParameterField.ParameterValueType.ToString & Chr(13)
    DisplayText = DisplayText & "Prompting Text: " &
    ParameterField.PromptText & Chr(13)
    DisplayText = DisplayText & "Report Name: " &
    ParameterField.ReportName & Chr(13)
    DisplayText = DisplayText & "Has Current Value: " &
    ParameterField.HasCurrentValue & Chr(13)
    DisplayText = DisplayText & "Minimum Value: " &
    ParameterField.MinimumValue & Chr(13)
    DisplayText = DisplayText & "Maximum Value: " &
    ParameterField.MaximumValue & Chr(13)
    DisplayText = DisplayText & "Edit Mask: " &
    ParameterField.EditMask & Chr(13)
    MsgBox(DisplayText)
 Next
```

8. Click Debug > Start or press the F5 key to start your application. A message box like the one shown in Figure 9.12 opens and displays information about the parameter fields in your report.

FIGURE 9.12   Parameter field information displayed in a message box.

9. Click OK to continue. Enter a parameter value, and click OK to view the report.

Save your project as VB_Parameters.

You will notice that immediately after the message box appears, the report viewer prompts you for your parameter value. Remember, at this point we are just retrieving information about the parameter but haven't set any parameter values—that is covered in the next section.

10. These simple properties give you a first glimpse into working with parameters. You could use the same technique to populate an array of information about each parameter in your report and build a custom user interface to match the parameters. Or you could store this information in a database table and define prompting dialog boxes or a wizard to prompt the user for parameter values.

11. But before we get too far, we need to dig a bit deeper into working with parameters. In our next example, we will see how to access the current and default values stored with your parameter fields, to help you start to build a custom user interface for selecting values.

Retrieving and Setting Discrete Parameter Values

When you create parameter fields in Crystal Reports, you can create a static list of values from which the user can select when the report is run. This list, called the *default values* for the parameter, can consist of a description and a value.

For example, if you had a State parameter, you could create default values that included a description of New York and a value of NY, which is actually what is passed to the parameter. In addition to creating default values in Crystal Reports, you can also select the sort method used when displaying these values. These default values are entered when you create the parameter in Crystal Reports, as shown in Figure 9.13.

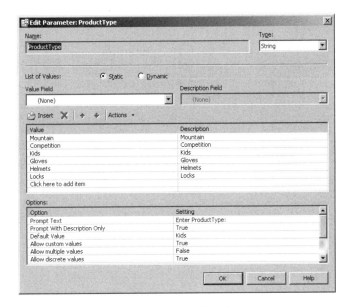

FIGURE 9.13 Setting up default values for a parameter.

When the user is prompted to enter a parameter, this list of default values will be shown. When you actually enter a value into a parameter field (either from the default values or by typing it in yourself), these values are considered the current value, and depending on the type of parameter, there may be one value or multiple values. An example of the default Crystal Reports parameter dialog box showing both the current and multiple default values is shown in Figure 9.14.

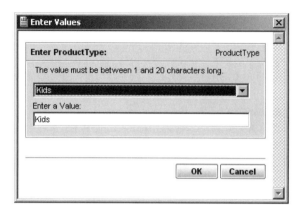

FIGURE 9.14 Current and multiple default values.

To demonstrate how to work with parameter fields, to the project we just worked on we will add a drop-down list to display these default values, as well as pass the value selected to your report as the current value. Because this is such a big project, we are going to break it into two parts, starting first with retrieving the default and current values from your report.

To retrieve the default values, we are going to read through a collection of values called `DefaultValues` and then use those values to populate a combo box at the top of our form. Once we have filled the combo box with these values, the user can then select a parameter value and click a button to run the report again, passing the parameter value to the report.

In this example, the report has only a single parameter, which makes our job a bit easier. In addition, the parameter field was defined as a discrete parameter, so it expects only one value to be returned. A little later in this section we will look at how to pass other parameter value types to your report, but for now, use the following steps to retrieve and set your parameter field:

1. From the Start menu, open Visual Studio .NET 2003.
2. Click File > Open > Project.
3. Open the VB_Parameters project you were working with earlier in this section.
4. At the top of your form, add a label, a combo box, and a button. Change the combo box text to be blank, and change the text on the button to read View Report. Your form should now look like the one shown in Figure 9.15.

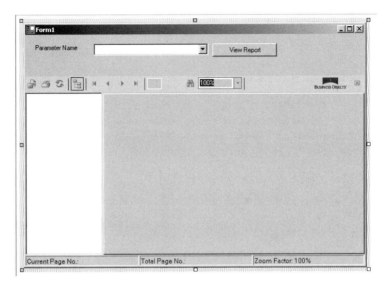

FIGURE 9.15   The completed form.

5. Double-click your form to open the code view, and replace the code in the Form Load section with the following code:

VB .NET:

```
CrystalReportViewer1.ReportSource = "d:\projects\DYNPARAM.rpt"
CrystalReportViewer1.DisplayGroupTree = False
ParameterFields = CrystalReportViewer1.ParameterFieldInfo

ParameterField = ParameterFields(0)
Label1.Text = ParameterField.PromptText

Dim i
For i = 0 To (ParameterField.DefaultValues.Count - 1)
ComboBox1.Items.Add(ParameterField.DefaultValues.Item(i).
Description)
Next

ParameterDiscreteValue = New
CrystalDecisions.Shared.ParameterDiscreteValue
ParameterDiscreteValue.Value = " "
ParameterField.CurrentValues.Add(ParameterDiscreteValue)
```

6. Double-click the View Report button you placed on your form, and enter the following code:

VB .NET:

```
CrystalReportViewer1.ReportSource = "d:\projects\DYNPARAM.rpt"
ParameterFields = CrystalReportViewer1.ParameterFieldInfo
ParameterField = ParameterFields(0)
ParameterDiscreteValue = New
CrystalDecisions.Shared.ParameterDiscreteValue
ParameterDiscreteValue.Value = ComboBox1.SelectedItem
ParameterField.CurrentValues.Add(ParameterDiscreteValue)
```

7. Click Debug > Start or press the F5 key to start your application. The combo box at the top of the form should be populated with the default values from your report, as shown in Figure 9.16.

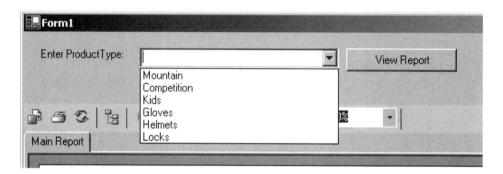

FIGURE 9.16 The finished form with the drop-down list for the default values.

8. Select a value and click the View Report button. Your report now reflects the parameter value that you selected.
9. This is just one example of how you could use the default values to set a discrete parameter. You may also encounter a situation where a parameter in your report has been set to accept multiple values. If this is the case, you can recursively call the CurrentValues.Add method to pass these additional values to your parameter before running your report.

Another handy trick: when working with a report that has subreports and the subreports themselves have parameters, you can reference them using the name of the subreport (for example, ParameterField = ParameterFields(0, "SubReport1").

NOTE

Setting Ranged Parameter Field Values

Another popular type of parameter field is a ranged parameter. A ranged parameter is one that has been created to accept a range of values through entering start and end values. Ranged parameter fields are often used with date-type fields or numbers. For example, you could create a ranged parameter that would allow you to select customers with orders between $10,000 and $20,000. Or you could create a ranged parameter that would allow you to enter a start date and an end date for orders so you could select all records in between. An example of this type of parameter field is shown in Figure 9.17.

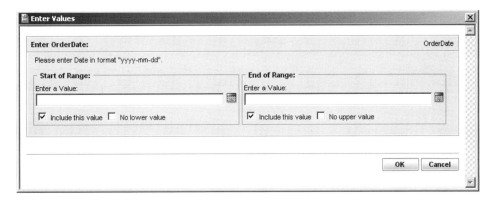

FIGURE 9.17   An example of a ranged date parameter.

You can set the current value for this type of parameter just as you normally would set a parameter. However, instead of creating a single discrete value, you will be passing both a start value and an end value. In our next example, we create a custom user interface to accept a start date and an end date and then pass these values to our report along the way. To create this application, use the following steps:

1. From the Start menu, open Visual Studio .NET 2003. Click File > New > Project.
2. From the New Project window, click the Visual Basic Projects folder, and then select Windows Application.
3. Enter a name and location for your project, and click OK. For this example, we have called the project VB_RangeParam.
4. A new project will open with a blank Windows form. Click View > Toolbox, and locate the CrystalReportViewer control. Drag the control on to your form, and set the Dock property to Fill. Set the Dock Padding > Top

property to 50. This will give us some room at the top of the form to add some extra features later.

5. Next, double-click the form to access the code behind it, and add the following line in the Form Load subroutine. The sample report, RANGEPARAM.RPT, is included in the PROJECTS folder on the CD-ROM. You may need to modify the file location depending on where you have saved this file.

ON THE CD

VB .NET:

```
CrystalReportViewer1.ReportSource = "d:\projects\rangeparam.rpt"
CrystalReportViewer1.DisplayGroupTree = False
```

6. Now, with the report viewer control in place and the report source set, you can do a quick check to make sure that you can preview your report. Click Debug > Start or press the F5 key to start your application. The form opens and displays your report.

7. Next, add two text boxes and three buttons, and set the text for each text box to blank and on two of the buttons enter "..." for the text. On the last button, enter View Report. Add some labels to mark each text box as the Start Date and End Date. Your form should now look like the one shown in Figure 9.18.

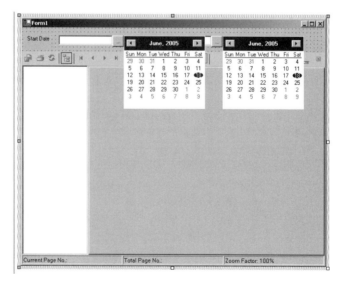

FIGURE 9.18 The finished form.

8. To make selecting dates a bit easier, locate the `MonthCalendar` control in the toolbox, and drag and drop two copies of it onto your form, one beside each button marked "...". This button will show the calendar and allow the user to select a date.

9. Change the Visible property on the two `MonthCalendar` controls to be False.

10. Next, we need to put some code behind our buttons. Double-click each button marked "...", and enter the following code:

VB .NET:

```
MonthCalendar1.Show()
```

11. Now switch to the code view of your form, and create the subroutine for when the user selects a date. This has two purposes: we want to pass the date selected back to the text box, and we want to close the calendar control. The code looks like the following lines. Remember to repeat the same code for the start and end date (...) buttons, changing the text box and calendar number.

VB .NET:

```
Private Sub MonthCalendar1_DateSelected(ByVal sender As
System.Object,
ByVal e As System.Windows.Forms.DateRangeEventArgs) Handles
MonthCalendar1.DateSelected

    TextBox1.Text = MonthCalendar1.SelectionEnd
    MonthCalendar1.Hide()

End Sub
```

You may want to run your application at this point, just to make sure that the calendar controls are working correctly. When you click the (...) button, the calendar should appear. Click to select a date. The calendar should disappear, and the value you selected should be shown in the appropriate text box.

12. Now we are ready to get down to the coding to pass the parameters! First things first—we need to declare the required variables. In the code view of your form, scroll up to the class declaration, and paste the following code underneath the `Inherits System.Windows.Forms.Form` statement:

VB .NET:

```
Dim ParameterFields As CrystalDecisions.Shared.ParameterFields
Dim ParameterField As CrystalDecisions.Shared.ParameterField
Dim ParameterRangeValue As CrystalDecisions.Shared.Parameter
RangeValue
```

13. Now scroll down to the Form Load subroutine, and add in the following code. This code snippet will set the ReportSource to the report we are using and set up the parameter fields for use. You will notice in this snippet that the start value and the end value have been given an initial value of 1/1/1. When the user selects a new start value and end value, those values will be passed to the report instead.

VB .NET:

```
CrystalReportViewer1.ReportSource = "d:\projects\RANGEPARAM.rpt"
CrystalReportViewer1.DisplayGroupTree = False
ParameterFields = CrystalReportViewer1.ParameterFieldInfo
ParameterField = ParameterFields(0)

ParameterRangeValue = New CrystalDecisions.Shared.Parameter
RangeValue
ParameterRangeValue.StartValue = "1/1/1"
ParameterRangeValue.EndValue = "1/1/1"
ParameterRangeValue.LowerBoundType =
CrystalDecisions.[Shared].RangeBoundType.BoundInclusive
ParameterRangeValue.UpperBoundType =
CrystalDecisions.[Shared].RangeBoundType.BoundInclusive
ParameterField.CurrentValues.Add(ParameterRangeValue)
```

15. Finally, back on your form, double-click the View Report button, and enter the following code to fire when the button is clicked. This code is almost identical to the code used in the Form Load section, except it passes the dates the user selected to the report for processing.

VB .NET:

```
CrystalReportViewer1.ReportSource = "d:\projects\RANGEPARAM.rpt"
CrystalReportViewer1.DisplayGroupTree = False
ParameterFields = CrystalReportViewer1.ParameterFieldInfo
ParameterField = ParameterFields(0)
```

```
ParameterRangeValue = New CrystalDecisions.Shared.Parameter
RangeValue
ParameterRangeValue.StartValue = TextBox1.Text
ParameterRangeValue.EndValue = TextBox2.Text
ParameterRangeValue.LowerBoundType =
CrystalDecisions.[Shared].RangeBoundType.BoundInclusive
ParameterRangeValue.UpperBoundType =
CrystalDecisions.[Shared].RangeBoundType.BoundInclusive
ParameterField.CurrentValues.Add(ParameterRangeValue)
```

16. Click Debug > Start or press the F5 key to start your application. The form opens and displays your text boxes at the top of the page where you can enter a start date and an end date. Click the (…) buttons to open a calendar to select your dates, and then click the View Report button to pass these values and view the report.

Many report developers use parameters to control report formatting and output; you could use a range parameter to run the report for only a certain section of your customers (for example, A to K, L to Z, and so on). You could also use ranged parameters to create a flexible report that can be run on a daily, weekly, monthly, or ad-hoc basis, eliminating the need to create separate reports for each use.

 Remember, this is not the final word on working with parameter fields—in the second half of the chapter we will be looking at how to interact with parameter fields using the ReportDocument *object model.*

Working with Database Logons

We have been working with reports created from an unsecured Access database—that is, no user name or password is required to access the data. Unfortunately, these days most databases and other data sources require a login using a valid user name and password. If you have integrated a report that is built on a secured data source, users will be prompted to enter a user name and password using a dialog box similar to the one shown in Figure 9.19.

The good news is that the CrystalReportViewer object model caters for programmatically logging in to your data source, but there is a catch. Because a single report can be based on multiple tables from multiple data sources, you will need to loop through all of the tables in use in your report and set the logon credentials for each. And because the CrystalReportViewer doesn't have access to the rich object model provided through the ReportDocument interface, you will need to know the name of each of the tables in your report and manually add them to your code.

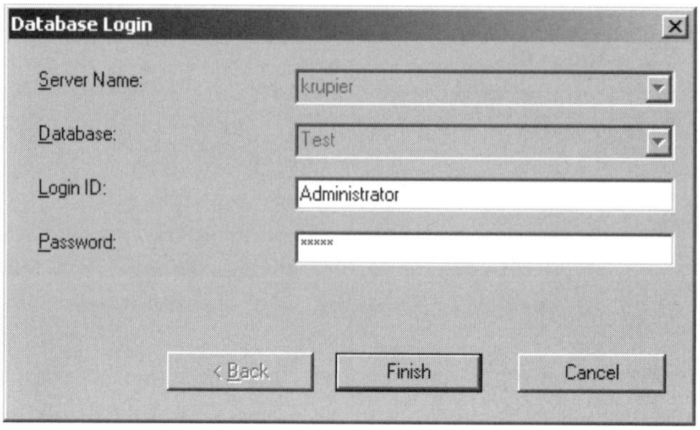

FIGURE 9.19   A typical secure data source login dialog box.

With that said, there is not too much work involved in actually setting the login credentials. To start, you will need to create a LogonInfo object and then specify a table name and the user name and password for each table, as shown in the following code snippet:

VB .NET:

```
Dim LogonInfo As CrystalDecisions.Shared.TableLogOnInfo
CrystalReportViewer1.LogOnInfo = New
CrystalDecisions.Shared.TableLogOnInfos
LogonInfo = New CrystalDecisions.Shared.TableLogOnInfo
LogonInfo.TableName = "Products"
LogonInfo.ConnectionInfo.UserID = "Admin"
LogonInfo.ConnectionInfo.Password = ""
CrystalReportViewer1.LogOnInfo.Add(LogonInfo)
```

This is one of the areas where you may want to consider using the ReportDocument object model instead of CrystalReportViewer. The ReportDocument object model allows you to loop through all of the tables in your report and retrieve information about each, making setting the login credentials easy. That said, if your reports are based on a single summary table or view, this process may not be that arduous.

WORKING WITH THE REPORT DOCUMENT OBJECT MODEL

At the beginning of the chapter I mentioned there are two object models we would be working with in this chapter. Everything you have read up until this point has described features and functionality available in the `CrystalReportViewer` object model. This simple object model provides the majority of functionality you may need for simple applications but for more fine control over the report, you will need to use the `ReportDocument` object model.

The `ReportDocument` object model provides the most control over the report and can be used to navigate through the structure of a report and features all of the properties, methods, and events you can use to interact with the report.

The Crystal Reports XI .NET SDK provides a detailed diagram of the Report-Document object model that shows all of the different components of a report, as well as all of the related collections, objects, properties, etc.

And since it would be tough to cover the entire object model in a single chapter (or even a single book) we have covered the most commonly used features and functionality from the object model and included additional samples on the Web site that accompanies the book at www.crystalxibook.com.

Selecting a Binding Method

All of the reports you have been working with in this chapter have been viewed and manipulated through the viewer object model by setting the `ReportSource` property to a specific file location, as shown below:

```
CrystalReportViewer1.ReportSource = "c:\myreport.rpt"
```

But this is not the only way you can access reports from your application (although it is considered the easiest). When integrating Crystal Reports into your own applications, you have a choice of either leaving the report outside of the application itself or embedded within the application.

For example, if you were creating a commercial application and wanted to give users the ability to create their own custom reports and add them to your user interface, you could create a /REPORTS directory under your application folder structure, so any reports added to that location could be easily exposed through your user interface.

Likewise, if you were developing an internal application for use within your own organization, you could create a /REPORTS folder on a shared network drive, so you could add reports from time to time and have these reports appear in your application. The benefit of storing reports external to your application is that your application is flexible and can be extended with new reports or by modifying existing reports.

To bind to a report stored external to your application, follow these steps:

1. From the Start menu, open Visual Studio .NET 2003.
2. Click File > New > Project.
3. From the New Project window, click the Visual Basic Projects folder, and then select Windows Application.
4. Enter a name and location for your project, and click OK. For this example, we have called the project VB_ExternalBind. A new project will open with a blank Windows form.
5. Double-click the form to access the code view and add the following to the top above the class definition:

VB.NET

```
Imports CrystalDecisions.CrystalReports.Engine
```

6. Next, add the Crystal Report Viewer control to your form and set the dock property to Fill.
7. Double-click the form to access the code behind and in the Form Load section; add the following code:

VB.NET

```
Dim ExternalBindReport As ReportDocument = New ReportDocument
ExternalBindReport.Load("c:\binding.rpt")
CrystalReportViewer1.ReportSource = ExternalBindReport
```

8. Finally, click Debug > Start or press the F5 key to start your application. Your application is now bound to an external report.

This demonstrates how you can store reports externally—on the other hand, if you want more control over your reports you could embed them into the application itself so that they were not editable or exposed to the rest of the world. This would mean that every time you want to update a report, you would need to modify the report, recompile and distribute the application.

To bind to a report stored within your application, follow these steps:

1. From the Start menu, open Visual Studio .NET 2003.
2. Click File > New > Project.

3. From the New Project window, click the Visual Basic Projects folder, and then select Windows Application.

4. Enter a name and location for your project, and click OK. For this example, we have called the project VB_EmbeddedBind. A new project will open with a blank Windows form.

5. The first thing we need to do is specify the report we want to work with. To add a report to your project, select Project > Add Existing Item and browse for your report file. A sample report, BINDING.RPT, is included in the PROJECTS folder on the CD-ROM.

6. From the toolbox, drag the `ReportDocument` icon onto your form. This will open a dialog that will allow you to select the report you just added from a drop-down list; then click OK.

7. Next, double-click the form to open the code view and enter the following in the form load section:

VB.NET

```
Dim EmbeddedBindReport As New binding
```

8. You can now work with this report using all of the properties, methods, and events associated with the `ReportDocument` object model (i.e., print, export, etc.) To view the report, add the Crystal Report viewer control to your form and add the following line to your form load subroutine:

VB.NET

```
CrystalReportViewer1.ReportSource = EmbeddedBindReport
```

9. And lastly, click Debug > Start or press the F5 key to start your application. Your application is now bound to an report embedded into the application itself.

Now that you have seen both methods, it's time for my two cents—if I had to recommend an approach, it would be to leave the reports external to your application and do the work up-front to create a simple user interface for adding custom reports, whether it be by adding reports to a fixed directory or by specifying the location through a report menu option or wizard. End-users will be happy, as they can add additional reports without any additional coding and you can get back to what you like doing best—developing software!

Printing Your Report

Even though the viewer provides a print preview of the report, you may encounter situations where you want to print directly from your application. Using the ReportDocument object model, you can print directly to a printer and specify printer options, like the number of pages, printer trays, etc. In the following sections, this will be our first look at the functionality in the ReportDocument object model, as we look at how to print your report and control the output.

The easiest method to get your report to print out is PrintToPrinter, which can be used to print your report to the default printer. This method accepts four properties, which include:

- Number of Copies
- Collation (True/False)
- Start page
- End Page

So to use this method to print your report to the default printer, follow these steps:

1. From the Start menu, open Visual Studio .NET 2003.
2. Click File > New > Project.
3. From the New Project window, click the Visual Basic Projects folder, and then select Windows Application.
4. Enter a name and location for your project, and click OK. For this example, we have called the project VB_PrintReport. A new project will open with a blank Windows form.
5. The first thing we need to do is specify the report we want to work with. To add a report to your project, select Project > Add Existing Item and browse for your report file. A sample report, INVOICEREPORT.RPT, is included in the PROJECTS folder on the CD-ROM.

ON THE CD

6. Next, double-click the form to open the code view and enter the following in the form load section:

VB.NET

```
Dim InvoiceReport As New invoicereport()
```

7. From the toolbox, draw a command button on your form.
8. Double-click the command button to open the code behind it and enter the following:

VB.NET

```
InvoiceReport.PrintToPrinter(1, True, 0, 0)
```

9. Finally, click Debug > Start or press the F5 key to start your application. Your report will now be printed to your default printer.

By setting the page numbers to zeros, all of the pages in the report will be printed, although you may see some developers use "1" and "999" as the page range by default. The only problem is that there are some reports out there that may be more than a 1,000 pages, so make sure you use zeros if you want to be sure to get every page.

And it is not just the default printer you can print to—you can specify the printer name, paper size, orientation, etc. using the following properties:

VB.NET

```
With InvoiceReport.PrintOptions
    .PrinterName = "Canon PIXMA iP1000"
    .PaperSize = CrystalDecisions.[Shared].PaperSize.PaperA4
    .PaperOrientation = CrystalDecisions.[Shared].Paper
    Orientation.Landscape
End With
```

These options would print the report to the Canon printer on A4 sized paper, with landscape orientation.

The ReportDocument API also includes the ability to set a custom paper source and duplex printing options—for more information, check out the Crystal Reports XI .NET SDK developer help and search for the "Printing and Setting Print Options" tutorial.

Exporting Your Report

While Crystal Reports is the default choice for developers, end-users may want to export their report into another format that they can manipulate more easily. And Crystal Reports supports a wide variety of export file formats, so there is usually a file format to suit just about every need. Using the ReportDocument object model, you have a number of different exporting options that you can set, depending on your requirements. Here is a quick run-down of what you need to know.

There are a couple of different exporting methods available to you—the first, ExportToDisk is the easiest to use and only requires you to specify the export format and the file name to be exported to. The second, Export is a little more complex, as it allows you to set more options around the export formats and different destinations that are available.

But before we can start exporting your report, you will need to know three things: a format, a destination and any options required. The ReportDocument SDK supports exporting to the destinations detailed in Table 9.2.

TABLE 9.2   Format Options

Description	Export Format
Adobe Acrobat PDF	PortableDocFormat
Crystal Reports	CrystalReport
HTML 3.2	HTML32
HTML 4.0	HTML40
Microsoft Excel	Excel
Microsoft Excel (Data Only)	ExcelRecord
Microsoft Word	WordForWindows
No Format	NoFormat
Rich Text	RichText
Rich Text (Editable)	EditableRTF
Text	Text
Text (Character Seperated)	CharacterSeparatedValues
Text (Tab Seperated)	TabSeparatedText

So to use our simple ExportToDisk method, all you would need to do is combine one of these formats with a file path and location. To use this method to export your report, follow these steps:

1. From the Start menu, open Visual Studio .NET 2003.
2. Click File > New > Project.
3. From the New Project window, click the Visual Basic Projects folder, and then select Windows Application.

4. Enter a name and location for your project, and click OK. For this example, we have called the project VB_SimpleExportReport. A new project will open with a blank Windows form.

5. The first thing we need to do is specify the report we want to work with. To add a report to your project, select Project > Add Existing Item and browse for your report file. A sample report, EXPORTREPORT.RPT, is included in the PROJECTS folder on the CD-ROM.

ON THE CD

6. From the toolbox, drag the Report Document object from the Components section on to your form—this will open a dialog with a drop-down box. Use the drop-down box to select the report you just added.

7. Next, double-click the form to open the code view and enter the following in the form load section:

VB.NET

```
Dim ReportToExport As New exportreport()
ReportToExport.ExportToDisk(CrystalDecisions.[Shared].Export
FormatType.Excel, "c:\simpleexport.xls")
```

8. And last, click Debug > Start or press the F5 key to start your application. Your report should now be exported to your C: drive in Excel format.

With all of these file formats, try exporting from the Crystal Reports designer to determine the correct format for you—you may decide that you like the output better from one format over another. Also, the quality of exported files can be improved by focusing on the report design. There are a number of white papers on the Business Objects knowledgebase about optimizing reports for exporting to various formats. There is also a handy guide to what components of a report will and won't be exported to various formats. To find these documents, visit http://support.businessobjects.com *and search the Knowledge Base for the keyword "Export."*

9. While the `ExportToDisk` method is quick and easy, you may want more control over the export process—in that case, you will need to use the `Export` method and set the related export options for the format you have selected. The first thing you will need to decide in addition to the format is the destination for your exported file—the `ReportDocument` object model supports the destinations shown in Table 9.3 below.

TABLE 9.3 Destination Options

Description	Destination
To Disk	DiskFile
To an Exchange Folder	ExchangeFolder
To Email (MAPI)	MicrosoftMail
No Destination	NoDestination

In addition to these destinations, Crystal Reports XI also introduced two new methods ExportToHttpResponse() *and* ExportToStream() *specifically for Web applications. To learn about these two new options, search for either method name in the .NET developer help that ships with Crystal Reports XI.*

It goes without saying that if you plan to export to Microsoft Exchange or to an email, you will need to have a working mail client on the same computer where your application is running. A good test for Exchange accessibility is to log in using the same user account that will run your application and try to open Outlook and Access and the Exchange public folder. If you can browse the folder, see its contents, and add items to the folder, chances are that your report export will work correctly. For the email destination, if you can click a link on a Web page and a blank email form opens, this is also a good sign that MAPI is working and you should be able to export your report successfully to this destination.

And finally, once you have picked the destination and export format, you will need to set any options that are related to that format. For example, if you pick a destination of disk, you will need to set the disk filename/path, etc. in a collection of DiskFileDestinationOptions related to that destination. Or for Word, for instance, there is a collection of PdfRtfWordFormatOptions related to these three export options.

An easy way to keep track of what properties, options, etc. you need to set when exporting is to think of the three things you need to set: destination, format, and options, keeping in mind that some destinations and formats will have options of their own. To pull all of this together, the following example demonstrates how to export a report to PDF format and save to your local hard drive. To create this example for yourself, follow these steps:

1. From the Start menu, open Visual Studio .NET 2003.
2. Click File > New > Project.
3. From the New Project window, click the Visual Basic Projects folder, and then select Windows Application.

4. Enter a name and location for your project, and click OK. For this example, we have called the project VB_ExportReport. A new project will open with a blank Windows form.

5. The first thing we need to do is specify the report we want to work with. To add a report to your project, select Project > Add Existing Item and browse for your report file. A sample report, EXPORTREPORT.RPT, is included in the PROJECTS folder on the CD-ROM.

ON THE CD

6. From the toolbox, drag the Report Document object from the Components section on to your form—this will open a dialog with a drop-down box. Use the drop-down box to select the report you just added.

7. Next, double-click the form to open the code view and enter the following in the form load section:

VB.NET

```
Dim ReportToExport As New ReportToExport

ReportToExport.Load()

Dim ExportOptions As New CrystalDecisions.Shared.ExportOptions
Dim DiskFileDestinationOptions As New CrystalDecisions.Shared.
DiskFileDestinationOptions
Dim FormatTypeOptions As New CrystalDecisions.Shared.PdfRtf
WordFormatOptions

ExportOptions = ReportToExport.ExportOptions

With FormatTypeOptions
    .FirstPageNumber = 1
    .LastPageNumber = 10
End With

With DiskFileDestinationOptions
    .DiskFileName = "c:\advancedexport.pdf"
End With

With ExportOptions
    .ExportDestinationType = CrystalDecisions.Shared.Export
     DestinationType.DiskFile
    .ExportFormatType = CrystalDecisions.Shared.ExportFormat
    Type.PortableDocFormat
    .DestinationOptions = DiskFileDestinationOptions
    .FormatOptions = FormatTypeOptions
End With
```

```
ReportToExport.Export()
```

8. And last, click Debug > Start or press the F5 key to start your application. Your report should now be exported to your C: drive.

This is just one example of how you could use the export functionality in your own application—you could combine the different destinations and export formats to give users the ability to deliver report content anyway they like. At first glance this code is probably a bit confusing. The destination options can all be summarized into one table, as shown in Table 9.4.

TABLE 9.4 Destination Options

Disk File (`DiskFileOptions`)
DiskFileName

Exchange Folders (`ExchangeFolderDestinationOptions`)
DestinationType
EncodedPassword
FolderPath
Password
Profile

Email (`MicrosoftMailExportOptions`)
MailCCList
MailMessage
MailSubject
MailToList
Password
UserName

So if you wanted to export to an Exchange Folder, you would need to provide the profile name, password, folder path, etc. You can get a full description of each of these properties by using the Object Browser within Visual Studio.NET. The "intellisense" feature within Visual Studio should also show you what values are expected by each of these properties, but most are self-explanatory.

For understanding export format options, the best place to start is within the Crystal Reports designer itself. Open a report and then try exporting to various formats and note the different options that appear in the export dialogs as you select the different formats (Excel, Word, HTML, etc.). The same options can be set programmatically through the properties shown below in Table 9.5.

TABLE 9.5 Export Format Options

HTML (HTMLFormatOptions)

FirstPageNumber

HTMLBaseFolderName

HTMLEnableSeparatedPages

HTMLFileName

HTMLHasPageNavigator

LastPageNumber

UsePageRange

Excel (**ExcelFormatOptions**)

ConvertDateValuesToString

ExcelAreaGroupNumber

ExcelAreaType

ExcelConstantColumnWidth

ExcelTabHasColumnHeadings

ExcelUseConstantColumnWidth

ExportPageBreaksForEachPage

ExportPageHeadersAndFooters

FirstPageNumber

LastPageNumber

ShowGridLines

UsePageRange   →

DataOnlyExcelFormatOptions

ExcelAreaGroupNumber

ExcelAreaType

ExcelConstantColumnWidth

ExcelUseConstantColumnWidth

ExportImages

ExportObjectFormatting

ExportPageHeaderAndPageFooter

MaintainColumnAlignment

MaintainRelativeObjectPosition

SimplifyPageHeaders

UseWorksheetFunctionsForSummaries

PDF, RTF, Word (**PdfRtfWordFormatOptions**)

FirstPageNumber

LastPageNumber

UsePageRange

RTF Editable (**EditableRTFExportFormatOptions**)

InsertPageBreaks

Text (**TextFormatOptions**)

CharactersPerInch

LinesPerPage

Text, Character Separated (**CharacterSeparatedValuesFormatOptions**)

Delimiter

PreserveDateFormatting

PreserveNumberFormatting

SeparatorText

So by combining the different export destinations, formats, and options, you could have hundreds of combinations of different ways to export your report. Remember to always set the options that are appropriate for your export format and when in doubt, select View > Object Browser within Visual Studio.NET and have a look at the options for the export and destination formats you have selected to make sure you are working with the right set.

Working with Parameters

Parameters are a great way of adding interactivity to reports and you can easily set parameter values from your own application and user interface; this offers users a tight integration with existing functionality. When we looked at the viewer object model earlier in this chapter, you got a look at the default parameter dialogs that Crystal Reports offers—if the parameter field value was not set, this dialog would appear and prompt the user for a value. And in addition to using the parameter value entered in your report, you could also use the parameter field and value in conjunction with record selection to filter your report data.

 And like the viewer object model, the `ReportDocument` *object model also includes a* `RecordSelectionFormula` *property which you can use to get or set the record selection formula for the report, which provides an easy way to directly work with the report's record selection.*

The `ReportDocument` model also provides the ability to work with parameter fields that appear in your report, and the interfaces work in a similar manner to the way parameters are handled by the viewer.

Most parameter fields can be classed by the input they accept—parameter fields will have a "type" (string, number, etc.) as well as an input method, whether the parameter accepts discrete values, a range of values, or a combination of the two. Discrete parameters are the most common type of parameters used in Crystal Reports, as they are flexible and can be combined to create complex record selection and formulas.

Parameter fields can be accessed through the `ReportDocument` object model through the `ParameterFieldDefinitions` collection of `ParameterFieldDefinition` objects. There is one `ParameterFieldDefinition` for every parameter that appears in your report.

Each of those parameter fields in your report can have default values and current values associated with it. The default values are stored in a similar fashion, where you have a collection of `ParameterValues`, comprised of many different `ParameterValue` objects. And to make things even more complex, these values can either be discrete values or ranged values, with a start and end.

In the project that follows, we are going to look at how to look into a report document and retrieve up to five parameter fields and the prompting text and default values associated with those fields. The user can then select values from the default list and click a button to pass these values to the report and then view the report itself. To get started with this project, follow these steps:

1. From the Start menu, open Visual Studio .NET 2003.
2. Click File > New > Project.
3. From the New Project window, click the Visual Basic Projects folder, and then select Windows Application.
4. Enter a name and location for your project, and click OK. For this example, we have called the project VB_ParameterValues. A new project will open with a blank Windows form.
5. The first thing we need to do is specify the report we want to work with. To add a report to your project, select Project > Add Existing Item and browse for your report file. A sample report, CITYSALES.RPT, is included in the PROJECTS folder on the CD-ROM.

6. From the toolbox, drag the Report Document object from the Components section onto your form—this will open a dialog with a drop-down box. Use the drop-down box to select the report you just added.
7. Next, switch to the Form view for the default form created with your project (Form1) and on the left-hand side of the dialog, add five labels from the toolbox, along with five combo boxes. These controls will be used to display the prompting text and the default values from the parameter fields in your report.
8. Under the combo boxes on the left-hand side, add a command button and change the text to read "View Report."
9. Finally, add the Crystal Report Viewer to the right-hand side of the page. With that, your form design is complete and we can get on with the coding.
10. Next, double-click the form and in the Public Class definition for the form, add the following code, after Inherits System.Windows.Forms.Form:

VB.NET

```
Dim ReportDocument = New citysales

Dim ParameterFieldDefinitions As CrystalDecisions.Crystal
Reports.Engine.ParameterFieldDefinitions
Dim ParameterFieldDefinition As
CrystalDecisions.CrystalReports.Engine.ParameterFieldDefinition
```

```
Dim defaultParameterValues As CrystalDecisions.Shared.Parameter
Values
Dim defaultParameterValue As CrystalDecisions.Shared.Parameter
Value

Dim currentParameterValues As CrystalDecisions.Shared.Parameter
Values
Dim currentParameterValue As CrystalDecisions.Shared.Parameter
Value

Dim ParameterDiscreteValue As CrystalDecisions.Shared.Parameter
DiscreteValue
```

11. This has established the variables we will need to work with the parameter fields found in the report document, as well as the related default and current values. Next, we need to add some code behind our user interface. Double-click the form to open the code view and in the Form Load section, enter the following:

VB.NET

```
Here we are looping through all of the parameters in the
report, displaying the prompting text for each using the
labels you added earlier, as well as displaying the default
values in each combo box.

ParameterFieldDefinitions = ReportDocumentwithParameters.Data
Definition.ParameterFields

        Dim i
        For i = 0 To ParameterFieldDefinitions.Count - 1

            ParameterFieldDefinition = ParameterField
            Definitions(i)defaultParameterValues = Parameter
            FieldDefinition. Default Values

            If i = 0 Then
                Label1.Text = ParameterFieldDefinition.Prompt
                Text.ToString

                For Each defaultParameterValue In default
                ParameterValues
                    ParameterDiscreteValue = CType(default
```

```
                                  ParameterValue, CrystalDecisions.Shared.
                                  ParameterDiscreteValue)
            ComboBox1.Items.Add(ParameterDiscreteValue.Value.ToString())
                          Next
                    End If

                    If i = 1 Then
                          Label2.Text = ParameterFieldDefinition.Prompt
                          Text.ToString
                          For Each defaultParameterValue In default
                          ParameterValues
                                ParameterDiscreteValue = CType(default
                                Parameter Value, CrystalDecisions.Shared.
                                ParameterDiscreteValue)

            ComboBox2.Items.Add(ParameterDiscreteValue.Value.ToString())
                          Next
                    End If

                    If i = 2 Then
                          Label3.Text = ParameterFieldDefinition.Prompt
                          Text.ToString
                          For Each defaultParameterValue In default
                          ParameterValues
                                ParameterDiscreteValue = CType(default
                                Parameter Value, CrystalDecisions.Shared.
                                ParameterDiscreteValue)
            ComboBox3.Items.Add(ParameterDiscreteValue.Value.ToString())
                          Next
                    End If

                    If i = 3 Then
                          Label4.Text = ParameterFieldDefinition.Prompt
                          Text.ToString
                          For Each defaultParameterValue In default
                          ParameterValues
                                ParameterDiscreteValue = CType(default
                                ParameterValue, CrystalDecisions.Shared.
                                ParameterDiscreteValue)
            ComboBox4.Items.Add(ParameterDiscreteValue.Value.ToString())
                          Next
                    End If
```

```
             If i = 4 Then
             Label5.Text ParameterFieldDefinition.Prompt
             Text.ToString
             For Each defaultParameterValue In defaultParameter
             Values
                  ParameterDiscreteValue = CType(defaultParameter
                  Value, CrystalDecisions.Shared.Parameter
                  DiscreteValue)
     ComboBox5.Items.Add(ParameterDiscreteValue.Value.ToString())
                  Next
             End If

        Next
```

12. Next, we need to add some code behind our command button to pass the values to the report and view the report itself. From your form design, double-click the command button and add the following code behind it:

VB.NET

```
Again, we are looping through all of the parameters in the
report, setting the current value based on what the user has
selected from the corresponding combo box on the form

ParameterFieldDefinitions = ReportDocument.DataDefinition.
Parameter Fields

        Dim i
        For i = 0 To ParameterFieldDefinitions.Count - 1

             ParameterFieldDefinition = ParameterField
             Definitions(i)

             currentParameterValues = ParameterFieldDefinition.
             CurrentValues

             Dim ParameterDiscreteValue As CrystalDecisions.
             Shared. ParameterDiscreteValue = New Crystal
             Decisions.Shared. ParameterDiscreteValue

             If i = 0 Then

                  ParameterDiscreteValue.Value = ComboBox1.
                  Selected Item
```

```
                            currentParameterValues.Clear()
                            currentParameterValues.Add(Parameter
                            DiscreteValue)
                            ParameterFieldDefinition.ApplyCurrentValues
                            (current ParameterValues)

                   End If

                   If i = 1 Then

                            ParameterDiscreteValue.Value = ComboBox2.
                            Selected Item
                            currentParameterValues.Clear()
                            currentParameterValues.Add(Parameter
                            DiscreteValue)
                            ParameterFieldDefinition.ApplyCurrentValues
                            (current ParameterValues)

                   End If

                   If i = 2 Then

                   ParameterDiscreteValue.Value = ComboBox3.Selected
                   Item
                   currentParameterValues.Clear()
                   currentParameterValues.Add(ParameterDiscreteValue)
                   ParameterFieldDefinition.ApplyCurrentValues(current
                   ParameterValues)

                   End If

                   If i = 3 Then

                            ParameterDiscreteValue.Value = ComboBox4.
                            Selected Item
                            currentParameterValues.Clear()
                            currentParameterValues.Add(Parameter
                            DiscreteValue)
                            ParameterFieldDefinition.ApplyCurrentValues
                            (current ParameterValues)

                   End If

                   If i = 4 Then
```

```
                    ParameterDiscreteValue.Value = ComboBox5.
                    Selected Item
                    currentParameterValues.Clear()
                    currentParameterValues.Add(ParameterDiscrete
                    Value)
                    ParameterFieldDefinition.ApplyCurrentValues
                    (current ParameterValues)
              End If

        CrystalReportViewer1.ReportSource = ReportDocument
```

13. When finished adding, click Debug > Start or press the F5 key to start your application. Your form should now display the prompting text for your parameter fields, as well as the default values shown in each of the combo boxes. When you select some values and click the "View Report" button, your report should now display in the viewer, with the values shown.

This example demonstrates the most common method of setting parameter fields from your own code and can be applied to not only Windows applications, but Web applications as well. You will also find that application developers will skip using the default values collection altogether, in favor of displaying data from a particular database field.

For example, instead of displaying all of the countries stored in the default values of a report, they will actually bind the combo box to application data already in memory or to a database table and field where this information can be found. Part of this functionality can be accomplished with the use of dynamic parameter fields, a new feature in Crystal Reports XI which will retrieve the values from the database when the report is run. Some developers, however, will still want to have control over the values that are displayed.

If your are using ranged parameters, this sample code can easily be adapted to work with that type of parameter as well—instead of creating a value as `Crystal Decisions.Shared.ParameterDiscreteValue`, you could create a value as `CrystalDecisions.Shared.ParameterRangeValue` and instead of setting a single value, you could set both the `StartValue` and `EndValue`.

For an example of setting ranged parameters from your application, visit www.crystalxibook.com *and search for "Range Example."*

Reporting from ADO.NET Datasets

When Microsoft first introduced Visual Studio .NET and the .NET framework, one of the major enhancements was to ADO and a new version, ADO.NET, was born. Crystal Reports can use ADO.NET data sets as a source of data for developing reports. In addition, you can set this data source at runtime so application data can be passed directly to the report, eliminating the need to make another round-trip to the database to get the data again (after all the application has already retrieved it once).

To create an ADO.NET data set for this example, follow these steps:

1. From the Start menu, open Visual Studio .NET 2003.
2. Click File > New > Project.
3. From the New Project window, click the Visual Basic Projects folder, and then select Windows Application.
4. Enter a name and location for your project, and click OK. For this example, we have called the project VB_DataSet. A new project will open with a blank Windows form.
5. Click Project > Add New Item.
6. Click the option for "Dataset" and name it "Customer.xsd."
7. Next, click View > Server Explorer and navigate to the Database Connections node. Right-click and select Add Connection.
8. On the Data Link Properties page, switch to the Provider tab and select the "OLE DB for ODBC Provider" option and click Next.
9. Using the drop-down box, select the Xtreme Sample Database 11 DSN from the list and click OK.
10. Expand the data source you just added and expand the tables section.
11. Drag the Customer table directly onto your dataset design.
12. Save your project.

So there is the first step out of the way—we have a simple ADO.NET data set now that you can use as the data source for your report. Next, we need to actually create the report that we are going to integrate into your application. To create a report based off of your ADO.NET data set, follow these steps:

1. From the Start Menu, open Crystal Reports XI.
2. Click File > New > Standard Report.
3. Expand the Create New Connection node and double-click the option for ADO.NET (XML).

4. Using the dialog that appears, browse for the location where you created your Visual Studio project and select the .XSD file that corresponds to your data set (i.e. CUSTOMERS.XSD) and click Finish.
5. Your data set will now be listed as an available data source—expand the data set and you will see all of the tables it contains (in this instance, only one). Double click Customers to add it from the list on the left to the list on the right.
6. Click Next to select fields to appear on your report, grouping, etc.
7. When finished with the wizard, click Finish to return to the report designer.
8. Click File > Save and save your report file as "DataSetReport.rpt" as we will need it later.

You may notice that when you preview your report in the report designer, there is no data—that is because we created the report just off of the structure of the dataset. At runtime, we will actually use the ADO.NET data set that is generated to "fill" the report with data. But before we can do that, we need to put these two pieces of the puzzle together. To modify your application, follow these steps:

1. Open the application you were working with earlier.
2. Add the Crystal Report View to the form from the toolbox.
3. Click Project > Add Existing Item and browse for and select the report you just created.
4. Next, double-click the form to access the code behind and enter the following:

VB.NET

```
Dim ConnectionString As String = "Provider=Microsoft.Jet.
OLEDB.4.0;Data Source= C:\\Program Files\\Business Objects\\
Crystal Reports 11\\Samples\\en\\Databases\\xtreme.MDB"Dim
DatabaseConnection As OleDbConnection = New OleDbConnection
DatabaseConnection.ConnectionString = connString
Dim DataAdapter As OleDbDataAdapter = New OleDbDataAdapter
("Select * from Customer", DatabaseConnection)
Dim ReportDataSet As DataSet = New DataSet
DataAdapter.Fill(ReportDataSet, "Customer")

Dim DataSetReport As New DSREPORT
DataSetReport.SetDataSource(ReportDataSet)
CrystalReportViewer1.ReportSource = DataSetReport
```

5. And finally, click Debug > Start or press the F5 key to start your application. Your report will be populated with data from the data set you created and should be displayed in the preview window.

And the good news is that whether you are using SQL Server, Oracle, DB2, etc., the procedure is always the same—you fill the data set using your own connection information and database-specific information, then use the `SetDataSource` method to set the data source for the report. With that said, there are some "gotchas" to watch out for—first and foremost, the dataset that you created the report from and the data set you are passing to the report at runtime must be the same. So if you have deleted a field out of the data set, make sure you go back and update the report design to match.

Working with Database Logons

Earlier in the chapter, we looked at how to set the database logon information for reports based on secure data sources. This process was a bit tricky, because from the report viewer itself we don't have the ability to delve into the structure of the report to determine all of the different data sources that have been used. Luckly, the `ReportDocument` object model allows us to navigate through all of the different data sources in use in the report and set the credentials for each.

To start, each report will have a collection of `Tables` and for each `Table`, there will be `TableLogonInfo`. For example, if you had a report based on three tables from the same SQL Server database, you could very easily set the same `TableLogonInfo` for each of them. But if you had a report based on one table from Oracle and one table from SQL Server, you would need to pass separate credentials for each database table. And that is where being able to enumerate through the tables in a report comes in very handy.

In the following sample project, we are going to loop through all of the tables that exist within a particular report, and set the connection info for each as we go through. To create this project and set the database information for the report, follow these steps:

1. From the Start menu, open Visual Studio .NET 2003.
2. Click File > New > Project.
3. From the New Project window, click the Visual Basic Projects folder, and then select Windows Application.
4. Enter a name and location for your project, and click OK. For this example, we have called the project VB_SecureDatasource. A new project will open with a blank Windows form.

5. The first thing we need to do is specify the report we want to work with. To add a report to your project, select Project > Add Existing Item and browse for your report file. A sample report, SECUREREPORT.RPT, is included in the PROJECTS folder on the CD-ROM.

6. From the toolbox, drag the Report Document object from the Components section on to your form—this will open a dialog with a drop-down box. Use the drop-down box to select the report you just added.

7. Also from the Toolbox, drag the Crystal Report view onto your form and set the docking to full screen.

8. Next, double-click the form to access the code behind it and enter the following (remembering to change the values for your own SQL Server, where you have installed and configuring the Northwind sample database):

VB.NET

```
Dim SecureReport As securereport

    Dim tables As CrystalDecisions.CrystalReports.Engine.Tables
    Dim table As CrystalDecisions.CrystalReports.Engine.Table

    Dim tableLogonInfo As CrystalDecisions.Shared.TableLogOnInfo

    Dim LogonInfos As CrystalDecisions.Shared.TableLogOnInfos
    Dim LogonInfo As CrystalDecisions.Shared.TableLogOnInfo

    Dim ConnectionInfo As CrystalDecisions.Shared.Connection
    Info = New CrystalDecisions.Shared.ConnectionInfo

    ConnectionInfo.ServerName = "(local)"
    ConnectionInfo.DatabaseName = "Northwind"
    ConnectionInfo.UserID = "sa"
    ConnectionInfo.Password = "admin"

    tables = SecureReport.Database.Tables

    For Each table In tables
        tableLogonInfo = table.LogOnInfo
        tableLogonInfo.ConnectionInfo = ConnectionInfo
        table.ApplyLogOnInfo(tableLogonInfo)
    Next
CrystalReportViewer1.ReportSource = securereport
```

9. When finished, click Debug > Start or press the F5 key to start your appli-
    cation. The database credentials will be passed to the server and your report
    will run without error.

You can use this same technique to set the database credentials for a number of
other database platforms as well—whether the report is based on a single data
source or multiple. When reporting off of multiple data sources, some developers
will even go so far as to establish a database table with the required credentials for
each data source or table. So as you are looping through the different tables, you
can look them up in the table and pass a standard set of credentials. It is also a good
idea not to hard-code the database credentials in your application, as they could
change over time—there are a couple of different ways you can do this, from storing the details in encrypted registry keys to securely storing them on-shared network location where the application can read these values. Alternately, some
organizations provide a "generic" username and password that is used for reporting and that does not expire or change.

SUMMARY

So whether you are looking for a simple Windows application to view reports or a
more complex integration with your own custom application, Crystal Reports has
the tools you need. From easy integration with the Crystal Reports viewer to complex customization with the ReportDocument object model, you have almost complete control over the report and its presentation. And some of the techniques you
learned how to use with the ReportDocument object model can also be applied to
Web applications, which is what we start looking at in the next chapter.

10 Integrating Reports into Web Applications

In This Chapter

- Getting Started
- Working with the Report Viewer Object Model

INTRODUCTION

When the Internet first started to gain popularity almost a decade ago, users saw a powerful tool for bringing together people and information; application developers saw a brave new world where a Web browser was the only requirement to run an application. And aside from a few skirmishes in the browser wars over standards and operability, that dream has become a reality. It is now possible to create robust Web applications that can be accessed from a simple Web browser, with no setup or local installation required.

The history of Web development can be traced back to a few key Web technologies and platforms, and none have been more prevalent than the tools and technology provided by Microsoft. With the introduction of Active Server Pages (ASP), Microsoft was able to inspire a whole generation of Web developers to create more than just static HTML pages. As tools evolve, so does the underlying framework, and in 2002, Microsoft introduced ASP .NET, an updated version of ASP designed to run on a common language runtime (CLR) that supported multiple languages.

And as a longtime OEM partner, Crystal Reports was right there as well. A copy of Crystal Reports was included with Visual Studio .NET 2002, so reports could be viewed and manipulated from ASP .NET applications. And just as Web development tools have advanced, Crystal Reports has also advanced in features and functionality to make it the perfect choice for ASP .NET developers looking to integrate reports into their applications.

The main focus of this chapter is on integrating Crystal Reports into ASP .NET Web applications created using Visual Studio .NET 2003 and the .NET framework. Although Crystal Reports can be used with a number of Web development tools and platforms, ASP .NET provides a rich platform for developing robust, scalable Web applications.

And like the previous chapter, this chapter includes code examples written in VB .NET with C# available for download, so you use the same code in your own application even if you don't use Visual Studio .NET.

Because quite a few developers still using "classic" ASP want to integrate reports into their applications, a list of resources, tutorials, and links to sample applications are available on the Web site accompanying this book (www.crystalxibook.com).

Just like the previous chapter, the examples and walk-throughs in this chapter assume that you have Visual Studio .NET 2003 installed with either the VB .NET or C# language option enabled. In addition, it is assumed that you have Crystal Reports XI Developer Edition installed on the same machine. This will update the OEM version of Crystal Reports that is included with Visual Studio .NET 2003, so you can edit any reports embedded in your project directly from within the IDE. Alternatively, if you would like to use the stand-alone report designer, right-click your report and select Open With to open a dialog box in which you can select the application to associate.

Select the option for crw32 to edit your report using the stand-alone report designer that ships with Crystal Reports XI.

In addition to the application requirements, you will also need to have a local IIS Web server installed and configured. Most of the examples and projects in this chapter will assume that you are using this local server to debug and run your applications.

Finally, the majority of the sample reports used in this chapter are based on the Xtreme Sample Database 11, which is an Access database that is installed and configured by default when Crystal Reports is installed. In addition to this sample database, some of the examples show code that is specific for SQL Server, Oracle, and other databases. You will need to have the correct database platform and sample databases installed and configured for these examples to work.

All of the sample applications and reports are located on the CD-ROM that accompanies this book. You can find also find additional samples and code at the companion Web site at *www.crystalxibook.com*.

GETTING STARTED

As with Windows applications, covered in Chapter 9, you can use two main object models to integrate reporting into your .NET applications. The first is the `Crystal ReportViewer` object model, which provides all of the properties, methods, and events you will need to view your report and provide some simple customization of the report at runtime.

This object model could be considered a "cousin" to the object model used in Windows applications; some properties and methods are different between the two, but its purpose is the same: to provide a way to view reports from your application and pass a few simple options to control the report output.

For complete control over the report, you will need to use the `ReportDocument` object model, which provides a rich set of properties, methods, and events that you can use to work with the report itself.

This object model is identical to the `ReportDocument` object model we looked at in the previous chapter, so you will see some overlap toward the end of the chapter. This overlap is on purpose—Windows and Web applications behave differently, and some techniques are more appropriate for one platform than the other.

Which object model you decide to use depends on the type of Web application you are looking to create. In Chapter 8, we looked at the different type of integration methods that you could use in your applications, including view only and view with parameters. For these simple Web applications, the Web version of the `CrystalReportViewer` object model is a good choice because it provides the basic options you will need to preview, set record selection, and so on, for reports from within your application. You can see this viewer in action on a Web form below in Figure 10.1.

You may notice that this viewer is slightly different from the one used in Windows applications. This viewer features a toolbar both at the top and bottom of the screen and can't be docked to the Web form window. However, this viewer shares many of the same features as the Windows report viewer. Also, you can pass parameters to the viewer using this viewer object model, as well as log on to secure databases.

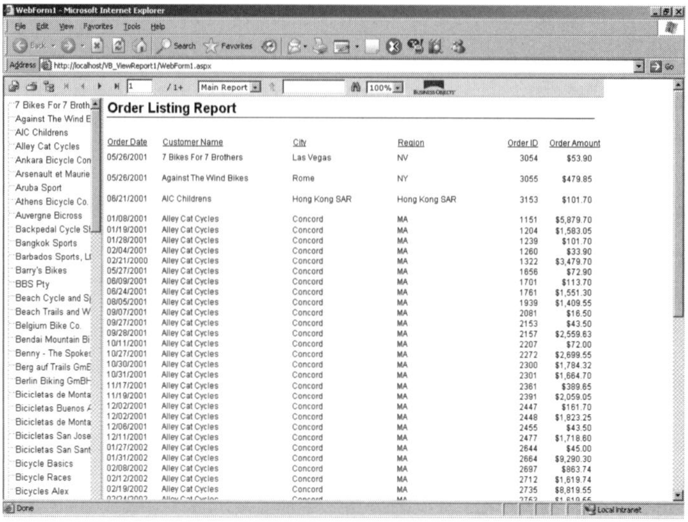

FIGURE 10.1 The Crystal Reports Report Viewer for Web forms.

If you have more complex integration requirements, such as passing ADO or ADO .NET data sets to the report, printing to a specific printer or printer tray, exporting to a specific format, and controlling formula fields and report formatting, you will need to use the ReportDocument object model.

In this chapter we will look first at the CrystalReportViewer object model and run through its features and functionality. In the second half of the chapter, we will look at the ReportDocument object model and see what it has to offer. There will be some duplication of topics as we go through each of the object models. For example, when we look at working with parameter fields, there will be a section near the front of the chapter on how they work with the CrystalReportViewer object model. Toward the end of the chapter, you may see the same topic again, only this time covering how parameters work with the ReportDocument object model and any advanced features this object model provides.

You must never mix the two object models. If you do have a look through the CrystalReportViewer object model and decide that you need more control over the report, make sure that you write all of your code using the ReportDocument object model and use the CrystalReportViewer object model only to view the resulting report.

Not only is mixing the two object models a bad programming practice, it can lead to unpredictable results when running reports, especially if you set some properties in one object model and some properties in the other.

WORKING WITH THE REPORT VIEWER OBJECT MODEL

You use two components to view a report from your Web application using the `CrystalReportViewer` object model. The first is a .NET control that you can drag and drop onto your Web forms; the second is the actual code behind it that controls the appearance and behavior of the viewer itself. You can use the properties, methods, and events associated with the object model to control both the report and viewer itself.

Throughout the rest of this section, we will be looking at some of the most common customizations that Web developers make to the viewer and how it is used with their reports, including viewing a report in a Web browser, setting the print method, and passing parameters. These customizations are grouped together logically based on their function, making it easier to find what you need.

For a complete list of all of the properties, methods, and events in the `Crystal ReportViewer` *object model, use the Visual Studio .NET Object Browser to browse through the class under the* `CrystalDecisions.Web` *namespace.*

Viewing Your Report on the Web

To view your report from within your ASP .NET application, all you need is a single line of code. Drag the Crystal Reports Viewer onto your Web form and set the `ReportSource` property. (And if you set the property through the property page, you don't even need that single line of code.)

Once you have added the viewer and set this property, you can then build and run your application and the Web form. The report viewer will be displayed with a preview of your report. To see this one line of code in action, use the following steps:

1. From the Start menu, open Visual Studio .NET 2003.
2. Click File > New > Project.
3. From the New Project window, click the Visual Basic Projects folder, and then select ASP .NET Web application.
4. Enter a name and location for your project, and click OK. For this example, we have called the project VB_WebViewReport. (The C# version of this project is called C#_WebViewReport.)
5. A new project will open with a blank Web form. Click View > Toolbox, and locate the `CrystalReportViewer` control. Drag the control onto your form
6. Next, double-click the form to access the code behind it, and add the following line in the Form Load subroutine. The sample report, WEBSALES.RPT, is included in the PROJECTS folder on the CD-ROM. You may need to modify the file location depending on where you have saved this file.

ON THE CD

VB .NET:

```
CrystalReportViewer1.ReportSource = "d:\projects\websales.rpt"
```

C#:

```
CrystalReportViewer1.ReportSource = "d:\projects\websales.rpt"
```

7. Finally, click Debug > Start or press the F5 key to start your application. Your browser window should open to display your Web form, and the viewer that you added to the page earlier should now display the Internet Sales report, as shown in Figure 10.2.

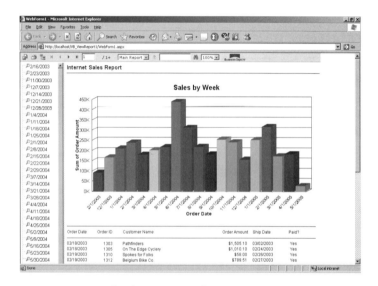

FIGURE 10.2 A simple report preview.

For some developers, this may be the only line of code you need, depending on the level of report integration you are trying to achieve. By default, the viewer is displayed with a toolbar at the top that includes the following buttons:

Export: Opens a Save dialog box that you can use to export your report to Word, Excel, PDF, and so on

Print: Opens the Print dialog box

Group Tree: Shows or hides the group tree on the left side of the report

Page Navigation Buttons: Provides navigation through report pages

Find: Opens the Find dialog box for entering text to find in the report

Zoom: Controls the magnification factor

Chances are, you may want to use the viewer just as it is, but there are some options, which we will look at in the next section, that you can set to customize the look and feel of the viewer.

Changing Viewer Appearance

The viewer itself has a number of properties that you can use to set different options for controlling its appearance. The first set of properties has to do with the overall appearance of the viewer; the second set deals with specific icons that appear on the viewer's toolbar.

The first set of properties are shown in Table 10.1.

TABLE 10.1 Viewer Properties

Method	Description	Type
DisplayToolbar	Controls whether to display the toolbar at the top of the viewer	Boolean
DisplayBottomToolbar	Controls whether to display the toolbar at the bottom of the viewer	Boolean
DisplayGroupTree	Controls the display of the group tree on the left side of the viewer	Boolean
PageToTreeRatio	Controls how large the group tree will appear in relation to your report page	Integer

One property you probably haven't seen before when working with the Windows report viewer is the page-to-tree ratio. This ratio determines how big your group tree will be in relation to the rest of your page. By default, this setting is set to 6 meaning the group tree is approximately 1.5 nches wide but you can set this value to any number.

If you wanted to not show the viewer's toolbar and adjust the group tree to be smaller, you could add the following code to the Form Load code we looked at before:

VB .NET:

```
CrystalReportViewer1.DisplayToolbar = False
CrystalReportViewer1.DisplayBottomToolbar = False
CrystalReportViewer1.PageToTreeRatio = 8
```

C#:

```
CrystalReportViewer1.DisplayToolbar = False
CrystalReportViewer1.DisplayBottomToolbar = False
CrystalReportViewer1.PageToTreeRation - 8
```

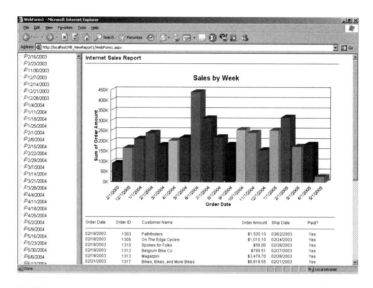

FIGURE 10.3 The report viewer minus the toolbar and with a different size group tree..

If you use this code to turn off the toolbars and change the ratio, the report viewer would now look like the one shown in Figure 10.3.

As mentioned earlier in the chapter, the viewer provides two sets of properties for controlling its appearance and functionality. This second property set is for controlling the individual icons that appear on the toolbar. By controlling the icons on the toolbar, you also control how users interact with the report. For example, if you don't display a print button, users won't be able to print their reports from the viewer.

These properties follow:

- `HasCrystalLogo`
- `HasDrillUpButton`
- `HasExportButton`
- `HasPageNavigationButtons`

- HasPrintButton
- HasRefreshButton
- HasSearchButton
- HasToggleGroupTreeButton
- HasViewList
- HasZoomFactorList

All of these properties are Boolean, so to hide the Print button from our earlier example, the code would look like the following example:

VB .NET:

```
CrystalReportViewer1.HasPrintButton = False
```

C#:

```
CrystalReportViewer1.HasPrintButton = False
```

FIGURE 10.4   The report viewer minus the Print button.

When you view your report, the viewer would now omit the Print button, as shown in Figure 10.4.

In addition to the properties to control the toolbar and buttons, there are also a number of properties you can use to format the contents of the group tree that appears on the left side of the report viewer. This group tree is an easy way for users to navigate through the report, but you may want to change the formatting to match your report design. You can edit the GroupTreeStyle properties from the viewer's property page, or you can access the collection of settings from within your application, as shown in the following code snippet:

VB .NET:

```
CrystalReportViewer1.GroupTreeStyle.Font.Name = "Arial"
```

C#:

```
CrystalReportViewer1.GroupTreeStyle.Font.Name = "Arial"
```

Selecting a Print Mode

One of the new features in Crystal Reports XI is the ability print from the Web report viewer. This print functionality can be delivered in two ways. The first uses an Adobe® Acrobat® (PDF) file as an intermediary file, with the print functionality provided through the Adobe Acrobat Reader, which is installed locally on a user's computer. When the user clicks the Print button, the dialog box shown in Figure 10.5 opens and instructs him how to print the report from Acrobat Reader.

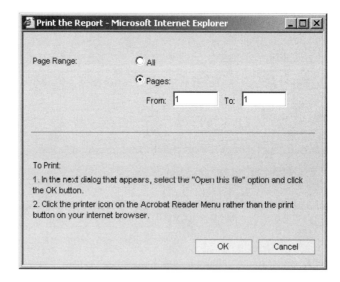

FIGURE 10.5   The Print the Report dialog box.

Because most users are familiar with PDF files, this is the default printing method and doesn't require any additional software or components to be installed (other than Acrobat Reader on the user's local machine).

The second method of printing is provided through a small ActiveX control for Internet Explorer that provides direct printing to your local printer. When this option is enabled and a user clicks the Print button in the report viewer, the ActiveX control is automatically downloaded and installed behind the scenes. A small intermediary window like the one shown in Figure 10.6 opens, and the standard Windows Print dialog box opens, in which the user can select a printer and define printer options.

You can control which printing method is used through the `PrintMode` property associated with the report viewer. You can use the following two print modes:

- `CrystalDecisions.Web.PrintMode.Pdf`
- `CrystalDecisions.Web.PrintMode.ActiveX`

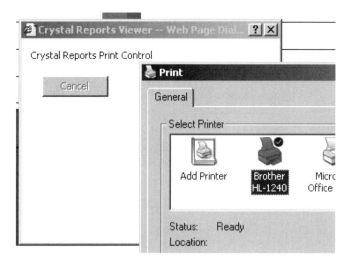

FIGURE 10.6   The ActiveX Printer Control in action.

To set the print mode to use ActiveX and print directly to the printer, the code would look like the following:

VB .NET:

```
CrystalReportViewer1.PrintMode = CrystalDecisions.Web.PrintMode.
ActiveX
```

C#:

```
CrystalReportViewer1.PrintMode = CrystalDecisions.Web.PrintMode.
ActiveX
```

You may have noticed as you were looking through the `CrystalReportViewer` object model that there is no equivalent function to the `PrintReport` method found in the Windows report viewer. This has more to do with the nature of Web applications than anything else. It is difficult for Web developers to call a Print dialog box directly from their application, because that application may be viewed on many different Web browsers and operating systems.

For commercial applications where you don't know what browsers or operating systems are in use, you should use the PDF print method. There may be an extra step in the middle before you can actually print the report, but it does provide consistent results. Also, if you are developing an internal application and know all of your users will be using Internet Explorer, then by all means use the ActiveX control.

Modifying Report Record Selection

Record selection is the process Crystal Reports uses to filter report records. It accomplishes this through the use of a record-selection formula, as follows:

```
{Customer.Country} = "USA"
```

Record-selection formulas are written using Crystal syntax and can be created when you design the report or at runtime when you are viewing the report. You can view any record selection currently in use in your reports by opening the report in Crystal Reports and clicking Report > Selection Formulas > Record to open the Record Selection Formula Editor.

Any record selection you create in this editor is saved with your report. When integrating reports into your application, you can use two properties to set the record selection at runtime. The first property, SelectionFormula, can be used to get or set the record-selection formula. This property can be used to overwrite any existing record selection that is present in the report, in effect giving you complete control over the records that are returned.

The second property, ViewTimeSelectionFormula, is used to append a record-selection formula onto the existing record-selection formula used in the report.

For example, if your report already had an existing record selection of

```
{Customer.Country} = "USA"
```

and you were to use the ViewTimeSelectionFormula property to set the record-selection formula to bring back a specific state in Australia, as follows:

```
{Customer.State} = "NSW"
```

the resulting record-selection formula would become

```
{Customer.Country} = "USA" AND {Customer.State} = "NSW"
```

This combination would not actually bring back any records—the first part of the record selection would look for all customers who are in the United States, whereas the second part would look for customers who are in the state of New South Wales. Therefore, you need to be careful if you plan to use the ViewTime SelectionFormula property, because you could end up not showing any records at all if the formula doesn't work out correctly.

Let's look at an application that sets the record-selection formula at runtime. To create this application, use the following steps:

■ From the Start menu, open Visual Studio .NET 2003.

1. Click File > New > Project.
2. From the New Project window, click the Visual Basic Projects folder and then select ASP .NET Web Application.
3. Enter a name and location for your project, and click OK. For this example, we have called the project VB_WebRecordSelection. (The C# version of this project is called C#_WebRecordSelection.)
4. A new project will open with a blank Web form labeled WebForm1.aspx. Click View > Toolbox, and drag a drop-down list and button onto your form.
5. Next, edit the Items property of the drop-down list using the dialog box shown in Figure 10.7. Enter the following items:

   ■ All Countries
   ■ USA
   ■ Australia
   ■ Canada
   ■ Mexico

6. The text and value for each option should be the same.

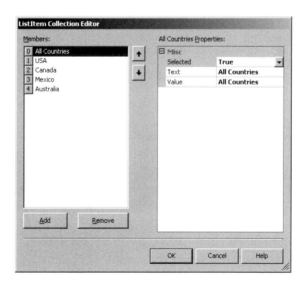

FIGURE 10.7   The ListItem Collection Editor.

7. Next, change the text property of the button to read View Report. Your form should now look like the one shown in Figure 10.8.

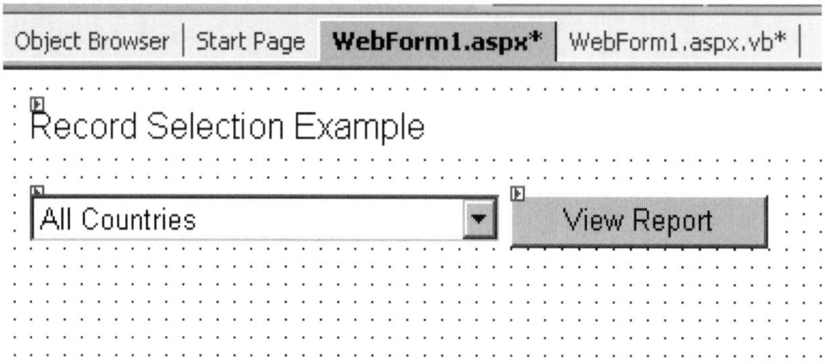

| Object Browser | Start Page | **WebForm1.aspx*** | WebForm1.aspx.vb* |

Record Selection Example

All Countries ▾   View Report

FIGURE 10.8 The completed form.

8. From this form we are going to allow the user to pick a value from the drop-down list and then click the View Report button to move to the next form, where this value will be used to create and set the record-selection formula for the report. Double-click the View Report button, and enter the following code:

VB .NET:

```
Server.Transfer("WebForm2.aspx", True)
```

C#:

```
Server.Transfer("WebForm2.aspx", True)
```

9. Next, we need to create the second form where the record-selection formula will be calculated and the report will be viewed. To create this form, click Project > Add Web Form and use the default form name of Web-Form2.aspx. Click OK.

10. Double-click this form in the Solution Explorer to open the design view, and drag two label fields from the toolbox to the top of the form.

11. Next, locate the CrystalReportViewer control. Drag the control onto the bottom half of your form.

12. Once you have the viewer in place, double-click the form to access the code behind it, and add the following line in the Form Load subroutine:

VB .NET:

```
Dim RecordSelectFormula As String
Dim PassedValue As String

PassedValue = Request.Form("DropDownList1")
RecordSelectFormula = "{Customer.Country} = '" & PassedValue & "'"
Label1.Text = "You selected to run the report for " & PassedValue
Label2.Text = "The resulting Record Selection Formula is " &
RecordSelectFormula

CrystalReportViewer1.ReportSource = "d:\projects\dynselect.rpt"
CrystalReportViewer1.SelectionFormula = RecordSelectFormula
```

C#:

```
Dim RecordSelectFormula As String
Dim PassedValue      As String

PassedValue = Request.Form("DropDownList1")
RecordSelectFormula = "{Customer.Country} = '" & PassedValue & "'"
Label1.Text = "You selected to run the report for " & PassedValue
Label2.Text = "The resulting Record Selection Formula is " &
RecordSelectFormula

CrystalReportViewer1.ReportSource = "d:\projects\dynselect.rpt"
CrystalReportViewer1.SelectionFormula = RecordSelectFormula
```

13. Now all that remains is to run your application and see the record selection filter your report. Click Debug > Start or press the F5 key to start your application. Your browser window will open and display your application, as shown in Figure 10.9.

14. Select a value from the drop-down list and click View Report to proceed to the second page, and preview your report with the record-selection formula applied.

This is just a simple example of how record selection can be used. You could create a record-selection formula as complex as you require.

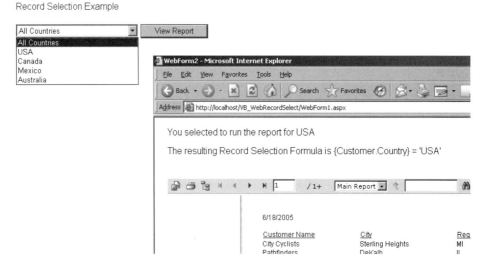

FIGURE 10.9   The completed sample application.

Working with Parameter Fields

Parameter fields have always been a problem when working with previous versions of Crystal Reports. The default parameter dialog boxes were ugly and unwieldy, and most developers preferred to re-create them rather than use them in their application. With Crystal Reports XI, these dialog boxes have come a long way and can use both dynamic and cascading parameters. You can read values from a data source and then pass the selected values back to your report (even in Web applications).

These enhanced parameter fields and dialog boxes make using the default Web viewer dialog boxes (shown in Figure 10.10) a viable option for developers who have simple integration requirements.

If you need more control over the parameter dialog box, or if you want to create your own, you will need to pass the parameter values to the report viewer using the `ParameterField` class. This class contains the properties you will need to retrieve and set parameter information at runtime. Also, there is another class called `ParameterFields` (note the plural), which holds all of the parameter fields in your report.

To start working with parameter fields, we are going to look at how to retrieve information from the report about the parameter fields in your report.

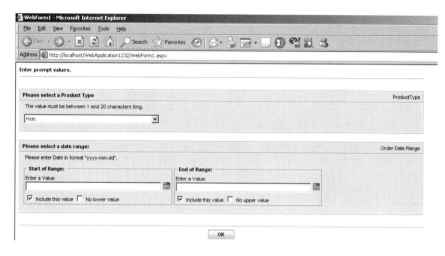

FIGURE 10.10   Default Crystal Reports parameter dialog boxes on the Web.

Retrieving and Setting Discrete Parameter Values

When you create parameter fields in Crystal Reports, you have the option of creating a static list of values from which the user can select when the report is run. This list, called the default values for the parameter, can consist of a description and a value.

For example, if you had a Country parameter, you could create default values that included a description of Australia and a value of AU, which is actually what is passed to the parameter. In addition to creating default values in Crystal Reports, you can also select the sort method used when displaying these values. These default values are entered when you create the parameter in Crystal Reports.

When the user is prompted to enter a parameter, this list of default values will be shown. When you actually enter a value into a parameter field (either from the default values or by typing it in yourself), these values are considered the current value, and depending on the type of parameter, there may be one value or multiple values.

To demonstrate how to work with parameter fields, to the project we just worked on we will add a drop-down list to display these default values, as well as pass the value selected to your report as the current value. Because this is such a big project, we are going to break it into two parts, starting first with retrieving the default and current values from your report.

To retrieve the default values, we are going to read through a collection of values called `DefaultValues` and then use those values to populate a combo box at the top of our form. Once we have filled the combo box with these values, the user can then select a parameter value and click a button to run the report again, passing the parameter value to the report.

In this example, the report has only a single parameter, which makes our job a bit easier. In addition, the parameter field was defined as a discrete parameter, so it expects only one value to be returned. A little later in this section we will look at how to pass other parameter value types to your report, but for now, use the following steps to retrieve and set your parameter field:

1. From the Start menu, open Visual Studio .NET 2003.
2. Click File > New > Project.
3. From the New Project window, click the Visual Basic Projects folder, and then select ASP .NET Web Application.
4. Enter a name and location for your project, and click OK. For this example, we have called the project VB_WebRecordSelection. (The C# version of this project is called C#_WebRecordSelection.)
5. A new project will open with a blank Web form labeled WebForm1.aspx. Click View > Toolbox, and drag a label, drop-down list, and button onto your form.
6. Double-click your form to open the code view, and declare the following variables just underneath the `Inherits System.Web.UI.Page` declaration:

VB .NET:

```
Dim ParameterFields As CrystalDecisions.Shared.ParameterFields
Dim ParameterField As CrystalDecisions.Shared.ParameterField
Dim ParameterDiscreteValue As
CrystalDecisions.Shared.ParameterDiscreteValue
```

C#:

```
Dim ParameterFields As CrystalDecisions.Shared.ParameterFields
Dim ParameterField As CrystalDecisions.Shared.ParameterField
Dim ParameterDiscreteValue As
CrystalDecisions.Shared.ParameterDiscreteValue
```

7. In the Form Load subroutine, add the following code:

VB .NET:

```
CrystalReportViewer1.ReportSource = "d:\projects\DYNPARAM.rpt"
CrystalReportViewer1.DisplayGroupTree = False
ParameterFields = CrystalReportViewer1.ParameterFieldInfo
ParameterField = ParameterFields(0)
Label1.Text = ParameterField.PromptText
```

```
Dim i
For i = 0 To (ParameterField.DefaultValues.Count - 1)
DropDownList1.Items.Add(ParameterField.DefaultValues.Item(i).
Description)
Next

ParameterDiscreteValue = New CrystalDecisions.Shared.Parameter
DiscreteValue
ParameterDiscreteValue.Value = " "
ParameterField.CurrentValues.Add(ParameterDiscreteValue)
```

C#:

```
CrystalReportViewer1.ReportSource = "d:\projects\DYNPARAM.rpt"
CrystalReportViewer1.DisplayGroupTree = False
ParameterFields = CrystalReportViewer1.ParameterFieldInfo
ParameterField = ParameterFields(0)
Label1.Text = ParameterField.PromptText

Dim i
For i = 0 To (ParameterField.DefaultValues.Count - 1)
DropDownList1.Items.Add(ParameterField.DefaultValues.Item(i).
Description)
Next

ParameterDiscreteValue = New CrystalDecisions.Shared.Parameter
DiscreteValue
ParameterDiscreteValue.Value = " "
ParameterField.CurrentValues.Add(ParameterDiscreteValue)
```

8. Next, switch back to the Design view of your form, and rename the Text property on the command button to read View Report.
9. Double-click the View Report button you placed on your form, and enter the following code:

VB .NET:

```
Server.Transfer("WebForm2.aspx", True)
```

C#:

```
Server.Transfer("WebForm2.aspx", True)
```

10. From the Project Explorer, double-click the WebForm2.aspx form, and add two labels from the toolbox, as well as the Crystal Reports viewer control.
11. Double-click your form to open the code view, and declare the following variables just underneath the `Inherits System.Web.UI.Page` declaration:

VB .NET:

```
Dim ParameterFields As CrystalDecisions.Shared.ParameterFields
Dim ParameterField As CrystalDecisions.Shared.ParameterField
Dim ParameterDiscreteValue As
CrystalDecisions.Shared.ParameterDiscreteValue
```

C#:

```
Dim ParameterFields As CrystalDecisions.Shared.ParameterFields
Dim ParameterField As CrystalDecisions.Shared.ParameterField
Dim ParameterDiscreteValue As
CrystalDecisions.Shared.ParameterDiscreteValue
```

12. Locate the Form Load subroutine, and enter the following code:

VB .NET:

```
CrystalReportViewer1.ReportSource = "d:\projects\DYNPARAM.rpt"
      Dim PassedValue
      PassedValue = Request.Form("DropDownList1")
      ParameterFields = CrystalReportViewer1.ParameterFieldInfo
      ParameterField = ParameterFields(0)
ParameterDiscreteValue = New
CrystalDecisions.Shared.ParameterDiscreteValue
      ParameterDiscreteValue.Value = PassedValue
ParameterField.CurrentValues.Add(ParameterDiscreteValue)
```

C#:

```
CrystalReportViewer1.ReportSource = "d:\projects\DYNPARAM.rpt"
      Dim PassedValue
      PassedValue = Request.Form("DropDownList1")
      ParameterFields = CrystalReportViewer1.ParameterFieldInfo
      ParameterField = ParameterFields(0)
ParameterDiscreteValue = New
CrystalDecisions.Shared.ParameterDiscreteValue
      ParameterDiscreteValue.Value = PassedValue
ParameterField.CurrentValues.Add(ParameterDiscreteValue)
```

13. Click Debug > Start or press the F5 key to start your application. The combo box at the top of the form should be populated with the default values from your report, as shown in Figure 10.11.

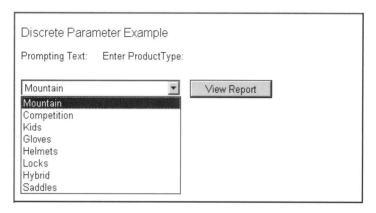

FIGURE 10.11   The finished form with the drop-down list for the default values.

14. Select a value, and click the View Report button. Your report should now reflect the parameter value that you selected.

This is just one example of how you could use the default values to set a discrete parameter. You may also encounter a situation where a parameter in your report has been set to accept multiple values. If this is the case, you can recursively call the `CurrentValues.Add` method to pass these additional values to your parameter before running your report.

Another handy trick: when working with a report that has subreports and the subreports themselves have parameters, you can reference them using the name of the subreport (for example, `ParameterField = ParameterFields(0, "SubReport1")`*).*

Setting Ranged Parameter Field Values

In addition to discrete parameters, which expect a single value, you may also run across reports that use ranged values, such as the report shown in Figure 10.12.

Ranged parameters accept both a start value and an end value and have a number of options that can be set, including whether to include the value in the range and whether there is any upper or lower bound.

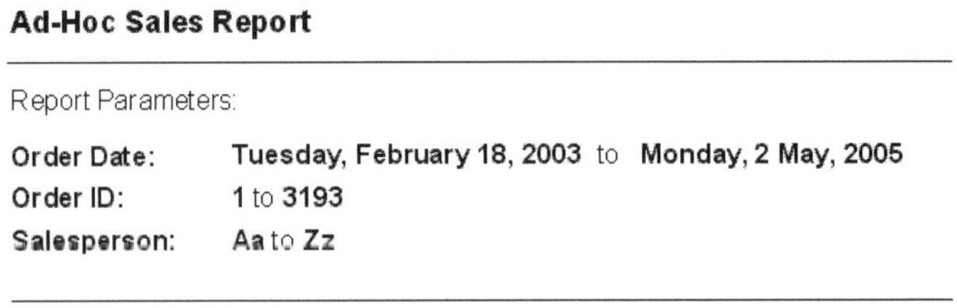

Ad-Hoc Sales Report

Report Parameters:

Order Date: Tuesday, February 18, 2003 to Monday, 2 May, 2005
Order ID: 1 to 3193
Salesperson: Aa to Zz

FIGURE 10.12   A typical report with a ranged parameter.

This type of parameter works in the exact same manner as discrete parameters, as shown in the following code snippet that can be used with one of the same reports included in the CD-ROM:

ON THE CD

VB .NET:

```
CrystalReportViewer1.ReportSource = "d:\projects\RANGEPARAM.rpt"
ParameterFields = CrystalReportViewer1.ParameterFieldInfo
ParameterField = ParameterFields(0)

ParameterRangeValue = New CrystalDecisions.Shared.ParameterRange
Value
ParameterRangeValue.StartValue = "12/31/2004"
ParameterRangeValue.EndValue = "01/01/2005"
ParameterRangeValue.LowerBoundType =
CrystalDecisions.[Shared].RangeBoundType.BoundInclusive
ParameterRangeValue.UpperBoundType =
CrystalDecisions.[Shared].RangeBoundType.BoundInclusive
ParameterField.CurrentValues.Add(ParameterRangeValue)
```

C#:

```
CrystalReportViewer1.ReportSource = "d:\projects\RANGEPARAM.rpt"
ParameterFields = CrystalReportViewer1.ParameterFieldInfo
ParameterField = ParameterFields(0)

ParameterRangeValue = New CrystalDecisions.Shared.ParameterRange
Value
ParameterRangeValue.StartValue = "12/31/2004"
ParameterRangeValue.EndValue = "01/01/2005"
ParameterRangeValue.LowerBoundType =
CrystalDecisions.[Shared].RangeBoundType.BoundInclusive
ParameterRangeValue.UpperBoundType =
CrystalDecisions.[Shared].RangeBoundType.BoundInclusive
```

```
ParameterField.CurrentValues.Add(ParameterRangeValue)
```

Working with Database Logons

When you create a report from a database or other data source, chances are you had to enter a user name and password to gain access to that particular database or source. When a report is run from your Web application, the user will be prompted for a user name and password each time unless you set these credentials before the user previews the report.

The Web version of the `CrystalReportViewer` object model caters to programmatically logging into your data source, but there is a catch. Because a single report can be based on multiple tables from multiple data sources, you will need to loop through all of the tables in use in your report and set the logon credentials for each. And because the `CrystalReportViewer` doesn't have access to the rich object model provided through the `ReportDocument` interface, you will need to know the name of each of the tables in your report and manually add them to your code. To log on to a secure data source from reports in your Web application, you will need to create a `LogonInfo` object and then specify a table name and the user name and password for each table, as shown in the following code snippet:

VB .NET:

```
Dim LogonInfo As CrystalDecisions.Shared.TableLogOnInfo
CrystalReportViewer1.LogOnInfo = New
CrystalDecisions.Shared.TableLogOnInfos
LogonInfo = New CrystalDecisions.Shared.TableLogOnInfo
LogonInfo.TableName = "Products"
LogonInfo.ConnectionInfo.UserID = "Admin"
LogonInfo.ConnectionInfo.Password = ""
CrystalReportViewer1.LogOnInfo.Add(LogonInfo)
```

C#:

```
Dim LogonInfo As CrystalDecisions.Shared.TableLogOnInfo
CrystalReportViewer1.LogOnInfo = New
CrystalDecisions.Shared.TableLogOnInfos
LogonInfo = New CrystalDecisions.Shared.TableLogOnInfo
LogonInfo.TableName = "Products"
LogonInfo.ConnectionInfo.UserID = "Admin"
LogonInfo.ConnectionInfo.Password = ""
CrystalReportViewer1.LogOnInfo.Add(LogonInfo)
```

This is one of the areas where you may want to consider using the `Report Document` object model instead of `CrystalReportViewer`. The `ReportDocument` object model allows you to loop through all of the tables in your report and retrieve information about each, making setting the login credentials easy. However, if your reports are based on a single summary table or view, it may not be a problem.

SUMMARY

ASP .NET is a popular platform for creating robust, scalable Web applications, and Crystal Reports plays an integral part in delivering reports and output from these applications. Using the combination of the two object models for viewing and manipulating reports, Crystal Reports provides a solution that is both easy to integrate and feature rich. If covering two platforms wasn't enough, in the next chapter we will look at integrating Crystal Reports into JSP applications.

11 Integrating Reports into Java Applications

In This Chapter

- Creating Reports for Use with JSP Applications
- Working with the Java Reporting Component
- Working with Parameter Fields
- Architecting Scalable Applications

INTRODUCTION

Crystal Reports has been well known among Microsoft developers, but it has less of a reputation with Java developers. This is in part because Crystal Reports is commonly associated with Visual Studio, but over the past few years BusinessObjects has worked with a number of developer tool vendors to integrate an OEM version of Crystal Reports and the Java Reporting Component into their Java tools. This list has now grown to include BEA Weblogic Workshop, Borland® JBuilder, IBM Rational Application Developer, and IBM Websphere® Studio.

This wide adoption has been driven by the decision to create a "100% Pure Java" implementation of the Crystal Reports engine, which is called the Java Reporting Component (JRC). This component, which was introduced with Crystal Reports version 10, is a rewrite of the same Crystal Reports engine that is used on

341

other platforms. The reasoning behind this move was to entice more Java developers to use Crystal Reports in their applications. The JRC features only a rough parity with the features in the other SDKs because it is a complete rewrite of the engine from the ground up. The JRC provides a powerful set of tools for integrating reports into your application with a minimum of custom code required.

Because the JRC is pure Java, it can be used with different Java development platforms and application servers, including WebLogic, WebSphere, and Tomcat. For a complete list of supported and tested platforms, check out the platforms.txt file available on your Crystal Reports CD-ROM.

In this chapter we look at using the JRC to add reporting to your own JSP applications. Although we won't be able to cover the entire set of features and functionality found in the JRC SDK, we will cover the most used features, including viewing a report, passing parameters, and database credentials. You may also notice that the layout of the examples in this chapter is different. In previous chapters we were using Visual Studio .NET to develop Windows and Web applications, so the tutorials and examples were geared to working within that environment.

With JSP development, there is no one dominant IDE used for development, and Java developers tend to use the IDE they are comfortable with, which could be anything from Eclipse to an advanced text editor. So the code examples in this chapter are listed in "long" form with the entire code listing in one go, ready for you to use in your own IDE or application as required.

Because every reporting application needs a report, it is a good place to start. In the next section we will be looking at some of the considerations for creating reports for use with JSP applications.

CREATING REPORTS FOR USE WITH JSP APPLICATIONS

Web applications represent a unique challenge for reporting—on one hand, a Web application provides an easy way to deliver reports to users without having to install an application locally; on the other hand, large reports and data sets may prove unwieldy when viewed through a Web browser. The following sections outline how to connect and report from your own data sources as well as some of the tricks of the trade to create quick, efficient reports that will make your JSP application fly.

Understanding JDBC

When working with Crystal Reports and Java, there are a couple of different ways you can access data in your reports. Java applications can use JDBC™ to connect to different data sources. This works in a similar manner to how ODBC is used in Crystal Reports, providing an abstraction layer between your report and the database.

JDBC is a well-accepted standard, and JDBC drivers are available for most popular database formats. Sun provides a searchable database of JDBC drivers that you can view at *http://developers.sun.com/product/jdbc/drivers*; DataDirect offers a suite of JDBC drivers that cover most major database platforms, including SQL Server, DB2, and Oracle and is detailed on their Web site at *www.datadirect.com*.

Another method you can use to access report data is an ODBC-to-JDBC bridging driver. The concept behind a bridging driver is that you can use any existing ODBC drivers without having to find the corresponding JDBC driver. The most popular ODBC-to-JDBC bridging driver is provided by Sun, but they do not recommend you use the driver unless no other driver is available. In addition to the Sun driver, there is also an ODBC-to-JDBC bridge available from EasySoft (www.easysoft. com), which is more robust and is suitable for most applications.

Regardless of where you purchase your JDBC driver, there is some setup that needs to be completed before you can use the driver with Crystal Reports. To start, you will need to install and configure your JDBC driver according to the vendor's instructions. Second, you will need to update the CRConfig.XML file usually found in *x*:\Program Files\Common Files\Business Objects\3.0\Java (where *x* is the drive where you installed Crystal Reports). Within this XML file are various configuration settings. You will need to update several elements relating to your JDBC driver, as shown in Table 11.1.

TABLE 11.1 JDBC Settings in CRConfig.XML

Element	Description	Example Value
JavaDir	Path to your Java implementation	`D:\Program Files\Java\jre1.5.0_02\bin`
ClassPath	Should include file path to JAR files for your JDBC driver, including full drive, path, and filename, as well as proper case	See Listing 11.1
JDBCURL	Corresponding URL to your JDBC driver, available from the driver documentation	`jdbc:oracle:oci8:scott/ tiger@myhost`
		→

Element	Description	Example Value
JDBCUserName	Initial user name to be used	Scott
JDBCClassName	Class name for your JDBC driver	com.oracle.jdbc.oracle.oci8

The majority of the values for this configuration file will come from the documentation that ships with your JDBC driver. Each driver will be different. There are some drivers that support different configurations of a single driver, so make sure that you get these settings correct.

When you have edited your CRConfig.XML file, it should look like the one shown in Listing 11.1, which shows how the configuration file would look if you were connecting to a SQL Server database.

LISTING 11.1   Updated CRConfig.XML

```
<?xml version="1.0" encoding="utf-8"?>
<CrystalReportEngine-configuration>
<reportlocation>../..</reportlocation>
<timeout>10</timeout>

<ExternalFunctionLibraryClassNames>
    <classname> </classname>
    <classname> </classname>
</ExternalFunctionLibraryClassNames>

<keycode>XXXXX-XXXXX-XXXXX-XXXX</keycode>
<Javaserver-configuration>
<DataDriverCommon>
<JavaDir>D:\Program Files\Java\jre1.5.0_02\bin</JavaDir>
<Classpath>C:\Program Files\Common Files\Business
Objects\3.0\java/lib/crlovmanifest.jar;C:\Program Files\Common
Files\Business Objects\3.0\java/lib/CRLOVExternal.jar;C:\Program
Files\Common Files\Business
Objects\3.0\java/lib/CRDBJavaServerCommon.jar;C:\Program Files\Common
Files\Business Objects\3.0\java/lib/CRDBJavaServer.jar;C:\Program
Files\Common Files\Business
Objects\3.0\java/lib/CRDBJDBCServer.jar;C:\Program Files\Common
```

```
Files\Business Objects\3.0\java/lib/CRDBXMLServer.jar;C:\Program
Files\Common Files\Business
Objects\3.0\java/lib/CRDBJavaBeansServer.jar;C:\Program Files\Common
Files\Business
Objects\3.0\java/lib/external/CRDBXMLExternal.jar;C:\Program Files\Common
Files\Business Objects\3.0\java/lib/external/log4j.jar;C:\Program
Files\Common Files\Business Objects\3.0\java/lib/cecore.jar;C:\Program
Files\Common Files\Business Objects\3.0\java/lib/celib.jar;C:\Program
Files\Common Files\Business Objects\3.0\java/lib/ebus405.jar;C:\Program
Files\Common Files\Business Objects\3.0\java/lib/corbaidl.jar;C:\Program
Files\Common Files\Business
Objects\3.0\java/lib/external/freessl201.jar;C:\Program Files\Common
Files\Business Objects\3.0\java/lib/external/asn1.jar;C:\Program
Files\Common Files\Business
Objects\3.0\java/lib/external/certj.jar;C:\Program Files\Common
Files\Business Objects\3.0\java/lib/external/jsafe.jar;C:\Program
Files\Common Files\Business
Objects\3.0\java/lib/external/sslj.jar;D:\Program Files\Microsoft SQL
Server 2000 Driver for JDBC\lib\msbase.jar;D:\Program Files\Microsoft SQL
Server 2000 Driver for JDBC\libmssqlserver.jar;D:\Program Files\Microsoft
SQL Server 2000 Driver for JDBC\lib\msutil.jar;${CLASSPATH}</Classpath>
    <IORFileLocation>${TEMP}</IORFileLocation>
    <JavaServerTimeout>1800</JavaServerTimeout>
    <JVMMaxHeap>64000000</JVMMaxHeap>
    <JVMMinHeap>32000000</JVMMinHeap>
    <NumberOfThreads>100</NumberOfThreads>
</DataDriverCommon>

<JDBC>
    <CacheRowSetSize>100</CacheRowSetSize>
    <JDBCURL>jdbc:microsoft:sqlserver://sqlserver01:1443</JDBCURL>
    <JDBCClassName>com.microsoft.jdbc.sqlserver.SQLServerDriver
    </JDBCClassName>
    <JDBCUserName>sa</JDBCUserName>
    <JNDIURL></JNDIURL>
    <JNDIConnectionFactory></JNDIConnectionFactory>
    <JNDIInitContext>/</JNDIInitContext>
    <JNDIUserName>weblogic</JNDIUserName>
    <GenericJDBCDriver>
        <Option>No</Option>
        <DatabaseStructure>catalogs,tables</DatabaseStructure>
        <StoredProcType>Standard</StoredProcType>
        <LogonStyle>SQLServer</LogonStyle>
```

```
        </GenericJDBCDriver>
    </JDBC>

    <XML>
        <CacheRowSetSize>100</CacheRowSetSize>
        <PreReadNBytes>4096</PreReadNBytes>
        <XMLLocalURL></XMLLocalURL>
        <SchemaLocalURL></SchemaLocalURL>
        <XMLHttpURL></XMLHttpURL>
        <SchemaHttpURL></SchemaHttpURL>
    </XML>
    <JavaBeans>
        <CacheRowSetSize>100</CacheRowSetSize>
        <JavaBeansClassPath></JavaBeansClassPath>
    </JavaBeans>
    </Javaserver-configuration>
    </CrystalReportEngine-configuration>
```

If you do have problems configuring the JDBC driver, see the knowledge base article c2017533 from BusinessObjects at http://support.businessobjects.com/library/ kbase/articles/c2017533.asp.

With the driver configured, the next step is to configure the JDBC driver within Crystal Reports. To demonstrate how this works, we will create a report based on a JDBC data source, in this case Microsoft SQL Server. Use the following steps to create reports from your JDBC data source:

1. From the Start menu, open Crystal Reports XI.
2. Click File > New > Blank Report. The Database Expert opens.
3. Double-click the Create New Connection folder.
4. Double-click the JDBC (JNDI) folder, The dialog shown in Figure 11.1 opens.
5. Enter a connection URL and database classname, using the same values that you entered in the CRConfig.XML file, and then click Next.
6. Using the dialog box shown in Figure 11.2, enter a username and password for your database server.
7. When complete, click the Finish button to connect to your data source. A list of available tables will appear below the data source name.

You can then select tables, fields, and so on as you normally would to create your report. As with all reporting in Web applications, make sure that your reports are efficient as possible. You may want to use stored procedures and/or summary tables for reports that require intense processing. JDBC is a convenient method for accessing data, but it also adds an additional layer between your report and the database itself.

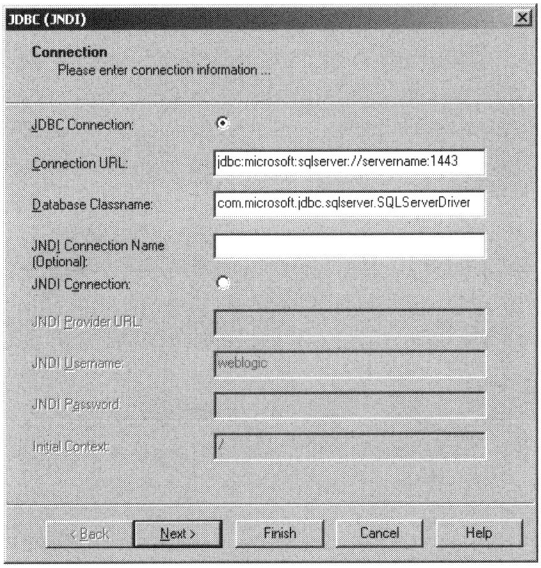

FIGURE 11.1 JDBC driver options.

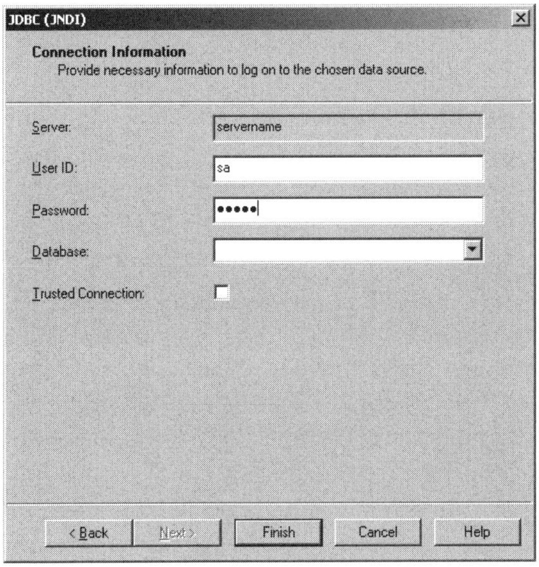

FIGURE 11.2 JDBC database credentials.

Working with XML Data Sources

If your data is not stored in a relational database, do not despair. Crystal Reports now ships with a native XML driver that can be used to access data held within static XML files or data served from Web services. This flexible driver is easy to install and configure and features a number of options for working with XML or XML-based data sources. The first option we are going to look at is for reporting from static XML files.

To create a report from a static XML file, use the following steps:

1. From the Start menu, open Crystal Reports.
2. Click File > New > Blank Report. The Database Expert opens.
3. Expand the Create New Connection folder, and then below this folder, expand the XML folder. The XML data source dialog box shown in Figure 11.3 opens.

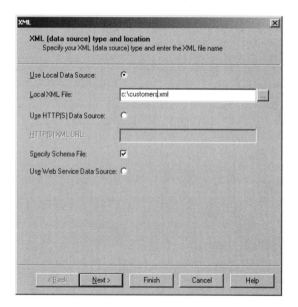

FIGURE 11.3 XML data driver options.

ON THE CD

4. Click the "..." button in the dialog box to browse for a local XML file stored on your hard drive or a network drive. For this example, you can use the sample CUSTOMERS.XML file that is included on the CD-ROM that accompanies this book. Click Finish to return to the Database Expert.
5. Your XML data file should now be shown below the XML data source. You can now create your report as you normally would, selecting fields, adding groups, sorting, and so on.

Crystal Reports will treat this file as if it is a table, and it will work out the appropriate data type for each of the fields it recognizes. You can also use this setup to connect to data served from Web services. Instead of specifying a static XML file, you could have specified a Web service data source.

The neat thing about Web services is that you can pass parameters to the Web service. For example, you could pass a string with a state value, and the Web service could return a list of all of the suppliers in that particular state. For more information on passing this type of Web service parameter, see the JRC Developer Help files and search for the topic "HTTP Parameters."

If you decide to use the XML driver to create reports, be aware that some additional setup is required to view these reports from your application. You will need to make sure you have the correct settings in the CRDB_JavaServer.ini file that is part of your application deployment. The following sections outline some of the setup requirements for successfully deploying your reporting applications using the JRC components.

WORKING WITH THE JAVA REPORTING COMPONENT

The Java Reporting Component (JRC) is a pure Java component created to enable developers to integrate reports into their applications. In the following sections we see how to use the JRC to add reports to your own application.

We do make some assumptions in the following section. The first is that you are an existing Java developer who is looking to integrate reports into your application; the second assumption is that you could be using any development environment (or none at all), so our code examples are in list form, which you can then use in the IDE of your choice.

As with all of the examples and projects in this book, the source code for the sample applications we will see are available on the CD-ROM, should you wish to use these examples as a starting point for your own integration.

Another good reference can be found in the form of the JRC Developer Help Files, which can be downloaded from *http://support.businessobjects.com/library/docfiles/cps10/downloads/en/crXI_JavaReportingComponent_en.zip*.

But before we get knee-deep in code, we need to look at how to actually configure the development environment to make sure your reports can be viewed from your JSP application.

Configuring the Development Environment

One of the first things you will need to do when you start working with the JRC is to configure your development environment and application. To make this a bit easier, we have broken down this configuration into steps that you can use as a checklist. We will go through each of the following steps in turn:

Verify the structure of your Web application folder.

1. Copy the crystalreportviewers11 folder to your Web application folder.
2. Copy the Java Reporting Component JAR files to your WEB-INF\lib folder.
3. Copy the crystal-tags-reportviewer.tld file to your WEB-INF\lib folder.
4. Copy the CRConfig.XML file to your WEB-INF\classes folder.
5. Modify your web.xml file.

Step 1: Verify the structure of your Web application folder

Make sure that your Web application folder has a WEB-INF subfolder and that within that folder there are subfolders marked \lib and \classes. Most JDEs will create this folder structure automatically when you create a new project.

Step 2: Copy the crystalreportviewers11 folder to your Web application folder

This folder contains all of the required files for the different viewers that Crystal Reports supports. You can find this folder under *x*:\Program Files\Common Files\Business Objects\3.0\crystalreportviewers11 (where *x* is the drive on which you have installed Crystal Reports).

Step 3: Copy the Java Reporting Component JAR files to your WEB-INF\lib folder

The JAR files for the JRC are located in *x*:\Program Files\Common Files\Business Objects\3.0\java\lib. You will need to copy all of these files into the \lib subfolder of your application folder. Also make sure that you copy any additional JAR files found in subfolders to ensure you have all of the third-party components that the JRE needs.

Step 4: Copy the crystal-tags-reportviewer.tld file to your WEB-INF\lib folder

This file is required if you are using the Crystal report viewer tags, which can simplify deploying the viewer. You can find this file at *x*:\Program Files\Common Files\Business Objects\3.0\java\lib\taglib. For more information on using the Crystal Report viewer tags, check out the Java SDK docs that ship with Crystal Reports XI.

Step 5: Copy the CRConfig.XML file to your WEB-INF\classes folder

This file contains configuration settings for the report engine itself and needs to be copied to the \classes sub folder. Do not modify this file to specify the location of your reports if you plan to use an absolute path to your report file. For example, with an absolute path, you can put your reports into your \classes folder and then reference the name of the report directly.

Step 6: Modify your web.xml file

The final step involves modifications to your applications web.xml file. You will need to add the following section:

```
<context-param>
<param-name>crystal_image_uri</param-name>
<param-value>crystalreportviewers11</param-value>
</context-param>
```

And if you are planning on using the Crystal viewer tag libraries, you will need to add the following section as well:

```
<taglib>
<taglib-url>
/crystal-tags-reportviewer.tld
</taglib-url>
<taglib-location>
/WEB-INF/crystal-tags-reportviewer.tld
</taglib-location>
</taglib>
```

Once you have completed these steps, you should be ready to begin integrating reports into your application using the JRC. When you create the WAR file to distribute your application, keep in mind the previous steps to ensure that your application can be deployed successfully. Also, watch the version numbers of the components provided with the JRC. BusinessObjects makes updates or patches available on their Web site—if you download and install these updates to fix a problem or issue you are experiencing, make sure you update the files everywhere they are used.

Viewing Your Report on the Web

One of the most common integration requests is a very simple one—to view a report from your application. To view a report using the JRC, we need to have a look at the `CrystalReportViewer` class included with the JRC. Just like with other platforms we have seen, the viewer class contains all of the properties and methods used to display your report and control the appearance of the viewer itself.

To view a report from your JSP page, the first thing you need to do is reference this class at the top of your JSP page, as shown in the next code:

```
<%@page import="com.crystaldecisions.report.web.viewer.*"%>
<%@page import="com.crystaldecisions.reports.sdk.*"%>
```

In that same code snippet, you will also notice that we are referencing the SDK itself, because we will be using it a little later as well.

Once you have referenced the viewer class, you need to open the report document and then set the report source property of the viewer to the report. The first thing we are going to do is create a variable to use to set the report name. Then we will create a new ReportClientDocument and open the specified report, as shown in the following code:

```
String MyReportName = "WEBSALES.rpt";
ReportClientDocument myReportClientDocument = new ReportClientDocument();
myReportClientDocument.open(MyReportName, 0);
```

You may also notice that we have prefixed all of our variable names with "my"—this is to eliminate any confusion when using variables that have a similar name to the property or method we are using. Anywhere you see the "my" prefix, you know that is an application variable that we have created ourselves. You can name the variable anything you like in your own application.

The next step to viewing our report is to get the ReportSource object, using the ReportClientDocument we have just opened, as shown in the next example:

```
Object MyReportSource;
MyReportSource = myReportClientDocument.getReportSource();
```

Next, now that we have the object we can look at working with the viewer itself. The first thing we will need to do is actually create the viewer, then set its report source using the setReportSource property. This property tells the viewer which report should be displayed. We can also set viewer options at this point, as shown in the next sample:

```
// Create the viewer and set its report source to your report
CrystalReportViewer myCrystalReportViewer = new CrystalReportViewer();
myCrystalReportViewer.setReportSource(MyReportSource);
// Set viewer options
```

```
myCrystalReportViewer.setOwnPage(true);
myCrystalReportViewer.setOwnForm(true);
```

Finally, we can refresh the report itself to get the latest data and then use the processHTTPRequest method to process our request and view the report.

```
// Make sure we refresh the report
myCrystalReportViewer.refresh();
myCrystalReportViewer.processHttpRequest(request, response,
getServletConfig().getServletContext(), null);
```

When you build and test your application page, your report should be displayed using the HTML viewer that is provided with Crystal Reports 11 and should look something like the one shown in Figure 11.4.

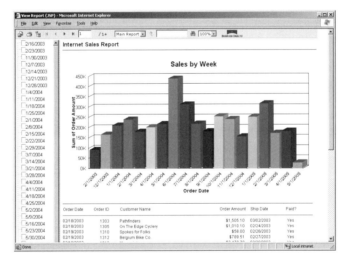

FIGURE 11.4   HTML report viewer.

If you are unable to compile and run your application, make sure that you have followed the setup instructions found earlier, and check to make sure that your report is in the correct location. (In this example, the report should be in the root of your Web application folder.) Listing 11.2 provides the complete listings for the steps we have just walked through and can be reused in your own application:

LISTING 11.2   VIEWREPORT.JSP listing

```
<%@page import="com.crystaldecisions.report.web.viewer.*"%>
<%@page import="com.crystaldecisions.reports.sdk.*"%>
```

```
<%
// Open your report document
String MyReportName = "WEBSALES.rpt";
ReportClientDocument myReportClientDocument = new ReportClientDocument();
myReportClientDocument.open(MyReportName, 0);
// Get the report source
Object MyReportSource;
MyReportSource = myReportClientDocument.getReportSource();
// Create the viewer and set its report source to your report
CrystalReportViewer myCrystalReportViewer = new CrystalReportViewer();
myCrystalReportViewer.setReportSource(MyReportSource);
// Set viewer options
myCrystalReportViewer.setOwnPage(true);
myCrystalReportViewer.setOwnForm(true);
// Make sure we refresh the report
myCrystalReportViewer.refresh();
myCrystalReportViewer.processHttpRequest(request, response,
getServletConfig().getServletContext(), null);
%>
```

Changing Viewer Appearance

If you are working on a simple report integration, this may be sufficient for your needs—you can change the name of the report opened or give users a selection of reports from which they can pick. But if you need more control over the report viewer that is used, we have some properties you should be aware of. By default, the viewer is displayed with a toolbar at the top that includes the following buttons:

Export: Opens a File > Save dialog box that you can use to export your report to Word, Excel, PDF, and so on.

Print: Opens the Print dialog box and prints your report.

Group Tree: Shows or hides the group tree on the left side of the report.

Page Navigation Buttons: Navigates through report pages.

Find: Opens a simple dialog box for entering text to find in the report.

Zoom: Controls the magnification factor.

Most developers use the viewer just as it is, but there are some options that you can set to customize the look and feel of the viewer that we will look at in the next section.

Changing Viewer Appearance

The viewer class has a number of properties that you can use to set different options for controlling the appearance of the viewer itself. The first set of properties has to do with the overall appearance of the viewer, whereas the second set deals with specific icons that appear on the toolbar within the viewer. The first set of properties is shown in Table 11.2.

TABLE 11.2   Viewer Properties

Method	Description	Type
setDisplayToolbar	Controls whether to display the toolbar at the top of the viewer	Boolean
SetDisplayBottomToolbar	Controls whether to display the toolbar at the bottom of the viewer	Boolean
SetDisplayGroupTree	Controls the display of the group tree on the left side of the viewer	Boolean
SetGroupTreeWidth	Controls how large the group tree will appear in relation to your report page	Integer

One property you probably haven't seen before when working with the Windows report viewer is the page-to-tree ratio. This ratio determines how big your group tree will be in relation to the rest of your page. If you wanted to not show the toolbar on the viewer and adjust the group tree to be smaller, you could add the following code to the Form Load code we looked at before:

```
MyCrystalReportViewer.setDisplayToolbar(false);
MyCrystalReportViewer.setDisplayToolbar(false);
MyCrystalReportViewer.setGroupTreeWidth(6);
```

As mentioned earlier in the chapter, there are two sets of properties when working with the appearance and functionality provided in the viewer itself. This second property set is for controlling the individual icons that will appear on the toolbar itself. By controlling the icons on the toolbar, you also control how the user interacts with the report itself. For example, if you don't display a print button, the user won't be able to print their report from the viewer.

These properties include the following:

- `SetHasLogo`
- `SetHasDrillUpButton`
- `SetHasExportButton`
- `SetHasPageNavigationButtons`
- `SetHasPrintButton`
- `SetHasRefreshButton`
- `SetHasSearchButton`
- `SetHasToggleGroupTreeButton`
- `SetHasViewList`
- `SetHasZoomFactorList`

All of these properties are Boolean, so to hide the Print button from our earlier example, the code would look like the following:

```
MyCrystalReportViewer1.SetHasPrintButton(false);
```

When you viewed your report, the viewer would now omit the Print button.

Selecting a Print Mode

One of the new features in Crystal Reports XI and the JRC is the ability to print from the Web report viewer. This print functionality can be delivered in two different ways. The first uses an Adobe Acrobat (PDF) file as an intermediary file, and the print functionality is provided through the Adobe Acrobat Reader, which is installed locally on a user's computer. When the user clicks the print button, a dialog box opens and instructs them how to print the report from Acrobat Reader.

Because most users are familiar with PDF files, this is the default printing method and doesn't require any additional software or components to be installed (other than Acrobat Reader on the user's local machine).

The second method of printing is provided through a small ActiveX control for Internet Explorer that provides direct printing to your local printer. When this option is enabled and a user clicks the print button in the report viewer, the ActiveX control is automatically downloaded and installed behind the scenes. A small intermediary window opens and the standard Windows print dialog box is opened for the user to select their printer, printer options, and so on.

You can control which printing method is used through the `CrPrintMode` property associated with the report viewer. You can use the following two print modes:

- `CrPrintMode.ACTIVEX`
- `CrPrintMode.PDF`

To set the print mode to use ActiveX and print directly to the printer, the code would look like the following:

```
MyCrystalReportViewer.setPrintMode(CrPrintMode.ACTIVEX);
```

The use of the ActiveX raises an interesting problem with applications that are viewed from computers where installing ActiveX is prohibited, for example in a locked-down corporate environment. If this is a concern, your best bet would be to use the PDF method to print the report. Both print methods provide a WYSIWYG print option for your reports, but the ActiveX control has fewer steps.

Exporting Your Report

Crystal Reports XI supports a number of different export formats, providing a way to distribute reports to users in a format that users can develop further or distribute. From the HTML viewer, users can export their report directly without any additional coding required.

If you want to generate the exported file for your users, you can use the JRC to export the report directly with a few lines of code. The key to exporting from your application is setting the export options first, then using the export control to actually export the requested file.

First, we need to set up the ExportOptions for your export, as shown in the next example:

```
// Set Export options
ExportOptions MyExportOptions = new ExportOptions();
MyExportOptions.setExportFormatType(ReportExportFormat.PDF);
```

In this example, we are exporting to PDF, but you could specify the other file formats that the JRC supports. Table 11.3 shows the available formats, as well as their corresponding constant values.

TABLE 11.3   Export Formats and Constants

Format	Constant
Crystal Reports	RPT
Portable Document Format	PDF
Rich Text Format	RTF

Once you have set the exporting options, we can then create the export control itself and then set the report source as well as our export options. We will also use this opportunity to specify how the file is actually going to be exported. If you set the setExportAsAttachment property to true, then the user will be prompted to save the file; false will display the file in the current browser window.

```
// Create the export control, set the report source and options
ReportExportControl MyReportExportControl = new ReportExportControl();
MyReportExportControl.setReportSource(MyReportSource);
MyReportExportControl.setExportOptions(MyExportOptions);
MyReportExportControl.setExportAsAttachment(true);
```

Finally, with all of these options set, you can then use the export control to process the HTTP request to fire up the report engine, run your report, and prepare it in the export format you selected. Listing 11.3 brings together all of these elements to export a report to PDF format from a single JSP page.

LISTING 11.3   EXPORTREPORT.JSP code listing

```
<%@page import="com.crystaldecisions.report.web.viewer.*"%>
<%@page import="com.crystaldecisions.reports.sdk.*"%>
<%@page import="com.crystaldecisions.sdk.occa.report.lib.*"%>
<%@page import="com.crystaldecisions.sdk.occa.report.exportoptions.*"%>
<%@page import="com.crystaldecisions.sdk.occa.report.reportsource.*"%>
<%
// Open your report document
String MyReportName = "export.rpt";
ReportClientDocument MyReportClientDocument = new ReportClientDocument();
MyReportClientDocument.open(MyReportName, 0);
// Get the report
Object MyReportSource;
MyReportSource = MyReportClientDocument.getReportSource();
// Set Export options
ExportOptions MyExportOptions = new ExportOptions();
MyExportOptions.setExportFormatType(ReportExportFormat.PDF);
// Create the export control, set the report source and options
ReportExportControl MyReportExportControl = new ReportExportControl();
MyReportExportControl.setReportSource(MyReportSource);
MyReportExportControl.setExportOptions(MyExportOptions);
MyReportExportControl.setExportAsAttachment(true);
// Process the report for exporting
MyReportExportControl.processHttpRequest(request, response,
getServletConfig().getServletContext(), null);
%>
```

WORKING WITH PARAMETER FIELDS

Parameter fields in Crystal Reports can be used to display information on your report, filter its contents, and so forth. You can use the JRC to pass parameters at runtime using the `ParameterField` class. This class contains the properties you will need to retrieve and set parameter information at runtime and is pretty easy to use.

The most common type of parameter in Crystal Reports is a "discrete" parameter field, where a single value is entered by the user and passed to the report. Normally, if you are viewing a report that uses a parameter and haven't set the value behind the scenes, the user will be prompted to enter the parameter value. We can suppress this prompt dialog box by setting the parameter before we view the report.

The first step is to create a collection of fields, of which our parameter field will be one. We will also need to create a variable to hold our parameter value (that is, the value that is passed to the report parameter) as shown in the next example:

```
// Create the fields collection
Fields MyFields = new Fields();
// Create a new parameter value and set it to "USA"
String MyParameterValue = "USA";
```

You need to make sure that the parameter value you create is the same type as the parameter defined in the report. For example, if you created a string parameter in the report, you would need to create and pass a string parameter here; otherwise, you will receive an error.

With this basic housekeeping out of the way, we can then create the `Parameter Field` object and set the name of the report we are working with, as well as create a new parameter value to pass in and add this to our parameter collection as shown in the next example:

```
// Create the parameter field object
ParameterField MyParameterField = new ParameterField();
MyParameterField.setReportName(MyReportName);
Values MyParameterValues = new Values();
// Create the parameter field value
ParameterFieldDiscreteValue MyParameterFieldDiscreteValue = new
ParameterFieldDiscreteValue();
// Set the name of the parameter and parameter value
MyParameterField.setName("?EnterCountry");
MyParameterFieldDiscreteValue.setValue(MyParameterValue);
MyParameterValues.add(MyParameterFieldDiscreteValue);
```

```
MyParameterField.setCurrentValues(MyParameterValues);
MyFields.add(MyParameterField);
```

This will set the parameter value to "USA," so when the report is viewed, the user will not be prompted for the parameter and the report itself will be filtered to show only those customers that are in the United States. Listing 11.4 for the SET-PARAM.JSP page brings the entire workflow together.

This is just one example of setting a simple discrete parameter. For examples of how to pass other parameter types, check out the JSP samples available on www.crystalxibook.com.

LISTING 11.4 SETPARAM.JSP Code Listing

```
<%@ page import = "com.crystaldecisions.sdk.occa.report.data.*"%>
<%@ page import = "com.crystaldecisions.report.web.viewer.*"%>
<%@ page import = "com.crystaldecisions.sdk.occa.report.*"%>
<%@ page import = "com.crystaldecisions.sdk.occa.report.lib.*"%>
<%@ page import = "com.crystaldecisions.reports.sdk.ReportClientDocument"
%>


<%
// Open your report document
String MyReportName = "export.rpt";
ReportClientDocument MyReportClientDocument = new ReportClientDocument();
MyReportClientDocument.open(MyReportName, 0);
// Get the report
Objects MyReportSource;
MyReportSource = MyReportClientDocument.getReportSource();
// Create the fields collection
Fields MyFields = new Fields();
// Create a new parameter value and set it to "USA"
String MyParameterValue = "USA";
// Create the parameter field object
ParameterField MyParameterField = new ParameterField();
MyParameterField.setReportName(MyReportName);
Values MyParameterValues = new Values();
// Create the parameter field value
ParameterFieldDiscreteValue MyParameterFieldDiscreteValue = new
ParameterFieldDiscreteValue();
// Set the name of the parameter and parameter value
MyParameterField.setName(paramName);
```

```
MyParameterFieldDiscreteValue.setValue(MyParameterValue);
MyValues.add(MyParameterFieldDiscreteValue);
MyParameterField.setCurrentValues(MyParameterValues);
MyFields.add(MyParameterField);
// Create the viewer and set its report source to your report
CrystalReportViewer MyCrystalReportViewer = new CrystalReportViewer();
MyCrystalReportViewer.setReportSource(MyReportSource);
// Set viewer options
MyCrystalReportViewer.setOwnPage(true);
MyCrystalReportViewer.setOwnForm(true);
// Make sure we refresh the report
CrystalReportViewer.refresh();
MyCrystalReportViewer.processHttpRequest(request, response,
getServletConfig().getServletContext(), null);

%>
```

Working with Database Logons

When you create a report from a database or other data source, chances are you had to enter a username and password to gain access to that particular database or source. And when a report is run from your Web application, the user will be prompted for a username and password each time unless you set these credentials before the user previews the report.

Luckily, there is a ConnectionInfo object that we can use to set database credentials before viewing our report. In the next example, a user name of "sa" and a password of "admin" are passed via the ConnectionInfo object so the user will not be prompted for these values.

```
// Set the connection info
ConnectionInfos MyConnectionInfos = new ConnectionInfos();
ConnectionInfo MyConnectionInfo = new ConnectionInfo();
// Set the database user name and password
MyConnectionInfo.setUserName("sa");
MyConnectionInfo.setPassword("admin");
MyConnectionInfos.add(MyConnectionInfo);
```

Once you have set this connection info, you can then view the report as you normally would using the same code we looked at earlier. Listing 11.5 pulls all of this together into a simple page you can use to set the database logon details for a report and view the same.

LISTING 11.5   SETDB.JSP Code Listing

```
<%@page import="com.crystaldecisions.reports.sdk.*"%>
<%@page import="com.crystaldecisions.sdk.occa.report.reportsource.*"%>
<%@page import="com.crystaldecisions.sdk.occa.report.lib.*"%>
<%@page import="com.crystaldecisions.sdk.occa.report.data.*"%>

<%
// Open your report document
String MyReportName = "setdb.rpt";
ReportClientDocument MyReportClientDocument = new ReportClientDocument();
MyReportClientDocument.open(MyReportName, 0);
// Get the report
Objects MyReportSource;
MyReportSource = MyReportClientDocument.getReportSource();
// Set the connection info
ConnectionInfos MyConnectionInfos = new ConnectionInfos();
ConnectionInfo MyConnectionInfo = new ConnectionInfo();
// Set the database user name and password
MyConnectionInfo.setUserName("sa");
MyConnectionInfo.setPassword("admin");
MyConnectionInfos.add(MyConnectionInfo);
// Create the viewer and set its report source to your report
CrystalReportViewer MyCrystalReportViewer = new CrystalReportViewer();
MyCrystalReportViewer.setReportSource(MyReportSource);
// Set viewer options
MyCrystalReportViewer.setOwnPage(true);
MyCrystalReportViewer.setOwnForm(true);
MyCrystalReportViewer.setDatabaseLogonInfos(MyConnectionInfos);
// Make sure we refresh the report
MyCrystalReportViewer.refresh();
MyCrystalReportViewer.processHttpRequest(request, response,
getServletConfig().getServletContext(), null);
%>
```

ARCHITECTING SCALABLE APPLICATIONS

One of the most important factors to keep in mind when developing applications with the Java Reporting Component is scalability. When using the JRC, the reports are processed on the Web server itself. In addition, the JRC SDK does not provide features for scheduling or offloading process of reports to other servers. The good news is that both Crystal Reports Server XI and BusinessObjects Enterprise XI feature a rich Java SDK that can be used to create scalable reporting applications.

You can use both products to offload processing from your Web application server to additional servers or tiers, enabling you to create a multitier application without having the write the back-end code. In addition, the servers within Crystal Reports Server XI and BusinessObjects Enterprise XI are split out by functionality, so if you need additional processing for scheduled reports, you can add an additional server to the architecture as required. Likewise, if your application delivers more on-demand reports, you could add additional server components to improve the performance of your own application.

For more information on Crystal Reports Server XI or BusinessObjects Enterprise XI, a good place to start is at *www.businessobjects.com/products*. You can also find links to additional sample applications for the different platforms and SDKs, white papers, and tutorials online at *www.crystalxibook.com*.

SUMMARY

Java and Java Server Pages are a powerful platform for application development, and having a pure Java component for reporting means you can quickly integrate Crystal Reports into your application. In this chapter we have barely scratched the surface of what you can do with JSP and Crystal Reports, but it should be enough to get you started. In the next chapter we will dive a bit deeper into extending your applications by leveraging the enterprise servers offered from BusinessObjects.

12 Extending Reporting Applications

In This Chapter

- Understanding the Server Architecture
- Installation Options for Windows
- Before You Install
- Installing BusinessObjects Enterprise XI
- Checking Your Installation
- Working with Enterprise Services
- Development Overview
- Working with URL Reporting
- Viewing a Report
- Developing Applications with the .NET SDK

INTRODUCTION

Crystal Reports provides a powerful report-design tool and development platform for integrating reports into your applications, but it does have limitations. With the advent of client-server technology, in early versions of Crystal Reports Business Objects looked for a way to leverage the processing power on servers to generate and view reports.

When Crystal Reports 4.5 was released in 1996, the Crystal Reports print engine was combined with a scheduling engine, and a server-based reporting product called Crystal Info was born. This product and its successors have had many names over the years, including Crystal Info, Seagate Info, then Crystal Info again, then Crystal Enterprise, and finally BusinessObjects Enterprise.

The features and functionality have changed over these many releases, but the core concept of offloading a report process to a server or multiple servers has remained the same. BusinessObjects Enterprise integrates technology both from the old Crystal Enterprise product as well as technology from the BusinessObjects product line, but the basic application framework and security is inherited from Crystal Enterprise, and it provides a robust, scalable platform for creating reporting applications.

As a developer, BusinessObjects Enterprise represents a tremendous "shortcut" for creating scalable applications, because all of the hard work has been done for you. Its features include a secure Web framework for distributing, a powerful scheduling and distribution engine, and a rich set of tools (not just Crystal Reports) for developing reports, ad-hoc queries, OLAP applications, and more. Business Objects also provides a rich set of developer APIs for .NET, Java, and Web services that you can use to leverage BusinessObjects Enterprise features, including the following:

- Secure Web-based platform for publishing, organizing, categorizing, and securing reports
- Robust architecture to offload report processing to multiple servers
- Powerful server-based technology for viewing reports on demand in a Web browser
- Flexible scheduling engine for scheduling reports, whether in batches, at a specific time and date, using a set schedule, based on an event, calendar, and so on
- Numerous distribution options, including scheduling reports to different destinations, including email, printer, disk, FTP, and so on
- Ability to export to a wide range of file formats, including Adobe Acrobat, Excel, Word, RTF, text, and more
- Detailed auditing and notification of report processing, success, or failure

For more information on the features that are provided in BusinessObjects Enterprise XI, see www.businessobjects.com/products/platform/enterprise.asp.

For developers who don't need the full feature set that BusinessObjects Enterprise provides, a new product called Crystal Reports Server XI was introduced with the XI release. This product was built on the same framework with the same server technology as BusinessObjects Enterprise, but it comes with a subset of the features and can be used only to distribute reports created with Crystal Reports. This server solution is also limited to a maximum of 20 users, but it is a fraction of the price of the full product with a Crystal Reports Server license for five concurrent users costing only $7,500.

This application has been a real breakthrough for application developers, because you can now integrate this powerful server technology into your own applications without breaking the bank. And the good news is the APIs, management tools, report designer, and so on in both Crystal Reports Server and Business Objects Enterprise are identical, providing a migration path when you need to leverage some of the OLAP, ad hoc, and other features in BusinessObjects Enterprise.

Throughout this chapter, we will see examples related to BusinessObjects Enterprise, but keep in mind that the same concepts and code can be used with Crystal Reports Server. You can download Crystal Reports Server for evaluation at www.businessobjects.com/products/reporting/crystalreports/evalxi/.

In that age-old struggle or "build versus buy," it is easy to see how Business Objects Enterprise can offer a host of features to your application with a minimum of cost and effort. And that is what this chapter is all about—leveraging the BusinessObjects server tools to extend your reporting applications to hundreds or even thousands of users.

But before we get too far into developing applications for BusinessObjects Enterprise, we need to first have a look "under the hood" to understand the servers that work together to make up a BusinessObjects Enterprise implementation.

UNDERSTANDING THE SERVER ARCHITECTURE

BusinessObjects Enterprise provides a multiserver architecture with servers that handle different processing tasks. You can have multiple instances of these servers to handle a greater number of client requests. The diagram shown in Figure 12.1 illustrates some of the servers related to report processing and providing the basic architecture diagram for BusinessObjects Enterprise.

Two main groups of servers relate to Crystal Reports and delivering reports within the Enterprise framework. The first are known as management servers because they handle system management tasks that are key to BusinessObjects Enterprise.

The first management server we will look at is the central management server, or CMS. The CMS handles incoming requests from third-party Web servers (like IIS and Apache) for authentication, viewing reports, scheduling reports, and so on, and serves as the "brains" of the system. Behind the scenes, a system database is used to keep track of users, groups, folders, reports, objects, schedules, and more.

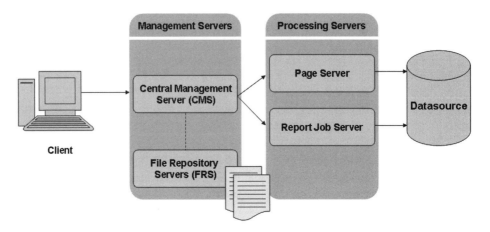

FIGURE 12.1 Basic BusinessObjects Enterprise Architecture

One of the most important features of the CMS is to authenticate users and provide access to the content held within BusinessObjects Enterprise. To understand where this content is stored, we need to have a look at a typical scenario that a report developer may encounter when creating a reporting application leveraging BusinessObjects Enterprise.

Crystal Reports provides the report designer for BusinessObjects Enterprise. The first thing a developer must do is create a report with the content he wants to add to his application. Once the report is designed, it will need to be uploaded or saved to BusinessObjects Enterprise. This can occur in one of the following three ways:

- From within Crystal Reports, the report developer clicks File > Save As and clicks the Enterprise icon to log on to BusinessObjects Enterprise and save his report to a particular folder.
- The report developer uses the Crystal Management Console, a packaged Web administration tool, to publish the report file from his Web browser.
- The report developer uses the Report Publishing Wizard, a packaged Windows application, to publish the report from his desktop.

When the developer saves or publishes his report, an entry for the report is written into the CMS system database, and the report itself is copied to one of the file repository servers (FRS). This is the second type of management server we will look at. There are actually two separate servers in use here. There is an "input" FRS that is used to store all of the report "templates" and an "output" FRS that is used to store reports that have been run and have data stored with them. These reports with saved data, called *instances*, are the output from when a report is scheduled and run.

So once a report has been published to BusinessObjects Enterprise, now what? Well, if the user wants to view the report, that request goes through the Web server to the CMS. Then the page server takes the report template and runs the report for the user to view.

On the other hand, if the user wants to schedule the report to view later, this scheduling request is also put through the Web server to the CMS, and the report job server then takes the report template and runs the report, only this time it places an instance with saved data into the output FRS, ready for the user to view.

From even this simple example you should be able to see some of the advantages of using BusinessObjects Enterprise and its distributed server architecture. If you needed to increase performance for view-on-demand reports, you could increase the number of page servers. Likewise, if you ran a heavy schedule of reports at night, you could increase the number of report job servers to compensate.

This simple architecture diagram by no means represents all of the servers and technologies that are available with BusinessObjects Enterprise. For more information on BusinessObjects Enterprise and a detailed architecture diagram see the BusinessObjects Enterprise Administrator's Guide under the topic "Architecture."

To see this architecture in action, we will see how to install BusinessObjects Enterprise on a standalone server or workstation. This is the most common installation type for development environments or developer desktop machines, and it provides a quick way of getting all of the different components up and running quickly.

INSTALLATION OPTIONS FOR WINDOWS

When installing BusinessObjects Enterprise XI on the Windows platform, you have a number of choices for how you actually install the software.

But before we get into actually installing the software we need to have a look at some of the prerequisites for installing BusinessObjects Enterprise XI and things you should take into consideration before proceeding.

BEFORE YOU INSTALL

On your BusinessObjects Enterprise XI CD-ROM in the platforms.txt file and also on the BusinessObjects Web Site (*www.businessobjects.com*) you will find both the detailed list of minimum system requirements and a list of supported platforms for operating system, databases, browsers, and so on. Take a moment to check these requirements and platforms before you begin your installation to ensure you have everything you need.

In addition, ensure that you have all of the required network and local machine access and that you have set up all of the network accounts, databases, email accounts, and so on that you will need to install and configure BusinessObjects Enterprise. For example, if you plan to report from an Oracle database, it is a good idea to have the Oracle client installed and configured in advance.

If you don't have full control over your network or environment, you may also want to notify your network administrator, database administrator, and any other relevant parties that you are about to perform the installation in case anything should go wrong in the middle of the installation process. If you are confident that you have all of this in place and are ready to proceed, you can start the installation.

INSTALLING BUSINESSOBJECTS ENTERPRISE XI

To install BusinessObjects Enterprise XI, place the product CD-ROM in your CD-ROM drive and run setup.exe to start the BusinessObjects Enterprise XI Installation Wizard. After a brief check for other installed software and components, the Installation Wizard will present a welcome dialog box like the one shown in Figure 12.2.

Throughout the installation wizard you can use the Next button to proceed and the Back button to return to the previous step in the installation process. The next step of the installation process is accepting the licensing agreement using the dialog box shown in Figure 12.3.

In addition to being displayed in this dialog box, the license agreement is also available on the BusinessObjects Enterprise XI CD-ROM as license.pdf in the /DOCS directory.

Once you have accepted the licensing agreement, you will need to enter your name, organization, and product key code using the User Information dialog box. You can find the product key code on the back of the CD-ROM sleeve, usually printed on a red sticker. If you purchased BusinessObjects Enterprise XI as part of a larger software purchase from BusinessObjects, the product key code can be found on the licensing certificate that was provided with your CD-ROM media kit.

Next, using the dialog box shown in Figure 12.4 you will need to define where to install Crystal Reports Server. The default location is X:\Program Files\Crystal Decisions\Enterprise 10\. You can change this location by clicking the Browse button on the right side of the dialog box.

FIGURE 12.2   BusinessObjects Enterprise XI Installation Wizard.

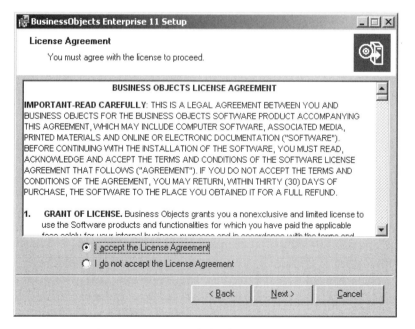

FIGURE 12.3   License agreement dialog box.

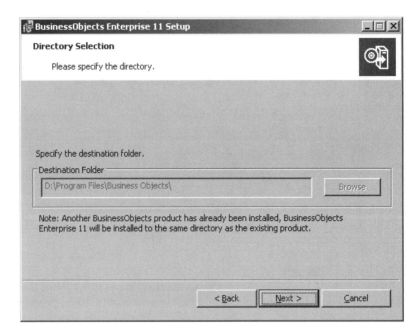

FIGURE 12.4 Directory selection

A standalone installation of BusinessObjects Enterprise XI requires at least 480 MB of hard drive space with all components installed and configured (and not including report and output files), so make sure that you have enough room at the location you select.

Selecting an Installation Type

In the next dialog box, you are prompted to select the type of installation you are performing. The New installation option allows you to install a standalone BusinessObjects Enterprise server with all of the required server components. Choose this installation type if you are setting up the first BusinessObjects Enterprise XI server in your architecture, or if you plan to run all of the components on a single server. You should also choose this option if you are installing BusinessObjects Enterprise XI on your local machine for application development purposes.

If you are adding additional servers or components to your BusinessObjects Enterprise XI implementation, use the Expand installation option to expand an existing BusinessObjects Enterprise XI installation. This installation type allows you to select the servers and components that you want to install; you should choose this option whenever adding new servers to your topology.

Finally, the Custom installation option allows you to select the components to be installed on your server, using the dialog box shown in Figure 12.5.

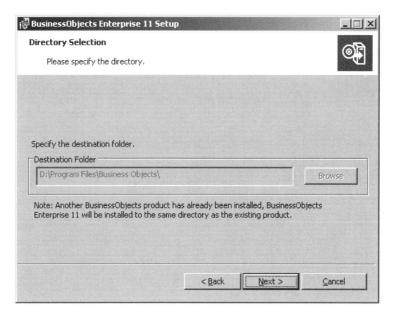

FIGURE 12.5   Feature selection dialog box.

Selecting Components

When selecting the features to install with your BusinessObjects Enterprise XI installation, you can select from the options using the drop-down list beside each feature. The majority of components are selected to be installed on your local computer, but there may be some components listed as Install on Demand. It is a good practice to change these components to be installed anyway—they won't take up much room, and it is easier to install them now than to look for an installation CD-ROM later when they are required.

The next dialog box, shown in Figure 12.6, is for selecting the database server where your system database will reside.

By default, BusinessObjects Enterprise XI installs a copy of the Microsoft Database Engine (MSDE) if it does not find SQL Server installed locally on your computer. This installation will be performed without any prompting dialog box. Another dialog box appears only if the setup has detected that you have SQL Server installed. You must enter the credentials for the server where your system database will reside.

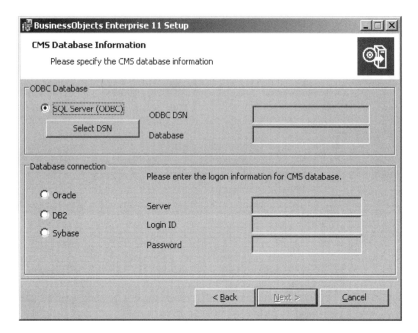

FIGURE 12.6   CMS database information.

Remember, BusinessObjects supports a number of different databases for storing its system database, including Oracle and Sybase. For more information on using a different system database, see the Administrator's Guide available in the /DOCS directory of your product CD-ROM.

Completing the Installation

Once you are finished answering the prompts in the Installation Wizard, the file installation will begin and a standard progress dialog box with a blue bar indicating progress appears. The installation process can take anywhere from 10 to 30 minutes, depending on the specs of the server in which you are installing BusinessObjects Enterprise. During this process the installation may seem to hang from time to time as BusinessObjects Enterprise XI installs additional third-party components. This hang time shouldn't last for very long, and the time estimates presented by the setup program are reasonably accurate.

When the installation process is finished, you will be prompted to register your copy of BusinessObjects Enterprise XI. Registration is free and can be done online. A registration number, which is different from the product keys you entered earlier, enables you to access technical support content, notifications, and so on.

Immediately after the registration screen appears, you may be prompted to log on to BusinessObjects Enterprise XI using the dialog box shown in Figure 12.7.

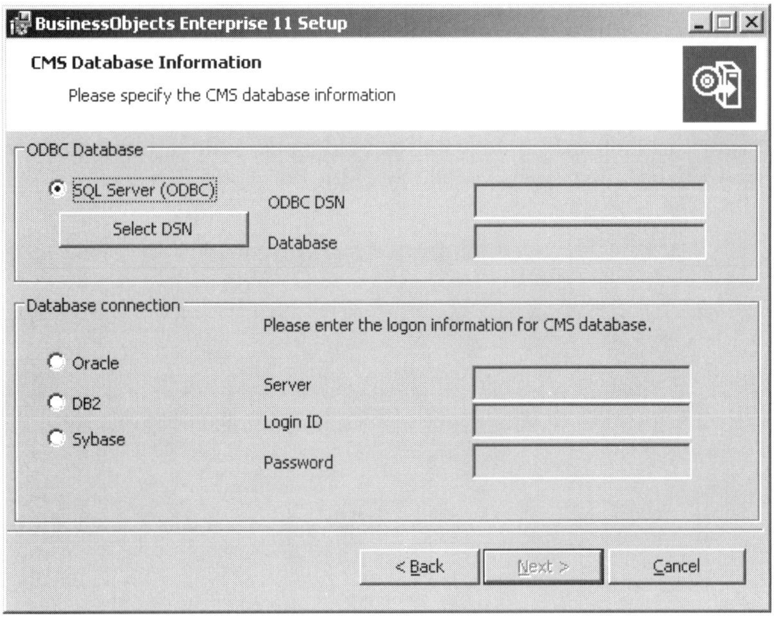

FIGURE 12.7   CMS Logon dialog box.

By default, BusinessObjects Enterprise XI is installed with a default username of Administrator and a blank password. You can use this username to log on to BusinessObjects Enterprise XI, but you should create a password for this account as one of your first tasks.

You can change the Administrator password by opening the Start menu and clicking Programs > BusinessObjects Enterprise XI > .NET Administration Launchpad. Log onto the Crystal Management Console. Click the icon for Users and then Administrator to open a dialog box in which you can enter a new password.

You may also receive a confirmation message confirming that all of the Enterprise services have been enabled and started, indicating that you are ready to get started working with BusinessObjects Enterprise.

CHECKING YOUR INSTALLATION

The easiest way to check that your installation went smoothly is to use InfoView (the default client interface) to see if you can view and schedule reports using BusinesObjects Enterprise. To open InfoView, open the Start menu and click Programs > BusinessObjects Enterprise XI > .NET InfoView. The application opens and allow you to log on. Once you are logged in, a folder named Report Samples, shown in Figure 12.8, is installed by default. You can schedule and view these reports from InfoView without any errors.

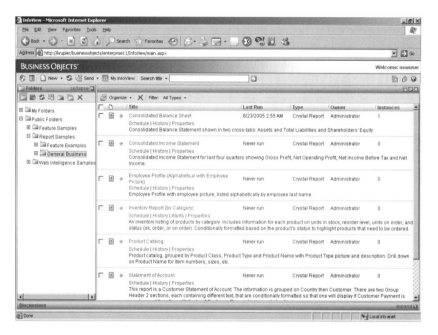

FIGURE 12.8 Sample reports provided with BusinessObjects Enterprise.

You also may want to verify that you can use the Central Management Console, which you can open by opening the Start menu and clicking Programs > BusinessObjects Enterprise XI > .NET Administration Launchpad. A Web page opens, where you can click to launch the Central Management Console. You can log on to the Crystal Management Console and manage users, groups, folders, and so on from the Admin interface. You can also publish your reports to BusinessObjects Enterprise for testing. To publish a report, use the following steps:

1. Open the Start menu, and click Programs > BusinessObjects Enterprise XI > .NET Administration Launchpad.

2. Click the link to open the Central Management Console.
3. Log on to the CMS with a username of Administrator and no password.
4. Click the Folders icon to open a list of available folders, and then click the Report Samples folder.
5. Next, click the Objects tab, and then click the New Object button to open the dialog box shown in Figure 12.9.

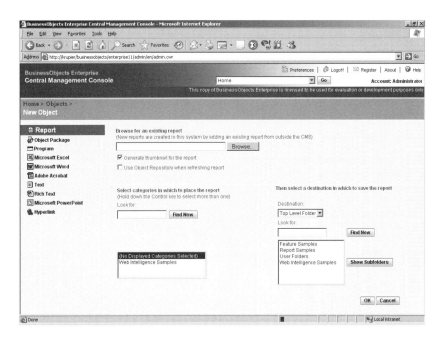

FIGURE 12.9   New object options.

6. Use the Browse button to browse for the report you want to publish. Select a report, and click the Open button.
7. Click OK at the bottom-right corner of the page to complete the publish procedure. Your report will be uploaded to BusinessObjects Enterprise, and you will be presented with a set of property pages for the report, as shown in Figure 12.10.
8. Click the Process tab, then the Database option to go to the dialog box in which you can enter any database usernames or passwords for your data source.
9. To test your report, click the Properties tab, and then click the Preview button to view your report.

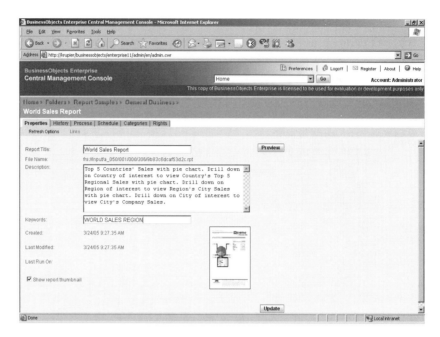

FIGURE 12.10 Report properties.

If you can successfully preview your own report from the CMC, you will be able to view your report from the applications we will be creating a little later in the chapter.

WORKING WITH ENTERPRISE SERVICES

The last topic in this section deals with how to work with the services that BusinessObjects Enterprise XI installs. By default, most of the server components we saw in Chapter 1 manifest themselves as Windows services, which can be controlled by the Central Configuration Manager, shown in Figure 12.11.

To launch the Central Configuration Manager (CCM), open the Start menu and click Programs > BusinessObjects Enterprise XI > Central Configuration Manager. The CCM presents a list of BusinessObjects Enterprise XI services (and any Web-related services). You can stop and start the services from this dialog box.

Service Dependencies

By default, all of the BusinessObjects Enterprise XI services should be running and displaying a green-light icon beside the service name. If for any reason this icon does not appear, one of the areas to look at first is the service's dependencies.

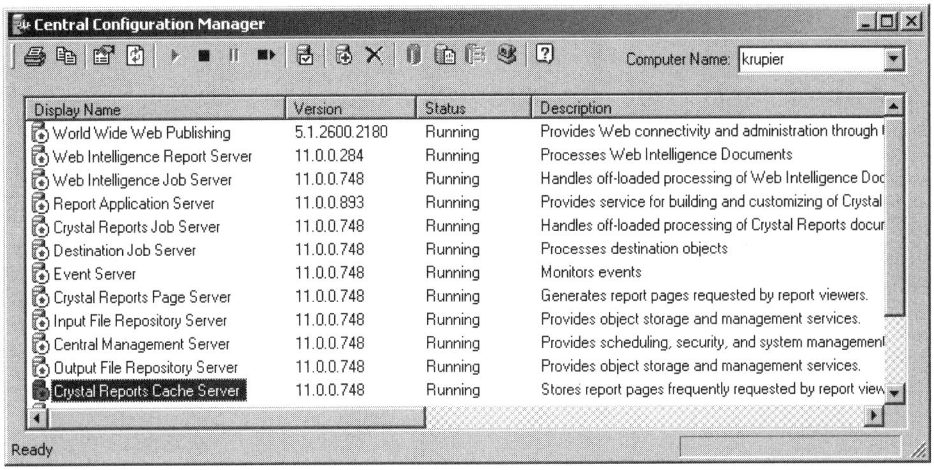

FIGURE 12.11   Central Configuration Manager.

To see the dependencies for a particular service, double-click the service name, and click the Dependencies tab to open the dialog box shown in Figure 12.12.

FIGURE 12.12   Service dependencies.

Dependencies are services that must be running for a particular BusinessObjects Enterprise XI service to run. For example, the Event Service is a common dependency, because BusinessObjects Enterprise XI uses event logs to log system performance and display error messages. If your BusinessObjects Enterprise XI service won't start, check the services in the dependency list to make sure that they are all running before moving on to other troubleshooting methods.

Starting and Stopping Enterprise Services

If you need to stop or start a BusinessObjects Enterprise XI service, you can do so using the icons at the top of the CCM. Highlight a service (or multiple services) and use the icons at the top to start, stop, and restart these services. You can also use the refresh icon to see the current status of these services.

DEVELOPMENT OVERVIEW

When BusinessObjects Enterprise was first introduced, the development team needed a solution to an age-old problem—cross-platform development. With support for Windows, Linux, and Unix servers, there was no one programming language that they could use easily across all of the supported platforms. So, with the introduction of BusinessObjects Enterprise 8, Crystal Server Pages (CSP) was introduced. Loosely based on Microsoft Active Server Pages (ASP), Crystal Server Pages offered developers a method to develop and deploy applications across a wide range of platforms. The default client application, e-Portfolio, was written using CSP and could be deployed on different platforms or customized to suit the developer's requirements.

In addition, the similarities between CSP and ASP meant a short learning curve for developers who were already familiar with Microsoft Web technologies. But with this ease of use came a new problem: Web developers using other platforms had to learn a new language (or derivative, as the case may be) to leverage BusinessObjects Enterprise. For Microsoft developers, this was not a real issue because COM factored heavily in the BusinessObjects Enterprise SDK, and a .NET SDK was also introduced to enable integration with ASP.NET applications. For Java developers, it has taken a little longer for the SDK to come up to "rough parity" with what is offered for Microsoft developers, but we have finally reached a point where either the .NET or JSP SDK is a viable platform for creating reporting applications.

The client application or desktop that ships with BusinessObjects Enterprise (now called InfoView instead of e-Portfolio) is available either in a .NET or JSP version. Unfortunately, the source code is no longer shipped with the application, as it was for e-Portfolio in previous versions. As a result it is more difficult to customize these client applications, whereas with the old CSP files you could simply copy the entire e-Portfolio directory and modify the pages as required.

However, there are still a number of different ways you can leverage BusinessObjects Enterprise functionality in your application using the existing SDKs, tools, and techniques outlined in this chapter.

You may notice one gap in our coverage in this chapter—when we look at integrating BusinessObjects Enterprise into your own applications, our focus will be on the .NET API and .NET Server Controls, but we will not be covering JSP integration in this chapter. The accompanying Web site for the book (www.crystal xibook.com) does, however, provide a number of JSP sample applications for BusinessObjects Enterprise and augments the material found in the final chapter.

It is always best to start with the simple integration methods first, so the first thing we are going to look our review of the APIs and techniques is how to launch and view reports from your Web browser via a simple URL string.

WORKING WITH URL REPORTING

You can leverage BusinessObjects Enterprise to view reports from a custom application in a couple of ways, depending on your requirements. For simple report-viewing applications, you may want to consider using URL reporting, where a report ID and related report commands are passed directly through the URL. This is the simplest method you can use to view a report from BusinessObjects Enterprise, and it doesn't require delving into the object model or writing any additional code (other than the code in your existing application to launch the appropriate URL).

The URL reporting method will allow you to perform the following tasks:

- View the report
- Log on to BusinessObjects Enterprise
- Specify which viewer to use (ActiveX, HTML, Java, and so on)
- Log on to a secure database
- Pass parameter fields
- Set a record-selection formula
- Export the report and specify the format

As you can see, a lot of functionality is included in this simple integration method, considering most developers put viewing reports as their primary objective when using Crystal Reports or related server technologies. However, if you need more control over how you view the report or if you want to schedule or distribute the report from your application using BusinessObjects features, then URL reporting is not for you.

Also, if your reports are large in size (20,000 records and up), you may want to consider scheduling these reports, as opposed to viewing them on demand using URL reporting. Viewing a large report with URL reporting may time-out the application if the time it takes to process the first page exceeds the timeout for the browser. (This is more common sense than a Crystal limitation—why would you try to run a 7,000-page report on-demand in a Web browser?) So as with all decisions regarding tools and techniques, make sure you pick the appropriate tool for the job.

However, if you need a quick and easy method to view reports from your application with a minimum of fuss, URL reporting may be the way to go.

VIEWING A REPORT

Viewing a report from BusinessObjects Enterprise can be as easy as putting together a simple URL with the report ID that you want to view. When a report is published, it is assigned a report ID that is stored in the system database. This ID, rather than the report name (which could be the same as another report in another folder) is used to reference the report.

Previous versions of the platform supported the concept of "unmanaged reports," which were reports that were stored outside of BusinessObjects Enterprise that could still be viewed using Enterprise components. With Crystal Enterprise 9 this feature was downgraded but continued to work in version 10. Unmanaged reporting is not supported in BusinessObjects Enterprise, so any reports you want to view through a URL need to be published to BusinessObjects Enterprise using one of the techniques we looked at earlier.

To find the ID of your report, use the API to query for the report ID given the report name (which we will look at a little later in the chapter when creating .NET applications from scratch). To keep things simple we are just going to look in the Central Management Console to find the report ID. To find this ID, use the following steps:

1. From the Start menu, click Programs > BusinessObjects 11 > BusinessObjects Enterprise > .NET Administration Launchpad.
2. Click the link to open the Central Management Console.
3. Log on as Administrator with no password.

4. Click the Folders icon, and navigate to the folder where the report has been published. In this example, we are going to use one of the sample reports that ships with BusinessObjects Enterprise, so navigate to Report Samples > General Business and locate the World Sales report.
5. Click the World Sales Report to open its property pages and then click the Preview button to preview the report.
6. Look at the URL that is used to view the report, and note the ID number that is represented (in our example, the ID number is 306, but it may be different on your server).

Now, to view a report using a URL, we need to build up the URL to include this report ID. The basic syntax for URL report is

```
http://servername/businessobjects/viewrpt.cwr?id=306
```

The only required parameter that you will need to pass to this page is the report ID. As we go through some more advanced uses, you will see that you can pass additional information through the URL to control the viewer or report features, but the ID is the only required component. If you were to use this URL to view the World Sales report from your own server, it should look something like the one shown in Figure 12.13.

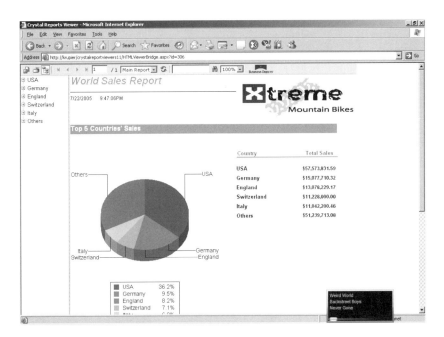

FIGURE 12.13 The World Sales Report viewed from a URL.

You may notice that when you view a report using URL reporting, you are actually forwarded to a .NET or JSP page to view the report. This is due in part to the changes that were introduced in BusinessObjects Enterprise XI to move to a more application-server approach where requests are routed through either the .NET or JSP framework. This technique is also used to keep backward compatibility with previous versions of Crystal Enterprise.

Logging on to BusinessObjects Enterprise

Whenever you use a URL to view reports, you will be prompted to enter a user ID and password using the dialog box shown in Figure 12.14.

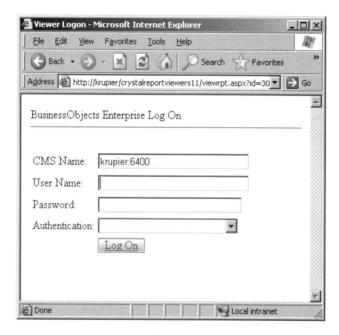

FIGURE 12.14 BusinessObjects logon page.

This dialog box appears BusinessObjects Enterprise provides a security layer for published reports to control access to report content. You can either use this default dialog box to allow the user to log on to Crystal Enterprise, or you can pass the logon details in the URL using the following URL parameters:

- APSUSER
- APSPASSWORD
- APSAUTHTYPE

If you haven't used Crystal Enterprise before, you may be wondering why the parameter is prefixed with "APS." In previous versions of the product, the Crystal Management Server was known as the Automated Process Scheduler, or APS.

To use these parameters to pass logon details, you append them to the basic URL using the & symbol, as shown in the following code listing:

```
http://servername/businessobjects/viewrpt.cwr?id=306&apsuser
=administrator&apspassword=admin123&apsauthtype=secEnterprise
```

In this example, the username is Administrator, the password is admin123, and the authentication type has been set to secEnterprise. The authentication type you pass will be determined by how your server is set up.

By default, BusinessObjects Enterprise is configured to use Enterprise authentication, where an administrator will maintain users, groups, and so on within BusinessObjects Enterprise. This information is stored in the system database, and as new users are required, they are added through the Crystal Management Console.

For users who use Windows Active Directory, you can also integrate Windows AD security directly into BusinessObjects Enterprise. To add new users to Business Objects Enterprise, you add them to the appropriate group in the Active Directory. The same concept is also available for you if your organization uses Windows Authentication or if you have an LDAP Server that you use to authenticate users and store user and group information. You can find out more about setting up these different security types in the BusinessObjects Enterprise *Administrator's Guide*, which is available in the /DOCS directory on your installation CD-ROM.

Table 12.1 shows the authentication types and their corresponding URL parameter value.

TABLE 12.1 URL Reporting Authentication Types

Authentication Type	Parameter Value
BusinessObjects Enterprise	secEnterprise
Windows Active Directory	secWindowsAD
Windows Security	secWindowsNT
LDAP Security	secLDAP

If your server was set up to authenticate against a Windows Active Directory account, your URL would look something like the following code:

```
http://servername/businessobjects/viewrpt.cwr?id=306&apsuser
=administrator&apspassword=admin123&apsauthtype=secWinAD
```

If your server has been configured to use single sign-on, you won't even need to pass the username or password. These values will be passed directly to Internet Explorer from the operating system. Again, for more information on setting up single sign-on, see the *Administrator's Guide* for BusinessObjects Enterprise.

Selecting a Viewer

BusinessObjects Enterprise offers a number of report viewers that you can use to view your reports. By default the DHTML viewer, which looks like the viewer shown in Figure 12.15, is used.

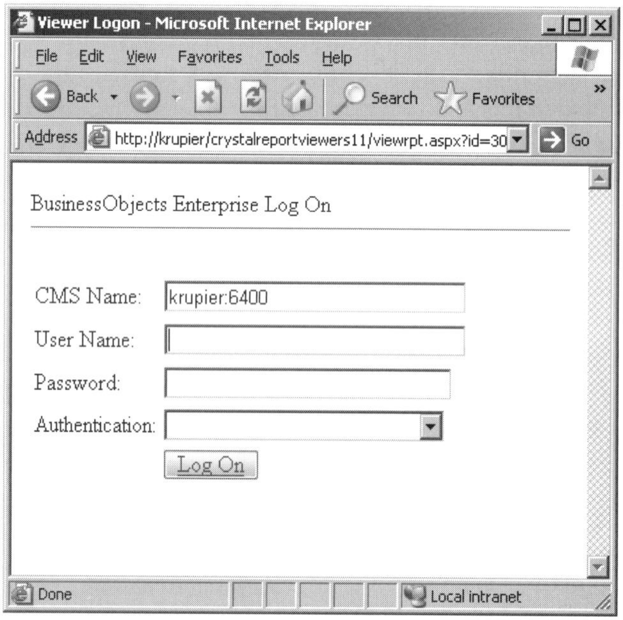

FIGURE 12.15   DHTML Viewer.

The DHTML viewer has the advantage of cross-platform support across multiple browsers and does not require any plug-ins or downloads to view reports. It provides the majority of functionality that anyone viewing the report will require (for example, drill-down, searching, printing, and so forth). Over the past few versions of the platform, the DHTML viewer has developed into a robust solution for viewing reports—so much so that it is the default viewer in BusinessObjects Enterprise.

The second viewer available in BusinessObjects Enterprise is the ActiveX viewer, shown in Figure 12.16.

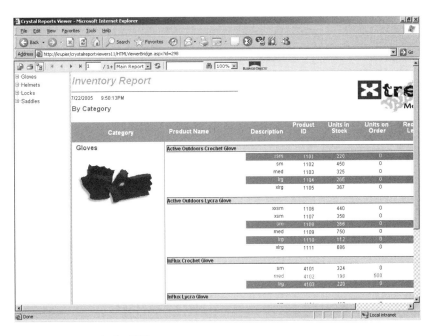

FIGURE 12.16   ActiveX Viewer.

The ActiveX viewer works with Internet Explorer and provides a much richer viewing experience, but it does require a one-time installation on the local machine. Because ActiveX controls are developed using the same tools as regular Windows applications, the dialog boxes used in the ActiveX viewer look and behave more like a Windows application than a Web application.

The third type of viewer available with BusinessObjects Enterprise is the Java viewer, shown in Figure 12.17.

The Java viewer is on par with the ActiveX viewer in terms of features and requires a Java-enabled browser in order to work correctly. You can control which of these viewers is used to view your report by using the INIT command in your URL. Table 12.2 shows the three possible values that you can pass to this command.

To view a report and use the ActiveX viewer, for example, your URL would look like the following example:

```
http://servername/businessobjects/viewrpt.cwr?id=306&init=actx
```

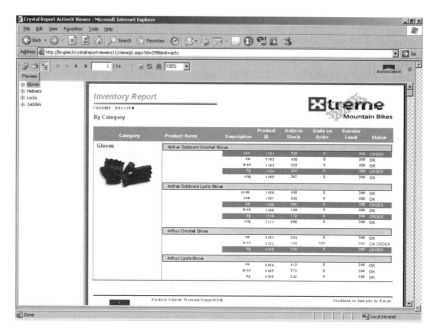

FIGURE 12.17 Java Viewer.

TABLE 12.2 URL Reporting Authentication Types

Authentication Type	Parameter Value
HTML Viewer	HTML
ActiveX Viewer	ACTX
Java	JAVA

This URL would open and display your report using the ActiveX viewer. If you had not used this viewer before you may be prompted to download and install this viewer in your Web browser, which should take only a few seconds because the viewer itself has a relatively small footprint.

Exporting Reports

In addition to viewing reports using URL reporting, you can also export reports to a variety of formats. The URL parameter for exporting reports actually consists of three parts—the first is the CMD parameter, which when set to EXPORT (for example, CMD=EXPORT) indicates that you want to export your report, and the EXPORT_FMT and `EXPORT_OPT` parameters, which specify the export format and the number of pages to be exported. A list of the available export formats is shown in Table 12.3.

TABLE 12.3   URL Reporting Authentication Types

Export Format	Parameter Value
Crystal Reports	U2FCR:0
Microsoft Excel	U2FXLS:3
Microsoft Excel (Data Only)	U2FXLS:4
Microsoft Word	U2FWORDW:0
Rich Text (Editable)	U2DRTF:0
Plain Text	U2FTEXT:1

To export your report to editable Rich Text using URL reporting, your URL would look like the one shown in the next example:

```
http://servername/businessobjects/viewrpt.cwr?id=306&cmd
=export&export_fmt= U2DRTF:0
```

In addition, you can specify the pages that are to be exported by using the `EX-PORT_OPT` parameter. This parameter accepts a page range enclosed in square brackets (for example, [1-20]), or you can pass a single dash to indicate all pages are to be exported. This parameter is optional but can be appended to the end of your URL, as shown the following code:

```
http://servername/businessobjects/viewrpt.cwr?id=306&cmd
=export&export_fmt= U2DRTF:0&EXPORT_OPT=[1-5]
```

In this example, only the first five pages of your report would be exported to RTF. This URL parameter is often handy if you are working with lengthy reports because you can export only the page ranges you require.

Working with Parameter Fields

Parameter fields are a powerful tool for filtering reports, and you can pass parameter values when viewing reports through the URL method. The URL command used to pass parameter values is `PROMPTEX`. This command is used in conjunction with the parameter name as it appears in your report. For example, if you had a report that had a parameter that was named `EnterCountry`, you would concatenate this name with the PROMPTEX command and a hyphen to indicate which parameter value you were passing (for example, PROMPTEX-EnterCountry). You can then set a value for this command as follows:

```
http://servername/businessobjects/viewrpt.cwr?id
=306&promptex-entercountry="Australia"
```

In this example we have passed a string value to the parameter, but you can also pass values for different types of parameters. For example, if you wanted to pass a numeric parameter you could either enclose the number in quotes or simply just pass the number, as follows:

```
http://servername/businessobjects/viewrpt.cwr?id
=306&promptex-refundcutoff=1500
```

You can also pass dates via the PROMPTEX command. For example, to pass a date value to a date parameter, you would use the DATE(YYYY,MM,DD) function to specify the date, as shown in the following code, where we are passing an OrderDate parameter to the report:

```
http://servername/businessobjects/viewrpt.cwr?id
=306&promptex-orderdate="Date(2006,01,01)"
```

Another handy URL command when working with parameter fields is PROMPTON REFRESH, *a Boolean command that you can use to control whether the user is prompted to enter new parameter values whenever they refresh the report. You can append this to your URL command using the ampersand (for example,* &PROMPTON REFRESH=0*) and pass a* 1 *for true or a* 0 *for false.*

If your report contains multiple parameter fields, you can pass values for each of the parameter fields by separating their PROMPTEX commands with an ampersand (&) as follows:

```
http://servername/businessobjects/viewrpt.cwr?id=306&promptex-
orderdate="Date(2006,01,01)"&promptex-orderthreshold=10000
```

And because parameters in Crystal Reports can also support multiple and ranged values, it probably wouldn't hurt to look at how to pass these as well. For multiple values, you use the same syntax as shown earlier, but separate each value with a comma in your URL. For example, if my EnterCountry parameter were set to accept multiple values in the report, we could pass the values Australia, USA, and Canada using the following URL:

```
http://servername/businessobjects/viewrpt.cwr?id
=306&promptex-entrycountry="Australia","USA","Canada"
```

To pass a range of parameter values, you can use two different sets of operators, depending on whether your range is to include the values passed or whether it should include just the values between the two values. For example, if you want to specify a range where the values include the start and end value in the selection, you would use square brackets to specify the range values. In the following example, we are passing a numeric parameter that would include all values from 10,000 to 20,000 including those values themselves:

```
http://servername/businessobjects/viewrpt.cwr?id=306&promptex-
orderamount=[10000-20000]
```

On the other hand, if you wanted to specify the same range but *not* include the values of 10,000 and 20,000 (just everything in between), your URL would use parentheses, as follows:

```
http://servername/businessobjects/viewrpt.cwr?id=306&promptex-
orderamount=(10000-20000)
```

Finally, to thoroughly confuse things, you can actually combine square brackets and parentheses in the same command. A square bracket on either side indicates that the value will be included; parentheses on either side indicates that the value will *not* be include. So, to pass a range of 10,000 to 20,000 where 10,000 will be included with the range but 20,000 will not, your URL would look like the following:

```
http://servername/businessobjects/viewrpt.cwr?id=306&promptex-
orderamount=[10000-20000)
```

The one exception to these rules is a date range parameter, which always must be passed using square brackets combined with the DATE(YYYY,MM,DD) *function we looked at earlier.*

Thankfully, mixing brackets and parentheses isn't done too often because it can become confusing. One technique we haven't looked at for parameters is actually passing parameters to subreports that appear in your report. A subreport can be linked to a main report, and any parameters that are passed to the main report can also be passed through to the subreport, eliminating the need to set the subreport parameter values separately.

However, you can have a situation where a subreport will have parameter fields that are independent of the main report and must be passed when the main report and subreport are run. In this instance, you can still use the PROMPTEX command, but you must specify the name of the subreport as well as the parameter name. In the example below, the report has a subreport named DAILYSALES that has a OrderID parameter that is set using the PROMPTEX command in the following URL:

```
http://servername/businessobjects/viewrpt.cwr?id=306&promptex-
orderid@dailysales=10
```

To check the name of your subreport, open the main report, click the subreport you want to check, and select Format Subreport. Click the Subreport tab, and look for the Subreport name shown at the top of the dialog box. You can also change the subreport name from the same location.

Setting Record Selection

Another handy feature of URL reporting is the ability to set record selection in the URL. A record-selection formula in a report is used to filter the records to return only the data that is required. Record-selection formulas are written using Crystal formula syntax and need to be valid and well formed; otherwise, an error message will be returned when you try to pass the formula in the URL.

A good way to test record-selection formulas is by actually pasting them into the report by opening the report and clicking Report > Selection Formulas > Record. The Record Selection Formula Editor, shown in Figure 12.18, opens.

You can then paste your record-selection formula into the editor and click the X+2 button to check the formula syntax. If the syntax checker returns "No Errors Found," then you can be sure that the syntax is correct.

Remember that the syntax checker checks only for correct spelling, field names, and so on. Your record-selection formula could still not return any records, depending on the logic you have used.

Once you have your selection formula, the SF command can be used to pass this record selection in the URL when viewing your report. If you wanted to filter your report to show only the customers from Australia, you could pass the following record-selection formula using the SF command in the URL:

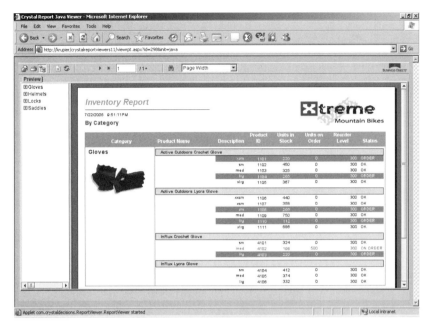

FIGURE 12.18   Record Selection Formula Editor.

```
http://servername/businessobjects/viewrpt.cwr?id=306&sf
={Customer.Country} = "Australia"
```

This formula will filter your report to show only the records that match the record-selection criteria. You can also pass multiple conditions in the selection formula, as follows:

```
http://servername/businessobjects/viewrpt.cwr?id=306&sf={Customer.
Region}
= "New South Wales" and {Customer.City} = "Sydney" and {Customer.
Country}
= "Australia" and {Orders.Order Amount} > $10000.00 and {Orders.Order
Date} > DateTime (2005, 01, 01, 00, 00, 00)
```

The one catch to using the SF command in a URL is that any record-selection formula you pass will actually be appended to the existing record-selection formula that appears in the report. If you do want to use this functionality as your primary filter for the report, you would need to go into the report designer and remove any existing record-selection formula. Otherwise, anything you pass using the SF command will be appended onto the end of this formula.

There is also a GF command that you can use in the same manner to set the Group Selection formula.

Working with Databases

Most reports are based on secure data sources, where a username and password are required to access the database. When working with reports based on secure data sources, you have a few choices when working with URL reporting. First, you can use the Central Management Console to set the database username and password for each report, so you won't need to specify this information each time the report is run.

To set the database information for a report published on BusinessObjects Enterprise, use the following steps:

1. From the Start menu, click Programs > BusinessObjects 11 > Business-Objects Enterprise > .NET Administration Launchpad.
2. Click the link for the Central Management Console.
3. Log on to the Crystal Management Console with the username Administrator and no password.
4. Click the Folders icon and navigate to the folder where your report resides.
5. Click the report name to open its property pages, as shown in Figure 12.19.

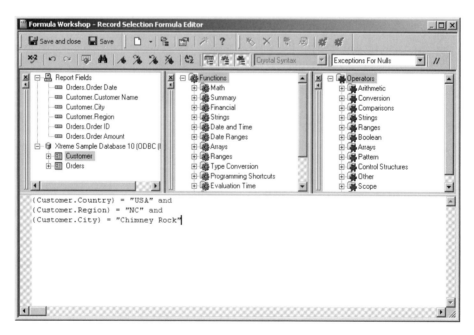

FIGURE 12.19 Report property pages

6. From here, click the Process tab, and then click the Database link immediately below the tab. The Database property page opens.
7. Enter a username and password to be used for this report.
8. Scroll down to the bottom of the page, and select the radio button marked Use Same Database Logon as When Report is Run.
9. Click the Update button at the bottom of the page.

Now whenever the report is run the user will not be prompted to enter a database username or password, and they will be taken to directly to the report preview.

The second method of dealing with the database credentials is to allow the user to enter them when the report is run. When a URL is used to launch a report based on a secure database that does not have its credentials set in the CMC, the dialog box shown in Figure 12.20 appears.

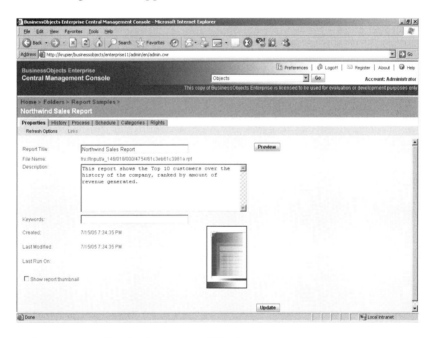

FIGURE 12.20 The database login dialog box.

Users can enter their database credentials here, then click OK to launch the preview of their report.

The third way you can deal with database credentials is to actually pass them in the URL itself when you pass the other report information. There are two URL commands, USER and PASSWORD, that are used to specify the database username and password for your data source. In the following example, a username of sa has been passed with a password admin via the URL as the first set of logon credentials to the report:

```
http://servername/businessobjects/viewrpt.cwr?id=4754&user0
="sa"&password0 ="admin"
```

Because a report can have any number of data sources and logons, index of the USER and PASSWORD commands can be incremented based on the number of data sources in the report.

If you had to choose between these three methods, the easiest would be to set the database logons within the Crystal Management Console. If you do need the user to pass the database credentials, your best bet is to either allow them to use the default log on dialog box or pass the credentials in the URL with the rest of the URL commands.

If you do some reading, you'll notice that the documentation does mention the ability to set database logons via a URL command using an alternate method, and even set the credentials for a specific server and database name. We haven't covered those methods here, because URL reporting should be for simple applications only. When you get into more complex requirements for working with databases, you need to start looking at using one of the more feature-rich APIs.

URL Encoding

Finally, let's look at preparing your URL commands using your own reports and parameters. You may have noticed in our examples that the parameter names have not included spaces: this is actually on purpose to keep the examples simple and easy to understand. In reality, when you use the URL method with your own reports, your parameter names may include spaces and other characters (for example "Customer Country"). You can still pass values to these parameters using the URL method, but you will need to use some escape characters to represent some of the characters in your parameter name, because URLs have their own special characters that they use for different things.

For example, the ampersand symbol is used to concatenate two or more PROMPTEX commands; if your parameter name itself contains an ampersand, the URL won't work correctly. Table 12.4 shows some common characters.

There are also some characters that you probably shouldn't in include parameter or field names, including the percent symbol (which is used to escape characters) and the pound or hash symbol, braces, and brackets because these all can be misinterpreted when used in a URL.

TABLE 12.4 Escape Characters

Original Character	Escaped Character
@ Symbol	%40
Ampersand	%26
Dollar Sign	%24
Equal Sign	%3D
Forward Slash	%2F
Question Mark	%3F
Period	%2E
Semicolon	%3B
Space	%20
Tilde	%7E

In addition to URL reporting, there is also an OpenDocument *method that can be used to open and view Crystal Reports and other content types from BusinessObjects Enterprise. Because this functionality was developed for use with report and content types other than Crystal Reports, we haven't covered it here. You can find out more about the* OpenDocument *method from the BusinessObjects SDK documentation that ships with the product.*

DEVELOPING APPLICATIONS WITH THE .NET SDK

If you find URL reporting is a bit too basic for your needs, you probably need to consider using the .NET SDK for BusinessObjects Enterprise. The .NET SDK gives you almost complete control over BusinessObjects Enterprise, including performing administration and configuration tasks, managing reports and other content, and scheduling and viewing reports. Because the SDK covers the all of the features and functionality that BusinessObjects provides, we have kept our coverage of the SDK limited to basic desktop operations that you may want to integrate into your own application, including the following functionalities:

- Logging on to BusinessObjects Enterprise
- Listing folders and reports
- Viewing report properties

- Viewing reports
- Scheduling reports

This list represents the most common functionalities that application developers want to integrate into their own applications. The decision to include only this material was a tough one, because the API presents a rich set of properties, methods, and events for controlling BusinessObjects Enterprise, but that material could be a complete book in itself.

In addition to the .NET SDK, BusinessObjects Enterprise also includes a number of .NET Server Controls that you can leverage to create reporting applications quickly using pre-built components that you can drag and drop on a page. For more information on these controls, visit www.crystaldevelopersjournal.com *and search for ".NET Server Controls."*

Several features in the .NET SDK deal specifically with administration or configuration features that you will not use in your own application. Therefore, we present the information you *will* need to leverage the power of BusinessObjects Enterprise to view reports from your own application, without the overhead of learning how the administration and configuration API works.

If you are interested in writing applications to manage or administer a Business Objects Enterprise framework, a good place to start is with the BOENET_SDK.CHM Help file available for download from http://support.businessobjects.com/library/docfiles/cps10/docs_en.asp.

Application Basics

The .NET SDK provides a powerful interface that you can use to integrate Business Objects features into your own custom applications. If you haven't worked with BusinessObjects Enterprise, a good place to start is by reviewing the default client interface for Enterprise, which is called InfoView (formerly e-Portfolio) and is shown in Figure 12.21.

To access InfoView, open the Start menu and click Programs > BusinessObjects 11 > BusinessObjects Enterprise 11 > .NET InfoView. You can log on with the default user account (Administrator, with no password) or any valid user account that has the rights to access InfoView.

One of the first things you will see is that BusinessObjects Enterprise provides a secure framework for distribution that requires authentication. Your custom applications will also need to authenticate users to determine what objects they can see and what actions they can perform.

FIGURE 12.21 InfoView, the default client application for BusinessObjects Enterprise

On the left side of the application window, you can see that reports published to BusinessObjects Enterprise are stored in folders and subfolders. When you click a folder, a list of reports is returned, along with the related actions that are available for each (schedule, history, and so forth).

This folder structure and the references to the report objects themselves are stored in the BusinessObjects Enterprise system database, which cannot be queried directly. To retrieve a list of folders, objects, or other elements, your application must query the SDK InfoStore object. This object can be queried using a SQL-like syntax to return a collection of objects or properties.

To view a report in InfoView, click the report title or name. The report will be run by the Page Server, and the report viewer will display the report in frame, as shown in Figure 12.22.

This type of report is called "on demand" because it is run when the report is viewed. If you want to integrate on-demand reporting into your application, you must use the SDK to run the report and then use the standard report viewer you worked with in Chapter 10 to actually view the report.

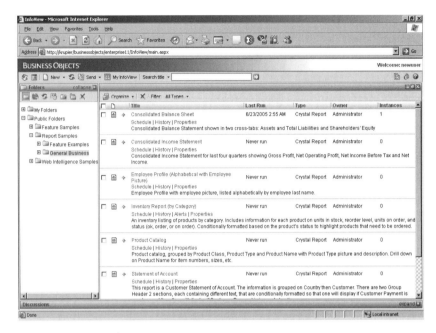

FIGURE 12.22 A report viewed in frame.

Also, you may notice that some reports have a Schedule option available. This option allows you to schedule a report sometime in the future, either at a specific time and date, when an event is triggered, on a recurring schedule, and so on using the dialog box shown in Figure 12.23.

When a report is run, by default it creates an output file, called an instance of the report, with the data saved in it. The History link in InfoView displays a list of all of the instances that have been run, as shown in Figure 12.24.

You can then click any of the instances to view the report using the standard report viewer we have used previously. To add scheduling to your application, you must use the SDK to retrieve the report you wanted to schedule and set any schedule options, including date, time, calendar, and format, and then commit these changes to the server.

If you are feeling a bit overwhelmed at this point, don't worry—the basic functions we have just seen are some of the same functions that we are going to build into a sample application to demonstrate using the BusinessObjects Enterprise SDK.

One of the downsides to using such a rich and flexible API is that you must accomplish a number of things in order to do a single task. For example, to view a report we must log on to BusinessObjects Enterprise, perform a query to get the report itself, and then run and view the report. To help out with the examples, we are going to build an entire reporting application in the projects that accompany this section.

FIGURE 12.23   InfoView scheduling options.

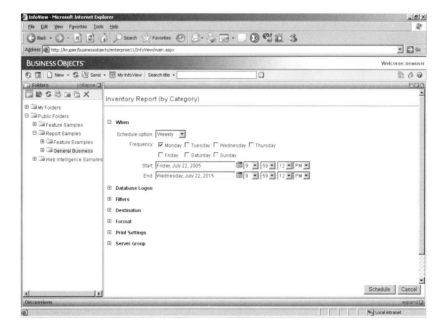

FIGURE 12.24   A history of reports that have been run.

This reporting application will have the structure shown in Figure 12.25. This diagram provides the blueprint for our application pages. Table 12.5 shows a brief description of each of these pages, as well as their function.

FIGURE 12.25   Sample application structure.

TABLE 12.5   Application Structure

Page Name	Description
logon.aspx	The initial logon form with fields for CMS, user name, password, authentication type, etc.
logonproc.aspx	Processes logon information from logon.aspx
main.aspx	Main frames page
header.aspx	Header frame page
main.aspx	Left-hand frames page, listing folders and reports
intro.aspx	Introductory page for the frames page
report.aspx	Summary page showing report properties
picture.aspx	Page used to display report thumbnail
viewreport.aspx	Page used to display report preview

Before we get started, a word about your development environment—to use the .NET SDK provided for BusinessObjects Enterprise on your development machine, you must perform a Client/SDK install from your BusinessObjects Enterprise CD-ROM to install the controls. In addition, it is recommended that you deploy and test your application on a server where BusinessObjects Enterprise has been correctly installed and configured.

Before you get started developing your application, use the .NET Administration Launchpad to log on to the Central Management Console, and verify that you can see all of the folders, reports, and so on and that you can view one of the sample reports from the CMC. The number-one problem when developing applications is that the environment has not been installed or configured correctly. Viewing and/or scheduling a sample report is a baseline test to ensure that everything is working correctly. Next, try viewing and/or scheduling a report build from your own data source that you have published to BusinessObjects Enterprise. If you are able to log on and view and schedule a report, you can be confident that your application can as well.

When you are confident that you can log on and view and schedule reports, the next trick is to set up your .NET project correctly, remembering to add the appropriate assemblies to your project. The assemblies you will need are either prefixed with `CrystalDecisions.Enterprise` or `BusinessObjects.Enterprise`. In addition, to view reports you will need to add the following assemblies:

- `CrystalDecisions.ReportAppServer.ClientDoc`
- `CrystalDecisions.ReportAppServer.Controllers`
- `CrystalDecisions.ReportSource`
- `CrystalDecisions.Web`

If you have had previous versions of BusinessObjects products installed on the same development machine and or server (such as Crystal Enterprise 10 or Crystal Enterprise 9), check out the version numbers of all of the assemblies to make sure you get the right version.

Logging on to BusinessObjects Enterprise

When integrating BusinessObjects Enterprise in your own application or creating an application from scratch, the first thing you will need to do to access BusinessObjects Enterprise is create a Session Manager object. The `SessionMgr` class provides an access point to the Central Management Server and has a `Logon` method that is used to pass the CMS server name, username, password, and authentication type to the server. Once you are logged in, a session will be created. The following code creates both the Session Manager object and a Session:

VB.NET

```
Dim SessionManager As SessionMgr = New SessionMgr
Dim EnterpriseSession As EnterpriseSession
```

Once you have created both of these, you can then use the Logon method of the Session Manager to attempt to log on to BusinessObjects Enterprise. The Logon method has four properties that need to be set—username, password, the CMS server name, and the authentication type—as follows:

VB.NET

```
EnterpriseSession = SessionManager.Logon("Administrator", "mypass
word",
"SERVER01", "secEnterprise")
```

In this example, the username is Administrator, the password is mypassword, the server is SERVER01 and the authentication type has been set to secEnterprise. The authentication type you pass will be determined by how your server is set up.

By default, BusinessObjects Enterprise is configured to use Enterprise authentication, where an administrator will maintain users, groups, and so on within BusinessObjects Enterprise. This information is stored in the system database, and as new users are required, they are added through the Central Management Console.

For organizations that use Windows Active Directory, you can also integrate Windows AD security directly into BusinessObjects Enterprise. To add new users to BusinessObjects Enterprise, you add them to the appropriate group in the Active Directory. The same concept is also available for you if your organization uses Windows Authentication or if you have an LDAP Server that you use to authentication users and store user and group information.

You can find out more about setting up these different security types in the BusinessObjects Enterprise Administrator's Guide, *which is available in the /DOCS directory on your installation CD-ROM.*

Table 12.6 shows the authentication types and their corresponding values.

TABLE 12.6 Authentication Types

Authentication Type	Parameter Value
BusinessObjects Enterprise	secEnterprise
Windows Active Directory	secWinAD
Windows Security	secWindowsNT
LDAP Security	secLDAP

When logging on with the Logon method, it is always a good idea to use a `Try...Catch` statement or other mechanism to catch any errors that may occur. You may also come across the situation where a user's password has expired and needs to be reset. In this the case, you need to create a form to accept the old and new passwords and reset them using the `SetPassword` method.

For more information on resetting passwords with `SetPassword`, *search for the method name in the BusinessObjects Enterprise XI SDK Help file.*

Once a user has logged in, it is time for some additional housekeeping. Remember earlier when we looked at the InfoView desktop application and saw all of the folders, reports, and so on? This information was provided through the `InfoStore` interface of the SDK. We will use this interface extensively through the different pages of your application, so we are going to create it here and store it in a session variable, along with the session itself, as shown in the following code:

VB.NET

```
Dim InfoStore As InfoStore
Dim EnterpriseService As EnterpriseService
EnterpriseService = EnterpriseSession.GetService("InfoStore")
InfoStore = New InfoStore(EnterpriseService)

Session("InfoStore") = InfoStore
Session("EnterpriseSession") = EnterpriseSession
```

With the user successfully logged in and some basic housekeeping out of the way, you can now proceed to the next page of your Web application to retrieve a list of available folders and reports. In our sample application, all of the code we have looked at will be contained in the `logon.aspx` page and the `logonproc.aspx` page. To create these two pages for your own application, use the following steps:

1. Open Visual Studio.NET 2003 from the Start menu.
2. Click File > New > Project.
3. From Visual Basic Projects, select ASP.NET Web Application, enter a name and location for your project, and click OK. In this example, we have called the project VB_CEApplication.
4. In the Solution Explorer, rename the default Web page WebForm1.aspx to Logon.aspx.
5. Double-click Logon.aspx to open the form in the designer. From the toolbar, drag five labels onto your form, as well as three text boxes and a drop-

down list. Arrange these controls and change the label text using the form shown in Figure 12.26 as a guide.

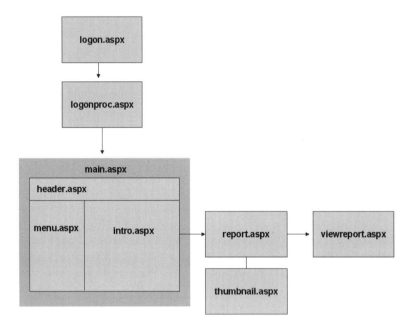

FIGURE 12.26 A typical logon form.

6. On the properties for each of the text boxes, rename them CMS, USER, and PASSWORD, respectively. Rename the drop-down list as AUTHEN-TICATION.
7. Modify the Items property of the AUTHENTICATION drop-down list to include the following text and values:

- Enterprise   `secEnterprise`
- Windows NT   `secWinNT`
- Windows Active Directory   `secWinAD`
- LDAP   `secLDAP`

8. Next, draw a button on your form, and change the text property to read Logon.
9. Double-click the button to access the code behind the button, and enter the following line of code:

VB.NET

```
Response.Redirect("logonproc.aspx")
```

10. Double-click the form to access the code behind it, and in the
    FORM_LOAD section, enter the following line of code. This is used to dis-
    play any error that is returned to the page.

VB.NET

```
ErrorLabel.Text = Request.Querystring("Error")
```

11. Next, click Project > Add Web Form to add a new Web form to your pro-
    ject. Name the Web form logonproc.aspx, and click Open.
12. Enter the following code behind the form in the FORM_LOAD section:

VB.NET

```
Dim logon_error As Boolean

'Retrieve the values from the previous page
Dim cms = Request.Form("cms")
Dim username = Request.Form("username")
Dim password = Request.Form("password")
Dim authentication = Request.Form("authentication")

'Create a new session manager, session, infostore and enterprise
service
Dim SessionManager As SessionMgr = New SessionMgr
Dim EnterpriseSession As EnterpriseSession

'Try to logon using the values passed from the previous page

Try
EnterpriseSession = SessionManager.Logon(username, password, cms,
authentication)
Catch ex As Exception
logon_error = True
Session("ErrorMessage") = Err.Description
Response.Redirect("logon.aspx?error=There was error logging in")
End Try

Dim InfoStore As InfoStore
```

```
Dim EnterpriseService As EnterpriseService
EnterpriseService = EnterpriseSession.GetService("InfoStore")
InfoStore = New InfoStore(EnterpriseService)

Session("InfoStore") = InfoStore
Session("EnterpriseSession") = EnterpriseSession

If logon_error = False Then
Response.Redirect("main.aspx")
Else
    Server.Transfer("logon.aspx?error=There was a logon error",
    True)
End If
```

13. With the code behind your LOGONPROC.ASPX page, click Project > Add Web form to add a new Web form to your project. Name the Web form MAIN.ASPX.
14. Next, click Debug > Start or press the F5 key to start your application. Your browser window will open and display the logon page.
15. Enter the CMS Server name, username, and password, select an authentication type, then click OK.

If you are successful, you will be directed from the logon page to main.aspx. If there was a problem with the logon, you will be returned to the logon page and an error will be displayed.

Working with Folders and Reports

Once you are logged in, you can start working with the InfoStore object to retrieve lists of folders and reports. For our sample application, we are going to create the main page of the application as a classic "header and side" frames page, as shown in Figure 12.27.

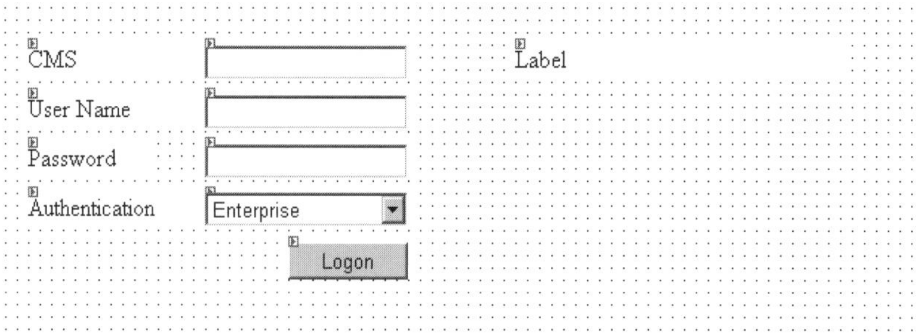

FIGURE 12.27 The main application user interface.

A list of folders and reports will be returned to the menu on the left side, and report information and viewing/scheduling options will be shown in the main part of the page once a user has selected a particular report.

When working with the `InfoStore` object to retrieve content stored in Business-Objects Enterprise, a good place to start is with folders. Folders help keep the content organized and provide a navigation method as well. Folders, like all objects in BusinessObjects, can be referenced by their ID or name and have a number of associated properties. We can use these properties to query for the parent of the folder we are working with or any child folders, making it easy to navigate up or down the folder structure.

The top-level parent folder in BusinessObjects Enterprise always is referenced as folder 0, making it easy to display a list of all of the folders below it or to jump directly to the top of the folder structure when needed.

To get a list of folders, we need to query the `InfoStore` object. As was mentioned earlier, the query language used with the `InfoStore` object closely resembles SQL, but instead of querying a database, it is used to query a store of information held within the BusinessObjects Enterprise system database and elsewhere.

When querying the InfoStore object, you can query the `CI_INFOOBJECTS` interface for a number of different properties that you specify in the `SELECT` clause of your query statement. In addition, you can also filter the results that are returned using a `WHERE` clause, just like SQL. So if you wanted to retrieve a list of top-level folders from BusinessObjects Enterprise, your query would look like the following:

```
Select SI_NAME, SI_ID From CI_INFOOBJECTS Where SI_PROGID =
'CrystalEnterprise.Folder' And SI_PARENT_FOLDER = 0
```

In this instance, we selected the ID and name of each folder (`SI_NAME`, `SI_ID`) and used the `WHERE` clause to filter for only folder objects where the parent folder is 0 (the top-level folder). There could be any number of folders returned in this query, so we could loop through them to display the folder name (`SI_NAME`) in our menu on the left side of the page (MENU.ASPX).

As you start learning about the query terms used with BusinessObjects Enterprise, you will be able to query for just about any object or property contained in the Enterprise framework. A reference for the query language is available in the BusinessObjects Enterprise XI .NET SDK Help file. Table 12.7 contains a list of the most commonly used properties or fields.

In addition to writing your own query statements, there is also a handy Query Builder utility available at *http://servername/businessobjects/enterprise11/WebTools/websamples/query/*.

TABLE 12.7 Common `InfoStore` Properties

Property	Description
SI_ID	ID number of the object
SI_NAME	Name of the object
SI_DESCRIPTION	Description associated with the object
SI_PROGID	Type of object (i.e. `CrystalEnterprise.Folder`, `CrystalEnterprise.Report`, etc.)
SI_UPDATE_TS	Update timestamp set the last time the object was updated
SI_PARENT_FOLDER	ID number of the parent folder for the object

This utility can be used to build queries that you can paste into your own code. The Query Builder is also a good way to learn what properties and attributes can be retrieved using the `InfoStore` object.

Once you have settled on the query that you want to pass, you will need to use the `Query` method of the `InfoStore` object to retrieve your result set, as shown in the following code:

VB.NET

```
Dim InfoStore
InfoStore = CType(Session("InfoStore"), InfoStore)
Dim query As String = "Select SI_NAME, SI_ID From CI_INFOOBJECTS
Where
SI_PROGID = 'CrystalEnterprise.Folder' And SI_PARENT_FOLDER = 0"
Dim myInfoObjects As InfoObjects = InfoStore.Query(query)
Dim myInfoObject As InfoObject
```

You'll notice that both an `InfoObjects` and an `InfoObject` variable were created. The `InfoObjects` (plural) object is used to hold the entire result set that is returned, whereas the `InfoObject` (singular) object is used to reference an item within that result set. These two variables will make it possible to look through all of the folders that are returned (that is, for each `myInfoObject` in `myInfoObjects`).

To put this all together and retrieve a list of folders for your sample application, use the following steps:

1. Open the project you have been working with in this section.
2. Double-click the MENU.ASPX page in your project, and click the HTML button at the bottom of the page to open the HTML view.

3. Add the following code to the HTML view of the page. This will create our frames page.

```
<frameset rows="64,*" border="0" frameSpacing="0" frameBorder="0">
<frame name="banner" src="header.aspx" scrolling="no" noresize>
    <frameset cols="239,66%">
        <frame name="contents" src="menu.aspx?parent_folder=0">
    <frame name="main" src="intro.aspx">
    </frameset>
```

4. Click Project > Add Web form to add a new Web form to your project, and name the Web form HEADER.ASPX.
5. Repeat this process and create a new page named INTRO.ASPX.
6. Next, switch back to the Design view of your form, and double-click the form to access the code view. Enter the following code in the FORM_ LOAD section:

VB.NET

```
Dim InfoStore
InfoStore = CType(Session("InfoStore"), InfoStore)

Dim parent_folder
parent_folder = CInt(Request.QueryString("parent_folder"))

Dim showfolderid
showfolderid = CInt(Request.QueryString("showfolderid"))

Dim query As String = "Select SI_NAME, SI_ID From CI_INFOOBJECTS
Where
SI_PROGID = 'CrystalEnterprise.Folder' And SI_PARENT_FOLDER = " &
showfolderid

    Dim myInfoObjects As InfoObjects = InfoStore.Query(query)
    Dim myInfoObject As InfoObject

    If showfolderid = 0 Then
        Response.Write("Top Level Folder<BR><BR>")
    Else
        Response.Write("<A HREF='menu.aspx?showfolderid=" &
        parent_folder & "&parentfolder=" & parent_folder & "'>Up a
        level</A><BR><BR>")
```

```
        End If

        Response.Write("Folders<BR>")

        If myInfoObjects.Count = 0 Then
            Response.Write("No subfolders<br>")
        End If
        For Each myInfoObject In myInfoObjects
            Response.Write("<A HREF='menu.aspx?showfolderid=" &
            myInfoObject.ID & "&parentfolder=" & showfolderid & "'>" &
            myInfoObject.Title & "</A><BR>")
        Next

        Response.Write("<BR>")
        Response.Write("Reports<BR>")
        Dim reportquery As String = "Select SI_NAME, SI_ID From
        CI_INFOOBJECTS Where SI_PROGID = 'CrystalEnterprise.Report' And
        SI_PARENT_FOLDER = " & showfolderid

        Dim ReportObjects As InfoObjects = InfoStore.Query(reportquery)
        Dim ReportObject As InfoObject

        If ReportObjects.Count = 0 Then
            Response.Write("No reports in this folder<BR>")
        End If
        For Each ReportObject In ReportObjects
            Response.Write("<A HREF='report.aspx?reportid=" &
            ReportObject.ID & "' target='main'>" & ReportObject.Title &
            "</A><BR>")

        Next
```

7. With the code entered behind, you can now click Debug > Start or press the F5 key to start your application. Your browser window will open and display the logon page.
8. Log on to the application using a valid user ID and password. You should be redirected to the main page, which now shows a list of available folders. When you click a folder, it shows the list of subfolders underneath this folder and any reports in the main folder.

You may have noticed in the code that we are using the same type of query to retrieve both the folders and reports in the folder. There is also a link on the page to enable users to go up a folder or to return to the top-level folder, if required. In the next section, we will be building the REPORT.ASPX page that will display report properties and give users a link to view a report.

Viewing Report Properties

Taking our `InfoObject` queries a little further, we are going to create a query to retrieve information about the report itself, including its description that appears in BusinessObjects Enterprise as well as its title and a thumbnail or preview image of the report itself.

From the previous section, we have a menu that lists folders, subfolders, and reports. You may have noticed that in the code there is a link on the name of each report that pointed to the REPORTS.ASPX page. This ID is passed to the page and then is used to query for the text-based information that we want to see.

To retrieve the thumbnail image of the report, a second utility page named PICTURE.ASPX is used to retrieve the preview image, because this is not a text property that can be accessed directly by querying the `InfoStore` object. Once you have retrieved the report object, there is a `GetPicture` method that you can use to retrieve the image. This functionality has been placed in a separate page, because this is a utility that you can use at various times to retrieve thumbnail images in your application. In addition, the image source on the page is set to this URL because the page is set to return a JPEG image.

To add the report information page to your application, use the following steps:

1. Open the project you have been working with in this section.
2. Click Project > Add Web Form to add a new Web form to your project. Name the Web form REPORT.ASPX.
3. Insert three text labels, a hyperlink, and an image control onto your form, using the form shown in Figure 12.28 as a guide.
4. Next, double-click the form and add the following code behind in the FORM_LOAD section:

VB.NET

```
Dim reportid = CInt(Request.QueryString("reportid"))
Session("reportid") = reportid

Dim InfoStore
InfoStore = CType(Session("InfoStore"), InfoStore)
Dim query As String = "Select * From CI_INFOOBJECTS Where SI_ID = " &
reportid

Dim myInfoObjects As InfoObjects = InfoStore.Query(query)
```

```
Dim myInfoObject As InfoObject = myInfoObjects(1)
report_id.Text = reportid
report_name.Text = myInfoObject.Title
report_description.Text = myInfoObject.Description
```

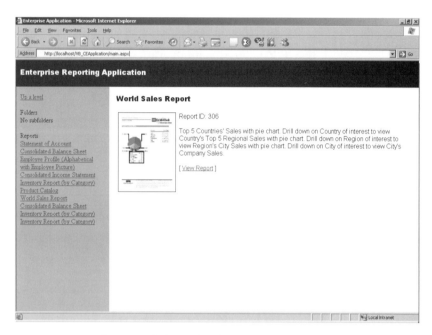

FIGURE 12.28 The report information form.

5. Now, to create the picture utility page, click Project > Add Web form to add a new Web form to your project. Name the Web form PICTURE.ASPX.
6. Double-click the form to open the code view, and enter the following code in the FORM_LOAD section:

VB.NET

```
Dim reportid = CInt(Session("reportid"))
Dim InfoStore
InfoStore = CType(Session("InfoStore"), InfoStore)

Dim query As String = "Select * From CI_INFOOBJECTS Where SI_ID = " &
reportid

Dim myInfoObjects As InfoObjects = InfoStore.Query(query)
```

```
Dim myInfoObject As InfoObject = myInfoObjects(1)

Dim imageByteArray As Byte() =
myInfoObject.GetPicture(CePictureState.cePictureThumbnail)
Response.ContentType = "image/jpeg"
Response.BinaryWrite(imageByteArray)
```

7. With the code entered behind, you can now click Debug > Start or press the F5 key to start your application. Your browser window will open and display the logon page.
8. Log on to the application using a valid username and password.
9. Navigate to a folder with reports, and click a report name to open the report information page. It should display the thumbnail image as well as summary information about your report.

And we are almost there—the last bit of functionality we are going to add to your report is actually the report viewer that we will use to view the report.

Viewing a Report

Now we see the most important part of the whole application—actually viewing the report itself. BusinessObjects Enterprise leverages the standard report viewer that is included with Visual Studio .NET 2003 and that you have been working with in previous chapters.

The process of actually viewing a report is a bit complicated using BusinessObjects Enterprise, because there is a little bit of manipulation actually required to get the report object itself and display it in the viewer. Remember, in previous chapters the viewer could actually run the report on demand on the local Web server. With the BusinessObjects Enterprise framework in place, the report is run on the Page Server and is simply viewed through the viewer.

Although the following code for viewing a report is a bit complicated, you should have to use it only once in each application because you can pass the report ID to the page for the report you want to view. To add viewing functionality to your application, use the following steps:

1. Open the project you have been working with in this section.
2. Click Project > Add Web Form to add a new Web form to your project. Name the Web form REPORT.ASPX.
3. From the Toolbox, drag the Crystal Report Viewer control from the BusinessObjects 11 section onto your form.

4. Double-click the form to open the code view, and enter the following code behind in the FORM_LOAD section:

VB.NET

```
Dim SessionManager As SessionMgr = New SessionMgr
Dim EnterpriseSession As EnterpriseSession = Session("Enterprise
Session")
Dim InfoStore As InfoStore
Dim EnterpriseService As EnterpriseService =
EnterpriseSession.GetService("PSReportFactory")
Dim ServiceAsObject As Object = EnterpriseService.Interface
Dim PSReportFactory As PSReportFactory = CType(ServiceAsObject,
PSReportFactory)
Dim PSReportFactory As PSReportFactory = CType(ServiceAsObject,
PSReportFactory)
Dim ReportSource As ReportSource =
PSReportFactory.OpenReportSource(reportid)
Dim ISCRReportSource As ISCRReportSource = ReportSource
```

```
CrystalReportViewer1.EnterpriseLogon = EnterpriseSession
CrystalReportViewer1.ReportSource = myISCRReportSource
```

5. To test your application, click Debug > Start or press the F5 key to start your application. Your browser window will open and display the logon page.
6. Log on to the application using a valid username and password.
7. Navigate to a folder with reports, and click a report name to open the report information page.
8. Click the View Report link, as shown in Figure 12.29, to open the report viewer.

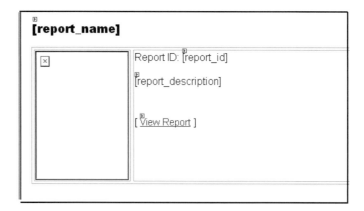

FIGURE 12.29 The View Report link.

A separate window opens when you click the link, and the report viewer displays your report. You can use same viewer formatting tricks and techniques we saw in Chapter 10 to modify the appearance and functionality of the viewer to suit your own application.

SUMMARY

Whether you are building an application for one report or one hundred, Business-Objects Enterprise and Crystal Reports Server offers a powerful report management and distributed architecture framework that you can leverage in your application. Whether it is through simple URL reporting or creating reporting applications from scratch, BusinessObjects Enterprise provides the ability to make your reporting applications even more robust without a lot of custom coding or re-inventing the wheel.

A
Working with the Repository

In This Appendix

- What Is the Respository?
- Working with the Repository
- Working with Repository Objects

INTRODUCTION

The Crystal Repository is a feature of Crystal Reports and BusinessObjects Enterprise that allows you to reuse report components in multiple reports. For example, you may have a company logo or header that must appear on every report. You can now store these objects in the Repository and use them in your reports. When an object is updated in the Repository, it can also be updated in all of the reports where it appears. In this appendix, we will take a look at the Repository and how it can be used to save time when creating reports.

WHAT IS THE REPOSITORY?

The Crystal Repository is a collection of objects that can be used in your report. It is accessed by clicking View > Repository Explorer. By default, no folders or objects will be shown until you provide your logon details for the server. These are the same logon details you would use to log in to your Crystal Reports Server or BusinessObjects Enterprise Server. To log on to the server, click the Logon button in the Repository Explorer to open the dialog box shown in Figure A.1.

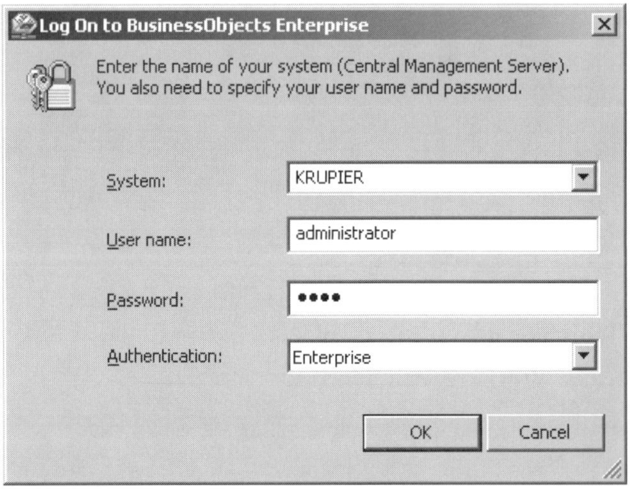

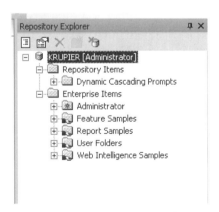

FIGURE A.1   Server logon details.

Select a system (or server), and enter your user name and password. Select an authentication type, and then click OK. Once you have logged in successfully, the Respository Explorer will display items from the Repository as well as reports and other objects from your Crystal Reports Server or BusinessObjects Enterprise system, as shown in Figure A.2.

FIGURE A.2   Default view of the Repository Explorer.

From within Crystal Reports you can store and use a number of different types of objects from the Repository, including

- Text objects
- Bitmaps
- Custom functions
- Report SQL Commands

These objects can be added to the Repository and shared between multiple reports and report developers, allowing report developers to create a single text object, custom function, and so on that can be reused as required. This means that the resulting reports are more consistent across the board. When it comes time to change a function, an SQL Command, and so on, it has to be updated in only one place. But before we can get started looking at the Repository, we need to create some folders to hold our Repository objects.

You can also view all the folders, reports, and other objects that have been published to your Crystal Reports Server or BusinessObjects Enterprise Server. To open a report, double-click it in its folder. You can also manage report and server settings, such as database logins and scheduling options, by right-clicking the report and selecting Manage Report. For more information on managing reports in Crystal Reports Server or BusinessObjects Enterprise, see the Administrator's Guide in the /DOCS directory on your server product CD-ROM.

WORKING WITH THE REPOSITORY

The Repository itself is stored in a database alongside the system database used by Crystal Reports Server or BusinessObjects Enterprise. The folders that we will create to organize the Repository don't actually exist on a file system anywhere—they are stored in the database, along with all of the items themselves.

Viewing and Filtering the Repository

By default the Repository displays the entire contents of the Repository, which can make things difficult to find, especially you do not have a good organization system in place. You can, however, use the view and filtering settings to help you find Repository objects more quickly. To change the default view, right-click the Repository server name, and select Change View Settings from the shortcut menu. The dialog box shown in Figure A.3 opens.

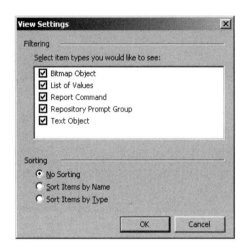

FIGURE A.3 Repository view options.

You can select the type of objects you want displayed as well as the sort order for items within the Repository. These filtering settings apply only to your current Crystal Reports session, so if you were to close and reopen Crystal Reports, you would need to change these settings again.

Another easy way to find objects in the Repository (especially your own) is to filter them by searching on either name or author. To filter the Repository, right-click the server name and select Advanced Filtering from the shortcut menu. A dialog box opens at the bottom of the Repository Explorer, as shown in Figure A.4.

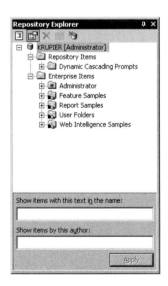

FIGURE A.4 Filtering options.

You can enter the name of an object or the name of the author. When you click the Apply button, the Repository will be filtered to display only the objects that meet the criteria you entered. To remove the filter, click the Apply box again with both fields blank.

Logging Off of the Repository

The final function you will need to know about is logging off—this is handy if you want to log off of one Repository and onto another (for example, logging off of a development server Repository and onto a test or production server). To log off, click the Logoff Server icon at the top of the Repository. To log on to a second Repository source, wait until the connection is cleared, and then click the Logon button to log on to the new data source.

Setting up Folders

By default, the Repository contains only a single folder, but you will probably want to do some initial setup to help keep your Repository contents organized.

You may notice that the default folder under Repository Items is Dynamic Cascading Prompts. If you are using Crystal Reports Server or BusinessObjects Enterprise, you can share dynamic parameters and pick lists between reports. You create and configure these parameters within the Business View Manager that ships with these server products. Any parameters you create will appear here in the Repository Explorer and are read-only from Crystal Reports.

You may find you want to create folders for each of the different types of items (text objects, bitmaps, functions, SQL commands, and so on). You may choose to create folders that relate to the different types of reports you are creating (sales, finance, and so on), depending on the type of objects you have and how you plan to use them.

It is a good idea to create a central corporate folder where you store your company's logo and other images as well as any standard disclaimers you want to appear on each report. Therefore, when a report developer is looking for this information, he won't have to dig through the various folders to find it. Also, when working with a team of report developers, it is important to create some policies and procedures around Repository use so developers don't accidentally remove or modify items that are in use in other reports.

To get yourself organized and create some new folders, use the following steps:

1. From within Crystal Reports, click View > Repository Explorer.
2. Click the Logon button to log on to your server.

3. Right-click the top-level folder marked Repository Items.
4. From the shortcut menu, select New Folder. A new folder is created, and your cursor will be placed in Edit Mode, which will allow you to type the name of your folder.
5. Type a name for your folder, and press Enter.

Your folder is now set up and ready for you to save some items to it. If you want to remove a folder, click to select the folder, and then click the Delete icon or select Delete from the shortcut menu. To safeguard against deleting an entire folder of objects, you won't be able to delete a folder unless it's completely empty. To delete a folder with objects, move or delete all of the objects within it first.

WORKING WITH REPOSITORY OBJECTS

The Repository features have been designed to be as intuitive as possible, making it easier to share common components between report developers and reports. In the following sections, we are going to walk through some of the basic tasks you will need to know to successfully work with the Repository and its objects.

Text Objects and Images

The easiest method to add a new text object or bitmap to the Repository is to drag it directly from your report into the Repository. To see this technique in action, use the following steps:

ON THE CD

1. Open Crystal Reports, and open the REPOSITORY.RPT report from the CD-ROM.
2. Click View > Repository Explorer.
3. Click the Logon button, and enter your user name and password, then click Logon.
4. Add a text object to your report (for example, by clicking Insert > Text Object) or picture object (click Insert > Picture), and format the object as you would like it to appear.
5. Drag the object into the Repository folder where you want to publish it.
6. A dialog box like the one shown in Figure A.5 will appear and prompt you to name the object and enter an author name and some description. The only information required is the name of the object—the other information is optional, but it could be helpful later.

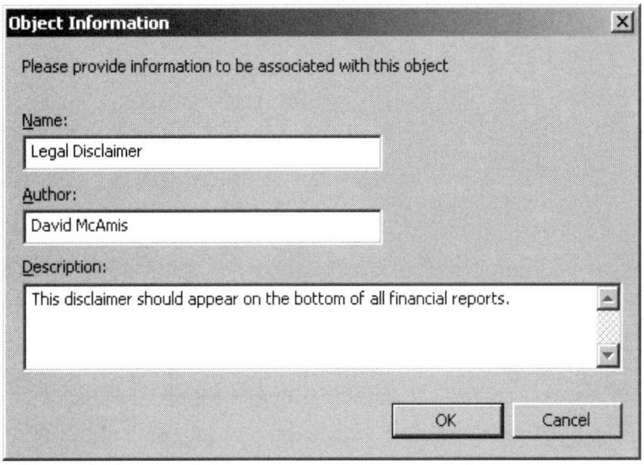

FIGURE A.5   Object options.

Once you have entered a name and clicked OK, the object is published to the Repository and ready to be used in reports. Alternatively, you can add text objects and images to the Repository by right-clicking the object and selecting Add to Repository from the shortcut menu. This action opens the dialog box shown in Figure A.6, in which you can enter a name and description and select a location for the object.

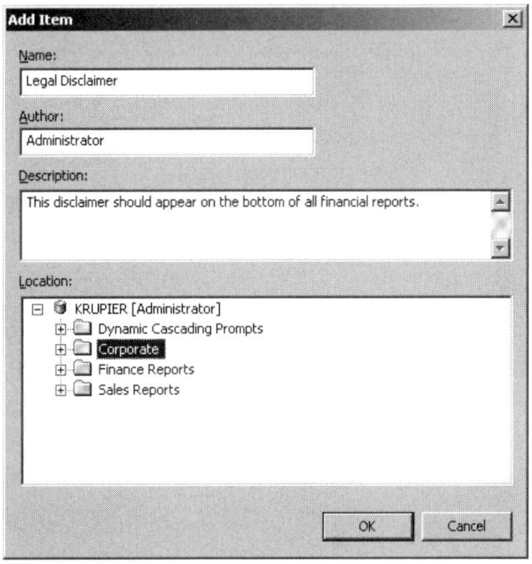

FIGURE A.6   Add to Repository dialog box.

You can now use this object in other reports as required by dragging the object from the Repository onto your report. By default, this object will stay connected to the Repository, so you will notice that when you right-click the object in your report, some menus for formatting or editing your object are missing. This is because the formatting is derived from the Repository object, so to change the formatting or edit the text, for example, you would need to right-click the text object and select Disconnect from Repository from the shortcut menu. This action will break the link with the Repository and allow you to edit the field.

SQL Command

Another handy use for the Repository is to store SQL Commands. SQL Commands are SQL statements that Crystal Reports can use as the data set for a particular report. To add an SQL Command to the Repository, use the following:

ON THE CD

1. Open Crystal Reports, and open the SQLREPOSITORY.RPT report from the CD-ROM.
2. Click Database > Database Expert to open the Database Expert dialog box.
3. Locate the SQL Command in which this report is based—it will be shown in the right column of selected tables and is named COMMAND.
4. Right-click the SQL Command name and select Add to Repository to open the dialog box shown in Figure A.7.

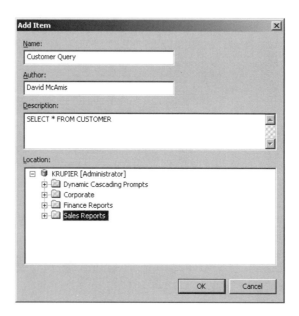

FIGURE A.7 Options for adding an SQL Command to the Repository.

5. Enter a name for your SQL Command (in this example, MyData), select a location using the folder structure, and click OK to add your object.

You can now use this SQL Command in other reports as required. You will notice in the Database Expert that the name of the SQL Command now displays a small icon beside it that looks like a pipe. This icon indicates that this SQL Command is tied to the Repository and can't be edited here. To create a report from this SQL Command, use the following steps:

1. Open Crystal Reports from the Start menu.
2. Click File > New > Standard Report. The Standard Report Wizard opens.
3. On the first step of the wizard, double-click the Repository data source.
4. Enter your logon credentials, and click OK. The Repository opens and displays a list of available SQL Commands.
5. Click to select your SQL Command (in this example, MyData), and click Open.
6. Click the Next button to continue with the Standard Report Wizard, selecting fields, grouping, sorting, and so on.
7. When finished, click the Finish button to preview your report.

This report is tied to the SQL Command until you remove or disconnect it—any changes to the SQL Command in the Repository will mean that the SQL Command changes everywhere it is used.

Custom Functions

The Repository also supports custom functions. We saw custom functions earlier in the book—basically, they are Crystal Reports formulas that can be reused as many times as required. Until now, we have looked at how to create them only in individual reports (meaning you have to re-create them each time you want to use them). But using the Repository, we can store this type of function centrally and reference it from multiple reports.

To show how you can add custom functions to the Repository, we are going to create a custom function from scratch, only this time instead of saving it with the report, we are going to save it in the Repository so it can be reused. To create your function, use the following steps:

ON THE CD

1. Open FUNCTIONFORMULA.RPT from the CD-ROM.
2. Click View > Field Explorer to open the list of available fields.
3. Expand the Formula Fields section, right-click any of the formulas, and select Edit. The Formula Editor opens.

4. Using the drop-down menu beside the New icon, select Custom Function. A dialog box appears and prompts you for the name of the function. Enter `CountryGrouping`, and then click the Use Editor button. The Crystal Reports Formula Editor opens.

5. Enter the formula text as follows:

```
Function  (stringVar Country)
If Country= "USA" then "Domestic" else
If (Country = "Mexico" or Country = "Canada") then "North
America" else
"Rest of World"
```

6. Next, click the Add to Repository icon from the toolbar. The custom function is added to the Repository and now appears in the list on the left side with the connected icon next to it.

7. To see this function in use in the report, click View > Field Explorer.

8. Right-click the Formula Field heading, and select New from the shortcut menu.

9. Enter a name for your formula—in this example, name the formula Country Flag.

10. Next, enter the formula text as follows:

```
CountryGrouping({Customer.Country})
```

11. When finished, click the Save and Close button to return to your report's Design view.

12. From the Field Explorer, drag this formula field onto your report into the Detail section.

You can update this function as required by opening the function from the Repository and disconnecting the function by right-clicking the function name in the Formula Editor, then selecting Disconnect from Repository from the shortcut menu. Edit the function as required, then click the Add to Repository button to update the function. You may see a warning message about updating the function, so click OK to accept your changes and update the function text.

SUMMARY

The Repository is a handy tool you can use to reduce the amount of duplication between reports and report developers. It also provides a handy place to store key report components and access reports held on either Crystal Reports Server or Business Objects Enterprise.

Appendix

B About the CD-ROM

The CD-ROM included with *Crystal Reports XI for Developers* includes all the sample reports, code, and projects from the various examples found in the book.

CD-ROM FOLDERS

Projects: Contains all the sample reports and code from examples covered in the book. The sample reports, code and projects are listed by the chapter they appear in. The code is listed in text files (.txt) which you can copy and paste into your own application.

Images: Contains all the images in the book, in color, by chapter.

OVERALL SYSTEM REQUIREMENTS

This book covers a number of different development platforms and technologies. The list below is a complete list of all of the components required depending on your requirements and development platform.

Report Development

- CD-ROM drive
- Window XP
- Hard drive
- 128 MB of RAM minimum, 256 MB is recommended
- Crystal Reports XI Professional or Developer Edition

.NET Development

- Windows XP
- CD-ROM drive
- Hard drive
- 128 MB of RAM minimum, 256 MB is recommended
- Visual Studio.NET 2003 or above
- Internet Information Server (IIS) for ASP.NET
- Crystal Reports XI Developer Edition
- Crystal Reports Server XI or Business Objects Enterprise XI (optional)

JSP Development

- Windows XP
- CD-ROM drive
- Hard drive
- 128 MB of RAM minimum, 256 MB is recommended
- Java Application Server (Tomcat, WebLogic, etc.)
- Crystal Reports XI Developer Edition
- Crystal Reports Server XI or Business Objects Enterprise XI (optional)

Index

Symbols

\# (hash symbol), appearance before running totals, 119

\$ (dollar sign), escaped character for, 397

& (ampersand)
  as concatenation operator, 169
  escaped character for, 397

() (parentheses)
  using with period functions and Date fields, 173
  using with square brackets in BusinessObjects Enterprise XI, 391

. (period), escaped character for, 397

/ (forward slash), escaped character for, 397

? (question mark), escaped character for, 397

@ (at) symbol, escaped character for, 397

[] (square brackets), using with parentheses in BusinessObjects Enterprise XI, 391

~ (tilde), escaped character for, 397

+ (plus sign) operator, using, 168

= (equal sign), escaped character for, 397

; (semicolon), escaped character for, 397

" " (double quotation marks), using with formulas, 168

A

ActiveX printer control, using, 326–327

ActiveX viewer, using with BusinessObjects Enterprise XI, 387

AD (Active Directory), integrating into BusinessObjects Enterprise, 404

Administrator password, changing for BusinessObjects Enterprise XI, 375

ADO.NET datasets, reporting from, 312–314

advanced charts
  adding to reports, 228
  inserting, 229–232
  options for, 230

ampersand (&)
  as concatenation operator, 169
  escaped character for, 397

ANALYSISREPORT.RPT file, using Group Sorting feature with, 115–116

APIs, availability of, 3

application data, using as data sources, 257

applications, architecting scalable applications, 362–363

APS prefix for URL parameters, explanation of, 385

area graphs, controlling chart grid lines and scale for, 243–244

arithmetic formulas, creating, 162–164. *See also* formulas

ascending sort order, explanation of, 37

ASP (Active Server Pages)
  versus CSP (Crystal Server Pages), 380
  introduction of, 317

ASP.NET, introduction of, 318

assemblies, adding for .NET projects, 403

at (@) symbol, escaped character for, 397

authentication types for BusinessObjects Enterprise XI, 404

Average summary function
  description of, 109
  syntax for and usage of, 168
  using with charts, 236

B

bar graphs, controlling chart grid lines and scale for, 243–244

Basic versus Crystal syntax, 156–158

BeforeReadingRecords evaluation time function, using with formulas, 176

binding method, selecting for ReportDocument object model, 293–295

binding process, explanation of, 267

BINDING.RPT file, using, 295

bitmaps, adding to Repository, 424–426